EFFECTIVE WEB DESIGN

Master the Essentials

EFFECTIVE WEB DESIGN

Master the Essentials™

Ann Navarro
Tabinda Khan

SYBEX®

San Francisco • Paris • Düsseldorf • Soest

Associate Publisher: Amy Romanoff
Contracts and Licensing Manager: Kristine Plachy
Acquisitions & Developmental Editor: Suzanne Rotondo
Editor: Brenda Frink
Technical Editors: Will Kelly and Kynn Bartlett
Book Designers: Patrick Dintino and Catalin Dulfu
Graphic Illustrator: Andrew Benzie
Electronic Publishing Specialist: Robin Kibby
Production Coordinator: Katherine Cooley
Production Assistant: Beth Moynihan
Indexer: Lynnzee Elze
Companion CD: Molly Sharp and John D. Wright
Cover Designer: Design Site

Screen reproductions produced with Collage Complete.

Collage Complete is a trademark of Inner Media Inc.

SYBEX is a registered trademark of SYBEX Inc.

Master the Essentials is a trademark of SYBEX Inc.

TRADEMARKS: SYBEX has attempted throughout this book to distinguish proprietary trademarks from descriptive terms by following the capitalization style used by the manufacturer.

Netscape Communications, the Netscape Communications logo, Netscape, and Netscape Navigator are trademarks of Netscape Communications Corporation.
Netscape Communications Corporation has not authorized, sponsored, endorsed, or approved this publication and is not responsible for its content. Netscape and the Netscape Communications Corporate Logos are trademarks and trade names of Netscape Communications Corporation. All other product names and/or logos are trademarks of their respective owners.

The CD Interface music is from GIRA Sound AURIA Music Library © GIRA Sound 1996.

The author and publisher have made their best efforts to prepare this book, and the content is based upon final release software whenever possible. Portions of the manuscript may be based upon pre-release versions supplied by software manufacturer(s). The author and the publisher make no representation or warranties of any kind with regard to the completeness or accuracy of the contents herein and accept no liability of any kind including but not limited to performance, merchantability, fitness for any particular purpose, or any losses or damages of any kind caused or alleged to be caused directly or indirectly from this book.

Photographs and illustrations used in this book have been downloaded from publicly accessible file archives and are used in this book for news reportage purposes only to demonstrate the variety of graphics resources available via electronic access. Text and images available over the Internet may be subject to copyright and other rights owned by third parties. Online availability of text and images does not imply that they may be reused without the permission of rights holders, although the Copyright Act does permit certain unauthorized reuse as fair use under 17 U.S.C. Section 107.

Library of Congress Card Number: 97-80781
ISBN: 0-7821-2278-7

Manufactured in the United States of America

10 9 8 7 6 5 4 3 2

Software License Agreement: Terms and Conditions

The media and/or any online materials accompanying this book that are available now or in the future contain programs and/or text files (the "Software") to be used in connection with the book. SYBEX hereby grants to you a license to use the Software, subject to the terms that follow. Your purchase, acceptance, or use of the Software will constitute your acceptance of such terms.

The Software compilation is the property of SYBEX unless otherwise indicated and is protected by copyright to SYBEX or other copyright owner(s) as indicated in the media files (the "Owner(s)"). You are hereby granted a single-user license to use the Software for your personal, noncommercial use only. You may not reproduce, sell, distribute, publish, circulate, or commercially exploit the Software, or any portion thereof, without the written consent of SYBEX and the specific copyright owner(s) of any component software included on this media.

In the event that the Software or components include specific license requirements or end-user agreements, statements of condition, disclaimers, limitations or warranties ("End-User License"), those End-User Licenses supersede the terms and conditions herein as to that particular Software component. Your purchase, acceptance, or use of the Software will constitute your acceptance of such End-User Licenses.

By purchase, use or acceptance of the Software you further agree to comply with all export laws and regulations of the United States as such laws and regulations may exist from time to time.

Software Support

Components of the supplemental Software and any offers associated with them may be supported by the specific Owner(s) of that material but they are not supported by SYBEX. Information regarding any available support may be obtained from the Owner(s) using the information provided in the appropriate read.me files or listed elsewhere on the media.

Should the manufacturer(s) or other Owner(s) cease to offer support or decline to honor any offer, SYBEX bears no responsibility. This notice concerning support for the Software is provided for your information only. SYBEX is not the agent or principal of the Owner(s), and SYBEX is in no way responsible for providing any support for the Software, nor is it liable or responsible for any support provided, or not provided, by the Owner(s).

Warranty

SYBEX warrants the enclosed media to be free of physical defects for a period of ninety (90) days after purchase. The Software is not available from SYBEX in any other form or media than that enclosed herein or posted to *www.sybex.com*. If you discover a defect in the media during this warranty period, you may obtain a replacement of identical format at no charge by sending the defective media, postage prepaid, with proof of purchase to:

SYBEX Inc.
Customer Service Department
1151 Marina Village Parkway
Alameda, CA 94501
(510) 523-8233
Fax: (510) 523-2373
e-mail: info@sybex.com
WEB: HTTP://WWW.SYBEX.COM

After the 90-day period, you can obtain replacement media of identical format by sending us the defective disk, proof of purchase, and a check or money order for $10, payable to SYBEX.

Disclaimer

SYBEX makes no warranty or representation, either expressed or implied, with respect to the Software or its contents, quality, performance, merchantability, or fitness for a particular purpose. In no event will SYBEX, its distributors, or dealers be liable to you or any other party for direct, indirect, special, incidental, consequential, or other damages arising out of the use of or inability to use the Software or its contents even if advised of the possibility of such damage. In the event that the Software includes an online update feature, SYBEX further disclaims any obligation to provide this feature for any specific duration other than the initial posting.

The exclusion of implied warranties is not permitted by some states. Therefore, the above exclusion may not apply to you. This warranty provides you with specific legal rights; there may be other rights that you may have that vary from state to state. The pricing of the book with the Software by SYBEX reflects the allocation of risk and limitations on liability contained in this agreement of Terms and Conditions.

Shareware Distribution

This Software may contain various programs that are distributed as shareware. Copyright laws apply to both shareware and ordinary commercial software, and the copyright Owner(s) retains all rights. If you try a shareware program and continue using it, you are expected to register it. Individual programs differ on details of trial periods, registration, and payment. Please observe the requirements stated in appropriate files.

Copy Protection

The Software in whole or in part may or may not be copy-protected or encrypted. However, in all cases, reselling or redistributing these files without authorization is expressly forbidden except as specifically provided for by the Owner(s) therein.

For Beth, Cat, and Liz: Yes, there is life
"off the air" and after 911—
reach out and grab it!

ACKNOWLEDGEMENTS

As I finish this, I sit back in amazement at where I've wound up and how quickly the years have passed since I entered this crazy whirlpool that's a career in Web development. Through it all I have many people to thank for their encouragement and support at each step of the way: Kynn Bartlett, Aliza Sherman, Faith Sloan, Cindy Svec, Rachel Waddington, Jerry Muelver, and Rich Roth.

To Brian Gill, of StudioB: For believing in me, and for the work you're about to undertake as we go on to the next one.

To Cindy Svec, who allowed me to tap the incredible breadth of knowledge she possesses on topics graphical, and for her considerable effort in illustrating and providing excellent draft material for much of the graphical components of this book.

To Dave Navarro: my hero, my friend, and my husband. Who could have imagined when we chose to follow this path that it would turn out like this? What a long strange trip it's been! Your love, encouragement, and support have kept me going through seemingly impossible deadlines. Thank you for suffering in silence (well, mostly silence!) as I abandoned you to take-out and grilled cheese while I spent many hours in front of the computer over dinner. I love you.

—*Ann Navarro*

To my Mom, Dad, and my brother Rahman, for supporting me endlessly in all of my endeavors.

To my dear friend Michael Baxter for his bottomless well of support, faith, and help, and for his generous donations of meals, facilities, and computer equipment.

To my wonderful friend Nathan "Acorn" Pooley, for providing support, encouragement, Pepsi, and a Windows machine, plus ice cream the night before the deadline.

To all my friends who were so patient and supportive, including Scott Klein, Thor Ekstrom, Clary Alward, Becky Hainz-Baxter, Karl Miyajima, and many others.

To Ann Navarro for giving me the opportunity to co-author this book.

To my colleagues at DigitalThink who were so understanding of my need for a flexible schedule and for our constant discussions about this book.

To Sybex, Inc.; my developmental editor, Suzanne Rotondo; and my editor, Brenda Frink, for publishing this material and being so helpful. Thanks also to Katherine Cooley for coordinating the production, Robin Kibby for desktop publishing, Andrew Benzie for illustration, Molly Sharp and Dale Wright for the companion CD, and Lynnzee Elze for indexing the book. A special thanks to Kynn Bartlett and Will Kelly for such a great tech edit.

And finally, this book is for designers who aspire to make the Web a well-designed place, accessible to everyone.

—*Tabinda Khan*

Contents at a Glance

Table of Contents

Introduction

The World Wide Web is a venue where anyone can express themselves. Individuals create sites that detail their interests or display their resumes. Businesses use the Web for sales and marketing efforts, as well as for consumer support. Educational organizations conduct classes online or make research material available to the general public.

Behind each of these sites is a Web designer. As the complexity of the content on each site grows, the Web designer must be more knowledgeable in order to be *effective*. Effective design incorporates elements that consider not only the Web site's content but also what browser it will be viewed in, on what platform that browser is running, and how graphics, text, and other visual elements are displayed on computer monitors at varying color depths and screen resolutions.

Why This Book?

In our many years of browsing the offerings of innumerable HTML, design, and programming books, one question always seemed to be left unanswered: how should designers deal with the fact that Web pages don't always show up as expected?

While plenty of texts tell you how to use *this* tag or *that* program, very few of them explain the practical implications of your design and technical choices. *Effective Web Design* gives you a solid foundation in HTML, layout techniques, and design applications. At the same time it teaches you how your creations will display in most browsers and where optimizing for Web presentation can really assist in the production process.

Who Should Read This Book?

Any Web designer—from the hobbyist to the student to the Web professional—will find value in the issues discussed in this book. If you've come from an artistic background, the skills on learning raw HTML and other technical topics can round out your creative efforts. For those coming from the technical side of computing, the skills on color, creating graphics, and other presentational material can help you think in terms of the visual experience, not just the functionality of the site. Code warriors and artists alike will find new tidbits even in their own areas of expertise to enhance their online skills.

The Companion CD-ROM

The HTML files created in many chapters as examples can be found in their entirety on the companion CD found at the back of this book. Any corrections found after press time will be posted at `http://www.sybex.com/` and at `http://www.webgeek .com/ewd/`.

Even though we've provided the sample files on the CD, you're strongly encouraged to complete them on your own, in the text editor of your choosing (see Skill 3 for help in selecting an editor). One of the best ways to learn HTML is to create HTML. By walking through each example yourself, you'll be able to get a better feel for the techniques than you would by only reading about them.

Many of the graphics seen in Skills 14, 16, and 17 deal with specific color issues. The differences can be subtle, and difficult to discern in the greyscale print process used. All of these graphics can be found on the CD, in folders labeled for the appropriate skill number. You're encouraged to load them and view them on screen.

Many of the shareware tools mentioned in the text are included on the CD for you to try and out and perhaps purchase, including TextPad, Tex-Edit Plus, CuteFTP, and more.

A Note about URLs

The Web is an ever-changing digital organism. Each of the URLs included in the text have been checked several times: by the authors as we wrote each chapter and by the technical editors as the book went into production. However, by the time you read this, some sites may have moved or changed, invalidating the pages we've cited. We apologize in advance for any inconvenience this may cause (and we welcome e-mail to `ewd@webgeek.com` alerting us if something has changed!).

Conventions Used in This Book

Some URLs are unfortunately longer than a single "book line" long. When this occurs, we've taken every effort to break the URL at a reasonable point, either after a slash (/) before or a period. Should you encounter such a URL, continue typing the data on the next line immediately; no extra hyphens have been added to the text.

When we introduce a new concept or phrase, you'll see it in *italics* the first time it's mentioned. HTML code, URLs, and e-mail addresses are presented in monospaced font.

NOTE Notes alert you to details of special interest.

COMPATIBILITY NOTE Compatibility Notes are items of special concern to cross-compatibility. These tidbits are key points to remember for effective design!

TIP Tips provide extra information that will be helpful in completing the task at hand.

WARNING Warning icons alert you to situations where particular care must be taken to avoid problems in your design.

Above all, have fun!

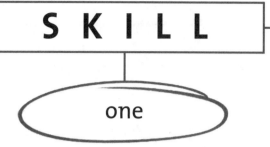

HTML and the
Cross-Compatibility Concept

- ❏ What makes design effective?

- ❏ How the Web was born

- ❏ Evolutions in HTML

- ❏ The cross-compatibility concept

What makes a specific Web design effective? The answer to that takes up the remaining 22 skills that make up this book. Effectiveness is a subjective measurement. How can we judge whether something is effective? For Web designers, the criteria can include:

- Is your site being used?

- Can the visitors you hope to attract access your site without barriers?

- Do visitors experience your site in the manner in which you intended?

- Does your site get your message across?

- Can you quantify the site's success through increased sales, decreased support calls, or inquiries from markets you've not previously been able to enter?

This list is not exhaustive but should spark your imagination into thinking about the multitude of ways that *effectiveness* can be defined on the Web.

In the Beginning

As improbable as it may now seem, the vast infrastructure and massive network we now know as the World Wide Web was the brainchild of a single man. Tim Berners-Lee was a scientist at CERN (http://www.cern.ch), the European Laboratory for Particle Physics. He had become frustrated by the necessity of using several computer terminals to access various stores of information belonging to the laboratory. Even more frustrating was the need to acquire proficiency using multiple programs that were peculiar to each terminal type.

Berners-Lee envisioned a world in which access to data would be a simple task, accomplished in a consistent manner regardless of the terminal or program in use. The concept of *universal readership* was formed, embracing the idea that any individual, on any type of computer, in any location, should be able to access data using only one simple and common program.

 NOTE   We don't believe Berners-Lee could have envisioned the browser wars of today, but in many ways his ideas and proposals have survived and flourished on the "modern" Web. He remains an integral part of the Web community, serving as director of the W3C—the World Wide Web Consortium. (For more about the W3C, see Skill 3.)

Linked Information Systems

Most information storage and retrieval methods that you've previously been familiar with are *hierarchical* in nature. This means that each bit of data is sorted in a structured manner: The files on your computer are sorted in such a way by default; files that begin with numbers come first as a group, followed by files that begin with letters. Within each group, files are sorted from lowest value (*0* in the numbers group, *A* in the letters group) to highest value.

A linked information system doesn't require such order or structure. You can travel from the number *1* to the letter *Q* and back to the number *9*, all the while having the information in each bit of data relate appropriately. This is the basic structure—or perhaps we should say nonstructure—of the World Wide Web. Documents are stored on thousands of computers, or *nodes*, around the world. Despite the unordered nature of the storage system, a document on a server in California can provide an entry point, or *link*, to a document stored on a server in Finland. Furthermore, you can link directly to the pertinent information; your users won't have to search through the entire site to locate what you are referring to.

This fluidity, combined with the programming efforts that brought about what we now know as browsers, has fulfilled the vision that Tim Berners-Lee had way back in the virtual "dark ages" of the Internet: The World Wide Web.

From Links to Hypertext

When Berners-Lee began laying out his plan for a linked information system, he was unaware that a term already existed for the process—*hypertext*—which was coined in the 1950s by Ted Nelson. It can be defined as "human readable information linked together in an unconstrained way."

In the beginning, these systems often used proprietary interfaces. Work was being done as early as the late 1980s to standardize hypertext systems. These efforts converged in the Internet arena as the development of the HyperText Markup Language, or HTML, established by Berners-Lee. This original version is now known as HTML 1.

In 1993, a young student at the National Center for Supercomputing Applications at the University of Illinois at Urbana-Champaign named Marc Andreesen created a graphical user interface for the Web known as Mosaic. It was originally developed on the X Windows platform, a Unix-based environment. (At the time, Unix was the most common operating system for Internet-connected computing systems.)

Later that year, the Mosaic programmers began devising custom extensions to HTML to expand on the capabilities of the Mosaic browser. Little did they know the trend that they would set in motion!

These advances, and suggestions from other individuals and institutions, were combined into an updated version of HTML, HTML 2, under the supervision of the Internet Engineering Task Force (IETF) in mid-1994.

The W3C was formed in late 1994, with guiding the structure and growth of HTML a top priority for the organization's efforts. The W3C has published an activity statement that summarizes its involvement in the standards process and defines its goals and directional vision for the future. You can find this document online at http://www.w3.org/MarkUp/Activity.

Spanning Platforms and Versions

When asked which Web browser they use, there's a good chance the average surfer will respond, "Netscape." But what exactly does *Netscape* mean? Netscape is the name of a company; so this answer is like saying you drive a Ford when asked what kind of car you own. Ford produces dozens of different models in any number of model years and sells them under a variety of nameplates (Ford, Mercury, Lincoln, and so on). The same goes for Web browsers. They are categorized by *platform* (the operating system being used on the computer in question, for example; Windows, Mac, or Unix) and by *version number* (similar to the model year of a car, though they often come out more frequently than that).

As you might suspect, the features of each browser are slightly different within the same version number across platforms and are often significantly different across versions. Differences may be as minor as which font is the default or as major as whether the browser supports Java. Appendix A, at the back of this book, outlines features and HTML tag support across major browser versions. Online, the BrowserCaps site has the results of several thousand browsers going up against a series of capability tests. You can take the test with your favorite browser or view the results at http://www.browsercaps.com/.

The Current State of HTML

Just before this book went to press, the W3C issued the working draft for HTML 4 as a proposed recommendation. All 220 W3C member organizations will be reviewing and voting on the proposal, a process that generally takes about six weeks. During this time, minor modifications may be made to the recommendation, based on comments from member organizations. Once voting is complete, the draft can either be accepted as an official recommendation, revert to working draft status for additional modification, or be abandoned as a W3C work project (a scenario that occurred with HTML 3—it was dropped in favor of moving forward with what became the HTML 3.2 recommendation).

Several exciting complementary projects are also underway, including:

Extensible Markup Language (XML)   A meta-language that allows you to create your own markup language along with making use of SGML concepts (Standard Generalized Markup Language, the superset of language that HTML was derived from).

Cascading Style Sheets 2   An expansion of the current CSS1 recommendation (discussed in detail in Skill 7) that combined with HTML 4 and XML forms the basis for the Document Object Model (DOM)—a language and platform independent interface that allows programs and scripts to access and update the content, style, and structure of documents dynamically. This system will complete the goal of separating a document's content from its presentation. You'll find a press release at `http://www.w3.org/Press/CSS2`.

Synchronized Multimedia Integration Language (SMIL)   Pronounced "smile," allows Web designers to bring televisionlike content to the Web, without the traditional constraints of massive bandwidth requirements or learning complicated programming languages. SMIL can be authored directly in a text-editor like HTML. You'll find the announcement of this first public draft at `http://www.w3.org/Press/SMIL`.

Dynamic HTML (DHTML)   A combination of CSS and JavaScript blended with HTML 4. Designers are given considerable new power over element placement and the overall look and feel of a Web site.

Innovations in Web technologies continue to come at a furious pace. As a Web designer, it's your job to keep yourself apprised of new developments. Not everyone will be able to immediately adopt each new technique as soon as the details hit the Net, nor should you expect everyone to do so.

Balancing the properties of current HTML recommendations, the abilities of the browsers in use by the general Web population, and the temptation to quickly incorporate new innovations in your designs can be a difficult task.

They Don't Call It the "Bleeding Edge" for Nothing

New technology is often described as "being on the cutting edge." The phrase sounds sexy, high-tech, and awe-inspiring. With the latest and greatest constantly evolving and changing in the online world, chasing after that cutting edge can be like juggling kitchen knives: you're likely to get nicked in the process.

How then, do you, a Web designer, balance the requirements of the existing technology with the frequent demands of clients or superiors that want the nifty new Web gizmo they saw on someone else's site last night?

The Cross-Compatibility Concept

Your goal is really quite simple; it stems from Tim Berners-Lee's original concept: anyone, on any type of computer, anywhere in the world, should be able to access your document and achieve the expected results. To maintain this tenet of universal readership, you need to keep in mind that:

- People access the Web from three major computing platforms—Windows, Macintosh, and Unix (including all *nix variants)—and on many less common platforms, such as NeXT, Be, VMS.

- Dozens of Web browsers are available for public use. Although the two most popular, Microsoft's Internet Explorer (IE) and Netscape's Navigator, are used by the vast majority of the installed user base, hundreds of thousands of netizens do use other browsers every day.

- Even among IE and Navigator users, there are half a dozen or more variations on *each platform*. Both IE and Navigator have had four major releases and several minor ones for each major release. (You can learn more about browsers in Skill 2.)

- Not every Web user is a Web junkie. Average users don't know how to upgrade their browsers, nor would they be particularly inclined to if they did. "If it ain't broke, don't fix it" is a common sentiment.

- Most computer users never change the defaults that were set on their systems at the factory. This often means they are browsing at a screen resolution of 640×480 pixels at 256 colors.

You *can* accommodate these often conflicting visitor needs with careful consideration and planning. By focusing your design efforts on the HTML features that can be interpreted by the widest array of browsers on the widest array of platforms, you'll accommodate the widest array of visitors. That doesn't mean, however, that you always have to cater to the lowest common denominator, which often ends up being the minimal abilities of Lynx, a text-based browser often found in academic settings (see Skill 2 for more information on Lynx).

In this book, you'll learn exactly which techniques work on which browsers. You'll become familiar with the HTML recommendations of the W3C and how to incorporate "valid" (correct) HTML markup into your documents. Every step of the way, we'll show you tips and tricks for including some of the more exciting cutting-edge Web design skills, all the while producing documents that *degrade gracefully* when viewed on less capable browsers.

Degrade? It's not as ugly as it sounds. Graceful degradation simply means that if a browser can't render your documents in the way that you intended, the end result is still visually and functionally acceptable.

Who's Out There?

Even though the Web originated in Europe, its growth exploded in the United States, in part due to the existing framework for the Internet through *ARPAnet*— the United States Defense Advanced Research Project Agency, a testing ground for new technologies that linked universities and research centers together—and in large part due to the intellectual gold rush that occurred in the computing industry in this country. In terms of raw numbers, the Web is still dominated by U.S. interests, but by no means should the Web be interpreted as a U.S.-only audience: there are more than 240 "wired" countries around the world.

TIP   You can find a list of all countries that have a two-character country code used for Internet addressing online at `http://www.ics.uci.edu/pub/websoft/wwwstat/country-codes.txt`.

Even in the United States, most of the population is not online. Among those who are, their hardware configurations are likely to be significantly less powerful than that used by those of us who frequent the Silicon Valley geek emporiums as often as most people zip through a drive-thru at the local burger joint.

In Georgia Tech's Graphics, Visualization, & Usability Center's eighth annual survey (http://www.gvu.gatech.edu/user_surveys/survey-1997-10/):

- Forty percent of U.S. respondents were women (up from just 5% in 1994).

- Most European respondents were male, at 78%.

- In higher age ranges there was a smaller pecentage of women online than in lower age ranges.

Additionally, other surveys (Baruch College-Harris Poll, IntelliQuest, FIND/SVP) found that:

- Total U.S. online users number between 40 and 47 million.

- Children account for almost 10 million of those users, a huge increase in that category since 1995.

- The average age of the online visitor is just over 35 years old. Forty-five percent of all users are over 40.

- Seventy-three percent of U.S. users have at least some college education.

- Forty-two percent of U.S. respondents have an annual income in excess of $50,000.

- Home access is still the most common, with 60% of U.S. users logging on there.

Hardware usage is also quite varied. Recent surveys have found that:

- Most online users still connect with a personal computer. Sixteen percent have begun using network computers or TV-based terminals.

- The browser wars (see Skill 2) have resulted in dozens of browser-usage statistic reports. Most tend to agree that at the time of this publication, Netscape still holds on to approximately 60% of the browser market and Microsoft to about 30. Other browsers make up about 10% of the market share, which could push the major browsers in either direction.

- Fifty-five percent of the GVU survey respondents connect via modems at 33.6K or slower.

- More than 70% of users haven't upgraded or switched browsers in more than a year.

Additionally, Web designers need to remember that the average CPU in many parts of the world (and in many educational settings in the United States) is still a 486 or a 386 (sometimes often just a 286!) class processor. This can prevent many users from installing the latest and greatest browsers and other Web software.

Have You Mastered the Essentials?

Now you can...

- ☑ Understand the origins of the Web.
- ☑ Follow the constant changes in HTML and related Web-design techniques.
- ☑ Explain the cross-browser and cross-platform philosophy.

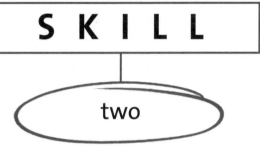

Browser Basics

- ❑ Browser history

- ❑ Browser wars

- ❑ Netscape Navigatore

- ❑ Microsoft Internet Explorer

- ❑ Lynx

- ❑ Mosaic

- ❑ AOL

- ❑ WebTV

Although most of us use either Netscape Navigator or Microsoft Internet Explorer, there are actually many other browsers available for the Web. In order to design accessible Web pages on your site, you should become familiar with not only the most common browsers, but also any others your audience might be using.

A Bit of Browser History

The World Wide Web was begun at *CERN (Conseil European pour la Recherche Nucleaire,* now known as European Laboratory for Particle Physics). Although the idea for the Web came from many different places, a proposal was initially written and circulated at CERN in 1989. CERN was also responsible for developing the first Web browser, which was released in 1990 (a very long time ago in Web years).

This first browser was developed as both a browser and editor on a NeXT-Step machine. Unlike the browsers with full graphical interfaces that we are used to seeing today, it only displayed text. Other browsers were soon developed, including Erwise, Viola, and Lynx. Today, many machines are still using these non-graphical browsers, especially Lynx. Lynx is used primarily on Unix and VMS systems, although it is available for all major platforms.

Later the NCSA (National Center for Supercomputing Applications), which is based at the University of Illinois at Urbana-Champaign, became involved with the Web and began developing a browser. This browser, Mosaic for X, was released to the public on X, PC/Windows, and Macintosh platforms in September of 1993.

One of the people who worked on the project as an undergraduate student at NCSA was Mark Andreessen. In 1994, he and five other people left NCSA to form the Mosaic Communications Corporation, which later became the Netscape Communications Corporation. Netscape released the first version of Netscape Navigator, nicknamed "Mozilla", at the end of 1994.

Meanwhile, it seemed like everyone was getting in on the browser craze. Microsoft developed Internet Explorer (IE), which has become Netscape's main competition; Sun Microsystems developed HotJava; and America Online (AOL) developed their own AOL browser. More recently, a company called WebTV has introduced a browser that runs though your television using what is commonly called a set-top box. Now you don't even need a computer to surf the Web!

Current Browser Usage

The two main browsers in use today are Netscape Navigator and Microsoft Internet Explorer. Together they comprise approximately 90% of the browser market. While it can be difficult to get accurate numbers, individual market-share (as of this book's press time) for these browsers puts Navigator at approximately 60% and IE at 30%.

As a Web site designer, it's important that you consider the 10 percent of people who are not using either Navigator or IE. While 10% does not sound like a lot, there are so many people on the Web that 10% can add up to a hefty number. For instance, if your potential audience numbered 10 million users (and there are even more people than that on the Web today), ten percent means that 1 million potential users are locked out of your site. Many of the features found in the two most popular browsers are not found in other, more basic browsers such as Lynx.

But different browsers are only part of your challenge. Along the way, browsers have been released in different versions, with each release supporting new features. When designing a Web site, it is important to realize that while the vast majority of your audience may be using Navigator or IE, a significant portion of them will not be using the latest version with the latest features. Even though it is fairly easy to get the latest version, browsers are released so often and so frequently contain bugs that many people are content staying with their current setup. Also, it seems like each release of a browser needs more computing power, and some people simply can't or won't upgrade their machines.

 NOTE   Most software companies undertake a period of end-user testing known as *beta testing*. A beta test is the second round of testing for a product (*alpha* testing normally being an internal test by company staff members). Microsoft and Netscape both release beta versions of their software to the general public. Many bugs and problem areas are resolved during this period, as well as improvements incorporated from user suggestions. Many Web developers love to live on this "bleeding edge" of cutting edge technology and download the new betas the minute they're available. Remember though that new features found in these betas are often not supported by earlier versions of the browser, and the general public is traditionally far slower to upgrade than the hard-core Net community.

You can see the interfaces for IE and Navigator browsers below. Figure 2.1 shows the IE 3 interface; Figure 2.2 shows the IE 4 interface. Figure 2.3 and Figure 2.4 show the interfaces of versions 3 and 4 of Navigator. All of the interfaces are shown on the Windows 95 platform. If you only have one browser on your machine now, consider downloading at least the latest versions of Navigator and IE. When visiting sites mentioned in upcoming skills, look at them through each browser. See if you can detect any subtle differences in the way the browsers render the pages.

 NOTE   Navigator can be downloaded from http://home.netscape.com/download/index.html. Microsoft's download page for IE can be found at http://www.microsoft.com/ie/download/.

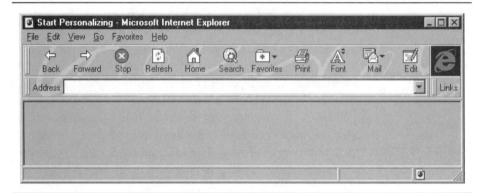

FIGURE 2.1: The IE 3.0 interface

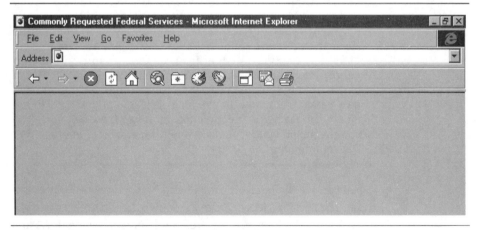

FIGURE 2.2: The IE 4.0 interface

FIGURE 2.3: The Navigator 3.0 interface

FIGURE 2.4: The Navigator 4.0 interface

The Browser Wars

Sometimes it seems that companies such as Netscape and Microsoft release new versions of their software constantly. While other types of software updates can take years, new browsers are released every few months. Probably the biggest reason for the frequent updates is what is commonly referred to as the *browser wars*.

What Are the Browser Wars?

The browsers wars are a race between companies (namely Netscape and Microsoft) to establish market dominance for their browser by being the first to release new features which work only with their particular browser.

The idea is that people (such as yourself) who develop Web sites will want to use a great new HTML tag even though it's only supported by one of the browsers, let's say in this case, IE. In order to take advantage of the tag, you'll attempt to get your users to use IE, perhaps by providing a link so they can download it.

Why Are the Browser Wars Happening?

If the browsers are often inexpensive or even free, then why is everyone clamoring to get their browser on your desktop? The answer is that companies such as Microsoft and Netscape make other software, such as server software, which is much more expensive. They are counting on the name recognition from all of the free or low-cost software to propel buyers to the higher priced purchases.

Another issue is that of standards. In the software industry, there is usually a push to develop standards, or protocols, that similar pieces of software all use. In the Web industry, these standards are often about HTML. The World Wide Web Consortium (http://www.w3.org/) is responsible for setting the standards for HTML, and for deciding what is "official" HTML and what isn't. Browser companies frequently release HTML tags that are not official HTML tags as defined by W3C. These browser-specific HTML tags are dubbed HTML extensions.

The setting of standards in software is not a one way street—it's not as if the World Wide Web Consortium decides the standards and everyone goes from there. Rather, there is a back and forth—extensions from companies such as Netscape and Microsoft are so commonly used that the software companies have a hand in setting the standards, not just following them. In Table 2.1, you'll see other examples of the browser companies and the World Wide Web Consor-tium working together to set standards. From a software company's point of view, the advantage of being the company to set the standards is that your company will already have the standard implemented, whereas your competition will now have to catch up. The downside, however, is that the W3C may decide against your implementation of a new feature, leaving you without support for their chosen path. The emergence of dynamic HTML and positioning methods used with cascading stylesheets (see Skill 7) is just one such example. Netscape's <LAYER> method was rejected by the W3C in favor of DHTML and CSS.

As a Web designer, you have a responsibility to keep up with which elements are "official" and which are browser-specific extensions. Always keep in mind that reliance on such "browserisms" can literally keep visitors from being able to view your site—and nobody wants that!

Browser Developments

So what about the developments in the browser wars? (And why should you care?) The reason that developments are so important is that they vastly affect your ability to design effective, accessible Web sites. It is the business of every professional Web designer to stay on top of browser developments and how they are going to affect Web design. Table 2.1 shows a timeline of browser developments which have already taken place.

TABLE 2.1: A brief history of browser development

Date	Development
October 1994	Netscape introduces Netscape Navigator 1.0 free to users via the Internet.
March 1995	Netscape Navigator 1.1 is announced. It includes support for advanced layout capabilities using HTML 3.0 tables and graphical backdrops. These capabilities allow more sophisticated page presentation, including multiple text columns and flexible image placement.
September 1995	Netscape introduces Netscape Navigator Gold 2.0, which enables users to easily create, edit, and navigate live online documents. Naturally, the editor that's a part of the Gold package supports the Netscape extensions. Capabilities include support for frames, a page presentation capability in Netscape Navigator 2.0 that enables the display of multiple, independently scrollable cells on a single screen; and HTML 3.0 tables and backdrops.
January 1996	Netscape announces plug-ins, which are small pieces of software that enhance browser capabilities.
April 1996	Netscape announces Netscape Navigator 3.0. It supports new HTML tags, including background colors in tables and audio and video embedding functions.
	Microsoft Internet Explorer 2.0 for Macintosh is released. It supports the Shockwave plug-in, HTML 2.0 and 3.0 tags, QuickTime, and Virtual Reality Modeling Language (VRML).
May 1996	Microsoft Internet Explorer 3.0 Beta becomes available.
June 1996	Netscape announces that more than 130 plug-in developers are creating plug-ins to work with Netscape Navigator. It also announces that its Internet site receives over 80 million hits a day and has accumulated a total of over 10 billion hits since its inception. Microsoft's team continues the furious pace of development of IE 3.0, which will introduce extensability through Active X controls.
August 1996	Netscape announces the availability of Netscape Navigator 3.0, which supports both Java and JavaScript. Several third-party developers make public plans to develop plug-ins to take advantage of Netscape Navigator 3.0 functionality. There are already 175 plug-ins announced for Netscape Navigator.
	Microsoft launches Internet Explorer 3.0. Top Web sites offer free content that can only be viewed by users with Internet Explorer 3.0.
October 1996	Netscape announces Netscape Communicator, which integrates Netscape Navigator 4.0 browser software, Netscape Composer HTML authoring software, Netscape Messenger electronic mail, Netscape Collabra group discussion software, and Netscape Conference real-time collaboration software.
	Netscape announces Netscape Navigator 4.0, which includes support for absolute positioning, layering and stylesheets, new HTML fonts for authoring, and support for Netscape ONE (the open network environment).

Skill 2

TABLE 2.1 CONTINUED: A brief history of browser development

Date	Development
January 1997	Microsoft ships the final Internet Explorer 3.0 for Macintosh. Microsoft Internet Explorer 3.0 offers full support for HTML 3.2, tables, frames, and enhanced frames (borderless and floating). With this version, Internet Explorer becomes the first browser to allow Macintosh users to view Web pages created using the HTML standard cascading stylesheets.
April 1997	Microsoft announces Microsoft Internet Explorer 4.0. Improved stylesheet support, Dynamic HTML , and the Active Desktop are touted as the new wave in browsing.
July 1997	Microsoft endorses the World Wide Web Consortium's HTML 4.0 and announces support in Microsoft Internet Explorer 4.0.

How Do Browser Wars Affect Users?

Now that you've looked at the history of browser developments, you can probably see how such developments affect your potential Web sites. Let's take a look at the ways the browser wars and the general evolution of Web standards affect your work, in both positive and negative ways.

The Upside

Browser wars result in newer, better features that you can implement on your Web sites. The blistering pace of development leads to regular updates and bug fixes in browsers as well as timely changes in the user interface brought about by consumer comments. If you've spent much time surfing the Web, you've probably seen excellent uses for advanced HTML capabilities such as tables, frames, and forms. These features allow users to view information in columns or cells, navigate sites using toolbars, and give and receive feedback.

You've probably also seen cool uses of Java and animation—everything from having information pop up when someone mouses over an image to calculating mortgage loans. Used in moderation, such advancements can add a lot to the user's Web experience.

Another example would be Netscape's invention of the plug-in interface, which we'll cover later on in Skill 20. By building a browser that worked with plug-ins, Netscape allowed users to add additional functionality by downloading relatively small pieces of software and simply storing them in the appropriate directory. This allowed users to be able to view video, hear audio, see 3D worlds, and so on. An alternative to plug-ins has been helper applications, or non-Netscape applications, which were launched when the user needed to use a file that was not supported by the browser. Many capabilities that used to be handled exclusively by helper applications are now handled directly by the browser or by plug-ins. Microsoft later adopted the plug-in interface for Internet Explorer.

 NOTE Browser releases also frequently contain additional features that enhance the user's experience but do not really affect how you design a Web site. One example is the ability to read e-mail from within the browser.

As the software companies continue to try and outdo each other, both in market share and in the standardization process, it is frequently the end users who benefit. But this is not the case for every user, especially not for those who do not keep up with the latest software, either because they are not able to or because they choose not to. That said, let's take a look at the challenges provided by the browser wars.

The Downside

As we've mentioned, the main challenge for the Web designer is designing a Web site that works for different browsers. To this end, the designer should keep several things in mind:

- The latest official World Wide Web Consortium HTML standards.

- Which features are supported by which browsers. This includes not only the two main browsers, but also the other browsers such as Lynx, Mosaic, AOL, and WebTV.

- Which features are supported by which *versions* of the browsers. An early version of a browser does not support all of the features supported by the latest version.

- Which types of browsers your audience will be using. If you are going to have a general interest or commercial Web site freely available to the public, you can expect to get all kinds of browsers. If you are designing a site which will only be available to people in your company, all of whom use Netscape Navigator 3.01 for Windows, you might be able to get away with a bit more.

- The fact that, depending on how you choose to design your site, your audience can have the choice of which fonts and font sizes they use to view your site.

- The fact that the audience may choose to come to your site with the images turned off.

- Whether a feature that requires certain browser capabilities is really worth it. That is, whether it adds enough value to the site to justify locking out users whose browsers do not support the feature.

- Whether there is another way to achieve a desired result that is supported by more browsers. (This may not always be the case, but it's great if you can come up with it.)

- The likely speed of the connection your viewers will use to access the site. We haven't really discussed this, but it helps to know if a lot of your users are coming in over a 14.4 modem (which is likely if your Web site is publicly accessible) or over a T1 connection (which may be the case over a closed corporate intranet).

As you can see, the real challenge is keeping on top of these issues and making sure that you take them into consideration when making Web site design decisions. While it may seem like a lot to consider, it's important that you have all of the facts in order to make informed decisions. Once you get used to considering these factors, it becomes second nature. Also, once you're caught up with the basics (hopefully, by reading this book), you just need to *maintain* your knowledge base.

Browser Security Issues

Another challenge that may not affect the design of your site as directly as other aspects, but is certainly worth mentioning in any discussion about browser wars, is that of security. Frequently in the race to get browsers out the door, companies do not adequately test the security of their browsers. Usually, if you wait a few weeks after a major browser release, someone will find a security problem with the browser and a patch will be issued. Recently, these security problems have been related to code that downloads and executes on the user's computer, such as Java and ActiveX controls. While patches have been released for these particular problems, they serve as key examples of how, in the race to beat the competition, software companies do not always test adequately.

Primary Features of Browsers

Sometimes the biggest battle, especially for the beginner, is figuring out what the browser features actually are and who supports them. Again, it's important that you are aware of which features are supported by which browsers and in which versions they were first implemented. Armed with this knowledge, you'll be able to make educated decisions about the design and features of your Web sites by analyzing your server statistics for which browsers your audience is using and how many of them may be unable to see features you have implemented. The process of analyzing your server logs is discussed in detail in Skill 12. In this section, we'll examine in more detail the browsers you are likely to encounter.

For a much more detailed list of which features and HTML tags are supported by different versions of each browser, please see Appendix A.

Netscape Navigator

Netscape Navigator is currently the most popular browser on the World Wide Web. As of this writing, Navigator is in various iterations of version 4. While the browser is available as a stand-alone application, Netscape has also bundled it into a suite of products named Netscape Communicator; Communicator includes not only the browser, but also other tools for collaboration. For purposes of this discussion, we're going to stick with just the browser.

Multimedia, Interaction, and Animations

There are many ways to implement interactivity or movement on a site. One way is by using animated GIFs, in which a series of GIF files load on the page in sequence. GIF is a graphics format—you can read more about it in Skill 16. Netscape Navigator supports animated GIFs.

Netscape Navigator also supports the EMBED tag, which is not official HTML, but which allows the embedding (for example) of an audio file. The EMBED tag works for versions of Navigator 2.0 and later. The embedded file is handled by a plug-in.

Another way to add interaction and multimedia to the Web is by using Java and JavaScript. Java is a full-featured object-oriented programming language and it can be used to insert applets into Web pages or to write stand-alone applications. Java can be inserted into an HTML page by using the APPLET tag, which is supported by Netscape 2.0 and later, although it did not appear in the official HTML specification until HTML 3.2. JavaScript, on the other hand, is a scripting language and is not used to develop stand-alone applications. It is implemented using the SCRIPT tag, which was not implemented in Navigator until version 3.05b.

Plug-ins, which are small pieces of software used to extend a software program's capabilities, were implemented in Web browsers by Netscape Communications for Navigator beginning with version 2.0. Plug-ins can be used for viewing audio, video, 3D, and many other things You can even use them to look at other users' desktops. It just depends on which plug-in you have (and how much RAM you can spare!).

You can add forms to your Web site by using the FORM tag. You can use forms to ask any questions you like, to gain information about your users, and to give them a chance to provide feedback. Forms have been supported by Navigator since version 1.1.

Tables, Layout, and Styles

Ah, tables. It was a great advancement when Web designers were finally able to lay information out in rows and columns by using tables instead of preformatted text (more on that in the HTML section). Netscape Navigator has been supporting tables since version 1.1, although some of the attributes to the TABLE tag were added later. Tables can be really handy.

If you've ever surfed the Web and come across Web sites that had several different "panes" or individual sections within the larger browser window, you've seen frames. Each of these frames can be scrolled through separately. Some people love them, others hate them. Navigator has supported simple frames since version 1.1. A lot of the fun features (such as frame colors) were not supported until version 3.05b, which came out at about the time frames were becoming much more popular.

The newest style advancement to hit the Web is stylesheets, a concept first implemented in a major browser by Microsoft Corporation. The idea behind stylesheets is that the Web designer can specify design elements for the entire site in one place. For example, a designer could say that all of the paragraphs should be in a blue font, and then every paragraph will automatically be blue. The paragraph gets the information that it's blue from the stylesheet (a separate document). What that means is that the designer needs only to specify the paragraph color in the style-sheet. This allows the designer to change all the paragraphs on the site to any other color by changing only the stylesheet rather than changing every paragraph. This is a huge timesaver.

There are many other advantages to stylesheets, such as the ability to send different stylesheets for different types of users. A user using a speech-based browser can request a very simple document, while a graphic designer can request a graphics-intensive page, for example.) Another advantage of stylesheets is that they make it much easier to make your Web site consistent—all of your tables can automatically look the same, for example. You'll learn more about styesheets in Skill 7. For now, just keep in mind that they are only supported by the newer browsers. Netscape did not support stylesheets until Navigator 4.0, so a lot of people cannot yet view them.

Images

The ability to have images is what gave the Web a tremendous advantage over Gopher, its predecessor. While not all browsers can view images *inline*, meaning on the same page as text, all browsers are capable of downloading images so you can view them. I'll cover images in much more depth in a later chapter, but I wanted to mention here that inline images have been supported by Navigator since version 1.0. Images are commonly used as links.

One use of images is as *imagemaps*. An imagemap is a clickable image divided into sections, each section linking you to a different place on the Web. Imagemaps, like images, have been implemented in Netscape since version 1.0. You'll learn how to create them in Skill 9.

NOTE   There are actually two kinds of imagemaps: client-side imagemaps and server-side imagemaps. Navigator supports both, but some other browsers, such as Lynx, do not. For more information, read the section about Lynx below.

Mail and News

Many browsers allow the user to read and send e-mail or Usenet newsgroup posts. This all-in-one approach is popular, in that it allows Web site designers to incorporate links to newsgroup archives or specific e-mail addresses right in their Web pages. Both news and mail have been featured by Navigator since version 1.0, although the interface has changed quite a bit with newer versions.

Secure Transactions

While there are many types of security and encryption on the Internet, you are probably most interested in secure purchasing. Beginning with Navigator 3.0, digital certificates have been supported. Newer versions of Netscape have a key icon at the bottom which lets you see if a transaction is secure. This will be more important if you plan to have a Web site where your users can purchase goods. See Skill 22 for a detailed discussion on Web commerce.

Microsoft Internet Explorer

Microsoft was a later contender in the browser wars and has quickly caught up with Netscape. Microsoft Internet Explorer is currently in version 4.0. Along the way, Microsoft has developed some technologies, including stylesheets and ActiveX.

Let's take a quick look at how IE supports the major features explained above.

Multimedia, Interaction, and Animations

As you might expect, IE supports GIF animations. It also has supported Java applets since version 3.0b2. The inclusion of the SCRIPT tag for JavaScript came with version 3.0. Microsoft also copied Netscape's plug-in idea—there are currently many plug-ins for both Navigator and IE. IE has supported forms from the very beginning—version 1.0.

Perhaps the most interesting twist in IE development has been the introduction of ActiveX. ActiveX was devised by Microsoft, adapting existing OLE 2.0 and OCX technologies for Internet applications. An ActiveX control is a cross between a plug-in and a Java applet—it adds functionality that acts like a plug-in, and it runs independently of the browser, like an applet. Unlike an applet, the ActiveX control is downloaded and stored on the user's hard disk. ActiveX controls currently are not supported by any browser other than IE, though there is a Navigator plug-in which will allow you to view ActiveX controls. Support for ActiveX began with IE 3.0.

Tables, Layout, and Styles

Microsoft Internet Explorer has supported tables since version 1.0 and frames since version 3.0. The options it supports for frames are a bit different from the ones supported by Netscape Navigator, though, and Microsoft also invented floating frames (using the IFRAME tag). You'll learn about frames in Skill 5.

Images

IE has supported images since version 2.0. It doesn't support a lot of image placement options, such as centering, or directing the flow of text around the image object. IE also supports imagemaps.

Mail and News

Beginning with version 2.0, IE has supported reading and sending e-mail, along with reading from and posting to newsgroups.

Secure Transactions

Like Navigator, IE supports digital certificates for security. Additionally, IE has a technology called Authenticode. Authenticode allows software creators to digitally sign their software so that users can be very sure that the software (including Java applets) originated where they think it did.

One feature in IE that many parents find attractive is the ability to use "parental controls" that are built into the browser. These settings will not allow the user to view Web sites that have unacceptable (as defined by the parent setting the controls) content ratings. You'll learn more about rating systems later in Skill 22.

Lynx

Lynx was developed at the University of Kansas to be used on their own system. The current version is 2.6. Lynx is an older "bare bones" text-based browser and has the advantage of running on older systems. It is used mostly on Unix and VMS systems, although you can get it for other platforms. It is particularly popular at universities and colleges, where students often have Unix shell accounts.

Lynx is also popular with some people with visual impairments because it can be configured as a text reader to read lines form Web pages. With their system configured with the proper audio hardware called a speech synthesizer, the computer reads out loud to the user. Additionally, many heavy Web users will fire up Lynx when they're looking for text-based information content in a hurry. Because the browser doesn't load images and many other large file-size objects, sites can be rapidly skimmed for relevant content.

Lynx is a text-only browser, so if you want to accommodate Lynx users, you'll have to provide alternatives to images or else let Lynx users download them. We'll go over the use of alternative text for images later, in Skill 5.

Lynx is a perfect example of something we see frequently in the software world—often there is a tradeoff between features (such as images, formatting, and frames) and system requirements (such as platform issues and RAM). While Lynx does not support many of the newer features, you also don't need a ton of RAM and a newer machine to run it. With Lynx's command line interface, it can take some getting used to if you are accustomed to pointing and clicking. You can see the Lynx interface below in Figure 2.5.

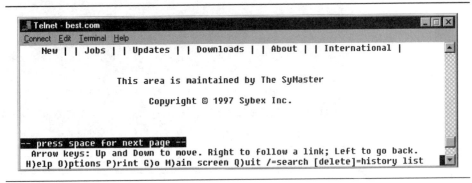

FIGURE 2.5: The Lynx browser interface

Multimedia, Interaction, and Animations

Lynx does not support animated GIFs, the EMBED tag, Java, JavaScript, plug-ins, or the ActiveX architecture. Lynx does support forms, although Lynx users have to navigate through them using the arrow keys or the TAB key on the keyboard rather than simply clicking in a field and typing in their content. Lynx can handle checkboxes, radio buttons, regular buttons, selection lists, and text submission areas.

Tables, Layout, and Styles

Lynx does support tables, although it does not necessarily display them as intended. It recognizes the TABLE tag and then breaks out the information into a sort of outline form. That is, all of the information is there and the user can figure out the hierarchy and follow the links if they exist, but you should not depend too heavily on the rows and columns. If you want to plan tables which make sense to Lynx users, you might want to use the PRE tag, discussed later in this book.

Figure 2.6 shows a basic table in Lynx 2.7 for Windows 95. It has three columns; first name, last name, and city. With just two rows, it's fairly easy to read. However, you can imagine how it would look with a dozen or more additional rows, all containing data of various lengths. It can get messy pretty quickly.

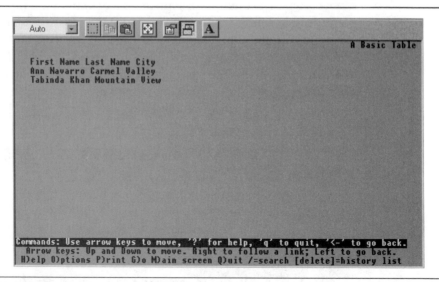

FIGURE 2.6: A basic table as seen in Lynx.

Frames in Lynx are a similar story to tables—while Lynx recognizes and handles the tags associated with frames, the results might be quite different from what you intended. Instead of rendering the frames, Lynx provides text links to the different frames on an HTML page. Later, as you learn how to create frames, you will learn more about the NOFRAMES tag, which is used to provide alternative content for browsers that don't support frames at all. Lynx does not support stylesheets.

Images

As noted earlier, the Lynx browser does not support images. However, it does work with imagemaps.

Lynx works better with client-side imagemaps because it is easier for the browser to figure out where different areas of the map lead. This is because on a client-side map, the browser has the chance to process alternate text. Remember, there are no images, so the map is displayed in Lynx as text links. On a server-side map, the browser clicks and a pair of coordinates is sent to the server. Lynx is only capable of sending the coordinates (0,0), and so this does not work well. There are workarounds, but they are not as elegant as having a client-side map to begin with. (To learn about the difference between client-side image maps and server-side image maps, refer to Skill 9.)

Mail and News

You cannot read your e-mail from within Lynx. However, you can send e-mail from Lynx if there is a link to an e-mail address or an author has been specified within the HTML page. Lynx supports the reading of newsgroups and replying to newsgroup posts.

Secure Transactions

Lynx does not currently support any extra security features.

NCSA Mosaic

Like Lynx, NCSA Mosaic is a university-developed browser. NCSA Mosaic is from the National Center for Supercomputing Applications at the University of Illinois at Urbana-Champaign. NCSA Mosaic was first released to the public in 1993. As you might recall form the section earlier in this skill on browser history, it was from NCSA that Mark Andreessen and some of his colleagues left to form Netscape Communications Corporation in 1994.

NCSA Mosaic is an older browser with limited capabilities, although it can handle many more HTML tags and file types than Lynx can. One of the biggest differences between NCSA Mosaic and Lynx is that Lynx supports graphics file formats.

As of January 1997, the Mosaic team has stopped development of any new versions of the browser. However, many people still use it faithfully. Mosaic is available for the X-Windows, Macintosh, and PC platforms.

Multimedia, Interaction, and Animations

NCSA Mosaic does not support animated GIFs, the EMBED tag, Java applets, JavaScript, or the plug-in or the ActiveX architecture. It does support forms.

Tables, Layout, and Styles

NCSA Mosaic does not support tables, frames, or stylesheets.

Images

This is one of the areas in which Mosaic is more advanced than Lynx. Beginning with version 2.0, Mosaic can display GIF and JPG image files. Earlier versions do not support images at all.

NCSA Mosaic does not support imagemaps.

Mail and News

NCSA Mosaic does not support mail and news reading.

Secure Transactions

Like Lynx, NCSA Mosaic does not have secure transaction systems built into the browser. It does not support a feature like digital certificates.

AOL

In 1995, the world's largest online service provider, America Online (AOL) developed a Web browser. The AOL browser was not very well-received and AOL moved over to allowing AOL users to choose which browser they would like to use with the AOL service. AOL has a huge installed base (over 8 million subscribers), and some of them still use the AOL browser. It's nearly impossible to know for sure just how many AOL members use the original AOL browser and how many have upgraded to mainstream offerings.

For the user, the benefit of using the AOL browser is that they get on the Web instantly—everything goes though AOL and there is very little that the user has to download and configure. The drawback is that the quality of the AOL browser is poor. Many a Web site which was designed to work fine on other browsers needed an new "AOL version." Version 3.0 is the last version. You can see the AOL 3.0 browser interface below in Figure 2.7.

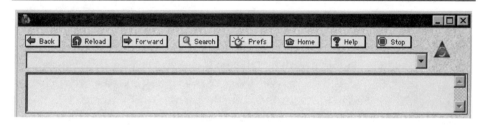

FIGURE 2.7: The AOL 3.0 browser interface. Copyright © 1997-98 America Online, Inc. All Rights Reserved.

Multimedia, Interaction, and Animations

The AOL browser does not support animated GIFs, the EMBED tag, Java, or JavaScript. It also does not support plug-ins or ActiveX components. It does support forms.

Tables, Layout, and Styles

The AOL browser supports tables and frames, although the frames are reported to be buggy. The browser recognizes the TABLE tag but not many of the attributes (options) for it. Both tables and frames were implemented beginning with version 3.0.

The AOL browser does not support stylesheets.

Images

All versions of the AOL browser support images and image maps.

Mail and News

The AOL browser lets the customer use mail and news, but access is limited to what AOL provides—there is no direct access to the Internet.

Secure Transactions

The AOL browser does not contain any features to increase the security of online transactions. It does not support digital certificates.

WebTV

On to the next idea for Web access—the WebTV browser lets the user access the Internet through a television set. The user environment is very different from a computer, so if you decide you want to include WebTV users as much as possible, you should definitely take the time to check how their extensions work.

At this writing, WebTV is just becoming a viable product and the browser version is 0.9. However, the future for WebTV (which was recently purchased by Microsoft) as an individual product is uncertain. Competing concepts include a set-top box being introduced by RCA and Zenith Electronics using Navio/NCI software and PC-TV and "PC Theater" products being developed by Philips Electronics, Gateway 2000, and Compaq. The existing WebTV market is still small, just over 100,000 subscribers currently online as of this writing. How WebTV and Microsoft will fare in this increasingly competitive segment is yet to be seen.

Multimedia, Interaction, and Animations

The WebTV browser version 0.9 supports animated GIFs and forms, although it does not support encryption (for security) for the information submitted via forms. It does not support the EMBED tag, Java applets, JavaScript, plug-ins, or ActiveX.

Tables, Layout, and Styles

WebTV supports tables, though in a non-traditional manner. The WebTV browser does not support frames or stylesheets. One of the most problematic conventions of WebTV is that the terminal is set to a fixed 544 pixels in width and it does not support horizontal scrolling. Users will likely run into display troubles when trying to view Web sites that make use of wider elements.

Images

The WebTV browser supports graphics. There are many extensions which are specific to WebTV. It also supports client-side imagemaps.

Mail and News

The WebTV browser allows users to send and receive e-mail but does not have a direct interface to Usenet news. Users can still read newsgroup postings which are mirrored on Web sites.

Secure Transactions

The WebTV browser does not contain any security elements, including support for digital certificates.

Have You Mastered the Essentials?

Now you can. . .

- ☑ Describe how browsers have changed and evolved.
- ☑ Understand how changes in browsers affect you and your ability to design an effective Web site.
- ☑ List the major features that are supported by browsers today.
- ☑ Make informed decisions about which features you want to consider including or excluding on your Web sites.

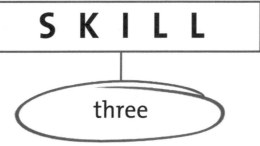

The HTML Document

- ❏ Selecting an Editor

- ❏ HTML must haves

- ❏ Describing your document with *TITLE* and *META* tags

- ❏ Defining text and background looks using the *BODY* tag

- ❏ Headings and text placement

By now you should be aware that an HTML document provides the structure for your Web page. In this skill you'll step through the creation of a basic HTML document. First we'll discuss HTML editors and how to select one, and then we'll move on to the actual document. We'll cover several types of HTML elements and how they are constructed along with any options you may have for their use.

The basic structure of the document is set up with the DOCTYPE, HTML and BODY tags, while the tags nested within the HEAD tag describe your document.

Selecting an Editor

Before you begin creating your first HTML document, you need to select a text editor to work in. There are lots to choose from, and which one you ultimately end up using is a matter of personal preference and availability.

Some HTML purists believe that using Windows' NotePad or Unix's vi editor is the only way to acquire your markup skills. We won't go that far, but we do have several suggestions.

What to Use

There are literally dozens of HTML authoring tools on the market today, in retail, shareware, or even freeware format. These may simply be enhanced text editors that automatically highlight your HTML tags in various colors or make a spellchecker available to you, or they may provide built-in macros to handle repetitive markup tasks. Quite a few of them profess to provide *WYSIWYG* control over your layout, that is: What You See Is What You Get. We'll amend that to: What You See Is What You *and Only You* Get. As you learned in Skill 2, each browser version may display document elements in a different manner. Sometimes a *very* different manner! So you know that a Pentium powered PC running Windows 95 and Netscape 3.01 will present a very different picture than the old 386 running Windows 3.1 and NCSA Mosaic that you sometimes use down at the university computer lab. So how can a tool guarantee that everyone will see your page the way you do? For the most part, *they can't*. At least not completely.

Now, no one is purporting that the creators of these tools have developed a group case of dottiness. To the contrary, many of these tools can be very handy, when—and only when—the user is aware of how the programs produce the resulting HTML document. Do they produce markup that makes use of browser-specific tags? Do they rely heavily on tables for layout? Will they allow you to tweak the HTML yourself?

The main thing to keep in mind is this: before you can use these tools intelligently, you must have a sound comprehension of the underlying HTML processes. Each skill in this book will provide you with the background behind each tag, in order to help you choose the best possible presentation for your projects. Once you become experienced in these tasks, you may choose an authoring tool that saves you time by automating some choices and processes for you. Until then, it's best to follow the tradition of "learning by doing."

Editors Available for the PC

Text Pad   A true favorite! Text Pad can be customized to behave like familiar programs such as Microsoft applications, WordStar, BRIEF and others. It provides integrated spell checking, a powerful search and replace utility, sticky indents, macro recording, and an innovative "clip library" for inserting frequently used text such as HTML tags. The winner of its class in the 1997 Ziff-Davis Shareware Awards, this Helios Software Solutions product is available for Windows 3.1 and Win95/NT. The Win95/NT version is included on the CD that comes with this book. (See Figure 3.1.)

Programmer's File Editor   As the name implies, this product is geared toward programmers. However, it carries several features that are handy for HTML markup. It also includes the ability to drag and drop files from File Manager or Explorer and multiple levels of undo and active buttons on a toolbar for the most frequently performed operations. Programmers File Editor is a freeware product that is available for Windows 3.1 and Windows 95/NT.

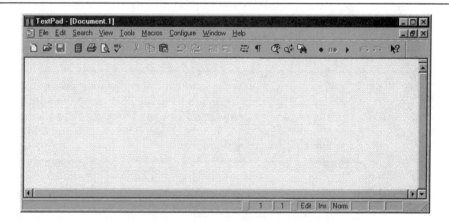

FIGURE 3.1:   The Text Pad 3.0 interface (Win95/NT version)

Notepad   The Microsoft Windows classic, Notepad is about as basic as it gets, with the capability for search, cut and paste, and word wrapping. Notepad ships and installs with the standard Windows 3.1 and Windows 95 setup.

WordPad   Microsoft's junior word processor, WordPad is a bit of a cross between Notepad and Word. It provides standard text formatting options for font choices, bullets, alignment, and so forth; and it can save files in Rich Text Format or Word 6 format. WordPad users should take care to save files as standard text documents rather than using the default and saving files as Word 6 documents, which contain control codes and other artifacts that can degrade your HTML documents. WordPad is a Microsoft product and ships with Windows 95.

Editors for the Mac

BBEdit   The 1996 winner of the MacUser Editors' Choice Award, this program includes a powerful search and replace mechanism, customizable behavior settings, macros, and much more. BBEdit is the standard in Mac-based HTML editing. It is available from Bare Bones Software and works with System 7 or later. (See Figure 3.2.)

Text-Edit Plus   When you need a more powerful text editor that includes drag and drop, multi-file search and replace, and even Speech Manager support, this shareware product from Trans-Tex Software fits the bill. You'll need System 7 or later to run it.

SimpleText   This classic Mac text editor is included with your OS software. File sizes are limited, which may inhibit your ability to do all of your Web editing with this program. This program is published by Apple Computer, Inc.

 NOTE   There are a slew of additional programs commonly available that you might want to take a look at. Two good resources for shareware, freeware, and product demos are Tucows (The Ultimate Collection of Windows Software) at http://www.tucows.com and CNet's Download.com at http://www.download.com.

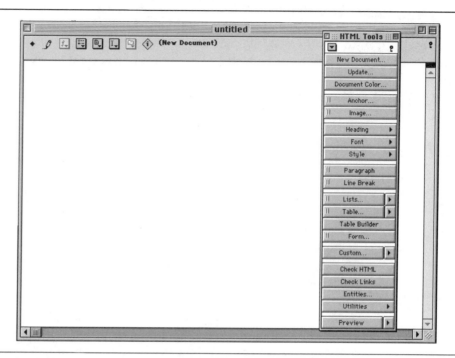

FIGURE 3.2:   The BBEdit interface on a Mac

In the Beginning

There are several components that every HTML document must have in order to be processed correctly: DOCYTPE, HTML, HEAD, TITLE, and META. We'll look at each of them in turn below. Some might go so far as to say that that a document simply isn't an HTML document without them—like fettuccini alfredo without sauce is no longer a lusciously creamy concoction, only noodles. No matter whom you ask they'll say that these tags are key components to any HTML document.

To begin creating your HTML file, you will choose what type of document to create. Sounds a bit rhetorical, doesn't it? You're working on an HTML file, right? But, there are actually many different versions or standards of HTML. You might compare them to dialects of a single language.

With HTML, there are dialects or versions that have evolved around specific browsers, and there are those browsers that strictly follow the standards published by the W3C. With the DOCTYPE tag, explained in detail in the next section, you'll be selecting which version of HTML you want to work with.

The Document Type

One of the most cryptic HTML components you'll run into is the DOCTYPE tag. This tag identifies your file as an HTML document and also identifies the specific *document type definition* (*DTD*) that your document makes use of. The DTD is a file that defines the syntax of a language based on SGML. You should remember from Skill 1 that HTML is a subset of SGML, so it too makes use of document type definitions.

An HTML DTD is the entire collection of tags that may be used in that version of HTML. It defines which tags are required and which are optional. The DTD also includes all the possible variations on a tag that are allowed under its particular structure. You might think of it as an HTML dictionary.

The Internet Engineering Task Force, in cooperation with the W3 Consortium created the DTDs for HTML 2.0 and HTML 3.0. Additional definitions have been created for specific browsers in an attempt to reproduce the behavior of the individual programs. This can be handy when you know that your Web audience will be using a specific browser publisher (such as Netscape) or a specific browser version. This scenario would be most commonly found in *intranet* settings—internal corporate Web sites that aren't accessible to anyone outside the company and where the system administrators would have greater control over what browser programs are used. While some of these new DTDs have not been developed or endorsed by the browser publishers, they will serve the purposes of most HTML developers in these situations with few to no difficulties.

The DOCTYPE tag is present to tell an SGML *parser*, or processor, what DTD it should use while processing the document. HTML documents don't go through an SGML parser before display, but the DOCTYPE tag is instrumental in allowing you to quickly review your HTML syntax for errors. Though you technically can leave it out of your document, it's best not to, for reasons that will be covered in the section on validation in Skill 8.

ALPHABET SOUP ORGANIZATIONS

Okay, so just who are the Internet Engineering Task Force and the W3 Consortium, and how do they impact what we're doing?

The IETF is an open community of network engineers, operators, vendors, and researchers who are concerned with smooth operation of the Internet and the development of net related architecture. The organization is open to any interested individual.

The IETF compiled the DTDs for HTML through version 3, at which time control over that activity was assumed by the W3C. They currently produce recommendations, specifications, and informational documents dealing with a wide variety of Internet protocols.

The W3 Consortium, or W3C, is an international industry consortium, jointly hosted by the Massachusetts Institute of Technology Laboratory for Computer Science (MIT/LCS) here in the United States, Institut National de Recherche en Informatique et en Automatique (INRIA) in Europe, and the Keio University Shonan Fujisawa Campus in Asia. The consortium was formed in 1994 to develop common protocols for use on the Web. Tim Berners-Lee, creator of the World Wide Web, serves as Director and Jean-François Abramatic is the current Chairman.

The W3C is funded by commercial members. Although those members may be key industry players like Netscape and Microsoft Corporation, the organization strives to remain "vendor neutral" while working to produce the specifications that will be recommended for inclusion in Internet related products.

The most commonly known recommendations delivered by the W3C are the specifications for each new version of HTML. Each version begins as a public draft, and after a period of comment and refinement it is published in final form.

continued ▶

With the rapid expansion of the Web and the extremely short development cycles for new browser products, developers will often incorporate draft versions of HTML long before they become a final standard.

Both the IETF and W3C are involved in far more than what we've mentioned here. For further information on their activities, you can visit their Web sites at http://www.ietf.org/ and http://www.w3.org/ respectively.

The *DOCTYPE* Tag

The DOCTYPE tag always appears in the first line of your HTML document. It takes the general form of:

```
<!DOCTYPE HTML PUBLIC "public identifier">
```

The public identifier is the assigned name for the document type declaration (DTD). Some common public identifiers are listed in Table 3.1.

TABLE 3.1: Common DTD Public Identifiers

Identifier	Used For
"-//W3C//DTD HTML 4.0 //EN"	The new HTML 4.0 recommendation (formerly known as Cougar)
"-//W3C//DTD HTML 3.2 Final//EN"	The final HTML 3.2 specification
"-//Microsoft//DTD Internet Explorer 3.0 HTML//EN"	IE 3.0 behavior
"-//Microsoft//DTD Internet Explorer 3.0 Tables//EN"	IE 3.0 behavior with tables
"-//Netscape Comm. Corp.//DTD HTML//EN"	Netscape Navigator extensions
"-//IETF//DTD HTML Level 3//EN"	HTML 3.0
"-//IETF//DTD HTML 2.0//EN"	HTML 2.0

NOTE   A very broad catalog of DTDs is available at http://ugweb.cs.ualberta.ca/~gerald/validate/lib/catalog. The list was compiled for use with the Kinder, Gentler HTML Validator developed by Gerald Oskoboiny.

In all of our HTML examples, we'll be using the DTD for the current HTML 4.0 draft. The construction of our DOCTYPE tag will then appear as:

```
<!DOCTYPE HTML PUBLIC "-//W3C//DTD HTML 4.0//EN">
```

WARNING   Public identifiers are case sensitive. When inserting them in your documents, be sure to keep capitalization, spelling and spacing exactly as shown.

Seems like an awful lot of information for just one tag, doesn't it? Don't worry, that's the worst of it for this section.

The *HTML* Tag

Each HTML document must be defined as such. After your DOCTYPE tag, the second line of each document will be your HTML tag. The tag has no options to keep track of—it is simply entered as:

```
<HTML>
```

This identifies the beginning of your HTML document. At the very end of each HTML document, the tag is *closed* with </HTML>.

NOTE   A closing tag is used when the tag is meant to provide a container of sorts. That is, an instruction to treat everything within it's bounds in a specific manner. Since the HTML tags defines the document as being HyperText Markup Language, it makes sense that the very last line of the document tells the browser "This is the end of the HTML."

The *HEAD* Tag

The HEAD tag identifies a section of your HTML document. Think of it as being like letterhead. It names the document, provides information about its contents, and names the author or contains other identifying information. Like the HTML tag, it has a closing tag since it is a demarcation of a specific section within your document. Most HTML authors place this tag on the third line of the document, following the DOCTYPE and HTML tags. The usage would appear as:

```
<HEAD>
additional stuff here
</HEAD>
```

The *TITLE* Tag

Inside the HEAD element you'll find a TITLE tag. <TITLE> is a container for the text describing your document, so a closing tag is required. There are two types of HTML tags: container tags and empty tags.

The text indicated by the TITLE tag will be displayed in the title bar of your Web browser, as shown in Figure 3.3.

Netscape - [THE SYBEX HOME PAGE]

FIGURE 3.3:   The title bar at http://www.sybex.com/.

The text used should be short but informative. The title seen in Figure 3.3 is self-explanatory. Your title can include accented characters or special characters, but it cannot contain additional tags. The markup in the HTML document would look like:

```
<TITLE>The Sybex Home Page</TITLE>
```

Many businesses like to keep the company name in the title of all pages and then add a brief description of what that particular page contains, such as:

```
<TITLE>Widgets, Inc: Product Catalog</TITLE>
```

Your choice of title text does have implications for when the site is bookmarked or indexed by a search engine, as we'll discuss in Skill 8, so choose your titles carefully.

The *META* Tags

The META tags are used to provide information that describes the properties of a document and assigns values to those properties. META tags are not typically displayed to people viewing your page but can be accessed by search engines and other programs designed to make use of them. The META tags use *attributes*.

N   NOTE

Each additional piece of information defined inside of a tag is called an *attribute*. The next section, *Understanding Attributes,* covers some common document properties you can set using attributes within META tags.

TIP   The HTML specifications, including the HTML 4.0 draft specification, don't provide a standard set of META properties. This allows for some creativity on your part, but your usage should be standardized at least across the Web site, if not across all of your work. The properties we'll describe below are those in common use on Web sites today.

Understanding Attributes   Let's look at how the META tag is constructed, as it is more complex than the tags we've looked at so far.

In the example below, name and content are attributes of the META tag. The attributes, in this case, are the names of the properties we'll be defining for the document. The information defined in the content quotation marks is the value for those properties. The equals sign equates the name of the property to its value. So, we now have a property of Author, which has a value of Ann Navarro. The Author property can be especially useful when more than one individual is working on a given Web site project because the author responsible for each page is clearly identified.

```
<META name="Author" content="Ann Navarro">
```

Other frequently seen document identification META tags include a copyright statement and a date. Both of these have some unique characteristics.

```
<META name="copyright" content="&copy; 1997 Foo Corporation">
```

The construction of the tag is the same as our previous author property. The name of this property is *copyright*, and the value is the text within the content attribute. But what does © mean?

The code © is a *character entity*, a description of a character in a format that the browser will understand and interpret for display. In this case, © is the character entity for the copyright symbol (©). For more about character entities, see Skill 5.

Our next sample, the date property, uses long-standing Internet traditions for date presentation.

```
<META name="date" content="22 Jul 1997 18:54:32 GMT">
```

The date itself is presented in what Americans generally think of as an international format of date-month-year. The month is entered with the standard three letter abbreviation, without any punctuation. The year should be the full four numerals.

18:54:32 GMT represents the current time in twenty-four hour hour:minutes: seconds format, at Greenwich Mean Time. (GMT is 8 hours ahead of Pacific Standard Time, or 7 hours ahead of Pacific Daylight Time. GMT is 5 hours ahead of Eastern Standard Time and 4 hours ahead of Eastern Daylight Time.)

 NOTE   Even if you're not familiar with working in twenty-four hour time formats, the calculation is pretty simple. Before noon, all times are as you would write them if you were using a.m. and p.m. notation. After the noon hour, simply add twelve to the p.m. formatted time. To translate our example time back into familiar notation, subtract 12 from the hour notation of 18, and you get 6. The time noted is 6:54:32 p.m. Greenwich Mean Time. (You may see references to Zulu or UCT instead of Greenwich Mean Time. Both refer to the same time, the current hour in the time zone for Greenwich, England.)

META Tags and Search Engines   Several of the major Internet search engines will first look for <META> information and make use of it in their listings before using their own pre-programmed method of collecting information from your pages. A solid understanding of what they're looking for can help your site find advantageous placement within search results.

The first of these two examples is the <META> property *description.* The value is a short description of your Web page.

```
<META name="description" content="Our first basic HTML document.">
```

Many search engines will limit your description to 20–25 words or about 200 characters. In order to avoid your descriptions display cutting off in mid-sentence or even worse, mid-word, you should limit yours too.

Next comes the META property *keywords.* This is a list of words or short phrases—separated by commas—that you want to be used to make reference to your Web page from an index. In our sample first HTML document, we might want to have the page indexed as a resource and example for beginning Web developers. We could choose a META tag that looks like this:

```
<META name="keywords" content="HTML, basic, beginner, Web developer,
Web design, tutorial">
```

As with the description property, some search engines will limit how many key words that they will index off any given page. Our recommendation is to pick no more than 20 and to list them in your view of their order of importance or relevance to your topic.

WARNING   An unfortunate by-product of a growing Internet has been the attempt by some to "tip the scales" in their favor on search engines by *loading* a document with keywords. Loading is the practice of entering a key word repetitively in the hope of a site earning a higher relevancy rating within the search results. Major search engine providers have countered this practice in a variety of ways, the most punitive being to completely remove any reference to that site from their archives.

Skill 3

IT'S ALL ABOUT READABILITY

Like the written page, an HTML document is easier for humans to read if it's organized into neatly defined sections of text. There are no hard and fast rules about how many tags or how much information may be on each line within your HTML document.

For example, you may string your HEAD elements all together in a single line, such as:

<HTML><HEAD><TITLE>*My Page*</TITLE></HEAD>

However, most people find an arrangement such as:

<HTML>

<HEAD>

<TITLE>*My Page*</TITLE>

</HEAD>

to be easier to follow and easier to locate errors in.

The issue becomes much clearer as your HTML documents become more complicated with the addition of tables, lists, frames and combinations of many other tags and elements. While it is a matter of personal choice, we believe that making a practice of "clean markup" will pay for itself quickly when viewed in hours saved in later modifications.

The <*BODY*> of Work

Now that your DOCTYPE has been set, you've opened the HTML container, and you've filled in all the HEAD elements, it's time to get down to the actual document.

If we collect all the example tags used so far, we have the following HTML document:

 A Basic HTML Document: *basic.html*

```
<!DOCTYPE HTML PUBLIC "-//W3C//DTD HTML 4.0//EN">
<HTML>
<HEAD>
<TITLE>A Basic HTML Document</TITLE>
<META name="author" content="Ann Navarro">
<META name="copyright" content="&copy; 1997 Foo Corporation">
<META name="date" content="22 Jul 1997 18:54:32 GMT">
<META name="description" content="Our first basic HTML document.">
<META name="keywords" content="HTML, basic, beginner, web developer,
web design, tutorial">
</HEAD>

</HTML>
```

The *BODY* Tag

Like <HEAD>, <BODY> is a container and the closing tag is required. It holds all of the information from the end of the HEAD container to the close of the HTML container. In other words, if it isn't in the <HEAD>, it goes in the <BODY>.

As with the META tags, <BODY> has a variety of possible attributes. The <BODY> attributes have more impact though, in that they control how a number of things happen or are displayed within the page itself. The most common attributes for <BODY> include settings for a page background color or graphic, text color and hypertext link colors.

We'll add the following tag to our HTML document and then dissect it attribute by attribute:

```
<BODY bgcolor="#FFFFFF" text="#000000" LINK="#0000FF" ALINK="#FF00FF"
VLINK="#800080">
```

Backgrounds

Web developers have two options for defining what appears as a background for their Web pages: a solid color or a graphic. Each has their strengths and limitations. Let's take a closer look at the pros and cons of each below.

Background Color   In the example markup above, we've used the attribute BGCOLOR to assign a specific color to our background. In this case, we've chosen the color white and have entered the *RGB value* of white in hexadecimal notation.

RGB is an abbreviation of Red-Green-Blue. Every color is divided into those three components, and a value is assigned to the amount of red, green and blue that are blended to create the intended color. Values can range from 0 (none) to 255 (full color saturation).

Hexadecimal, the base 16 numbering system, is used to store those values to keep the RGB value a 3-byte value. A numeric value, converted into the binary code that computers understand, can hold a value up to 255 to remain in a single byte of memory space. Perhaps through a cosmic coincidence, hexadecimal notation tops out at FF—the representation of the number 255—before moving into three characters. So, the full range of 0 to 255 can be arranged in 3 bytes by using only two characters per color component.

To further translate our choice of white, it breaks down to a red component of 0 (00 in hexadecimal), a green component of 0, and a blue component of 0, which is correct in that white is the absence of color. The value is preceded by the *hash symbol*—or # sign—to indicate that hex notation is being used. Table 3.2 shows 16 widely known color names and their corresponding RGB values in hex notation. For an in-depth look at color, RGB values, and hexadecimal notation, consult Skill 15.

T A B L E   3 . 2 :   Sixteen common color values

Color Name	Hexadecimal Value	Color Name	Hexadecimal Value
Black	#000000	Green	#008000
Silver	#C0C0C0	Lime	#00FF00
Gray	#808080	Olive	#808000
White	#FFFFFF	Yellow	#FFFF00
Maroon	#800000	Navy	#000080
Red	#FF0000	Blue	#0000FF
Purple	#800080	Teal	#008080
Fuchsia	#FF00FF	Aqua	#00FFFF

Background Graphics   Our other option for background treatment would be to choose a graphic as the background for all of our other text and images to come. Background graphics have a unique property applied to them known as *tiling*. Tiling is the endless repetition of an individual graphic. The browser will automatically tile background graphics if the Web page is larger in physical dimensions than the graphic. In most cases, this really is a good thing, in that the size of the graphic file is smaller and the page loads faster. On Web pages, this has the effect of placing the image in the top left corner of the document and then repeating it in a matrix to the right and down as many times as is necessary to appear behind all portions of the document.

Figure 3.4 illustrates what we'll add to our Basic.html document. It is a very wide graphic at 1400 pixels but very short at only 5 pixels. The image contains a red bar on the left side with some shading to provide the illusion of a depth change between the red and the white portions of the graphic.

FIGURE 3.4:   Our background graphic, bar.gif

The image is inserted into our HTML document with the following markup.

```
<BODY background="bar.gif" TEXT="#000000">
```

When using a graphic, the attribute used changes from the BGCOLOR used for solid color rendering, to BACKGROUND. The value for the attribute is the name of the graphic file being used in *URL* format. The Uniform Resource Locator—sometimes referred to as a URI or Uniform Resource Identifier—is what we typically refer to as a Web site address.

We'll discuss the topic of URLs in more detail in the upcoming section on *Linking Out*. For now it will suffice to say that the usage of just the file name is appropriate for graphics that reside in the same directory on the Web server as your HTML document.

When our new BODY tag is inserted within the basic.html document, and the background graphic tiles, our blank document now appears as it does in Figure 3.5.

So why hasn't our graphic tiled to the right as we explained above? In order to keep the intended appearance of a colored bar down only the left side of the page, we created our bar graphic at 1400 pixels wide. That width will accommodate almost every screen size and browser window width without running out of horizontal space. If the graphic can't tile to the right because of its width, it will only tile downward.

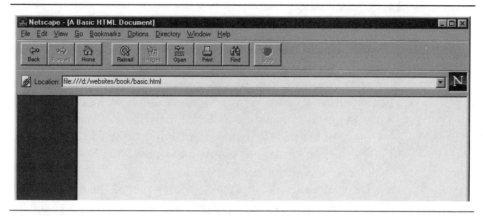

FIGURE 3.5: The Basic.html document with a tiling background graphic.

TIP

You may recall that the three most common *screen resolutions*—the number of pixels across and from top to bottom on a monitor—are 640 pixels wide by 480 pixels tall, 800 × 600, and 1024 × 768. What matters here is not monitor size, but the resolution chosen. At 640 × 480, everything appears larger. At 1024 × 768, you've increased your available space by fitting more (and smaller) pixels into the available space on your monitor. Several larger resolutions are available but are generally only used on screens at least 21 inches in size.

The Text Attribute

The default color of your page text is defined here; we've chosen a black to contrast well with our white background. The color is also stated in hexadecimal notation here, as it will be in all other attributes that define specific colors.

**WARNING**

You may occasionally see specific color names used in place of the hexadecimal notation we've stated are required. In some later versions of some browsers—primarily Netscape Navigator and Microsoft Internet Explorer—the browser will understand the 16 common color names shown in Table 3.2. However, the practice has not gained widespread support and this functionality may not remain an option. By using hexadecimal notation you can feel sure that your choices will last through new browser versions and future updates to the HTML specifications. Worse yet, use of "blue" as a color name may cause a browser to try to interpret the color as "B" "LU" "E", which ends up as "#0B000E", a near-black color.

Links

The remaining attributes of LINK, ALINK, and VLINK all deal with hypertext links in the various states that can be present on a Web page: visited, unvisited and *active*. An active link is that brief moment during a mouse click.

The LINK attribute defines the color of hypertext links that have not previously been activated by the viewer. In our example, we've chosen blue.

ALINK represents the color of the link while it is being activated. When we add a link to our basic HTML document, you'll be able to click on it to see this property in action. While your mouse button is down, the link changes color. Our choice for this attribute was the color red.

The VLINK attribute sets the color of hypertext links that your visitor has been to recently. Since Web sites aren't linear by design, it helps the reader remember where they've been and what information they may still want to view. We chose to use purple here.

NOTE Before the HTML 3.2 specification that allowed your markup to specify text and link color choices, link colors were determined by the visitor's browser settings. By tradition, those settings defaulted to blue for an unvisited link, and maroon or purple for visited links. This gave the viewer an instant visual clue as to what areas of a Web site had previously been experienced. Now that the document author can set these colors, care should be taken not to venture too far from these traditional expectations. If you wish to use different colors, we recommend choosing hues that contrast from the regular text and each other in the same manner as the traditional blue and purple do.

Headings

We're finally ready to add some text! HTML documents do carry over some conventions from the printed word. The heading element is used to briefly describe the topic of the section it precedes. There are six levels of headings available to you, from level 1, the highest level, through level 6, which is the lowest.

The tag is a container and has a simple construction of:

```
<H1>Your Heading Here</H1>
```

An attribute for this element that is commonly used is ALIGN. This will tell the browser how to align the text contained in the heading relative to the page. Values for ALIGN may be left, center, or right. In the absence of an ALIGN attribute, the element assumes an alignment to the left. Center is the most common usage and would be created as:

```
<H1 align="center">Your Heading Here</H1>
```

Adding Text

Are you ready for some typing? It's now time to actually write something in our document. HTML provides us with two basic elements that control text placement: a paragraph element and a line break.

QUOTABLE ATTRIBUTES

If viewing the source HTML of Web pages has become a habit of yours, as it does for many new Web page authors, you'll undoubtedly have noticed quite a few discrepancies when it comes to handling attribute values. Some are enclosed in quotes while others aren't. There may not even seem to be an obvious pattern to the usage that might help you deduce a set of rules.

There is only one rule that governs quotation mark use in these circumstances, which is:

The attribute value *must* be enclosed in quotes if it refers to a URL or if the value contains non-alphanumeric characters.

To be completely clear, let's define these conditions.

- We previously defined a URL as a Uniform Resource Locator, more commonly referred to as a Web site address. For our usage here, a URL also includes references to specific pages, images or other files that are linked to or embedded in your HTML.

- Non-alphanumeric characters are anything that is not of the alphabet (*A* through *Z*, in either case) or a number (*0* on up the line). The characters used for punctuation, or special characters such as the # mark used in assigning color values within the BODY tag would be non-alphanumeric characters.

That said, you would never be wrong if you enclose all of your attribute values in quotes. We advise new HTML authors to consider doing so in order to prevent unnecessary errors. We will be following this method throughout this text so that you will be able to immediately identify the attribute value when new concepts are introduced.

The Paragraph Tag

Each new paragraph begins with the P tag. This tag normally produces a single white space line before and after the paragraph text. The tag is a container, though the HTML specification does set its closing tag as optional. If the closing half is omitted, the closure is understood with the introduction of the next paragraph or block element. The default alignment for a paragraph is flush left, with a ragged right margin. The alignment may be set with the ALIGN attribute, using a value of left (implied), center, or right.

NOTE   None of the alignment options provide justification in relation to both margins. HTML currently does not allow for such treatment, as the specific boundaries of a given "page" aren't possible for the author to define. Monitor resolution and browser window size determines the dimensions of the viewable area.

The Line Break

There may be times when you wish to begin a new line without beginning a new paragraph that would bring white space with it. HTML provides for this with the BR tag. This tag may be placed within the paragraph container without triggering an implied close of the paragraph. The many uses of the BR element will be discussed in more detail in Skill 6.

After the addition of paragraph text, our basic HTML document now looks like this:

The updated document: *basic2.html*

```
<!DOCTYPE HTML PUBLIC "-//W3C//DTD HTML 4.0 Draft//EN">
<HTML>
<HEAD>
<TITLE>A Basic HTML Document</TITLE>
<META name="author" content="Ann Navarro">
<META name="copyright" content="&copy; 1997 Foo Corporation">
<META name="date" content="22 Jul 1997 18:54:32 GMT">
<META name="description" content="Our first basic HTML document.">
<META name="keywords" content="HTML, basic, beginner, web developer,
web design, tutorial">
</HEAD>
<BODY bgcolor="#FFFFFF" text="#000000" LINK="#0000FF" ALINK="#FF00FF"
VLINK="#800080">
```

```
<H1 align="center">About This Document</H1>
<P>This HTML document is our first full example document created within
this book. We will be creating additional documents to provide you with
working examples of the concepts presented in upcoming Skills.
</BODY>
</HTML>
```

The document now actually has something other than background to display!
The basic.html file is shown in Figure 3.6 within a Web browser.

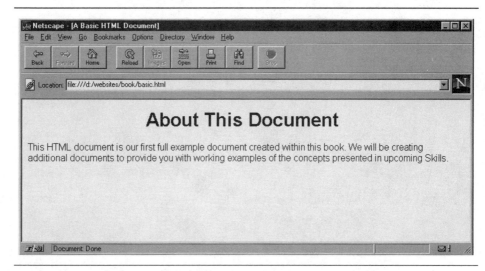

FIGURE 3.6:   The completed basic.html file as seen in a Web browser.

Have You Mastered the Essentials?

Now you can...

☑ Choose a text editor for your platform that has the features you desire.

☑ Determine which document type definition to use.

☑ Create the *HEAD* elements that are required for your document.

☑ Select which *META* elements you wish to include.

☑ Enter headings and basic text structures within your document.

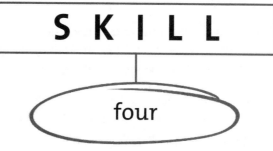

Handling Text with HTML

- ❑ Adding links to your Web page

- ❑ Lists, lists, and more lists!

- ❑ Quoting other material

- ❑ Modifying text display with styling

- ❑ Using special character sets

Now that you've learned how to create a basic Web page it's time to start exploring some of HTML's nifty tricks! In this skill you'll learn all about text treatment: using text to create links, applying special formatting to text, and using special text characters.

First, you'll learn to connect your Web pages to each other and to link out to pages half way around the world. Next, you'll learn about the HTML specification's wide variety of text placement and styling tools. You'll create numbered lists, lettered lists, bulleted lists, and definition lists, as well as quotations, citations, and preformatted text areas. Finally, you'll learn how the World Wide Web is truly world wide through the use of international character sets and special text characters that can be created even if you don't have the keys for them on your keyboard.

Linking Out

What makes the World Wide Web such an exciting place—and what makes it into a web of information—is the hyperlink. From any one Web page you can jump to another page in the same site or to a page in a site located way on the other side of the globe, all with a single click of a mouse.

Anchoring the Link

Links are created using a specific form of the *anchor* tag, <A>. This tag surrounds the text or object that is to be linked, so it can be said that the link is *anchored* to that object.

There are two ways to link to another file. You can link to the file itself, in which case a Web browser will display the file beginning at the top. Or, you can link to a specific point within a file, in which case the entire file will be loaded, but the browser will begin the display for you at the point specified.

To illustrate these two linking behaviors and their syntax, let's construct a new HTML file. The beginning of the file looks like this:

links.html

```
<!DOCTYPE HTML PUBLIC "-//W3C//DTD HTML 4.0//EN">
<HTML>
<HEAD>
<TITLE>Examples of Links</TITLE>
</HEAD>
<BODY bgcolor="#FFFFFF" text="#000000" LINK="#0000FF" ALINK="#FF00FF"
  VLINK="#800080">
```

```
<P>This page provides examples of two different types of links. The
   first is a link out to another page. This link is to the <A
   HREF="http://www.sybex.com">Sybex Web site</A>.

<P>The second link is to another file on this imaginary Web site. This
   link is to
<A HREF="page2.html">Page Two</A> of our site.

</BODY>
</HTML>
```

 WARNING   For the purposes of conserving space with these examples, only the imme-diately relevant portions of the file will be shown in this skill. So right here, that means the META tags will be omitted. As discussed in Skill 3, your work-ing documents should always include them.

The only unfamiliar item in the file is the anchor tag. As you can see from the example, the anchor tag is a container tag and has a corresponding closing tag.

The HREF is an attribute, which represents the *hyperlinked resource* that's being linked to. That's a fancy way of saying that the value of the HREF attribute is the URL of the file or site that you are linking to. As with all other attribute values, the URL must be contained within quotes.

The URL can be written in *absolute* form or in *relative* form. Absolute URLs can be thought of as the "entire" URL, including the protocol, the domain, the path, and the file name. The link to the Sybex Web site, which uses the URL http://www.sybex.com/, is written in absolute form.

Relative addressing is the path and file name within the URL *relative* to the location of the file that contains the tag. In its simplest form, only the file name is declared, as in the second link example above which only uses the file name page2.html. When that occurs, it is understood that this file *resides in the same directory* as the file that contains this tag. So instead of having to type

```
<a href="http://www.yourcompany.com/page2.html">
```

to link to a second page in the root directory of the Web site, you only need to type

```
<a href="page2.html">
```

and the system will know where to look for the page.

In the example above, regardless of whether the absolute or relative form of the URL was used a browser would display the new file from the top.

It's All Relative: Understanding Relative Hyperlinks

Relative addressing really comes in handy when you're dealing with multiple file directories and the logical structure that most Web sites make use of.

For example, suppose you are working on the Acme Widgets Web site at `http://www.widgets.com`. Their widget catalog is online, at `http://www.widgets.com/catalog/`. They also have a collection of FAQ files (Frequently Asked Questions) located at `http://www.widgets.com/faqs/`.

You can use a relative URL to link from the catalog to the FAQ about each product without having to use the full path of `http://www.widgets.com/faqs/` every time. To do so, you must determine where your Web page is in relation to the image file. In this case, the catalog directory is at the same "level" as the FAQ directory—one level down from the root level.

The Web server understands a bit of basic shorthand that says "go back up one level." In practice, that's the previous directory notation, written as:

```
../ (that's two periods followed by a forward slash)
```

To use the FAQ file named `faq1.html`, the anchor tag would be written as:

```
<A HREF="../faqs/faq1.html">
```

This tells the server "Go back up one directory level, then go down into the FAQ directory and display the file `faq1.html`." For Web design purposes, it is the same as writing:

```
<A HREF="http://www.widgets.com/faqs/faq1.html">
```

The directive can be used several times in succession. Let's imagine that Acme Widgets has two versions of their catalog—one written in English and the other in German—and that their Web site then has two appropriately named directories off the catalog directory.

continued on next page ▶

When working on a page within the English subdirectory, you still need to call FAQs from back in their own directory. How to do it? Again, compare where your current page is *relative* to the entire directory structure. The images directory was on the first level below the root. The English directory is on the *second* level below the root, since it is a subdirectory of catalog, which is at the same level as the FAQ directory. Confused? Visualize it as it would appear in a familiar directory tree on your hard drive, as shown below.

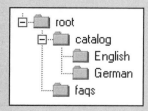

As with all relative addressing, you need to get back to the level *above* the one you ultimately want to go to, in order to allow yourself to go *down* into the directory desired. Because there are two levels to travel back through in order to be above the images directory, use the previous directory notation twice as seen here:

```
<A HREF="../../faqs/faq1.html">
```

That tells the server, go back into the catalog directory, back again into the root directory, then go down into faqs, and display the `faq1.html` file.

It may look a lot more complicated than it really is. If you ever find yourself stumped over how many previous directory notations to use, stop and draw yourself a small chart, and you'll soon find yourself hopping all over the place!

The second form of link behavior is to have the browser deliver the user to a specific point in the file being loaded. For that to work, the Web developer needs to give the browser an electronic roadmap of sorts. To link to Point A in the new file, there must be some sort of marker identifying where Point A is. For that, the anchor attribute *name* is used. Take a look at the file below, page2.html, which was linked to in the links.html file shown at the beginning of this section.

page2.html

```
<!DOCTYPE HTML PUBLIC "-//W3C//DTD HTML 4.0 Draft//EN">
<HTML>
<HEAD>
<TITLE>Examples of Links - Page Two</TITLE>
</HEAD>
<BODY bgcolor="#FFFFFF" text="#000000" LINK="#0000FF" ALINK="#FF00FF"
   VLINK="#800080">

<H1>Page Two</H1>
<P>You arrived at this page from a hyperlink on the links.html page.
   You can go back to the section of that page that discusses linking to
   a specific point in a page, by following
<A HREF="links.html#PointA">this link</A>.

</BODY>
</HTML>
```

The first thing you'll notice about the anchor tag on this page is that the URL contains a hash mark—the # symbol—commonly referred to in the U.S. as the "pound sign." That's the instruction to the browser to go not only to the links .html page but specifically to the section labeled with the text that follows the # symbol. In this case, it's PointA.

TIP   The labels used here follow the same naming conventions as traditional URLs. Spaces are discouraged, so many developers find using mixed case letters in place of spaces—PointA instead of Pointa—can increase readability.

Before this link will function correctly, we will need to make an adjustment to the links.html file, as shown below:

links2.html

```
<!DOCTYPE HTML PUBLIC "-//W3C//DTD HTML 4.0//EN">
<HTML>
<HEAD>
<TITLE>Examples of Links</TITLE>
</HEAD>
<BODY bgcolor="#FFFFFF" text="#000000" LINK="#0000FF" ALINK="#FF00FF"
   VLINK="#800080">
```

```
<P>This page provides examples of two different types of links. The
  first is a link out to another page. This link is to the <A
  HREF="http://www.sybex.com">Sybex Web site</A>.

<P>In order to illustrate the internal link to Point A in the next sec-
  tion, we need to fill up the page with additional text.

<P>Type several paragraphs here when you're creating your own file, so
  that you can't immediately see the Point A heading below when you
  first view the file in your Web browser.

<A NAME="PointA"><H2>Point A</H2></A>
<P>The is to another file on this imaginary Web site. This link is to
  <A HREF="page2.html">Page Two</A> of our site.

</BODY>
</HTML>
```

The new tag added was the anchor `<A NAME="PointA">` that is now anchored around the new heading tag `<H2>Point A</H2>`. The *name* attribute is the browser's road sign for Point A. The value is the label that will be used in all other anchor tags that want to link directly to that spot, as was shown in the listing for `page2.html`.

You can give the process a try using the following steps:

1. Using the text editor of your choice, copy and save both the `links.html` and `page2.html` files into a directory on your system dedicated to your test pages.

2. Add extra text as directed.

3. Launch your Web browser. Locate and open the `links.html` file.

4. Click on the link to `page2.html`. The browser will display Page 2.

5. Once there, click on the link to take you back to `links.html`. The browser will load the `links.html` page again, with Point A in focus.

The link may not appear to be doing anything special at this point, but that's only because the file being linked to—`links.html`—is short enough to display entirely within your browser without scrolling. You'll know that it worked though because the URL displayed in your browser's location box now includes the name anchor, as shown below.

Bookmarks & Go to: /Skill4/links.html#PointA

Experiment by adding additional paragraphs between the top of the links.html file and the anchor for Point A until you have to scroll in the browser in order to see it. Now you'll be able to click to the second page and then click back and better see the effect.

Block Elements

A block element is an HTML tag that causes a paragraph break. That means that a blank line is generally inserted before and after the tag. In Skill 3, you were introduced to the paragraph tag, <P>, and to the headings tags, <Hx>. This section will cover additional block elements, including lists, preformatted text areas, and block quotes.

Lists

In HTML 4.0, there are three formal types of lists: the *unordered* list, the *ordered* list, and the *definition* list. Each type of list can contain other block and text level elements, including additional lists nested within them. The only block elements that specifically are not allowed within lists are headings and the address tag.

Unordered Lists

An unordered list is what word processors typically call a *bulleted* list. Each item in the list begins on a new line, preceded by a round black dot. In HTML, the browsers do have some leeway in how to present such a list. Most commonly, you'll see the list indented from the current left margin and a round black disc used to set off each list item.

All lists are containers, so the unordered list tag, <UL>, has a closing partner of </UL>. Each item in the list is set off by its own list item tag, <LI>.

A basic unordered list would be constructed as follows:

```
<UL>
<LI>List item one
<LI>List item two
<LI>List item three
</UL>
```

The list would appear in a browser as shown below.

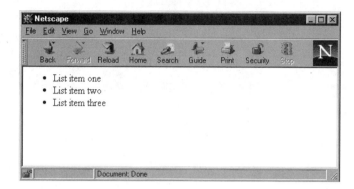

The unordered list tag has an attribute called TYPE that is available to change how the bullet is presented. The choices available are:

Disc(the default)	The familiar round black disk
Square	A small filled square
Circle	An unfilled circle

If, for example, the square option were chosen, the list tag syntax would become:

```
<UL TYPE="square">
```

COMPATIBILITY NOTE   While the choices for TYPE have been included in HTML since the recommendation for version 3.2, the major browsers have only begun supporting them in their 4.0 browser versions.

Ordered Lists

An ordered list is a list that has specific order; shown by numbering or lettering. The initial syntax is identical to the unordered list. It is a container, so the opening tag, <OL> requires a closing tag, </OL>. List items are included with one or more <LI> tags, as shown here:

```
<OL>
<LI>List item one
<LI>List item two
<LI>List item three
</OL>
```

The default display treatment for such a list is a numerical list beginning with the number 1, as shown below.

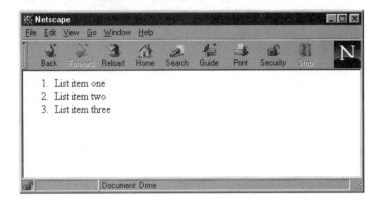

Ordered lists also make use of the TYPE attribute. Instead of changing bullet style, as the attribute does in unordered lists, it changes the numbering or lettering system to be used as shown in Table 4.1.

TABLE 4.1: Numbering Styles for Ordered Lists

Type	Style	Display
1	arabic numbers	1, 2, 3
a	lower case alphabet	a, b, c
A	upper case alphabet	A, B, C
i	lower case roman style	i, ii, iii
I	upper case roman style	I, II, III

Additionally, you can set the starting point for any of these numbering styles using the START attribute, or set the number value of a specific list item by using the VALUE attribute. Each of these attributes are used to produce the example below. (See Figure 4.1.)

```
<OL START="100">
<LI>This is list item 101
<LI>This is list item 102
<LI VALUE="110">This item skips to list item 110
<LI>This next item continues the numbering from the previous one, so it
    displays as list item 111.
</OL>
```

Experiment with different starting values and specific list item values. You should be beginning to see how well HTML handles lists.

Definition Lists

Definition lists are a little more complex than bulleted or numbered lists. They're most often used for things like glossaries or terminology references. The key is that you have a term that you are introducing and then the definition for that term.

Definition lists, like all other lists, are containers, so an opening <DL> is paired with the closing </DL>. Instead of having a single line item, <LI>, for each item in the list, a definition list has both a term tag, <DT>, and a definition tag, <DD>. At least one term and one definition must be included in the list.

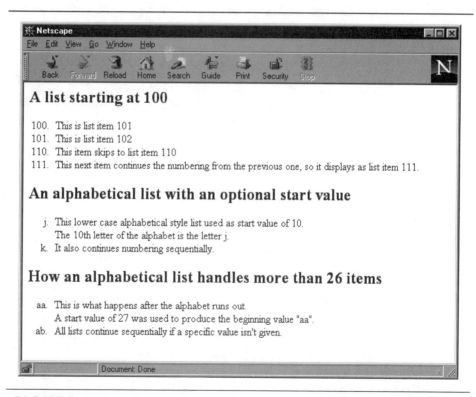

FIGURE 4.1:   Three examples of ordered lists using various numbering styles and START or VALUE attributess

If this book were an HTML page, a definition list could have been used to display the three bullet style options available within unordered lists. To do so, we'd use the following markup:

```
<DL>
<DT>disc
<DD>the familiar round black disc (default)
<DT>square
<DD>a small filled square
<DT>circle
<DD>an unfilled circle
</DL>
```

The display of such a list tends to vary in different browsers more than other list elements. However, Internet Explorer and Navigator both display this sample list as shown below:

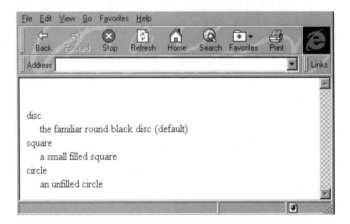

There are only two rules regarding what can or can't be included in these two tags. The term tag <DT> can only contain text level elements. The definition tag <DD>, on the other hand, can contain both text or block level elements which effectively allows paragraphs and other nested lists.

Quotations

As their name indicates, a quotation element is used when you are quoting a block of text. Real world applications of this are common. You might be converting a company employee manual into HTML for the intranet. The section on payroll practices may quote several pieces from your state's labor law. Your sales staff may want to include brief testimonials from satisfied customers on your public Web site. These and many other examples can make use of the two available tags for quotation.

The *BLOCKQUOTE* Tag

<BLOCKQUOTE> is a container, and as a container it requires the corresponding closing tag, </BLOCKQUOTE>. As a block level element, it can contain other block level elements such as paragraphs, lists, and text level formatting.

Most major browsers will display the contents of the BLOCKQUOTE tag by indenting from both left and right margins. Since it is a block element, paragraph breaks are seen both before and after the container contents.

The Quote Tag

New to HTML 4.0 is the quote tag <Q>. Quote is also a container and has a corresponding closing tag of </Q>. Quote is intended to be used for quoting short passages, which won't require other block level elements.

Preformatted Text

One of the most basic tenets of HTML has from the beginning been flexibility in display. Text lines will wrap based on the end user's screen resolution and browser window size rather than on pre-measured page widths. Even with the advent of layout control measures now available to the Web developer in stylesheets (covered in Skill 5), this inherent flexibility should only occasionally be interrupted for situations where the lack of absolute spacing will distort or destroy the informational content.

In order to preserve absolute text placement, HTML allows the use of a preformatted text area using the opening tag, <PRE>, and the corresponding closing tag, </PRE>.

When this tag is used, the data contained within the tag is displayed *exactly* as it is laid out in the source HTML file. Line breaks and the use of multiple space characters to produce white space is preserved. In order to keep the absolute formatting of the data, browsers will use a fixed-width font. The default font used in both Internet Explorer and Navigator on a Windows platform is Courier New.

Skill 4

Modifying Text Display

For some time now HTML has provided the Web developer with ways to produce basic text styling—the use of italics, boldface, underlines, and others. HTML has also allowed the Web developer to mark passages that should have emphasis and strong emphasis, letting the browser determine just how to present that visually rather than giving explicit directions such as italics and boldface. The use of emphasis over specific rendering instructions is known as providing the text's *structure* versus its display.

In the present, the argument over whether to use structural markup over display markup has become moot. The traditional means of rendering emphasis with the container <EM> and </EM> was with italic text. Strong emphasis, using the container <STRONG> and </STRONG>, generally produced bold text. The key here is that the browser isn't *required* to display those tags using those visual cues. The HTML specification doesn't tell the browser programmers *how* to display these structural elements, only that they need be different than the normal presentation. Emphasis could be displayed using a different font coloring or by increasing the font size by a single step. Strong emphasis might be displayed by turning the text into green italics, indented and at three font sizes larger than the original. There are no hard and fast rules. Some browsers let the user determine such visual cues, while others are programmed with just a single treatment. The bottom line is that you can't count on an EM container producing italicized text. It probably will for 95% or more of your visitors, but it's not guaranteed.

In order to counteract that uncertainty, tags were developed that specifi-cally produced *font styling*—rendering of the text with a visual enhancement such as italics, boldface, and underlines, without changes to color, font size, or font face.

Font Style Elements

Font style elements are text level elements. That means they can be used inline without creating paragraph breaks around them. A single word or phrase could be rendered with *italics* or in **boldface** type just as easily as it was done in this book. Each tag is a container that requires a corresponding closing tag.

The following HTML markup provides examples of the most commonly used font style elements.

 fontstyle.html

```
<HTML>
<HEAD>
<TITLE>Font Style Samples</TITLE>
```

```
<BODY BGCOLOR="#FFFFFF" TEXT="000000">

<H1>Font Style Samples</H1>

<P>The first example is the use of <I>italic text</I>. Some prefer to
   use the <EM>emphasis tag</EM> instead. Emphasis, however may be
   rendered with styling other than italics.

<P>Next is <B>bold text</B>. Some prefer to use the
   <STRONG>strong emphasis</STRONG> tag instead. Strong emphasis,
   like emphasis, can be rendered in ways other than as bold.

<P>Additional font styling includes the use of <TT>teletype text.</TT>
   Teletype text is displayed in a <TT>monospaced (fixed-width)</TT> font.

<P>Other options include using <BIG> big text</BIG>, using <SMALL>small
   text</SMALL>, using <STRIKE>text that has been struck
   through</STRIKE>, or using <U>text that has been underlined</U>.

</BODY>
</HTML>
```

Figure 4.2 shows `fontstyle.html` as it displays in Netscape Navigator 4.02 on a Windows 95 machine.

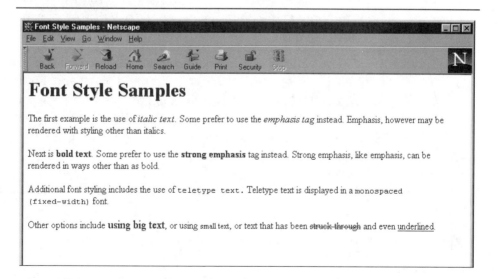

FIGURE 4.2:   How Navigator 4.02 displays the file fontstyle.html.

NOTE HTML 4.0 discourages the use of these individual tags for text styling effects in favor of using stylesheets. The W3C has gone so far as to *deprecate* the strikethrough and underline tags. When a tag is deprecated, it means that the WC3 recommends that it not be used and that they are likely to phase it out of future HTML versions.

An Emphasis on Suggestion

The distinction between a deprecation, as with the strikethrough and underline tags, and the W3C's suggestion to use stylesheets is an important one. Deprecation is a strong signal that says, "Don't use this any more. It's been done away with, or we've provided this other means of accomplishing the same thing." The W3C didn't do that with most of the text styling elements.

What they did do is express their confidence in stylesheets as a better means of managing styling issues. In many ways they're right. However, by only discouraging the use of text style elements in favor of stylesheets, they have effectively recognized the immediate reality that only a small minority of the Web viewing public has a browser capable of using those stylesheets.

Keep in mind when developing your sites that as of this printing, only Internet Explorer version 3.0 or higher and Netscape 4.0 or higher can support stylesheets. If text styling is critical to your message and you have determined that your audience is likely to be using other browsers (see Skill 12), it would be wise to consider using the individual text styling tags described in this section.

Special Character Entities

As its name implies, the World Wide Web is a huge entity, consisting of information in many languages. We've already talked about how the Web is intended to convey information across many types of machines and operating systems. How then, do we ensure that people who speak different languages and whose languages use symbols that are not found on standard Western keyboards can use the Web?

Character Sets

Character sets have been around for a long time, long before the Web. You might be familiar with term *ASCII*. ASCII, invented by the IBM Corporation in the 1960s, is one set of characters and can be used fairly commonly. If you're using a standard English keyboard, you might want to think of ASCII as the things you can type directly from the keyboard, without holding down any special keys (except the Shift key for capital letters). If you are used to typing characters by holding down the Option, Command, Control, or Alt keys, it's probably not ASCII.

HTML uses a particular *Document Character Set*, which simply means that there is a set of certain characters which are usable in HTML documents. The Document Character Set for HTML is ISO10646, also known as *the Universal Character Set, or UCS.*

 NOTE   *ISO* is the International Standards Organization. They are responsible for determining international standards for many types of things, not just for the computer industry. They also do all types of measurements and other industrial types of standards, such as those for the metal industry.

As in ASCII, there are certain characters that are part of the UCS and those which are not. Chances are, most characters you would be interested in using are in the UCS, but things are a bit more complicated than they might seem at first glance.

Browser Support of Character Sets

As you learned from the discussion of browser capabilities in Skill 2, the fact that a feature exists does not mean that a browser supports it. In fact, the default on most modern browsers is to support only a subset of the Universal Character Set. This subset is the ISO-1889-1 subset, also known as Latin-1. What this means is that your standard, Western version of Netscape Navigator, without any special configuration, will only correctly display the characters in this subset. However, browsers can recognize more than one type of subset. That is, they can recognize other subsets, or character encodings, of the UCS.

Why do browsers work this way? Why not just have every browser automatically work with the entire Universal Character Set? The answer is pretty simple—the UCS is very large, and because most documents are written in a single language (although, of course, that language may vary), it is easiest to let the author of each document choose the subset they wish to use.

 NOTE   If you are familiar with character sets in general, you might be interested to know that the Universal Character Set is the same as *Unicode2*. Both are 16-bit character sets. If you set the upper byte of the UCS to zero, the bottom 8 bits comprise the ASCII character set.

Characters That Are Not in the Latin-1 Subset

What if you want to use characters that are not in the Latin-1 subset? There are a couple of ways you can go. One option is to identify which type of encoding you would like to use by specifying it in META tag of the document. The second way you can use the characters is by specifying character entities, which are codes you can use to specify the character you wish to use. Let's take a look at each of these options.

Using the *META* Tag

Remember the META tag? In case you've forgotten, it's a tag that goes within the document's <HEAD> area. It allows the author of the HTML document to include extra information about the document. One of these extra pieces of information can be the document encoding. The actual character set (a.k.a. document encoding, a.k.a. character encoding) is defined by setting the character set to the code for the type of encoding you wish to use.

Here's an example:

```
<HTML>
<HEAD>
<META http-equiv="Content-Type" Content="text/html, charset=fr-FR">
```

In this example, the document encoding will be French for France (as opposed to French for Canada or French for Senegal). Just to give you an idea of some of the encoding options available, Table 4.2 shows the default list provided with Netscape Navigator Gold 3.01.

TABLE 4.2:   Common character encodings

Language	Character Set
English	en
English/United States	en-US
English/United Kingdom	en-GB
French	fr
French/France	fr-FR
French/Canada	fr-CA
German	de
Japanese	ja
Chinese	zh
Chinese/China	zh-CN
Chinese/Taiwan	zh-TW
Korean	ko
Italian	it
Spanish	es
Spanish/Spain	es-ES
Portuguese	pt
Portuguese/Brazil	pt-BR

WARNING   The browser cannot find out which type of encoding you have specified in the <META> tag if you have non-ASCII characters which appear before you specify the encoding.

Using the Character Entities

Character entities are numeric representations of characters and they display the desired character regardless of document encoding, which is handy. The issue of how to represent them in HTML can become a bit confusing, however, because there are several ways. Character entities can be represented three ways:

- By numerical entities that use decimal values

- By numerical entities that use hexadecimal values
- By named entities

Let's take a look at each of these.

Numerical Entities That Use Decimal Values

Numerical entities can be defined by decimal values. What does this mean? It means that you can specify the character you wish to use by using the syntax `&#Unicodevalue;` where Unicode value is a unique number assigned to this symbol.

NOTE   The Unicode values can be found in many places. You can get them from the World Wide Web Consortium at http://www.w3.org/. Sometimes text editors, such as BBEdit also give them. Look for something called an ASCII or Unicode table.

Let's look some sample HTML. We'll look at the results in a browser window in a minute. Here's how you would code the decimal numerical entity for the division sign:

```
<HTML>
<HEAD>
</HEAD>
<BODY>
I often use the &#247; sign.
</BODY>
</HTML>
```

COMPATIBILITY NOTE   Note the semicolon at the end of the entity. Some browsers consider it to be optional, but in the interest of cross-browser compatibility you should always use it.

Numerical Entities That Use Hexadecimal Values

Numerical representations of entities can also use the hexadecimal values of characters. Hex values can usually be found in the same locations as the decimal values—Web sites and text editors. To represent entities using hex values, you can use the following syntax `&#xHexadecimalvalue;` where the actual hexadecimal value of the character replaces `Hexadecimalvalue`.

Here is the same example using the hexadecimal representation of the division sign entity:

```
<HTML>
<HEAD>
</HEAD>
<BODY>
I often use the &#xF7; sign.
</BODY>
</HTML>
```

Referring to Entities by Name   Eventually it was realized that using the decimal and hexadecimal representations was not the most intuitive way to code entities. Slowly, names have been evolving for the entities. They are certainly more intuitive, but they are sometimes a bit odd.

Often, it's easy to think of several abbreviations for an entity. For example, you might wonder whether the named entity for the division sign is ÷, ÷, or &division;. It's ÷, and its use is demonstrated in the example below:

```
<HTML>
<HEAD>
</HEAD>
<BODY>
I often use the &divide sign.
</BODY>
</HTML>
```

TIP   Be sure to note that the named entities do *not* contain the # sign following the & sign. Also note that names do not exist for all the entities, at least not yet. For this reason, you may need to use the decimal or hex representations.

Some Character Entity Examples   The graphic below shows the results of using either ÷, ÷, or the &divide entities.

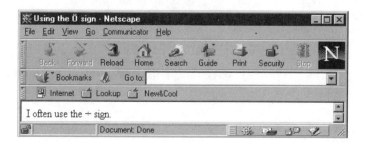

The image below shows the results of using the following HTML code (without replacing the division sign with an entity) and displaying it in Netscape Navigator Gold 3.01 for the Macintosh. On the Macintosh, the division sign is formed by holding down the Option key and typing **?**. Note that it is not possible to type the division sign without using a modifier key.

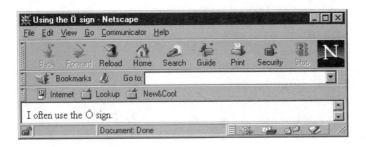

```
<HTML>
<HEAD>
</HEAD>
<BODY>
I often use the ÷ sign.
</BODY>
</HTML>
```

When to Use Character Entities

The Universal Character Set covers a lot of characters, including the standard ASCII characters on your keyboard. You may be wondering when to use entities and when it's acceptable to type the character you want. After all, if this book were on a Web page, the entire thing could have been written using decimal or hexadecimal entities.

NOTE   Now that you're an expert on character entities, it might be useful to know that in Web developer slang, to represent a character with an entity is to *escape* it.

The truth is, many Web browsers will be able to translate a lot of the characters you type. That is, it's okay to type a comma and a period rather than escaping them. And, you can type all of the letters of the alphabet and numbers without worrying.

After that, it gets trickier. If you're not sure about a certain character, it's best to escape it. You should always check to see how the character looks when viewed through the Web browsers you wish to support. You should always replace the following five items with their respective entities:

- Quotation marks (" and ")
- The less than and greater than signs (< and >)
- The ampersand (&)
- Any characters not commonly found in English
- Mathematical symbols

Let's look at each of these items in turn.

Quotation Marks   Quotation marks play an important role in HTML because they are used to surround attributes to HTML tags. For example: `<img src="foo.gif">`. Of course, quotation marks are also used to quote text on the page.

Generally speaking, it's best to escape all of the quotations in the general text. The most commonly used entity for this is the named one, &quot.

Here's an example:

```
<HTML>
<HEAD>
</HEAD>
<BODY>
&quot;I love HTML.&quot;
</BODY>
</HTML>
```

 WARNING   If you have "curly quotes" on in your word processor or whatever text editor you are using to create your HTML pages, be sure to turn them off. Curly quotes are tricky in that you can type them directly from your keyboard, but they don't work in HTML. This is true even if you choose to escape quotation marks, because you'll still use unescaped quotes to surround attributes in your HTML tags.

The Greater Than and Less Than Signs   These signs should always be escaped when used in text because unescaped, they represent the beginning and end of HTML tags. The more recent browsers understand that if there is a space around the unescaped signs, they are less than and greater than signs, which can actually be a problem if you meant to use the < and > to surround an HTML tag and you accidentally left a space within the brackets. The older browsers will ignore everything between the < and > tags, thinking that they are HTML tags.

The most common way to escape these characters is by using the named entities: < (less than) and > (greater than).

Here's an example:

```
<HTML>
<HEAD>
</HEAD>
<BODY>
5 &lt; 7
5 &gt; 3
</BODY>
</HTML>
```

Other Mathematical Symbols   The <, >, and ÷ symbols aside, you should always use entities to represent mathematical symbols such as +, =, ×, and ÷. Although the Web was initially invented as a way for scientists to easily share information, browsers vary quite a bit in their interpretations of mathematical symbols. It's best to use entities.

The Ampersand   Because the ampersand (&) is used to indicate the beginning of an entity, it is also frequently escaped. The entity used most often is & .

Here's an example:

```
<HTML>
<HEAD>
</HEAD>
<BODY>
The &amp; symbol is frequently escaped by using the &amp;amp; entity.
</BODY>
</HTML>
```

This example is a bit trickier. Note that the second ampersand is escaped and then immediately followed by amp;. Altogether, viewed in a browser, &amp looks like &. If you can't see this, try it for yourself.

Characters Not Commonly Found in English   Although the World Wide Web is obviously an international phenomenon, there are a few things to keep in mind.

First, the Internet was primarily built by the United States government. Next, although many browsers can be found, the primary ones used throughout the world were built to support ASCII automatically, other characters not so well. ASCII was invented by IBM, a U.S.-based company, and represents North American and European letterforms and punctuation.

All of these reasons fit together to make a world which basically supports certain letters and punctuation most easily and U.S.-based language the most. This is not to say that other languages cannot be supported or represented, but it does mean that you usually will have to escape any non-English characters, even European characters such as Å. Remember, if you can't type it directly from your keyboard without using special keys, it probably needs to be escaped.

Have You Mastered the Essentials?

Now you can. . .

☑ Create hyperlinks among Web pages and Web sites.

☑ Format numbered, lettered, bulleted, and definition lists within your text.

☑ Include material in your Web page that has been quoted from other sources.

☑ Preserve special alignment and text behavior using preformatted text areas.

☑ Adjust font styling using bold, italic and other text treatments.

☑ Make use of characters not available on your keyboard using special character sets.

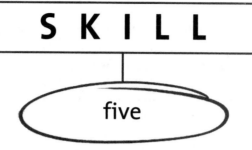

SKILL

five

Placing Pictures and Framing Content

❑ Placing images within the page

❑ Setting the flow of text around images

❑ Hints for optimal image behavior

❑ Bordering images with white space

❑ Using frames to set off content

❑ Creating the frame set

❑ Providing an alternative to frames for older browsers

❑ Inserting inline frames

Images are an integral part of Web site design. They are inserted into HTML files using the IMG tag. Attributes for the tag include the ability to position the image using alignment, setting aside white space using VSPACE or HSPACE, reserving image display area using WIDTH and HEIGHT, and providing alternative text for those users who cannot or have chosen not to load images.

Frames provide the Web designer with the ability to set off portions of the available browser window into independent smaller windows—frames. Frame support in its current state, is generally only available in IE 3.0 or Navigator 3.0 and higher.

Images

Text level elements don't cause paragraph breaks. They can be nested and can contain other text level elements but not block level elements. The IMG tag—pronounced as *image tag*—is used to insert images *inline* within your text. Inline refers to a layout that features text and images together; this layout is what you're used to seeing on Web pages and in modern magazines and books.

The IMG tag is an *empty tag*, that is, it is self-contained. It operates only on itself, not on text or other objects in your documents, so no closing tag will ever be used. At its most elementary, it identifies the location (URL) of an image file to be displayed on your Web page. The basic syntax is:

```
<IMG SRC="image.gif">
```

The IMG tag is an easy one to remember, as saying it out loud can readily identify the purpose of each of its parts. SRC is the HTML notation for *source*, which is the location of the file in URL form. Beyond the basic syntax of the IMG tag, there are six significant types of attributes that may be used within the tag. Each attribute is important in its own right and can significantly change the way in which the image is displayed.

Alignment

An image file can be displayed in different positions relative to the line where it occurs within the page. There are five possible values for this attribute (see Figure 5.1):

Top   The top of the image will be lined up with the top of the current line. When that line includes text, the top of the current line is where the top of capital letters extends.

Middle   The baseline of the current line—the line that touches the bottom of letters that don't "drop down" in any way—is aligned with the middle of the image.

Bottom   The bottom of the image sits on the baseline of the current line. This is the default alignment value; images will be aligned in this manner if the attribute is not declared within the tag.

Left   The image's left border is flush with the left margin. The text will flow around it, along its right border until the first new line can reach the left hand margin unimpeded by the bottom of the image.

Right   The image is docked to the right margin, its right border flush with it. The text will flow around the image, along its left border until the first new line can reach the right hand margin unimpeded by the bottom of the image.

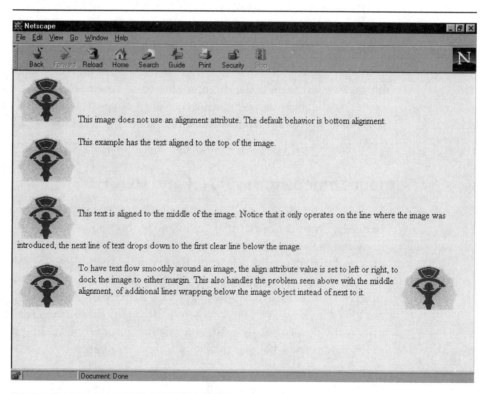

FIGURE 5.1:   The ALIGN attribute is a powerful layout aid.

COMPATIBILITY NOTE Special attention needs to be taken when using left or right alignment with images. Some older browsers, primarily from the Navigator and IE 2.*x* generation, may not "clear" an alignment if text lines haven't completely flowed around it. This older browsers will show a stair step effect. To make sure that the next line begins on a *completely* clear line, insert a line break—
—zadding an attribute for clear. The syntax is <BR CLEAR="ALL">. Alternative values for clear are LEFT and RIGHT, to drop to the first line clear to the left margin or clear to the right margin, respectively.

Images as Links

Even the newest Web surfer has likely seen images that have been used as links to other parts of a Web site. The process of creating a link using an image is simple. The markup includes the IMG tag nested within the anchor that provides the link, as shown below.

```
<A HREF="newfile.html"><IMG SRC="widget1.gif"></A>
```

Images used as links will default to being displayed with a single-pixel–wide border around them in the declared link color scheme. You have the option of changing that behavior by adding the *border* attribute to your IMG tag. A value of 0 removes the border from around the image. The markup would look like:

```
<A HREF="newfile.html"><IMG SRC="widget1.gif" BORDER="0"></A>
```

Image Dimensions: WIDTH and HEIGHT

The WIDTH and HEIGHT attributes describe the actual size of the image, measured in pixels. Browsers can display an image without knowing the image's size; but knowing the size allows the browser to reserve the space required for image display and to then continue loading the text lines that follow the inline image tag. As the images are sent from the Web server, they fill in the blocks of spaced reserved for them. This allows for faster display of the text, so your audience isn't kept looking at a blank screen, waiting for the entire page to finish loading. You've probably already seen this behavior while surfing the Web.

The syntax for a 100 pixel wide by 100 pixel tall graphic called widget1.gif would be:

```
<IMG SRC="widget1.gif" WIDTH="100" HEIGHT="100">
```

 **WARNING**   Avoid the temptation to resize a graphic by changing the width and height values within the IMG tag. Doing so will often greatly distort the image. If the image's physical size needs to be changed, use the resampling or cropping functions of your favorite graphics editor.

Alternative Text

Sometimes a visitor to your Web site can't see your images. Perhaps the visitor is using a text-only browser, such as Lynx (see Skill 2). Perhaps the visitor is vision-impaired and is using a speech synthesizer (see Skill 23). Perhaps the visitor is surfing the Web with their browser's option to auto-load images turned off, which is an option in both Internet Explorer and Navigator. Fortunately, HTML allows you to provide *alternative text* for your images.

 NOTE   IE, version 3.0 and higher, and Navigator, version 4.0 and higher, display the alternative text as a tool tip when a visitor's mouse is placed over an image.

So just what should be entered as alternative text? A short, concise description of the image itself or the destination or action to be taken if the graphic serves as a link. If you had a photo of a widget to be used with a specific gadget, your alternative text could be something like, "Widget 1 for use with Gadget 202." You could create that text by using the following syntax:

For images of purely decorative treatment, such as small bullets or other accents that don't provide information or navigation, an empty ALT attribute—ALT=""—should be used. Speech readers and other browsers that rely on ALT content then know they can safely ignore those images.

```
<IMG SRC="widget1.gif" ALT="Widget 1 for use with Gadget 202">
```

 NOTE   Almost any character can be used within an alternative text block. One that *can't* be used is the quotation mark. Because all attribute values are enclosed in quotes, a quote in the middle of your alternative text value will confuse the browser. The browser will interpret that first extra quote as the *end* of your alternative text, rather than as you intended. You can get around this problem by using a single quotes or by avoiding them all together.

White Space

Those familiar with the world of desktop publishing or other print processes will be familiar with the concept of *white space*. White space is the absence of printing around an element on a page.

The default spacing around a graphic is a single typed space between the graphic and the next character of text in the same line. The default often produces a crowded look and makes the text near the graphics difficult to read. Figure 5.2 shows an inline image using the default amount of white space and an inline image where we've added a little extra white space.

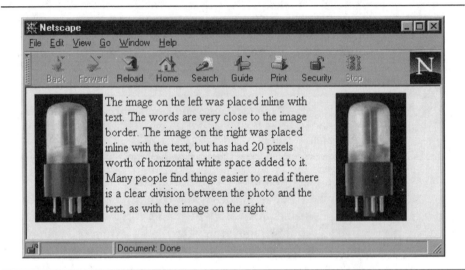

FIGURE 5.2:   An image without white space compared to an image with added white space

The image text on both sides of the image on the left crowds right up against it. On the right, there's more space, or "breathing room", for the image. It doesn't look squished.

The white space was added using the HSPACE attribute in the IMG tag. HSPACE and VSPACE provide horizontal white space and vertical white space, respectively. The value is measured in pixels, with syntax such as:

```
<IMG SRC="widget1.gif" HSPACE="10">
```

This syntax will cause 10 pixels of horizontal white space to be inserted on *both sides* of the graphic, in addition to the default single space that is found between all images and the remaining inline text.

If you want white space on all four sides of the image, both the HSPACE attribute and the VSPACE attribute can be used, as follows:

```
<IMG SRC="widget1.gif" HSPACE="10" VSPACE="10">
```

Image Mapping

When an image is going to be used as an image map, that fact can be declared in the IMG tag using either the USEMAP or ISMAP attribute. USEMAP is a function of client-side image maps, and ISMAP is used with server-side maps. The construction of image maps, including alternative methods of handling them such as the MAP element, are discussed in detail in Skill 9.

Frames

Sometimes it's desirable to have some content always remain visible within the page. For instance, most software programs have menu bars and icons at the top of the program window that will always remain in view, regardless of what else changes on the screen. Most often, Web designers wish to provide navigation content, or branding information, such as a logo, in a similarly static area. *Frames* were developed to fill this need. They divide the browser window into two or more individual frames or subsections, that will operate as if they were independent browsers.

HTML documents that make use of frames have a unique structure that may seem to violate many of the rules set down in previous skills. Figure 5.3 shows a site with a three frame layout.

The *FRAMESET* Tag

The FRAMESET tag is a container that defines the borders to be laid out for content presentation within the main browser window.

The individual frames within the browser window are defined in two dimensions: *rows* and *columns*. The row count is the number of horizontal sections to be created within the browser window. Thenumber of vertical sections represent the number of columns. Rows are described by the ROWS attribute and columns by the COLS attribute.

Skill 5

Each attribute has an implied value of 1. This means that if the attribute is not set within the FRAMESET tag, a frames-capable browser will assume a single horizontal or vertical space that results in a display across the full width or height of the browser window.

Let's take a look at the basic HTML for a <FRAMESET>.

```
<FRAMESET ROWS="value, value" COLS="value, value">
</FRAMESET>
```

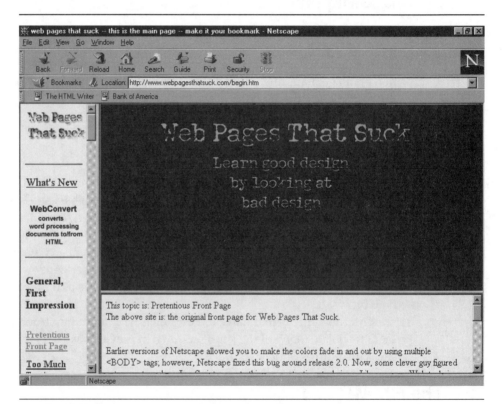

FIGURE 5.3   A Web site layout that makes use of frames

The first thing that's a little different in this tag is the format of the value for the ROW and COLS attributes. Each of these values contains a comma-delimited list of values. For example, you might want to divide a browser window into four equal quadrants. To do that, you need two rows and two columns. The size of each row or column is declared in the list of values for each of those attributes, as shown in the example FRAMESET container we just presented. What values should be placed used for each attribute? (The answer can be found in the upcoming section *Using a Percentage of the Browser Window.*)

Allocating Space between Frames

The values used for row widths and column lengths can be set in three different ways: in fixed pixel values, in a percentage of the browser window, or by using *relative spacing*.

Setting Fixed Pixel Sized Frames   Fixed pixel values are used when you want to present a frame of an exact size. Remember that a pixel remains a pixel, regardless of the visitor's screen resolution. A 200 pixel–wide frame will take up just under one third of the browser window when viewed at full screen on a monitor set to 640 × 480 resolution. But that same 200 pixel–wide frame will take up just one quarter of the browser window when viewed at full screen on a monitor set to 800 × 600 resolution. Frames with fixed pixel values are often used to hold logos in a horizontal frame across the top of a site or to hold navigational information in a fixed frame.

Using a Percentage of the Browser Window   The browser window can be divided up using percentages only if the dimensions of all frames can be expressed in percentages. For our example of dividing a browser window into four equal quadrants, the use of percentages would be the most obvious choice. The ROWS attribute would hold a value of "50%, 50%" and the COLS attribute would hold the same values of "50%, 50%". The result is the browser dividing the available window space in half, both horizontally and vertically, resulting in four evenly sized quadrants as shown in Figure 5.4 and in the file frames.html.

frames.html

```
<HTML>
<FRAMESET rows="50%, 50%" cols="50%, 50%">

<frame src="frame1.html" frameborder=1 name="q1">
<frame src="frame2.html" frameborder=1 name="q2">
<frame src="frame3.html" frameborder=1 name="q3">
<frame src="frame4.html" frameborder=1 name="q4">

</frameset>

</HTML>
```

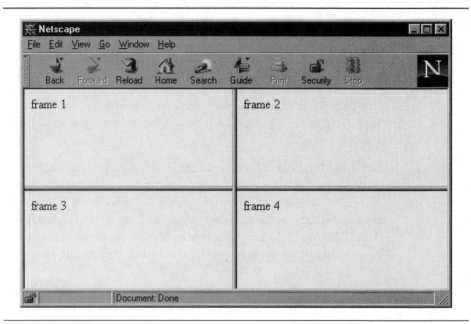

FIGURE 5.4:   A <FRAMESET> that divides the browser window into four evenly sized quadrants

The attributes for the frame tags used in this example file are discussed in the upcoming section *Filling the Frames with Content*. The four files used to fill each quadrant appear below:

frame1.html

```
<HTML>
<BODY BGCOLOR="#FFFFFF" TEXT="#000000">

<P>frame 1

</BODY>
</HTML>
```

frame2.html

```
<HTML>
<BODY BGCOLOR="#FFFFFF" TEXT="#000000">

<P>frame 2

</BODY>
</HTML>
```

frame3.html

```
<HTML>
<BODY BGCOLOR="#FFFFFF" TEXT="#000000">

<P>frame 3

</BODY>
</HTML>
```

frame4.html

```
<HTML>
<BODY BGCOLOR="#FFFFFF" TEXT="#000000">

<P>frame 4

</BODY>
</HTML>
```

Using percentages, your row or column values will always add up to 100%. But what happens when you want to use a combination of frames that includes one fixed pixel frame? How do you tell the browser to divide up the remainder of the available space? Percentages won't work because they are percentages of the *whole* window. This is where relative spacing comes in.

Handling Relative Spacing   The concept of relative spacing may on the surface appear to be similar to spacing by percentages. However, if you look closely, it's really very different.

In the example outlined previously in *Setting Fixed Pixel Sized Frames*, a 200 pixel–wide frame was created. Suppose that beyond that, you now have decided that you want the *remaining* space divided into two frames, one taking up three-quarters of the remaining space, the other taking up one quarter of the remaining space. The values for ROWS would then be defined as:

```
<FRAMESET ROWS="200,3*,1*">
```

The asterisks in this example tell the browser to make the second frame three times bigger than the third frame. Thus, the second frame is sized *in relation to* the third frame.

If the available width of the browser window is 600 pixels, the first row takes up its predefined width of 200 pixels, and the second is given 300 pixels to the third's 100 pixels. If this page were viewed on a monitor set to 800 × 600 resolution, with 760 pixels in available browser window width, the first row would take up 200 pixels, the second row would be set to 420 pixels (3/4 of 560), and the third would be set to 140 pixels.

Filling the Frames with Content

Now that you've allocated space for your frames, it's time to define each frame's content. The content is derived from individual HTML files that will be loaded into each frame. Each frame that was created by the rows and columns declared in the frameset must contain content, even if that content is an HTML file that simply has an empty body container.

It is possible to get really creative with frames making use of the attributes available to you. You can challenge traditional Web design by placing elements such as navigational tools in unexpected places. A fun example of this approach can be seen on Derek Powazek's Web site, at http://www.powazek.com/home/welcome.html (see Figure 5.5).

Derek combined several effects here. The first is a fixed size frame across the top without borders, which holds the site logo. The frame on the right contains the navigational tools and is set to scroll because the contents of that frame are longer than the available space within the browser. The main frame in the middle will also scroll when necessary.

The *FRAME* tag

The FRAME tag defines the individual frame contents. It has seven possible attributes: NAME, SRC, NORESIZE, SCROLLING, FRAMEBORDER, MARGINWIDTH, MARGINHEIGHT.

Some of these attributes will be familiar to you from other tags you've learned.

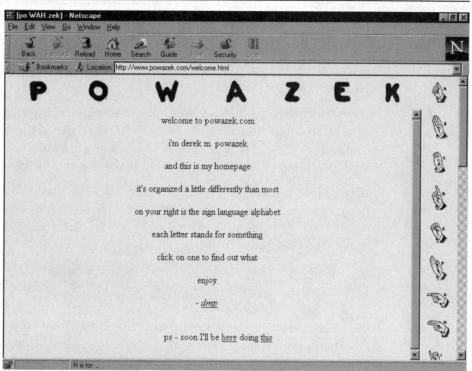

FIGURE 5.5:   Frames allow this site's creator to use a navigation tool on the right side of the browser display rather than the traditional left side or bottom.

Naming Frames   The NAME attribute is used to assign a name to your frame. Each frame should be named in a way that's meaningful. When links are used to load new HTML files into the various frames, the frame name will be used to target that process appropriately. Names such as main, NavWindow, header or footer can be envisioned easily.

Frames do have special naming conventions you'll need to remember. Frames that you create must have names that begin with an alphabetical character, that is any letter from A to Z in either lower or upper case. There are four reserved frame names that have special syntax and have been set aside to describe special behaviors: _blank, _self, _parent, and _top. Their special properties are described in the upcoming section *Targeting a Frame*.

Frame Source   The source (SRC) attribute should be a familiar one to you because we already used it when handling images. It is the source URL of the document to be contained within that frame. Following the concepts of relative path statements, you might use only a file name if the source file resides in the same directory as the file defining the FRAMESET, or you might include path information or a fully qualified URL.

No Resizing Allowed   The <FRAME> attribute NORESIZE is unique, in that it doesn't take a value. Simply by its presence, it tells the browser that the user should not be allowed to interactively drag and resize a frame's border. If the NORESIZE attribute is not present, the user is free to resize the frame as desired.

Independent Scrolling   HTML recognizes that the content of frames will often exceed their allotted viewing area. Just as scroll bars are provided for long or wide Web pages, they can be provided for individual frames. The SCROLLING attribute has three possible values:

AUTO   The default value. The browser will insert scroll bars when the length or width of the document loaded into the frame exceeds the available viewing space.

YES   When the attribute is set to a value of "yes", the browser is instructed to supply scroll bars, whether or not the document loaded into that frame exceeds the available viewing space.

NO   The browser is instructed to *not* provide scroll bars. Any content of that frame that exceeds the available viewing space will not be displayed. This value should be used with care and display tested for acceptable results on a variety of browser window sizes and screen resolutions.

Creating Bordered Frames   Figure 5.4 showed a browser window divided into four quadrants using frames. The gray bars are the frame borders. By default, the browser will include them. To proactively set the use of a border, set the FRAMEBORDER attribute to a value of 1. To instruct the browser not to use them, set the value to 0.

 NOTE   You might recognize these values from the boolean logic used in computer programming languages. A value of 1 represents True and a value of 0 represents False. The same concept has been carried over into HTML conventions. The value of 1 for a FRAMEBORDER attribute could said to be True for the instruction to include a border and False (a value of 0) for the instruction to not include a border.

Defining Margins   The attributes MARGINWIDTH and MARGINHEIGHT are used to determine the size of the left/right margins and top/bottom margins respectively. The values for these attributes are measured in pixels and *must* be greater than one.

COMPATIBILITY NOTE   If either attribute is not included within the FRAME tag, the default placement is left up to the browser. HTML does not provide a set default margin value for browsers to use, so the actual result does vary from browser to browser.

Derek Powazek also created a site that combines many of the attributes discussed here in a very unusual way. A story on his site *The Fray* (http://www.fray.com/hope/meeting) is actually "hidden" behind two other frames (see Figure 5.6). To get to the story, the reader resizes the two frames using the arrows shown.

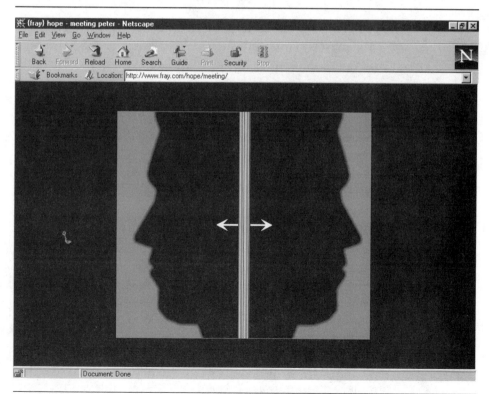

FIGURE 5.6:   Can you figure out how to reach the story?

Is Imitation *Really* the Sincerest Form of Flattery?

One issue that is most difficult for many new Web designers to understand is the application of copyright to HTML markup. How could simple BODY, P, and UL tags be copyrighted? Wouldn't other Web designers quickly control all possible variations of tags? Not really.

In practice, copyright attaches to a work—we traditionally think of works as drawings and paintings, or books like this one—at the moment of creation. When applied to HTML and the Web, copyright applies to the Web page content. When the tags used to create that content become the content itself, as with the design for the page captured in Figure 5.6, we enter a new, uncharted place in copyright law.

It's become almost a rite of passage among Web designers to view the HTML source of sites around the Web and to learn from the techniques used to create them. The key has always been the idea of learning by example: you then take the skills learned and apply them *in your own way* on your own Web sites.

The unique and creative methods used by Derek in creating the page pictured in Figure 5.6 have unfortunately been copied wholesale—someone simply used cut and paste—and used on other sites. It's certainly flattering, but it is also treading on very shaky legal ground. Derek was able to resolve his dispute with the other party when they agreed to include a short statement crediting him with the concept.

As a Web designer, you should take care to avoid situations like this one. Some developers might not have been as accommodating as Derek was or may have been "flattered" enough to call their intellectual property attorney.

The bottom line? Adhere to the tradition of learning by example. Take what you've seen and apply it to your work in a new and different way. If you find something you think is "just perfect" for your site, contact the original author and ask for permission to duplicate it. Above all, if you have concerns about whether or not incorporating ideas into your efforts is proper, consult your company's legal staff.

Targeting New Frame Content

Now that the browser window has been divided up into a set of frames, with their behavior and appearances defined, what happens when you need to create links in one frame that will display new content in another frame? The concept of a *target* for the link handles those instructions. A target is an attribute within a link. It defines the name of the frame in which the new content should be loaded. Let's take another look at the FRAMESET created in frames.html.

frames.html

```
<HTML>
<FRAMESET rows="50%, 50%" cols="50%, 50%">

<frame src="frame1.html" frameborder=1 name="q1">
<frame src="frame2.html" frameborder=1 name="q2">
<frame src="frame3.html" frameborder=1 name="q3">
<frame src="frame4.html" frameborder=1 name="q4">

</frameset>

</HTML>
```

A link will now be added to the frame1.html file as shown below. (This file is called frame1-1.html on the CD, to distinguish it from frame1.html earlier in the chapter. You should rename frame1-1.html to frame1.html before using it.)

frame1.html

```
<HTML>
<BODY BGCOLOR="#FFFFFF" TEXT="#000000">

<P>frame 1

<P>Link to new frame content, the file <A HREF="frame1a.html"
   TARGET="q1">frame1a.html</A>.

</BODY>
   </HTML>
```

Skill 5

The new content file will be created using:

frame1a.html

```
<HTML>
<BODY BGCOLOR="#FFFFFF" TEXT="#000000">
<P>This is frame 1a, displayed in this quadrant, q1, using the TARGET
    attributed
in the link you just followed.
</BODY>
</HTML>
```

Notice that after following the link, the only frame with new content is the upper left quadrant, q1, as shown in Figure 5.7.

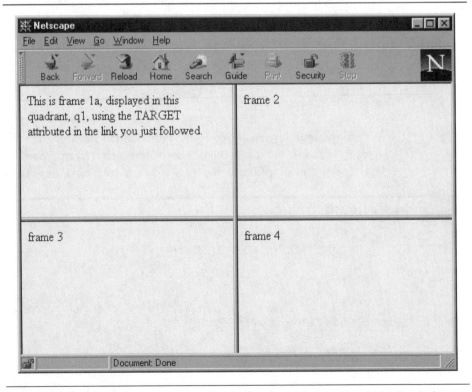

FIGURE 5.7:   The browser screen after frame1a.html has been loaded

Reserved Targets

In the earlier section *Naming Frames*, we introduced four reserved names: _blank, _self, _parent, and _top. These names have special meaning to the Web browser, and they initiate specific behavior when loading new content. Let's have a look.

A _blank TARGET   Table 5.1 shows that a TARGET value of _blank will result in the HTML file being loaded into a new, unnamed browser window. That means the user's computer system will actually launch the browser in a second instance and move the focus from the first instance where the link was clicked to the second instance of the browser where the new content is loading.

TABLE 5.1:   Reserved Frame Names

Name	Action
_blank	The linked file loads into a new and unnamed browser window.
_self	The document loads into the frame where the file containing thelink currently resides.
_parent	The browser loads the file into the closest outer or parent*<FRAMESET> from the current frame. This would occur if FRAMESET containers have been nested. The value will default to the behavior of _self if there is no parent frame.
_top	The document is displayed into the full original browser window, removing any other frame structure.

* Framesets are containers - A frame can hold another frameset, like nesting tupperware bowls. If you have a stack of 3, a file being loaded from inner bowl 3 would load in parent bowl 2, not the outmost bowl 1.

There are two issues of major significance to think about when using this approach. First, the user may or may not have recognized that a new browser has been launched. They may try to use their browser's back button to return to previous pages and be confused when they find they can't—the new browser window does not inherent the page access history from the original browser window. Your design should take this into consideration by at a minimum including links back to the original framed content.

Secondly, by launching a new browser, you're making an imposition on your visitor's computer resources. Those with less powerful computers may run into performance problems—potentially even system crashes—if their computers are overtaxed by running the additional instance of the browser program. As such, launching a new window should not be undertaken lightly. Consider all other design options before choosing to go forward here.

TARGETing *_self*   The _self TARGET value tells the browser to load the new content into the current frame. This behavior could be thought of as normal link behavior, if the frame is thought of as a full window. The previous example using a link from frame1.html to frame1a.html mimics this behavior. Instead of using the TARGET value q1, the value _self could have replaced it with identical results.

The *_parent* **Value**   The _parent TARGET value is one that can be handy when you have a layout that is several FRAMESET tags deep. It does, however, require a thorough understanding of the "family tree", of each <FRAMESET>. Rather than using _parent, it's often easiest to use the specific name of the frame you wish to target.

Climbing Out to the *_top TARGET*   When the TARGET value of _top is used, all <FRAMESET>s are pushed away, and the new content is displayed in the original full browser window. This behavior is greatly favored over loading new content into a new browser window using _blank because it doesn't tax the user's system by launching an entire new instance of the browser.

WARNING   Another key point in using the _top value occurs when you link to Web pages outside of your own site. If you don't use the _top value when linking from a document enclosed in a frame on your site, that new site will be displayed within your <FRAMESET>. Such browser behavior, while the default for a link without a TARGET, can land you in a pretty murky legal setting. Many a Web site owner has contended that by another Web developer displaying their content in that Web developer's frames, they have repurposed it for their own use or are intimating that the content is their own by enclosing it in their branded frames. As a result some feel they have moved over the line into copyright or trademark infringement. That's also beyond the more immediate degradation your user's experience of the new site by shoehorning it into a space that's smaller than what it was meant to be viewed in. All things considered? Use the TARGET value of _top when linking out to any other sites.

COMPATIBILITY NOTE   In several of the earliest frames supporting browsers, primarily Navigator 2.0, the browser's "back" button took the user all the way back out of the framed content, instead of just back one link. By providing navigation within your pages you can avoid this inconvenience to your visitors.

Providing for Browsers That Can't Display Frames

The concept of frames originated with an implementation by Netscape in their Navigator 2.0 browser. Any browsers in previous generations aren't able to display frames, and some less-used current browsers can't handle them either. How can a Web designer provide for both types of visitors in one site?

Some designers choose to provide a second complete set of Web pages that visitors can access separately. That's a plausible route when the framed layout makes use of nested frames and a significant number of screen divisions. However, the HTML specification for frames includes a provision for displaying content to those browsers that can't handle the frames by using the NOFRAMES element.

A common layout using frames provides a navigation menu in one small frame, the HTML file perhaps called nav.html and the content itself in a main frame with a file name of main.html. The <FRAMESET> itself is defined in the default file, in this case index.html. The markup in index.html could appear as simply as:

```
<HTML>
<FRAMESET COLS="30%, 70%">
    <FRAME SRC="nav.html">
    <FRAME SRC="main.html">
</FRAMESET>
</HTML>
```

If a user visited this site with a browser that didn't support frames, they'd be greeted by only a blank page. A short addition to the file can take care of this problem.

index.html

```
<HTML>
<FRAMESET COLS="30%, 70%">
    <FRAME SRC="nav.html">
    <FRAME SRC="main.html">
</FRAMESET>
<BODY>
<P>A <A HREF="main.html">no-frames version</A> is available here.
</BODY>
</HTML>
```

The user is then presented with the single sentence and link shown here in the BODY container (see Figure 5.8).

You'll notice that the link provided within `index.html` is to `main.html`, the same file used as the original SRC value of the second frame. That's where the NOFRAMES content will actually be presented, as shown here in the listing for `main.html`.

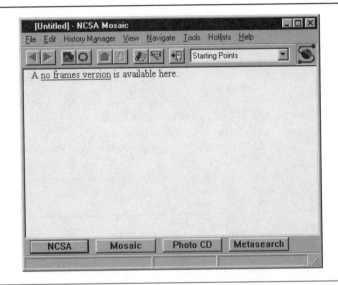

FIGURE 5.8: Index.html as seen in a non-frames compatible browser (NCSA Mosaic 3.0 for Win95).

main.html

```
<HTML>
<BODY BGCOLOR="#FFFFFF" TEXT="#000000">
<NOFRAMES>
<P>...the navigational content from nav.html here...
</NOFRAMES>
<P>...the original main.html document here...
</BODY>
</HTML>
```

While we didn't originally create a `main.html` file, the addition of the NOFRAMES element doesn't change anything else about the document. The NOFRAMES container is simply inserted immediately below the opening BODY tag and before any other

HTML markup. Figure 5.8 displays this short file in a non-frames compatible browser. Looks like a regular HTML page, doesn't it? That's the idea. The move from the framed content to a non-frames display should be as transparent as possible for the user without a frames capable browser.

 NOTE   The NOFRAMES example used here provides a simple transition between framed and unframed content. Designers who choose a more complex framed presentation—such as nested framesets or more than 2 or 3 frames in a single frameset—may be required to provide a full second set of HTML pages for non-framed presentation. At that point, a cost to benefit analysis should probably take place in order to evaluate how worthwhile such a presentation is compared to the cost of providing two complete versions of the site.

The Inline Frame

An inline frame—the IFRAME element—can be thought of like an image or other object that is inserted into an HTML document. They are presented in the space that you specify, and text and other elements can flow around them.

The attributes to the IFRAME element include most of those for the FRAME element (see *The FRAME Tag* earlier in this chapter). The additional attributes include WIDTH and HEIGHT, which are used as they are for setting aside space for images (see *Image Dimensions* earlier in this chapter). The only exception is the NORESIZE attribute. You can name the inline frame as well as determine its border, margin, and scrolling properties. As with FRAME, the information to be displayed in the inline frame is assigned in the SRC attribute. It can be an HTML file or any other file that would ordinarily be viewed through a link. Here's a short example:

```
<IFRAME SRC="info.html" WIDTH="300" HEIGHT="200" FRAMEBORDER="1"
   ALIGN="LEFT">
<P>Your browser apparently does not support frames. You may see the
   content intended to be displayed here by viewing <A
   HREF="info.html">this link</A>.
</IFRAME>
```

The contents of info.html, shown here, are then displayed in the frame as seen in Figure 5.9.

```
<HTML>
<BODY BGCOLOR="#FFFFFF" TEXT="#0000FF">
<P>This content is being presented within the inline frame.
</BODY>
</HTML>
```

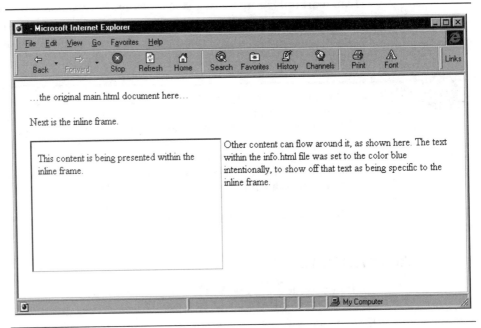

FIGURE 5.9: An inline frame as seen in IE 4.0

The newly modified `main.html` file is shown below. (This file is called `main1.html` on the CD to distinguish it from `main.html` earlier in the chapter. You should rename `main1.html` to `main.html` before using it.)

main.html

```
<HTML>
<BODY BGCOLOR="#FFFFFF">

<P>...the original main.html document here...

<P>Next is the inline frame.
<P>

<IFRAME SRC="info.html" WIDTH="300" HEIGHT="200" FRAMEBORDER=1
    ALIGN=LEFT>
<P>Your browser apparently does not support frames. You may see the
    content intended to be displayed here by viewing <A
    HREF="info.html">this link</A>.
</IFRAME>
```

```
<P>Other content can flow around it, as shown here. The text within the
    info.html file was set to
the color blue intentionally, to show off that text as being specific
    to the inline frame.

</BODY>
</HTML>
```

COMPATIBILITY NOTE At press time, the only major browser to support the IFRAME element was IE 4.0. As other browsers produce updated versions to support many of the new options included in HTML 4.0, additional support for inline frames could be expected.

Have You Mastered the Essentials?

Now you can...

- ☑ Include images in your documents.
- ☑ Create links using images.
- ☑ Align images to allow other content to flow around them.
- ☑ Design browser displays divided into several distinct frames.
- ☑ Provide an alternative for browsers that don't support frames.
- ☑ Use inline frames to set off additional HTML content.

Skill 5

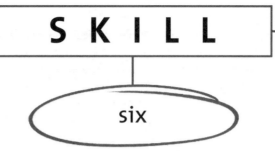

## 6

Tables

- ❏ Creating basic tables

- ❏ Table captions and borders

- ❏ Alignment of tables and cells

- ❏ Cell spacing and padding

- ❏ Grouping of columns and rows

More than many features, tables have had a large impact on the look and feel of Web pages. In this section, we'll look at basic table structures and how they are made. For information about how to make your tables accessible for visually impaired people or for those who are using browsers that do not support tables, see Skill 21.

The layout and structure of tables has changed quite a bit from HTML 3.2 to HTML 4.0 This skill will focus on HTML 4.0, and point out the 3.2 specifications where they are different. Currently, Netscape Navigator 4.*x* and Microsoft Internet Explorer 4.*x* sufficiently support HTML 4.0. If you wish to support older browsers, you should write to the HTML 3.2 specification for a while longer.

What Are Tables?

HTML tables consist of rows and columns, just like tables in print. The boxes formed by the intersection of the rows and columns are called *cells*. Tables can be used to format data, to make separate areas for toolbars, and to generally aid in the layout and design of information. Because tables have so many formatting options, they are a tremendous contribution to Web design. Not all browsers support tables, though, so you should read Skill 21 for alternatives.

Figure 6.1 shows the SFStation Web site (`http://www.sfstation.com`), which is a great example of what can be done with tables. All of the layout, including page divisions and the left-hand column of menu items, is possible because of tables. If you're interested in seeing a longer piece of sample HTML than this skill contains, go to this site and view the source code.

Creating a Basic Table

Let's take a look at the most basic HTML for making a table. The best way to learn how to build a table is to take a look at the HTML for a table and then examine the results in a browser.

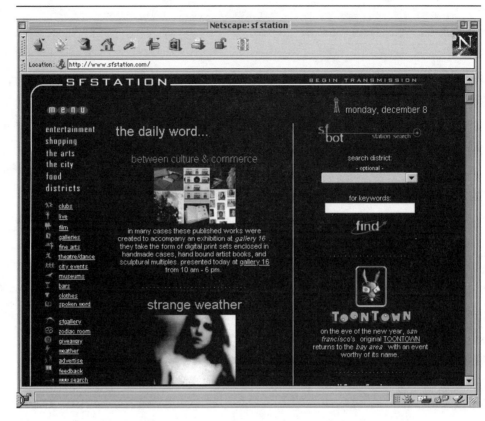

FIGURE 6.1: The SFStation Web site

basictable.html

```
<HTML>
<HEAD>
<TITLE>A Basic Table</TITLE>
</HEAD>
<BODY BGCOLOR="#FFFFFF"><TABLE>
<THEAD>
<TR>
<TD><strong>Grocery item</strong></TD>
```

```
<TD><strong>Quantity</strong></TD>
</TR>
</THEAD>
<TBODY>
<TR>
<TD>Apples</TD><TD>2</TD>
</TR>
<TR>
<TD>Oranges</TD><TD>1</TD>
</TR>
</TBODY>
</TABLE>
</BODY>
</HTML>
```

Figure 6.2 shows what the table looks like in Communicator 4.01 on the Macintosh.

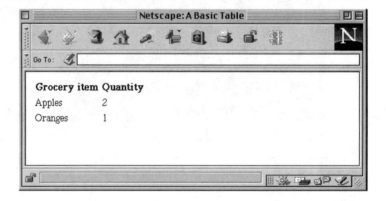

FIGURE 6.2:   `basictable.html` as viewed in Communicator 4.01 on the Mac.

The HTML tags we used are shown in Table 6.1. Let's examine them more closely.

Based on this information, you can see that the table in Figure 6.1 has two table rows defined by <TR> and </TR> and that each table row contains two table data cells. In the first cell of the first row, the data is *Grocery item*; in the second cell of the first row, the data is *Quantity*, and so on.

 NOTE   The cells of a table can contain many types of elements, including forms, images, lists, and other tables. They may also contain preformatted text and more than one paragraph.

TABLE 6.1: A closer look at the HTML elements used in basictable.html

HTML Element	Usage
<TABLE></TABLE>	These elements surround the table and delineate where it begins and ends.
<TR></TR>	These tags tell the browser there's a table row.
<TD></TD>	These tags tell the browser that there's a table cell. They also surround the data of the cell. That is, they say what's inside the defined cell.
<THEAD></THEAD>	These optional tags define a row as the table head. They work in exactly the same way as the TD tag. We'll discuss these tags in more detail later.

Table Formatting Options

Now you've created a simple table. If you want to spice it up, there's a lot of formatting you can try. In this section, we are going to add one feature at a time to the sample HTML and then look at what the table looks like in a browser.

Skill 6

 **WARNING**   The table in the last section works with both HTML 3.2 and HTML 4.0. For most of the fancier formatting, there usually needs to be differentiation between the two versions of HTML.

Captions

If you want, you can add a caption to your table, like the caption shown in Figure 6.3. To do so, you use the CAPTION element, as shown in the listing caption.html.

caption.html

```
<HTML>
<HEAD>
<TITLE>Sample Table with Caption</TITLE>
</HEAD>
<BODY BGCOLOR="#FFFFFF"><TABLE>
<CAPTION>Grocery List</CAPTION>
<THEAD>
```

```
<TR>
<TD><strong>Grocery item</strong></TD>
<TD><strong>Quantity</strong></TD>
</TR>
</THEAD>
<TBODY>
<TR>
<TD>Apples</TD><TD>2</TD>
</TR>
<TR>
<TD>Oranges</TD><TD>1</TD>
</TR>
</TBODY>
</TABLE>
</BODY>
</HTML>
```

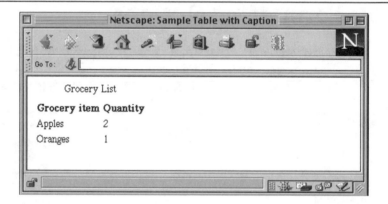

FIGURE 6.3: caption.html displayed in Communicator 4.01 on the Macintosh

You can specify where the caption is located relative to the table by using the ALIGN attribute. For example, using

```
<CAPTION ALIGN=BOTTOM>Your caption here</CAPTION>
```

places the caption beneath the table. Try it and see.

Borders

You've probably seen tables with borders around them There are lots of options for borders, including where they are and how thick they are. Let's take a quick look at a very simple border and then look at more sophisticated border options.

border.html

```
<HTML>
<HEAD>
<TITLE>Sample Table with Border</TITLE>
</HEAD>
<BODY BGCOLOR="#FFFFFF">
<TABLE frame border="1">
<CAPTION>Grocery List</CAPTION>
<TR>
<TD><strong>Grocery item</strong></TD>
<TD><strong>Quantity</strong></TD>
</TR>
<TR>
<TD>Apples</TD><TD>2</TD>
</TR>
<TR>
<TD>Oranges</TD><TD>1</TD>
</TR>
</TABLE>
</BODY>
</HTML>
```

Figure 6.4 displays what border.html looks like in Communicator 4.01 on the Macintosh.

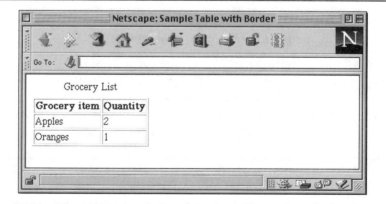

FIGURE 6.4: border.html as displayed in Communicator 4.01 on the Macintosh

Let's examine the sixth line of HTML:

```
<TABLE frame BORDER="1">
```

First, note the location of the frame attribute: it goes right in the TABLE element. The frame attribute, which describes the lines around the outside of the table, can be equal to a lot of things besides <BORDER>. Table 6.2 shows the possible values, taken from the World Wide Web Consortium HTML 4.0 specification.

TABLE 6.2: Possible values for the frame attribute

Value	Resulting Table
void	Creates a table with no sides. This is the default value.
above	Produces a border on the top side only.
below	Produces a border on the bottom side only.
lhs	Produces a border on the left side only.
rhs	Produces a border on the right side only.
hsides	Produces a border on the top and bottom sides.
vsides	Produces a border on the left and right sides.
box	Produces a border on all four sides.
border	Produces a border on all four sides. Box and border are interchangeable.

 WARNING   Be sure to use the lower case frame, as the uppercase FRAME is for defining frames for entire Web pages, not just tables.

Next, note that you can specify the width of the border, regardless of whether the frame is set to above, below, border, or any of the other options. To make the border twice as thick, the HTML would be <TABLE frame BORDER="2">. Be sure to try this on your own pages to see the difference.

 **COMPATIBILITY NOTE**   For pages which work with HTML 3.2 browsers, simply use the syntax <TABLE BORDER="1"> (or whatever number you choose).

Rules

The `frame` attribute covered in this skill applies to the entire table. In HTML 4.0, you can also specify the internal borders of rows and columns by using the `rule` attribute. Here's an example:

internalborders.html

```
<HTML>
<HEAD>
<TITLE>Sample Table with Internal Borders</TITLE>
</HEAD>
<BODY BGCOLOR="#FFFFFF">
<TABLE frame="hsides" border="1" rule="cols">
<CAPTION>Grocery List</CAPTION>
<TR>
<TD><strong>Grocery item</strong></TD>
<TD><strong>Quantity</strong></TD>
</TR>
<TR>
<TD>Apples</TD><TD>2</TD>
</TR>
<TR>
<TD>Oranges</TD><TD>1</TD>
</TR>
</TABLE>
</BODY>
</HTML>
```

COMPATIBILITY NOTE   At the time of this writing, rules are not supported by any of the major browser releases, although they support many other features of HTML 4.0. You should be particularly careful to test this feature before relying on it in your design.

In the above example, rules would only be applied between columns and not between rows. You could also choose between rows (`rules="rows"`) and between all cells (`rules="all"`). For reference, you can also use rules between cell groups (`rules="groups"`). Cell groups are covered later in this chapter.

Colors

You can also add color to a table. You have the option of adding it using the BGCOLOR attribute. This attribute uses the syntax BGCOLOR="#ColorHexNumber". Hex notation for color choices is covered in Skill 3. You can add color to the entire table by using the BGCOLOR attribute in the TABLE element, to a single row by adding it in the TR tag, or to a cell by adding it to a TD tag. In the following example we add gray to a row:

color.html

```
<HTML>
<HEAD>
<TITLE>Sample Table with Color</TITLE>
</HEAD>
<BODY BGCOLOR="#FFFFFF">
<TABLE frame border="1">
<CAPTION>Grocery List</CAPTION>
<TR BGCOLOR="#CCCCCC">
<TD><strong>Grocery item</strong></TD>
<TD><strong>Quantity</strong></TD>
</TR>
<TR>
<TD>Apples</TD><TD>2</TD>
</TR>
<TR>
<TD>Oranges</TD><TD>1</TD>
</TR>
</TABLE>
</BODY>
</HTML>
```

The color.html file as seen in Communicator 4.01 for the Mac is shown in Figure 6.5.

To color the entire table, the HTML would be

```
<TABLE frame="hsides" border="1" rule="rows" BGCOLOR="#CCCCC">.
```

COMPATIBILITY NOTE   These background colors work the same for HTML 3.2 and 4.0.

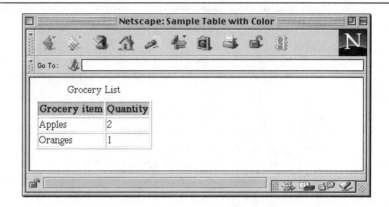

FIGURE 6.5: color.html as viewed on a Mac using Communicator 4.01

Alignment

Along with all the other types of formatting, HTML also allows the user to align text within the cells. There are three different types of alignments, two of which are supported by HTML 3.2 (horizontal and vertical), and one of which is new to HTML 4.0 (alignment by character). Alignments are defined by using the ALIGN attribute.

 NOTE   Even though the alignment refers to alignment of data within cells, you can use the ALIGN attribute like the BGCOLOR attribute—what it affects depends on where you place it. Place it in the TABLE element to align the entire table, in the TR tag to align the entire row, and in the TD tag to align the contents of a single cell.

Horizontal Alignment

In the following example, we'll align the contents of the second column to the right. For now, we are going to do each cell in the column individually. Later, when we cover groups of rows, you'll see how attributes can be applied to a group of rows in order to affect an entire column.

horizontal.html

```
<HTML>
<HEAD>
<TITLE>Sample Table with Horizontal Alignment</TITLE>
</HEAD>
<BODY BGCOLOR="#FFFFFF">
<TABLE frame border="1">
<CAPTION>Grocery List</CAPTION>
<TR BGCOLOR="#CCCCC">
<TD><strong>Grocery item</strong></TD>
<TD ALIGN="RIGHT"><strong>Quantity</strong></TD>
</TR>
<TR>
<TD>Apples</TD><TD ALIGN="RIGHT">2</TD>
</TR>
<TR>
<TD>Oranges</TD><TD ALIGN="RIGHT">1</TD>
</TR>
</TABLE>
</BODY>
</HTML>
```

Figure 6.6 shows how horizontal.html is rendered by a Mac with Communicator 4.01.

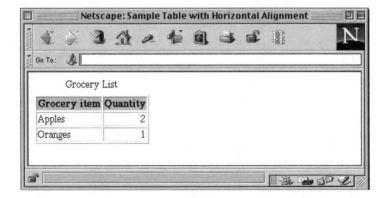

FIGURE 6.6: horizontal.html as seen in Communicator 4.01 on the Macintosh

Other horizontal alignments options include LEFT, CENTER, JUSTIFY, and CHAR. The first three of these work just like RIGHT. We'll cover CHAR later in this skill.

Vertical Alignment

You also have the option of aligning text vertically within a cell. This is done using the VALIGN attribute. Let's say that one of the table cells contained enough text to wrap within the cell. You have options about how you want to align material in the adjacent cells. Here's some sample HTML:

vertical.html

```
<HTML>
<HEAD>
<TITLE>Sample Table with Vertical Alignment</TITLE>
</HEAD>
<BODY BGCOLOR="#FFFFFF">
<TABLE frame border="1">
<CAPTION>Grocery List</CAPTION>
<TR BGCOLOR="#CCCCCC" VALIGN="TOP">
<TD><strong>Grocery item</strong></TD>
<TD ALIGN="RIGHT"><strong>Quantity</strong></TD></THEAD>
</TR>
<TR>
<TD width="25">Apples, bananas, pears, and bunches of grapes</TD><TD
  ALIGN="RIGHT" VALIGN="TOP">2 each</TD>
</TR>
<TR>
<TD>Oranges</TD><TD ALIGN="RIGHT">1</TD>
</TR>
</TABLE>
</BODY>
</HTML>
```

Figure 6.7 demonstrates how vertical.html is rendered by a Mac with Communicator 4.01.

In this example, the cell that contains the text "Apples, bananas, pears, and bunches of grapes" has left the cell with the text "2 each" fairly empty. By specifying VALIGN="TOP", we have lined up the text in the mostly empty cell. You also have the option to use BOTTOM, MIDDLE, and BASELINE. BASELINE simply means that the letters align with a baseline which corresponds to all the letters in a row. It only applies to the first line of text in a cell. Try this HTML with another value for VALIGN.

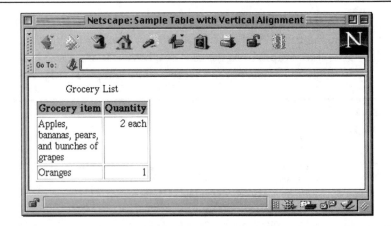

FIGURE 6.7: vertical.html as seen in Communicator 4.01 on the Macintosh

Character Alignment

A newer feature of HTML is that text can be aligned along a character, such as a decimal point. This can be handy for using HTML to display things like accounting procedures. Let's look at some sample HTML. The numbers of the items have been changed in order to show the decimal alignment.

character.html

```
<HTML>
<HEAD>
<TITLE>Sample Table with Character Alignment</TITLE>
</HEAD>
<BODY BGCOLOR="#FFFFFF">
<TABLE border="1">
<CAPTION>Grocery List</CAPTION>
<TR BGCOLOR="#CCCCCC">
<TD><strong>Grocery item</strong></TD>
```

```
<TD ALIGN="RIGHT"><strong>Quantity</strong></TD>
</TR>
<TR>
<TD>Apples</TD><TD ALIGN="char" char=".">2.0</TD>
</TR>
<TR>
<TD>Oranges</TD><TD ALIGN="char" char=".">100.00</TD>
</TR>
</TABLE>
</BODY>
</HTML>
```

 WARNING   At the time of this writing, there are no released browsers that support alignment by character.

Cell Margins

Another spacing option is the ability to specify the spacing within and in between cells. These attributes are called CELLPADDING and CELLSPACING, respectively. Both work for HTML 3.2 and HTML 4.0.

CELLPADDING

CELLPADDING is used to describe how much empty space is around the words in a cell. It can be specified as a number of pixels or as a percentage of the cell. When specified as a percentage of the cell, the percentage is divided by two horizontally and vertically. That is, if you specify that the padding equals 30% of the cell, then there will be a padding of 15% of the width of the cell above the data, 15% below the data, and 15% on either side of the data. If the cell is 100 pixels wide, and you specify a border of 30%, the browser will calculate that 30% of the 100 pixels, divide that number (30 pixels) by two and place a cell padding of 15 pixels all the way around the cell. That's because the browsers think of padding as being horizontal or vertical; and so if you say 30%, they think of dividing that 30% vertically and horizontally around the data (above and below it).

Let's add some padding to our sample table, as shown in Figure 6.8.

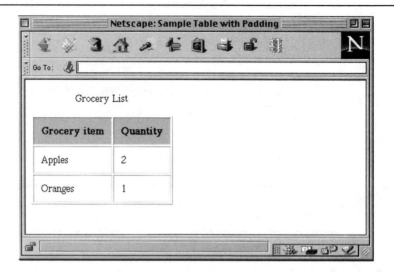

FIGURE 6.8: padding.html as displayed on the Mac using Communicator 4.01

padding.html

```
<HTML>
<HEAD>
<TITLE>Sample Table with Padding</TITLE>
</HEAD>
<BODY BGCOLOR="#FFFFFF">
<TABLE frame border="1" CELLPADDING="10">
<CAPTION>Grocery List</CAPTION>
<TR BGCOLOR="#CCCCC">
<TD><strong>Grocery item</strong></TD>
<TD><strong>Quantity</strong></TD>
</TR>
<TR>
<TD>Apples</TD><TD>2</TD>
</TR>
<TR>
<TD>Oranges</TD><TD>1</TD>
</TR>
</TABLE>
</BODY>
</HTML>
```

Note the new padding around the text. There are 10 pixels all around, but it does not look even because the text is aligned by default to the left side of the cell.

CELLSPACING

CELLSPACING is similar to CELLPADDING, but it adds space between cells rather than adding space within the cells. Without CELLSPACING, cells are right next to each other—they touch. Another way to think of CELLSPACING is to think of it as the width of the border between cells. In the example below, the border of the table has been left in to show where the space was added; if the border were off, then the table would simply appears as if there were more space between the cells.

spacing.html

```
<HTML>
<HEAD>
<TITLE>Sample Table with Spacing</TITLE>
</HEAD>
<BODY BGCOLOR="#FFFFFF">
<TABLE frame border="1" CELLSPACING="10">
<CAPTION>Grocery List</CAPTION>
<TR BGCOLOR="#CCCCCC">
<TD><strong>Grocery item</strong></TD>
<TD><strong>Quantity</strong></TD>
</TR>
<TR>
<TD>Apples</TD><TD>2</TD>
</TR>
<TR>
<TD>Oranges</TD><TD>1</TD>
</TR>
</TABLE>
</BODY>
</HTML>
```

The spacing.html file is shown in Figure 6.9. Notice where the spacing is placed in contrast to the padding in Figure 6.8. Try adding your own value for CELLSPACING to see what happens.

FIGURE 6.9: spacing.html as displayed on the Mac using Communicator 4.01

Grouping Rows and Columns

You've had a chance to see how to make a basic table and to do some fancier formatting. Now we're going to take a look at the process of grouping together rows and columns and how that affects their size. We're also going to learn how to specify that a cell span more than one row or column.

 NOTE You can apply the formatting you've already learned, such as color, borders, and alignment to groups.

Grouping is new to HTML 4.0, and it is a big advance because it allows the server to send the browser the overall table layout and begin to render the table without waiting for all of the actual table content.

Grouping Columns

In HTML 3.2, the width of columns was determined by using the WIDTH attribute. HTML 4.0 is pretty different, in that it allows you to specify column groups.

Column groups give the user more control over the final outcome of the table layout. Let's take a look at how column groups work.

The *COLGROUP* Tag

A column group is specified using the COLGROUP tag. You can also specify columns within the COLGROUP tag by using the COL tag. Every table must have a column group, and if groups are not spelled out in the HTML, then it's assumed that all of the columns in the table are in one group. Anything that you specify within the COLGROUP tag applies to the entire column group. Here is an example of how to specify a column group:

columngroup.html

```
<HTML>
<HEAD>
<TITLE>Sample Table with a Column Group</TITLE>
</HEAD>
<BODY BGCOLOR="#FFFFFF">
<TABLE frame border="1">
<CAPTION>Grocery List</CAPTION>
<COLGROUP span=2>
<TR BGCOLOR>
<TD><strong>Grocery item</strong></TD>
<TD><strong>Quantity</strong></TD>
</TR>
<TR>
<TD>Apples</TD><TD>2</TD>
</TR>
<TR>
<TD>Oranges</TD><TD>1</TD>
</TR>
</TABLE>
</BODY>
</HTML>
```

The columngroup.html file specifies a column group that contains two columns. If you type up and display the file, you'll notice that it doesn't look like the columns are grouped—it looks the same as the table in Figure 6.4. This is because a table that contains only one column group is exactly the same as a table that does not specify any column groups. Here's a table with two column groups instead of one.

Skill 6

twocolumn.html

```
<HTML>
<HEAD>
<TITLE>Sample Table with Two Column Groups</TITLE>
</HEAD>
<BODY BGCOLOR="#FFFFFF">
<TABLE frame border="1">
<CAPTION>Grocery List</CAPTION>
<COLGROUP span=1 align="left">
<COLGROUP span=1 align="center">
<TR BGCOLOR="">
<TD><strong>Grocery item</strong></TD>
<TD><strong>Quantity</strong></TD>
</TR>
<TR>
<TD>Apples</TD><TD>2</TD>
</TR>
<TR>
<TD>Oranges</TD><TD>1</TD>
</TR>
</TABLE>
</BODY>
</HTML>
```

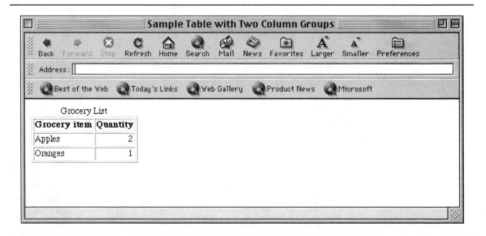

FIGURE 6.10: twocolumn.html as seen in IE 3.01 for the Mac.

The HTML markup for `twocolumn.html` defines two columns. The contents of the left-hand column (Grocery item, Carton of milk, and Carton of eggs) are all aligned on the left—you can see this if you look at the border in Figure 6.10. The contents of the right hand column group (Quantity, 1, and 2) are aligned center. Each column group spans one column. At the time of this writing, Communicator 4.01 did not support `COLGROUP` with the span attribute.

The *COL* Element

Now that you've seen how to define the column groups, let's take a closer look at the columns themselves. In HTML 4.0, they are defined within column groups by using the `COL` tag. The human perception is that data in a table is contained in columns and in rows. But in HTML, columns do not contain any information themselves—data is always contained in rows, placed within the `TD container`, which are in turn placed within the `TR container`—again, all of the data is defined as being in rows, not columns. Here's another way to think about it: when you start actually specifying which words or images go in which cell, you specify the cell by the row that contains the cell, not by the column.

Why does HTML have columns then? Because even though rows are used to define the *placement* of data, the reader still needs to perceive columns. The `COL` tag can be used to define attributes for a column or set of columns within a column group.

Here's another way to look at it. In the example `twocolumn.html`, we made a table with two column groups and defined each column group separately (one was left-aligned, one was center-aligned). Alternatively, we could have made them one column group and then defined two separate columns. The HTML would have looked like this:

definedcolumn.html

```
<HTML>
<HEAD>
<TITLE>Sample Table with Defined Columns</TITLE>
</HEAD>
<BODY BGCOLOR="#FFFFFF">
<TABLE frame border="1">
<CAPTION>Grocery List</CAPTION>
<COLGROUP span="2">
<COL ALIGN=LEFT">
<COL ALIGN="CENTER">
<TR BGCOLOR="#CCCCCC">
```

```
<TD><strong>Grocery item</strong></TD>
<TD><strong>Quantity</strong></TD>
</TR>
<TR>
<TD>Apples</TD><TD>2</TD>
</TR>
<TR>
<TD>Oranges</TD><TD>1</TD>
</TR>
</TABLE>
</BODY>
</HTML>
```

Note that the markup for `definedcolumn.html` will result in the same table as that pictured in Figure 6.10. Also, note that even though we have defined alignments in the column group by defining columns, we still define the placement of the information using table rows.

TIP   If you are having trouble seeing how this works, be sure to play with it. There's no substitute for trying HTML and changing attributes and tags to see how things change in the browser.

Column Widths   The COL tag can also be used to define the widths of columns. This means that your table may be rendered more quickly in browsers because the browser can define the columns without needing all of the data first. There are four ways to define column widths:

- By number of pixels

- By percentage of cell width

- By minimum width needed to hold the data

- By relative width

The syntax for defining columns widths is `<COL WIDTH="X">` where X depends on how you are defining your width. For a column that is 30 pixels wide, X would be 30. For a column that was 25% of the column group, X would be 25%. These examples are pretty obvious, but the next two cases take a tricky twist.

TIP   It's often better to size your columns with percentages rather than pixels. If you use an absolute number of pixels, you run the risk of not having a larger table fit on a small browser window..

If you want the columns to size themselves to fit the data, then you should make X equal to 0* (zero followed by an asterisk) so that the column will be defined by using <COL WIDTH="0*">.

WARNING   Making the columns size themselves in order to fit the data can slow down the formatting of the table. The browser will need to receive all of the data before it can size the columns correctly.

The last option for defining the width of columns is by using relative widths; that is, widths that are determined according to a number assigned to the column. (The number assigned to the column is always followed by an asterisk.) Take a look at the example below:

relativecolumn.html

```
<HTML>
<HEAD>
<TITLE>Sample Table with Relative Defined Column Widths</TITLE>
</HEAD>
<BODY BGCOLOR="#FFFFFF">
<TABLE>
<CAPTION>Grocery List</CAPTION>
<COLGROUP span="2">
<COL width="2*">
<COL width="1*">
<TR BGCOLOR="#CCCCC">
<TD><strong>Grocery item</strong></TD>
<TD><strong>Quantity</strong></TD>
</TR>
<TR>
<TD>Apples</TD><TD>2</TD>
</TR>
<TR>
<TD>Oranges</TD><TD>1</TD>
</TR>
</TABLE>
</BODY>
</HTML>
```

The first column will be twice the width of the second column.

It can be important to know how browsers prioritize your width assignments. Browsers will allocate the fixed or absolute widths you define first. Then they will take the remaining space and divide that according to percentages or relative numbers. This feature is important because a table can look very different from what you expected. Let's look at a small column group:

```
<COLGROUP span="2">
<COL="100">
<COL width="2*">
<COL width="1">
```

When the browser renders the table, it will first make a 100 pixel–wide column and will then divide the *remaining* space on a 2:1 basis to the last two columns. So, if the entire table is 400 pixels wide, the columns will respectively be 100 pixels, 200 pixels, and 100 pixels wide.

Column Spans Column spans are a lot easier to figure out than column widths. You can use SPAN to define how many columns in the group are spanned to represent one column. To span two columns, use <COL SPAN="2">. Figure 6.11 demonstrates the concept of column spanning.

WARNING   When you define a column group using <COLGROUP> and then define column widths using <COL="width">, the width you define applies individually to every column in the group. For example, if you define <COL SPAN="2" WIDTH="20">, you'll get a column that spans two columns, and the width of each of the spanned columns will be 20 pixels, for a total of 40 pixels.

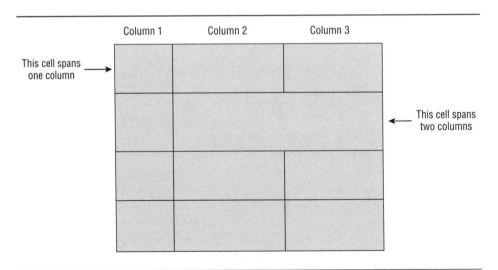

FIGURE 6.11: An illustration of column spanning

Grouping Rows

You've already seen the benefits of grouping columns. You can also group rows and use them to specify certain sections of the table, known as the table head, the table foot, and the table body.

The Table Head

Remember the THEAD container in the HTML for basictable.html at the beginning of this skill? These elements really are just like the TD element, and they are used in the same way. For a table to officially match the HTML 4.0 specification, though, it's necessary to specify the table head with the THEAD container.

The main practical reason for doing so is that if a table that is longer than a page is printed, the head will appear at the top of each page, making it easier to read the data. Also, if you decide to use stylesheets, you'll be able to specify that the table heads should look different from the table body, even though they look the same as a default.

From a functional aspect, table heads define a row, whichever row you consider to be the head of the table. This row is almost always at the top of the table. Defining a row as the table head does not guarantee that it gets any special formatting—that depends on the browser. Some browsers make the THEAD container contents look different from other cells, while others don't. It's best to test any formatting by viewing your HTML in the browsers you wish to support. The figures shown in this skill use the STRONG tag to emphasize the table head—the formatting is not automatic.

NOTE   If you choose to use the optional THEAD container or the optional TFOOT element discussed below, you must follow them with the TBODY elements as shown in the next example of HTML code.

The Table Foot

The foot of the table can be defined using the TFOOT container. As in the case of the table head, there is no guarantee of special formatting just because a row is defined as a table foot. The table foot is a section of the table that works just like any other table row—it can contain images, words, and can be divided into cells. The main practical reason for using the table foot is to have it appear at the bottom of each printed page if the table is printed to paper.

Also note that the TFOOT tag, although it defines the foot of the table, appears before the TBODY tag.

At the time this was written, Netscape 4.*x* and IE 4.*x* did not support <TFOOT>, nor did any other browser we're aware of. Therefore a sample display can't be included. However, the samplefoot.html listing that follows shows the tag in use.

samplefoot.html

```
<HTML>
<HEAD>
<TITLE>Sample Table Head, Foot, and Body</TITLE>
</HEAD>
<BODY BGCOLOR="#FFFFFF">
<TABLE>
<THEAD>
<TR>
<TD>
<strong>Grocery item</strong></TD>
<TD><strong>Quantity</strong></TD>
</TR>
</THEAD>
<TFOOT>
<TR>
<TD><strong>Grocery item</strong></TD>
<TD><strong>Quantity</strong></TD>
</TR>
</TFOOT>
<TBODY>
<TR>
<TD>Apples</TD><TD>2</TD>
</TR>
<TR>
<TD>Oranges</TD><TD>1</TD>
</TR>
</TBODY>
</TABLE>
</BODY>
</HTML>
```

Another reason to define all of the column groups, the table head, and the table foot is so the browser can begin laying out the table without waiting for all of the data. Specifying cell sizes is another way to sometimes make the table render more quickly. It also allows information on the same Web page but not in the table to flow around the table. The situation is analogous to specifying the size of images—the browser is able to set aside the space for the table without actually knowing what it contains.

Cells That Span More Than One Column or Row

Often, you'll want to have cells which span more than one column, as shown in Figure 6.12. You can do this by using the COLSPAN attribute for the TD tag. Here's an HTML example for a cell that spans two columns.

colspan.html

```
<HTML>
<HEAD>
<TITLE>Sample Table with COLSPAN</TITLE>
</HEAD>
<BODY BGCOLOR="#FFFFFF">
<TABLE frame border="1">
<CAPTION>Grocery List</CAPTION>
<TR>
<TD COLSPAN="2">Apples</TD><TD>1</TD>
</TR>
<TR>
<TD>Oranges</TD><TD>1</TD>
</TR>
</TABLE>
</BODY>
</HTML>
```

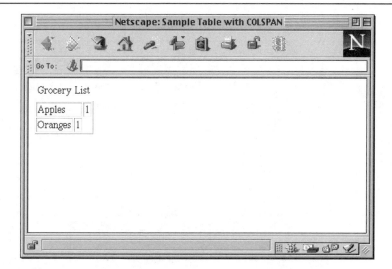

FIGURE 6.12: colspan.html as seen on the Mac using Communicator 4.01

Note in Figure 6.12 that the word "Apples" is still aligned to the left side of the cell even though the cell spans two columns. Also note that the "1" related to "Apples" has automatically moved over to a third column, while the "1" related to "Oranges" is still in he second column because the cell that contains "Oranges" does not span two columns.

Similarly, the ROWSPAN attribute may be used when you wish to have a cell span more than one row, as shown in Figure 6.13. Here's some sample HTML:

rowspan.html

```
<HTML>
<HEAD>
<TITLE>Sample Table with ROWSPAN</TITLE>
</HEAD>
<BODY BGCOLOR="#FFFFFF">
<TABLE frame border="1">
<CAPTION>Grocery List</CAPTION>
<TR>
<TD ROWSPAN="2">Apples</TD><TD>1</TD>
</TR>
<TR>
<TD>Oranges</TD><TD>1</TD>
</TR>
</TABLE>
</BODY>
</HTML>
```

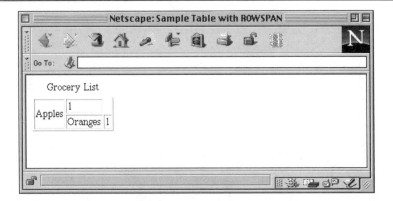

FIGURE 6:13: rowspan.html as seen in Communicator 4.01 on the Macintosh

Take a look at Figure 6.13 to see what has happened to the table. Because "Apples" has moved down to be centered between the two rows it spans, it has pushed "Oranges" and the "1" next to "Oranges" to the right. The "1" associated with "Apples" remains in the same place in the upper right corner of the table.

Have You Mastered the Essentials?

Now you can. . .

- ☑ Create a basic table.
- ☑ Add captions and borders to your tables.
- ☑ Use color and rules to set off individual columns, rows, or cells.
- ☑ Include cell padding and cell spacing to enhance readability.
- ☑ Apply attributes to groups of cells.
- ☑ Span cells across columns and rows.

Skill 6

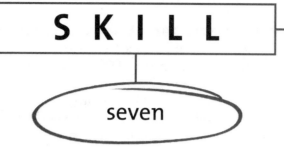

Stylesheets

- ❏ Why use stylesheets?

- ❏ Cascading Style Sheets

- ❏ Document specific styles

- ❏ Inline styles

- ❏ Referencing an external stylesheet

- ❏ Styles for fonts

- ❏ Text styles

When the general public gained interest in the Web and began developing their own Web pages, many people became frustrated at what they saw as the lack of design control provided in HTML. Word processors, desktop publishers, and employees of traditional print media such as magazines, newspapers, and books were all accustomed to being able to control the entire presentation of their work. Judgements could be made for the proper placement of elements within the page because the "canvas" had finite borders—the edges of the paper.

In traditional print media, for instance, a graphic can be placed exactly one and three sixteenths inches from the left margin while being exactly 2 inches from the top margin. Transferred to the computer screen, that precise placement often became a designer's nightmare. How could they move an image up by a half a line, in order to have a more pleasing flow of text around it? Could the spacing between lines be increased in order to accommodate a few lines that had superscript footnote markers? On paper, this is easily done. Within a browser, there were no mechanisms for nudging things about the screen in very small increments. That absolute control is sometimes called *pixel-level* control over presentation.

Quite a few "solutions" were created for dealing with traditional print concerns such as white space, setting margins, and many more presentational elements. The problem with these solutions is that they weren't reliable. Most either were browser-specific or used HTML tags in ways that weren't intended. Both of these situations create additional inconsistencies or flat out failures in display (see Skill 2).

Stylesheets have been developed as a means to define these visual instructions without resorting to misuse of HTML tags or solutions that can be implemented only by one browser or another. A stylesheet can be a set of instructions that can be applied to very specific portions of your document—highlight *this text* in *that color*—or a stylesheet can provide universal guidelines for document presentation, controlling font choices, colors, margins, heading styles, and almost any other visual detail you can think of. They can be developed in any *stylesheet language*—they are not produced in HTML. Each stylesheet language has its own syntax and rules, much like programming languages have their own rules. The initial language format is known as *Cascading Style Sheets*, commonly abbreviated as CSS. Cascading describes a behavior of precedence and order, as discussed in detail later in this skill.

One of the most visually identifiable features of Cascading Style Sheets is the ability to give the appearance of layered text, as seen on the W3C's Web site section dealing with stylesheets, shown in Figure 7.1.

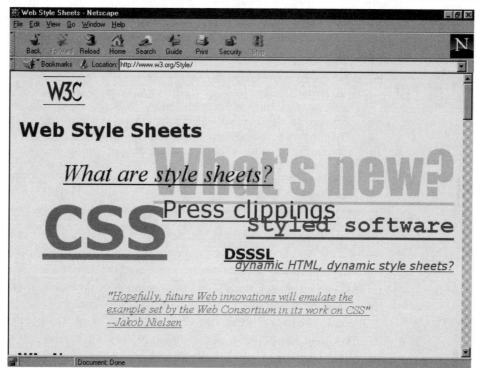

FIGURE 7.1: A layered look achieved through margin, heading, and font style manipulation.

 **COMPATIBILITY NOTE** Microsoft's Internet Explorer 3.0 for Windows 95/NT was the first browser to provide limited support for stylesheets—they actually began as the browser specific solution of Cascading Style Sheets. The concept was forwarded to the W3C, and stylesheets as a generic entity made their way into HTML 4.0. Netscape included support for the CSS format in their 4.0 versions of Navigator. Support beyond these two major browsers is still limited.

Selecting a Stylesheet Language

The HTML 4.0 stylesheet specification allows for any number of stylesheet languages to be developed. Most will likely come from the software firms that produce browsers, as the browser must be programmed to understand each new language. As of this writing, the only major language in this arena is Cascading Style Sheets.

NOTE   The terms *stylesheets*, *stylesheet language*, and *Cascading Style Sheets* are used nearly interchangeably in many Web developer communities, which can lead to some confusion as to just what each of them really means. *Stylesheets* is the generic term for a document that defines rules for the stylistic presentation of content. A *stylesheet language* defines the syntax of those rules. *Cascading Style Sheets* (CSS) is the name of the first mature stylesheet language that has been developed and has been implemented in both major browsers.

To many, stylesheets may seem like a whole lot of hoopla over nothing. If you want some text to be blue, you need to declare a style to make it blue rather than the "old-fashioned" way of using a FONT tag. So where's the improvement?

Taken as an entire concept, stylesheets can allow Web designers to exert as much visual control over their Web pages as they can over documents produced with tools like Microsoft Publisher or Adobe Acrobat. The truly creative among the Web designer population are rejoicing! Even those who prefer rather stark, text-based pages can benefit from stylesheets. They allow all of the visual issues such as font selection, colors, and emphasis treatments to be defined in one central location, allowing them to be referenced again and again from hundreds of different documents, saving the designer significant amounts of development time.

To get started, the Web designer needs to declare which stylesheet language they'll be using in their documents. This takes place in the document's HEAD container, using a META tag. (For information about META tag formats, see Skill 3.) The syntax below represents a declaration for the use of CSS.

```
<META NAME="Content-Style-Type" CONTENT="text/css">
```

NOTE   This META tag is equivalent to the HTTP header: Content-Style-Type: text/css. HTTP headers are bits of information that are passed back and forth between the server and the browser. The system was developed in such a way that the data is case-sensitive. Accordingly, be careful to maintain the exact capitalization and punctuation as shown in the example on the last page.

The Application of Style

Now that you've chosen a stylesheet language and have included a META tag defining that choice, it's time to start actually applying styles to your content. There are several ways of handling this; the two most flexible and time-saving are:

- Inserting a STYLE container into the document's <HEAD>

- Creating a separate document, the stylesheet, that defines the styles that will be global to all files that make reference to it.

Within the STYLE element are the specific instructions for handling the appearance of content within the document. The STYLE tag has one attribute, TYPE. The value defines what type of style you want to apply—Cascading Style Sheets—so the familiar text/css is entered here, as:

```
<STYLE TYPE="text/css">
```

These instructions to come are all enclosed in a *comment* so that they aren't misinterpreted by older browsers that don't support stylesheets and the STYLE element.

An HTML comment begins with a left angle bracket, an exclamation point and two dashes. It ends with two dashes and a right angle bracket. Any amount of text may be enclosed in a comment, but HTML tags may not. At least a single space must be left after the comment opens and before it closes.

```
<!-- This is a comment. -->
```

What Is a Style?

A style can be as simple as rendering some text in **boldface** or in *italic*. Or it can grow very complex with the adoption of print-based ideas such as line heights (double-spacing, etc) and font weights.

In a Web document, you might decide that you want to help your headings stand out a bit more by having all of them use a red font color. Without stylesheets, you'd need to make that instruction with each heading tag in your document. With stylesheets, that only needs to be declared once.

Style syntax is different than traditional HTML. Instead of tags or elements, the instructions are called *rules*. The basic syntax for a rule includes a *selector* and a *declaration*. A sample appears below:

```
H1 { color:red }
```

Skill 7

The selector is the HTML element that is being operated on, in this case, the H1 tag. The declaration is what the browser is supposed to do with it. The declaration will always be enclosed in braces, as shown here.

Inside the declaration, you have a *property* and a *value*, which are separated by a colon. A property is the stylesheet version of an attribute. A value carries the same meaning here. The `color` (property) of the `H1` element (selector) should be red (value).

You can save yourself some typing work by grouping selectors into a single rule. Let's say you wanted to have all of your headings rendered in red. Rather than typing out 6 rules in a row:

```
H1 { color:red }
H2 { color:red }
H3 { color:red }
H4 { color:red }
H5 { color:red }
H6 { color:red }
...
```

You can group them like this:

```
H1, H2, H3, H4, H5, H6 { color: red }
```

This rule will apply red color to all instances of headings in sizes 1 through 6.

COMPATIBILITY NOTE   For clarity in instructional examples, these rules used color names rather than hexadecimal notation. It is still best to use hex for broader browser support. This will become important as more browsers that are not enabled for color name support begin to adopt CSS support. See Skill 3 for more information on colors and color names.

Remember the old "structural markup versus display markup" argument for emphasizing and strongly emphasizing content? (See Skill 4.) Stylesheets provide the individual Web designer with the tools to change the rendering of emphasis rather than relying on the vagaries of a specific browser's rendering of them.

Let's say that you want to emphasize your text by using a purple colored Courier font type. The rule would be written as:

```
EM { color:purple; font-family:Courier }
```

The file `em.html` is the complete HTML source for applying this style, and Figure 7.2 shows how it would appear in Netscape 4.03.

em.html

```
<HTML>
<HEAD>
<STYLE TYPE="text/css">
<!- EM { color:purple; font-family:Courier; } ->
</STYLE>
</HEAD>

<BODY BGCOLOR="#FFFFFF" TEXT="#000000">

<P>This is normal text. On this browser, the default font is Times New
    Roman.

<P>This line has some <EM>emphasized text</EM>, which appears in a
    purple color and the font Courier.

</BODY>
</HTML>
```

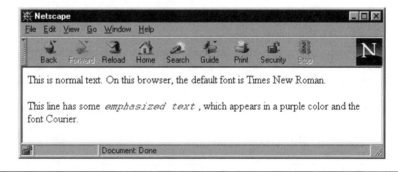

FIGURE 7.2:   Text emphasized with a color and font type change.

NOTE   In Figure 7.2, the emphasized section is also italicized. This is because the EM tag traditionally causes text to appear in italic. In our stylesheet, we added a color and a font change, but we did not take away the traditional change to italic. Unless you contradict the traditional rendering of a tag, the browser will apply that rendering in addition to the styles you've outlined. This idea is part of a concept called *inheritance*. You'll learn more about inheritance later in this skill.

Some Web designers find rules easier to read if only one *property:value* pair is written on each line. That sort of display would look like:

```
EM { color:purple
            font-family:Courier }
```

As long as all your rules are contained within the appropriate comment markers, you can format them any way you want.

Inline Style Applications

Styles can be applied not only globally to a document but also to specific instances of an element. This is known as *inline* style application.

Taking the example shown in Figure 7.2 one step further, suppose you wanted to use just one instance of strong emphasis (the STRONG tag in HTML) to be red as well as the traditional bold rendering, but you didn't define that ahead of time. You can do this by adding an additional *property:value* pair where the tag occurs, as shown in Figure 7.3 and in the markup seen in the file inline.html.

inline.html

```
<HTML>
<HEAD>
<STYLE TYPE="text/css">
<!- EM { color:purple; font-family:Courier } ->
</STYLE>
</HEAD>

<BODY BGCOLOR="#FFFFFF" TEXT="#000000">

<P>This is normal text. On this browser, the default font is Times New
    Roman.

<P>This line has some <EM>emphasized text</EM>, which appears in a
    purple color and the Courier font.

<P>This time, we'll use <STRONG STYLE="color:red">strong
    emphasis</STRONG> defined in-line for a red color.

</BODY>
</HTML>
```

NOTE   Yes, in this example it would be easier to use the old, non-stylesheet treatment. But, since non-stylesheet treatments are being deprecated, it's important that you learn the stylesheet way to handle this situation.

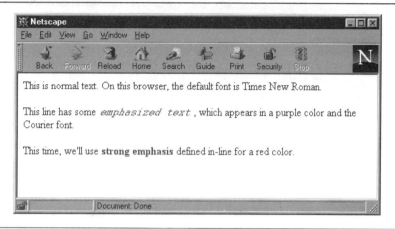

FIGURE 7.3: A font color modification made using inline styles.

Defining a Stylesheet

A stylesheet, as opposed to an inline application of styles, is a master document that defines the properties to be used in any individual document that makes reference to it. To reference it from your HTML documents, a new tag is used inside the HEAD element, as follows:

```
<LINK REL="stylesheet" HREF="mystyle.css">
```

The LINK tag links the stylesheet to the current document. The REL attribute defines the relationship between the current document and the document that it's being linked to—hence the value stylesheet. In this instance then, the link concept applies to the relationship rather than being a reference to a hyperlink. The two shouldn't be confused. The HREF attributed is familiar to you from hyperlinks, and its value is the URL of the external stylesheet.

WARNING You know that HTML files are conventionally named with the file extension .htm or .html. This standard practice allows browser and authoring tool software to recognize documents as HTML files, as well as allowing humans to know what to expect within the file simply by looking at the name. With stylesheets, the extension .css has become the traditional extension. This notation is not required by the stylesheet specification or by the Cascading Style Sheet language. However, it does provide a very helpful visual clue to the file's contents.

Skill 7

The file `styles.html`, shown here, links to the external stylesheet `mystyle.css`.

styles.html

```
<HTML>
<HEAD>
<TITLE>Styles</TITLE>
<LINK REL="stylesheet" HREF="mystyle.css">
</HEAD>

<BODY BGCOLOR="#FFFFFF">

<H1>External Style Sheets</H1>

<P>This file was created using an external style sheet named
   <EM>mystyle.css</EM>.
   The style sheet determined the color and justification of the
   heading,the font face, the alignment of this paragraph, and the
   application of color to the emphasis tag.

</BODY>
</HTML>
```

The file `mystyle.css`, as shown below, contains four rules that will be applied to the HTML document:

- Level 1 headings that are blue and centered

- A font face of Comic Sans MS (a fun font that is part of the Windows 95 standard set of fonts)

- Paragraph text that is center justified

- The addition of red coloring to text contained within the EM tag.

mystyle.css

```
BODY { font-family: "Comic Sans MS" }
H1 { color: blue; align:center }
P { text-align:center }
EM { color:red }
```

The results, as seen in Navigator 4.03, are shown in Figure 7.4.

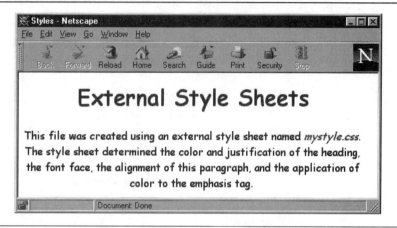

FIGURE 7.4:   The file `styles.html` rendered with a link to an external stylesheet.

The Cascading Concept

Many people use the terms stylesheets and Cascading Style Sheets interchangeably. That's a common habit among Web designers since the language of Cascading Style Sheets has been the only one to become readily available for them to use. However, it's important to remember the difference between the two and also to understand just what the *Cascading* in Cascading Style Sheets really means.

Stylesheets, as a generic entity, is the portion of the HTML 4.0 specification that provides for stylistic matters to be defined by an external document, in the <HEAD> of an individual document, or inline as needed. Cascading Style Sheets is a language—or perhaps better defined as a syntax—for defining those stylistic matters.

Cascading deals the order of relevance in style rules. What takes priority and when? Take another look at Figure 7.4, and the source file `styles.html`. What would happen to the heading if we applied an italics style to it in-line? Would that cancel out the previous style rules for <H1>, or would it add to it? Figure 7.5 provides the answer.

The heading was italicized, as instructed by the inline style, but it also took the rules from the external stylesheet that said an <H1> should be blue and centered.

This cascading can go through multiple levels. As a site grows more complex, an individual HTML file might draw style rules from an external stylesheet, as in `styles.html`, but also have its own rules defined in the <HEAD>, plus have additional rules applied inline.

Skill 7

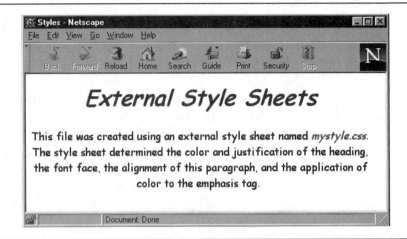

FIGURE 7.5: An inline style applied to a document already using an external stylesheet.

While cascading is a handy feature, what happens if you want to change the behavior of a particular element that has already had rules defined? Can they break out of the cascading model? Certainly! If, for instance, a second <H1> were to be added to `styles.html`, and we wanted to make it green, we could do so by overriding the original rule with an inline color change, as shown in the file listing for `styles2.html` and in Figure 7.6.

styles2.html

```
<HTML>
<HEAD>
<TITLE>Styles</TITLE>
<LINK REL="stylesheet" HREF="mystyle.css">
</HEAD>

<BODY BGCOLOR="#FFFFFF">

<H1>External Style Sheets</H1>

<P>This file was created using an external style sheet named
    <EM>mystyle.css</EM>. The style sheet determined the color and
    justification of the heading,the font face, the alignment of this
    paragraph, and the application of color to the emphasis tag.

<H1 STYLE="color:green">Overriding Style</H1>
```

```
<P>The color of this heading was changed by overriding the rule defined
   in the external style sheet with an inline style rule.

</BODY>
</HTML>
```

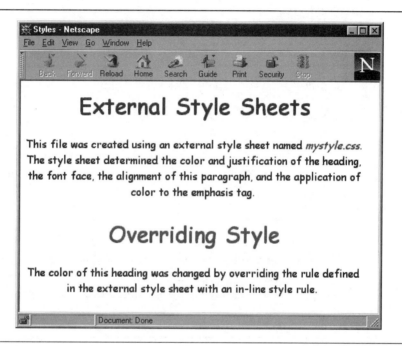

FIGURE 7.6:   Overriding an existing style rule

Inheritance

How are traits inherited? In people, traits are often inherited from the parents. A child can inherit blue eyes from a blue-eyed parent. In the Cascading Style Sheets language, styles are also inherited.

Though at first the ideas might sound similar, inheriting is different from cascading. Cascading means a document picks up styles as it goes down the line; kind of like water trickling down a few steps picking up some dirt, a twig and a leaf in the process. Inheritance, on the other hand, could be likened to what happens to the steps. Since water is present, the step inherits the property of being wet. The step won't be wet without the presence of water. Let's put that into HTML terms.

The file `inheritance.html` defines several styles in the HEAD container.

inheritance.html

```
<HTML>
<HEAD>
<STYLE>
<!- BODY { color:blue }
    H1 { color:black; align:center }
    ->
</STYLE>
</HEAD>
<BODY>
<H1>Tips about inheritance issues</H1>

<P>Many style rules are <EM>inherited</EM>. The emphasized word in the
    previous sentence <EM>inherited</EM> the blue coloring of the main
    body text.

</BODY>
</HTML>
```

The body text will be blue, we know that from the <BODY> style rule. There were no styles identified for the EM tag. What will happen when it is used? The EM container *inherits* the blue coloring of the main body text. Try out the code on your computer, and you'll see what we mean. You'll get the paragraph shown in Figure 7.7, all in blue.

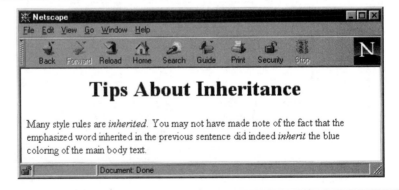

FIGURE 7.7: The EM tag used inherits the blue text from the style defined for the <BODY>.

Style Properties and Values

There are huge numbers of individual styles and properties available for you to use within Cascading Style Sheets—far more than it would be possible to cover here. In this section, you'll learn about styles that have been put into use on the Web previously, using HTML tags, and a few additions that Web designers have been yearning for. The full Cascading Style Sheets recommendation is available online at the W3C Web site, at `http://www.w3.org/TR/REC-CSS1`.

LET'S LEAVE PAPER OUT OF IT FOR A MOMENT

Long time inhabitants of the Web are often confounded by those who come from print media and insist on applying traditional print concepts to Web documents. The World Wide Web was created as a means of going beyond books and print, into a true "web" of hyperlinked information. The seemingly random paths that could be cut through widespread documents are most decidedly a non-linear means of communication.

Even the implementation of the first browser followed that free-form idea. Documents weren't confined to pages that were a strict 8.5×11 inches, with 1-inch margins, double spaced lines and 5 character indents. They flowed into the space available within the browser window—if the window was narrow, the document became long. If the window was wide, the document became short.

This is good, isn't it?

Or is it?

When business discovered the Web, many ad execs, art directors, and graphic designers were horrified by the structural format of the web. They asked, what do you mean emphasis might not always be 14 point Times Italic? Why can't I justify margins, use three column layouts, or flow text in around both sides of a centered image? *I can do that on paper!*

continued on next page ▶

Skill 7

Let's leave paper out of it for a moment. It may dismay some of the original, no-frills Web denizens, but the World Wide Web has become, and is evolving into, a truly multimedia environment. It no longer exists solely as a means of providing access to documents without regard to the viewer's computer configuration. This "new media" isn't tied to any one paradigm—not non-linear presentation, print, television, or movies.

When applying styles to your Web sites, reach beyond the confines of previous presentation traditions. Even though tools such as stylesheets are now becoming available and let you apply previous constraints to the Web, should you really do that? For instance, is your document truly enhanced by having one-inch margins around all sides, or are you simply used to viewing paper documents that way? The Web is neither print, nor television, nor radio, nor any other media that we've seen before, and we shouldn't try to make it those things.

This is good.

Styles for Fonts

Cascading Style Sheets provide five style properties for fonts: `font-family`, `font-style`, `font-size`, `font-weight`, and `font-variant`.

Font Family

A font family is a group of fonts derived from the same parent font. The font family *Arial* has several members; Arial Narrow and Arial Black are two of them. Each looks a lot like the others, much like children from the same two parents look alike. When you specify a font family in CSS, you want to use the family group name (in this case, Arial) rather than a specific family member name.

When setting a font-family choice in a style rule, listing several similar font families will increase your chances of the text being rendered as you intended if your first choice font isn't installed on the visitor's system. Using the Arial example, a rule with several font-family choices could look like:

```
{ font-family: Arial, Helvetica, AvantGarde, "Century Gothic", sans-serif }
```

The last font family is a generic font family of *sans-serif*, loosely translated as "without decoration." Serifs are the small flourishes on the tips and edges of letters, such as the foot on each leg of an n or m, and the small vertical line at the top of a capital S. A sans-serif font doesn't have those decorations. Should a visitor to the page using this style rule not have any of the four mentioned fonts installed, the inclusion of `sans-serif` will tell the visitor's computer to use an available sans-serif font rather than just the default font family, which might be serif or some other generic type.

 WARNING   If a font family name has spaces in it, as does the font Century Gothic, the name must be enclosed in quotation marks. Otherwise, the browser will condense what it sees as extraneous white space and look for a font called CenturyGothic, which it won't be able to properly locate.

There are five generic font families recognized by CSS, as shown in Table 7.1.

TABLE 7.1: The five generic font families supported by CSS.

Generic Family	Font Examples
serif	Times, Courier, Garamond, Palatino
sans-serif	Arial, Helvetica, Folio, Century Gothic
cursive	ShellyAllegro, Vivaldi, Nuptial
monospace	Courier, Lucida Console, QuickType Mono
fantasy	Western, Keyboard, Crayon

Font Style

There are three basic font face variations: normal, italic, and oblique. (Boldface, by the way, is not a font style, it's a font weight.) A normal font style is sometimes referred to as a "Roman" style. The type you are reading now is a normal font styling. You are probably familiar with italic, but you might not be familiar with

 oblique. An oblique style is a normal style, slanted to the right. The two letter As, shown here, illustrate the difference between normal and oblique.

Font Size

You're probably familiar with the print-world concept of font sizes if you've ever used a word processor. A typical default might be set to 10 or 12 "point" type. Using the font-size property, you can change the font size from the default size.

Your Web browser also uses a default font size setting. Take a look now to see what it is. In Navigator 4.0, select Edit ➢ Preferences ➢ Appearances ➢ Fonts. Other browsers will have different menu steps; the option will generally be available through a Preferences or Options menu.

There are three common ways to describe font sizes: absolute size, relative size, and percentages. Each of these descriptive methods does depend on the browser for interpretation. Not every browser will render the description in exactly the same manner as the others.

The possible values outlined in the next four sections should be thought of as a guide, understanding that values moving toward the extremes have less chance of being interpreted as you intended.

Absolute Size   Absolute sizing uses the keywords `small`, `medium`, and `large`. On either extreme, nomenclature that may be familiar to you from clothing sizes is used: `xx-small`, `x-small`, `x-large`, and `xx-large`. But how large is a large and how small is a small?

Each browser has its own internal table of font point sizes that correspond to these absolute sizes. The suggested difference between levels is one and a half times (1.5 times) the original. So, a medium is one and a half times the size of a small. A large is one and a half times the size of a medium and, as you can deduce, three times the size of a small. If the medium font size were 12 point, then large would be 18 point. An xx-small would be down near 5 point, which would be awfully hard to read on a computer monitor!

Relative Size   A relative size has only two possible values, `larger` and `smaller`. Those are both set *relative* to the current font size. If the suggested incrementing value of 1.5 times the original is kept, then an existing font size of 24 point, when styled to a property of `larger`, would become a size of 36 point.

Percentage   This method is probably the easiest for you to visualize. If you want a font to be changed to be half again as big as the current size, you'd increase it by 150%. The syntax used is { `font size:150%` }.

Font Variant

A font variant can be considered a further extension of font styles. The one currently supported by CSS is called `small-caps`. As you might imagine, in small-caps the text is rendered in capital letters smaller than the height normal for caps in that font. THIS SENTENCE IS IN CAPITAL LETTERS. THIS ONE IS IN SMALL CAPS.

Font Weights

The font weight relates to how dark or light a font would appear. For the most part, this applies best to the print world; however there is one weight that you should be used to seeing on Web pages, the **bold** weight.

Text Styles

Text styles are modifications made to the text as a whole, rather than the presentation of the individual characters as is done with font styles. Text styles you are likely to be familiar with include indenting and *justification* (the process of aligning each line of text to a given margin). Table 7.2 lists four common text styles that can be manipulated through the use of stylesheets.

T A B L E   7 . 2 : Four common text styles.

Property	Example Values/Effects
text-decoration	underline, strikethrough
vertical-align	baseline, top, middle
text-indent	indent by specified unit
text-align	left, right, center, justify

Text Decoration

The text decoration property in stylesheets is now the preferred method of handling situations such as underlining, strikethrough, as discussed in Skill 4. So instead of using the underline U container, we use the new SPAN tag along with the inline declaration of style. For example, without style sheets an underlined word would be marked up like this:

```
This sentence contains an <U>underlined</U> word.
```

Using CSS, the SPAN tag "spans" the block of text you want to apply a style to, as seen here, and in Figure 7.8:

```
This sentence contains an <SPAN STYLE="text-decoration:underline">
underlined</SPAN> word.
```

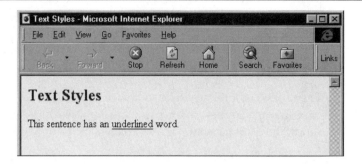

This implementation does generate a bit more typing for you when applying styles to single words or phrases as was done here. However, the W3C's decision to deprecate the underline and strikethrough containers keeps style elements consistently within the stylesheet realm instead of within HTML.

Vertical Alignment

This property is used to align text in relationship to other objects, such as images. Should the text align with the top of an image and flow down the side? Or should the text begin in the vertical middle of the image or even aligned with the bottom? In HTML, these issues were defined with the ALIGN attribute within the IMG (or other object) tag.

Indenting Text

Among all the tricks and work-arounds that Web designers have developed over the past few years, almost none have been attempted more times than finding a technically valid and visually acceptable form of indenting. Many designers have embraced the fact that the Web doesn't make use of indenting, but others aren't willing to give indents up yet.

The text-indent property takes a value that is a specific number of *em spaces*. (An em is the height of the current font.) If you want to indent three ems measured horizontally, express the style within the rule as { text-indent:3em }.

Text Alignment

Text alignment is one of the most common text positioning properties already in use on the Web. You'll very frequently encounter text or headings that have been aligned to the center or to one of the margins.

An alignment method that many designers have been waiting for is justify. This value will justify text to both margins rather than leaving the typical ragged right margin seen in Web documents.

Stylesheet Resources Online

There are several very thorough tutorials and reference works on the Web regarding stylesheets.

- Cascading Style Sheets, level 1 W3C recommendation can be found at http://www.w3.org/TR/REC-CSS1.

- C|Net's Builder.com area has a tutorial, a consolidated property reference table, and even a helpful tool called the *Style-o-Matic* at http://cnet.com/ Content/Builder/Authoring/CSS/index.html.

- Web Review has compiled a comprehensive Stylesheet Reference Guide with articles, tables and more. It's located at http://www.webreview.com/ guides/style/index.html.

- The HTML Writers Guild has a CSS Frequently Asked Questions list at: http://www.hwg.org/resources/faqs/cssFAQ.html.

Have You Mastered the Essentials?

Now you can...

- ☑ Differentiate between the stylesheet concept and a stylesheet language.

- ☑ Declare the default stylesheet language being used in your documents.

- ☑ Insert style rules within an HTML file using the *STYLE* tag within the *HEAD* container.

- ☑ Apply styles inline when they shouldn't be applied globally.

- ☑ Make reference to an external stylesheet that can be used by an unlimited number of documents.

- ☑ Visually enhance your Web documents with styles in ways that aren't bound to any traditional media.

Skill 7

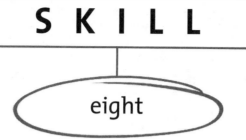

SKILL

eight

Communicating through Forms

- ❏ The *FORM* container

- ❏ Ten commonly used input controls

- ❏ Alignment and layout within the form

- ❏ Sending the data directly to e-mail

- ❏ Processing the response using CGI scripts

Communicating with the owners of a Web site has become an integral part of the World Wide Web experience. It occurs in dozens of formats—from a simple page that requests visitor feedback to complex order forms or even Web-based bulletin board messaging systems. The possibilities are limited only by your imagination, your visitor's interest in the product or service, and their willingness to spend the time required to complete a form.

The best forms not only combine the function of data collection but also retain the look and feel of the rest of the site. The form shown in Figure 8.1 is used by

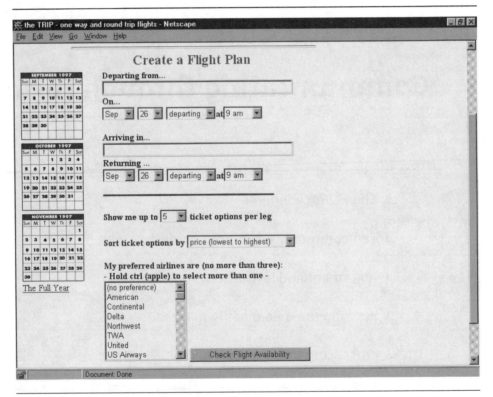

FIGURE 8.1:   The Trip.com invites members to Create a Flight with their well-planned flight availability query form.

members of The Trip.com, an online travel reservations service located at `http://www.thetrip.com`. In a very small space, the Create a Flight form collects the following information:

- where the trip is originating
- what date and time the flight should leave
- where the will flight go
- the date and time of the desired return flight
- how many flight options the traveler would like to see
- what airlines, if any, are preferred

This communication between the visitor and the Web site is successful on several fronts: all of this information is collected in a very small space, in a layout that blends beautifully with the rest of the site, and returns information to the user in a useful and meaningful format.

Preparing the Form

A basic form consists of the FORM container and two or more tags called *controls* that are placed within the container. A control is an HTML tag that provides a means for the user to enter data. That data can be a checkmark in a box, or it can be text-based information like a name or e-mail address. Regular text and image-based content can also be included within the form container. Let's take a look at a very basic form:

```
<FORM>
Please enter your name: <INPUT TYPE="text" NAME="name" SIZE="20">
<INPUT TYPE="submit" value="Submit">
</FORM>
```

The page resulting from this bit of HTML is shown in Figure 8.2. The INPUT tag is used for each of the controls. The TYPE attribute defines what kind of control it will be. The first example is a text control, which creates a box for the user to type in their name. The second control provides the button labeled Submit, which activates the form. Table 8.1 contains a list of ten controls available to you.

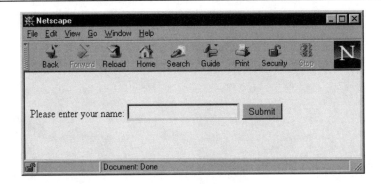

FIGURE 8.2: A basic form containing a text input control and a submit control

TABLE 8.1: Ten input control types

Input Control Type	Creates
text	A text input box. May only be a single line wide.
password	Also a text input box. The characters being typed are hidden from view to maintain security.
checkbox	A box that holds a check mark or ×when selected. Acts as a toggle between on and off.
radio	Similar to a checkbox but used in groups. Only one option per group may be active.
hidden	Allows inclusion of predetermined *key=value* pairs (See *Naming Controls* in the next section) to be submitted with the form. These fields are not displayed by the browser.
submit	Creates a standard button used for form submission.
image	Allows use of an image in place of the standard button for form submission.
reset	Inserts a standard button used to return the values of all input fields to their original state.
select	Provides a list of options for the user to choose from. May be in drop-down menu or list box form.
textarea	A text input area larger than a single line.

NOTE

The HTML 4.0 specifications provide for additional control types that require additional markup or programming techniques that reach beyond the scope of this text, or that aren't widely in use. At the time of this printing, the official documentation can be found at `http://www.w3.org/TR/WD-html30/interact/forms.html`.

Both of the `INPUT` tags in our example had additional attributes that we'll look at in turn by placing additional controls into the basic form.

The Text Box

The first control in our form was a text box. This is probably the most common control you'll see out on the Web because it's so versatile. Any information that you want to collect from a Web site visitor that can be expressed as a word, phrase, sentence, or even just a character or two can be placed into a text box. Visually, a text box can only span a single line of text. By visually, we mean that the control box rendered by the browser will sit on only one line—text boxes don't wrap as text lines do.

The `INPUT` tag used for the following control has two new attributes, `NAME` and `SIZE`:

```
<INPUT TYPE="text" NAME="name" SIZE="20">
```

In addition to these two, attributes of `VALUE` and `MAXLENGTH` are possible.

Naming Controls   Every control must have a name. Remember how the form is processed? The data is collected by the browser in *name=value* pairs and sent to the server in URL encoded form. The name half of the *name=value* pair is taken from the `NAME` attribute.

For clarity's sake, it's often easiest to think of a control's `NAME` as its label. If you're asking the user to input their first name, you might use a `NAME` value of `first name` or simply name as the example did.

WARNING

Because the values used in the `NAME` attribute are often operated on by the CGI programs this data is fed to, it's a good idea to be brief when choosing the value for this attribute. Common practices include using mixed case lettering instead of spaces—e.g. `FirstName` instead of `first name`—or even abbreviating it down to a single word such as `fname`. Whatever method you choose, be sure you can "decode" it later!

Skill 8

Defining a Control's Size   The SIZE attribute, as it applies to text boxes, defines how many characters wide the box will be. You might think of that as the number of characters that will fit *in view* within the text box rendered on the user's screen. If the user has a default font size of 36 points, the text box in the example would be twenty 36 point spaces wide. If instead, the default font size were a more customary 12 points, the text box would be twenty 12 point spaces wide.

The idea that SIZE is equal to the number of characters in view should tell you that the box can accept more input than the number of characters it is wide, and that's true. If more characters are entered than fit in the viewable area, the text should scroll as the user types. Even so, when choosing a text box size, be sure to use a value that would meet even one of the longest possible entries you could imagine. A control asking for the user's last name might be adequate for most respondents at a size of 10 characters but would serve almost all respondents at 15 or 20.

Limiting Response Length   There may be times when you want to limit the amount of information a user can enter in a text box. The MAXLENGTH attribute provides that. If the attribute is not present, the default behavior is to allow an unlimited length. As a practice, the MAXLENGTH value should never be set smaller than the SIZE of a text box; otherwise the intuitive response of the user may be to get confused.

Predefined Values   The attribute VALUE can be used to insert a predetermined string of text into the text box. While it's most often used in conjunction with other controls, it is available to you here. An addition could be inserted into the first control in the example such as:

```
<INPUT TYPE="text" NAME="name" SIZE="20" VALUE="Enter your name">
```

The result is shown in Figure 8.3.

Password Control

A special form of the TEXT control exists for the entry of sensitive information: the PASSWORD control. This special control accepts the same attributes as the TEXT control: NAME, SIZE, MAXLENGTH, and VALUE. The difference is in the display. When the user types in the password text box, the input is obscured from view by a series of asterisks or other characters, as shown in Figure 8.4. This prevents others from being able to read the password as it's being typed.

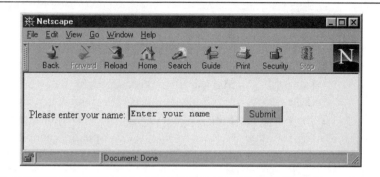

FIGURE 8.3: A text box with a defined value

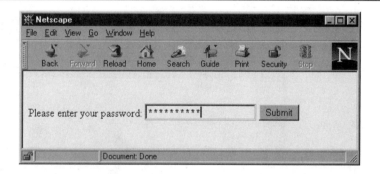

FIGURE 8.4: User input is obscured by asterisks within a PASSWORD control.

NOTE   Though the user can't view the input into a PASSWORD control, the data captured by the form is the actual entry. No decoding is necessary for processing.

Checkboxes: Letting the User Choose As Many As Apply

Forms allow a Web designer to collect very detailed information from their site visitors. In order to extract meaningful results from the responses, questions are often stated with a predefined set of answers to choose from. The visitor then checks each answer that applies to them.

In its most basic form, the CHECKBOX control uses only the TYPE and NAME attributes. A label can be made by placing text immediately to the right of the control.

```
<INPUT TYPE="checkbox" NAME="label"> label
```

Table 8.1 says that the checkbox toggles between an on and off state. The default state is off, which means no checkmark is present. This state is stored in the VALUE attribute when it is not otherwise defined. When the user places the mark, the state switches to on. If the sample here were to be used on a real form and the form submitted with the box checked, the *name=value* pair submitted would be *name=*on.

The file form2.html shown below, and the view in the browser shown in Figure 8.5, takes the original form example and add a question that uses checkboxes.

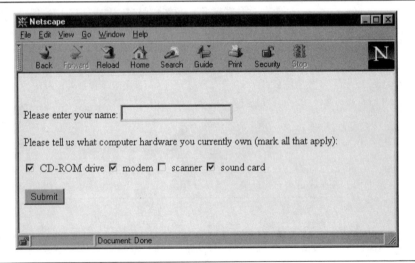

FIGURE 8.5:   A group of checkboxes with three items selected

form2.html

```
<HTML>
<BODY>

<FORM>

<P>Please enter your name: <INPUT TYPE="text" NAME="name" WIDTH=20>
```

```
<P>Please tell us what computer hardware you currently own (mark all
    that apply):

<P><INPUT TYPE="checkbox" NAME="hardware" VALUE="cdrom"> CD-ROM drive
<INPUT TYPE="checkbox" NAME="hardware" VALUE="modem"> modem
<INPUT TYPE="checkbox" NAME="hardware" VALUE="scanner"> scanner
<INPUT TYPE="checkbox" NAME="hardware" VALUE="sound"> sound card

<P><INPUT TYPE="submit" value="Submit">

</FORM>
```

The first thing that stands out when reviewing form2.html is that all four INPUT tags use the same NAME attribute of hardware and that the VALUE attribute is then set to specific pieces of hardware. How is the on/off state handled if a VALUE is already present? The VALUE attribute, when used with checkboxes, defines the value to be assumed only during the on state. It remains empty if the user leaves the box unchecked. By using the same NAME definition, the checked responses can be easily grouped together when the recipient reviews all the information that the form collected.

Radio Buttons: Letting the User Choose One and Only One

What about situations when a single choice needs to be made out of several available options? There isn't an attribute that would prevent a person from checking more than one checkbox. There is however, another control type that was made to handle just these scenarios: the RADIO control—often referred to as a *radio button*.

The RADIO control is presented visually as an empty circle. When marked, the circle contains a black dot much like a bullet.

The following snippet can be added to form2.html:

```
<P>Do you own a printer?
<INPUT TYPE="radio" NAME="printer" VALUE="yes"> yes
<INPUT TYPE="radio" NAME="printer" VALUE="no"> no
```

The VALUE attribute for the RADIO control is *required* and the NAME values *must* be identical in order for the control set to function properly. The *name=value* pair associated with this control inherits the value of the dot that's been selected, such as printer=yes.

PROVIDING A DEFAULT SELECTION

One nifty option for checkboxes and radio buttons is the ability to pre-select choices for your users. This technique can save the user some time, by setting the selections to the most commonly used choices, or it can subtly guide a user toward the choice that you prefer.

For example, many companies would prefer to send customers e-mail notices regarding new products and services rather than incur the expense of a paper mailing. A radio control could be added to the form asking for permission to send the respondent occasional news items via e-mail. A pre-defined selection of Yes means that the user must actively opt-out of such an arrangement.

E-mail traffic is a very sensitive issue on the Net these days. Always be very clear with your visitors as to what you will or won't do with their information. Assure them that you won't be selling or disclosing their data to any third parties if that is, in fact the case, and you'll likely get more positive responses.

This is accomplished by the addition of the CHECKED attribute, which is considered a *boolean* attribute. Boolean refers to the logical state of True or False (you can also think of it as on or off). If the attribute is present, the value is inherently true—no additional value needs to be declared—so it stands alone in your HTML source, as seen here:

```
<INPUT TYPE="radio" NAME="printer" VALUE="yes" CHECKED> yes
```

The user is presented with the Yes button already marked. The only action that must be taken is for the negative response rather than for either response.

Drop-Down Menus and List Boxes

Sometimes a question calls for too many possible responses to arrange neatly using radio buttons or checkboxes. The SELECT control addresses this scenario beautifully. A SELECT control can take two familiar forms:

drop-down menu   A list of choices that are revealed by "dropping down" when the user clicks on the arrow provided

list box   A list that presents choices in view bordered by a box

The list construction begins with the SELECT tag, which serves as a container for the list. Each individual list item is then entered using the OPTION tag, as follows:

```
<SELECT NAME="color">
<OPTION VALUE="red"> red
<OPTION VALUE="blue"> blue
<OPTION VALUE="green"> green
<OPTION VALUE="yellow"> yellow
</SELECT>
```

Because the SELECT container and its contents are all a part of the control, the SELECT tag contains the NAME attribute. The value of the control is determined by which OPTION is selected when the form is processed. This simple SELECT control is displayed as a drop-down menu, as shown to the right.

To turn this SELECT control into a list box, the SIZE attribute needs to be added. SIZE determines how many rows will be displayed at a given time. The default value is 1, which creates the drop-down list. A size of 2 or greater will create the list box display. The sample seen to the right has been set to a size of 4.

You aren't required to set the size of the list box to the number of options available. If the value is smaller, a scrolling mechanism is provided to let the user see all the choices, as shown to the right.

Users can be allowed to make multiple choices from a SELECT control with the addition of the MULTIPLE attribute:

```
<SELECT NAME="color" SIZE=6 MULTIPLE>
<OPTION VALUE="red"> red
<OPTION VALUE="blue"> blue
<OPTION VALUE="green"> green
<OPTION VALUE="yellow"> yellow
<OPTION VALUE="purple"> purple
<OPTION VALUE="brown"> brown
</SELECT>
```

By holding down the Ctrl key (apple on the Mac), the user can highlight more than one choice as seen here. Each value is then sent when the form is processed.

Extended User Input with *\<TEXTAREA\>*

A TEXTAREA control is defined as a multi-line field. Any time you want your visitors to be able to enter comments, ask questions, or provide information that may take up more than one line, a text area is the control to be used.

The syntax for the text area is a bit unusual. It takes the form of a container and has two new attributes: *rows* and *cols*.

```
<TEXTAREA NAME="comments" ROWS="5" COLS="60"></TEXTAREA>
```

As with all form controls, the TEXTAREA must be named. The attributes ROWS and COLS define the borders of the input area in terms of the number of lines high—rows—and the number of single-space columns wide—columns.

WHERE DID MY TEXT GO?

One of the most frustrating "features" of TEXTAREA controls is that some browsers don't provide the text-wrapping behavior that most people are used to when typing in a defined area, such as a word processor or in their e-mail software. For those who type while watching their keyboards, it can be disconcerting to look up and find that you've typed so far off to the right that a horizontal scroll bar is needed to get back to the beginning or even worse, that your cursor has disappeared off the edge of the text field.

Netscape originated an extension to the TEXTAREA control with the attribute WRAP. If you assign a value of virtual, Navigator will word-wrap at the right-hand boundary of the input area for the visual benefit of the user. A value of physical tells Navigator not only to word-wrap at the right boundary visually, but also to insert a CR LF—carriage return and line feed—when sending the form contents to the processing program or script.

Browsers that don't understand the WRAP attribute will ignore it and continue to handle the flow control of user input as they normally would have.

The TEXTAREA control also allows you to prompt the user by placing some text into the field for them. Anything contained between the opening and closing TEXTAREA tag will be displayed inside the field, as seen in Figure 8.6, and in the lines below:

```
<TEXTAREA NAME="comments" ROWS=5 COLS=60>Describe the problem in
    detail: </TEXTAREA>
```

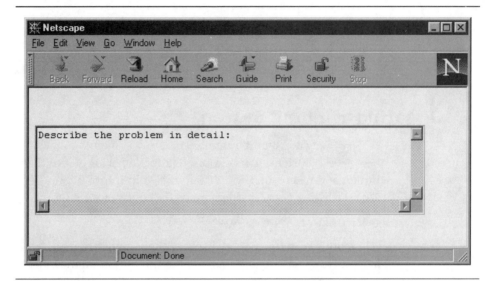

FIGURE 8.6: A TEXTAREA control with pre-defined text included

Supplying Hidden Details

In almost any informational exchange between you and your site visitors, there will be some information that you need every time that is static (it doesn't change). For instance, your site might have three forms on it: a survey, an order form, and a complaint form. When you receive responses, each one needs to be labeled properly with the form name. Instead of relying on the form processing method to do this for you, you can simply insert the form name using a hidden field. The syntax is very much like a text box with a preset value:

```
<INPUT TYPE="hidden" NAME="form" VALUE="survey">
```

This input tag will generate the *name=value* pair of form=survey and send it along with the rest of the data that was input directly by your visitor. If you place this tag before any other input fields, you'll be able to sort your responses with just a quick glance at the first *name=value* pair.

Submitting the Form

After your users fill out a form on your Web site, they need to be able to send the form to you. They can do so by clicking a button that sends the form. Or, if they want to start over and fill out the form from scratch, they can click on a Reset button.

Creating a Submit Button

 The Submit button seen here is something that almost any Web surfer will recognize. Its function is fairly intuitive—it looks like a button and when you click it it submits your information.

The file listing form2.html contains the control for a submit button:

```
<INPUT TYPE="submit" value="Submit">
```

This control can function by itself, without any attributes beyond the TYPE. Most browsers will default to insert the text *Submit* on the button if the value has not been set. To make sure all of your visitors see the same text or to provide something else entirely, use the VALUE attribute to define the button's label.

COMPATIBILITY NOTE With Navigator 4.0 Netscape broke with the tradition of the default value for a submit button, moving from simply *submit* to *submit query*. To accommodate an audience that may not understand why the term *query* would be attached to an order form or other response that isn't asking a question, consider making a habit of defining your own values for all submit controls.

Replacing Submit with an Image

The ubiquitous nature of the submit button has prompted many a Web designer to wish for an alternative. With the IMAGE input control type, you now have a choice. To replace the ordinary grey button with a custom image, replace the standard markup <INPUT TYPE="submit" value="Submit"> with the following:

```
<INPUT TYPE="image" SRC="mybutton.gif" HEIGHT="20" WIDTH="50"
   ALT="Submit Button">
```

This control includes the attributes you're familiar with from the IMG tag: source location, height, width, and alternative text. It's the input type that makes this control function as a submit button.

Resetting Form Defaults

If you've seen a few Submit buttons, you've undoubtedly seen them paired with a Reset button. When clicked, this button will reset all form fields to their original values: If no predetermined values were set, the form will be wiped clean. If fields did have predetermined values, the form will once again show those values.

Putting It All Together

When the time comes to build a form, it's helpful to visualize or even sketch out how the form would be laid out if you were developing it for paper. Forms can be hard to make look good if you just make them up as you go. Ask yourself the following questions:

- Are there questions that do best in a true/false format?
- Must the response be chosen from a finite set of options?
- Can more than one choice be made from that set?
- Should the user be able to write in their own choice if an appropriate one isn't present?
- Does the user need to have room to explain or comment at length?
- Do you need to limit the length of responses because of constraints in processing or field size limits in databases?

The answers to these questions will help you choose what input controls to use in each area of the form. The file listing form3.html shown here and in Figure 8.7 makes use of seven different control types: text, radio, checkbox, select list, text area, submit, and reset.

form3.html

```
<FORM METHOD="post" ACTION="http://www.webgeek.com/webgeek-cgi/book.cgi">

<INPUT TYPE="hidden" NAME="Form" VALUE="Tech Support Request Form">

<P>Please provide the following:

<P>Name: <INPUT TYPE="text" NAME="name" SIZE="30"><BR>
Email: <INPUT TYPE="text" NAME="email" SIZE="30"><BR>
Telephone: <INPUT TYPE="text" NAME="phone" SIZE="15">

<P>Please describe your computer system:

<P>Which platform do you use?

<INPUT TYPE="radio" NAME="OS" VALUE="Windows"> Windows
<INPUT TYPE="radio" NAME="OS" VALUE="Mac"> Mac
<INPUT TYPE="radio" NAME="OS" VALUE="Unix"> Unix

<P>Hardware (please mark all components present on your machine)

<P><INPUT TYPE="checkbox" NAME="hardware" VALUE="sound"> Sound Card
<INPUT TYPE="checkbox" NAME="hardware" VALUE="mouse"> Mouse
<INPUT TYPE="checkbox" NAME="hardware" VALUE="trackball"> Trackball
<INPUT TYPE="checkbox" NAME="hardware" VALUE="scanner"> Scanner
<INPUT TYPE="checkbox" NAME="hardware" VALUE="printer"> Printer
<INPUT TYPE="checkbox" NAME="hardware" VALUE="CDROM"> CDROM
<INPUT TYPE="checkbox" NAME="hardware" VALUE="tape"> Tape Back-up device

<P>How much RAM is installed?

<SELECT>
<OPTION VALUE="8mb"> 8 MB
<OPTION VALUE="16mb">16 MB
<OPTION VALUE="32mb">32 MB
<OPTION VALUE="64mb">64 MB
<OPTION VALUE="128mb">128 MB
</SELECT>

<P>Please describe the problem thoroughly:

<P><TEXTAREA NAME="problem" ROWS=6 COLS=70></TEXTAREA>

<P><INPUT TYPE="submit" VALUE="Submit"> <INPUT TYPE="reset" VALUE="Reset">

</FORM>
```

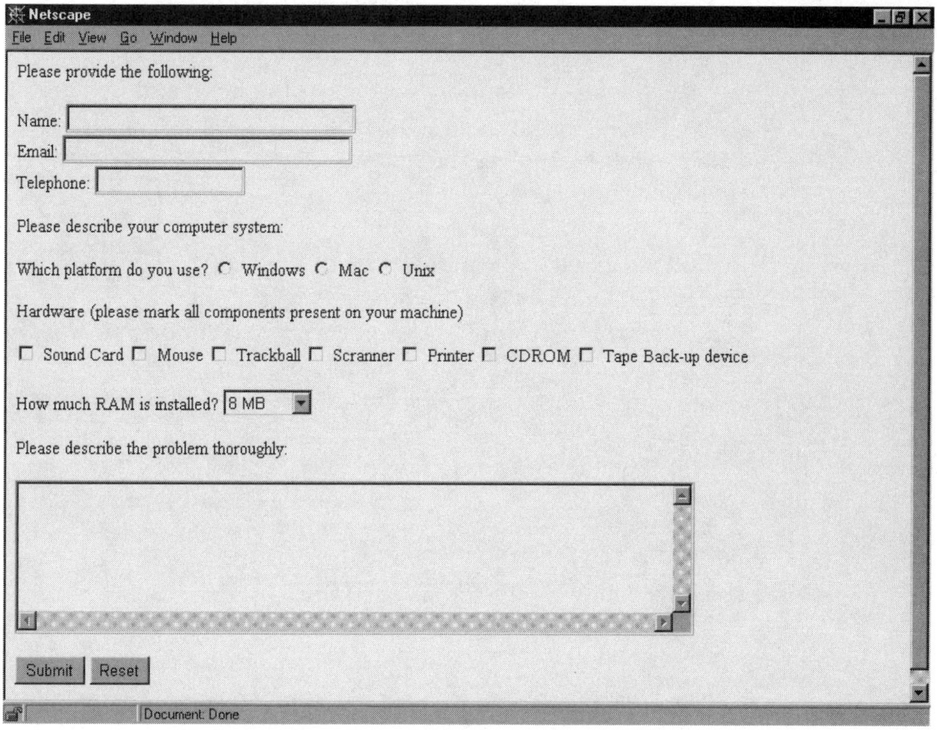

FIGURE 8.7:   A complete form

Though Figure 8.7 shows a fully functional form, it could use some improvement in layout:

- Notice that the top three text boxes are unevenly aligned.

- Having the hardware choices spread out across a single line makes them difficult to scan quickly.

Layout and presentation within forms can be improved upon with additional HTML markup or style sheet properties.

Aligning Form Fields

The reason that the three text boxes appear unaligned should be pretty obvious: the text that immediately precedes them contains a different number of characters on each line.

```
<P>Name: <INPUT TYPE="text" NAME="name" SIZE="30"><BR>
Email: <INPUT TYPE="text" NAME="email" SIZE="30"><BR>
Telephone: <INPUT TYPE="text" NAME="phone" SIZE="15">
```

A basic solution would be to enclose the fieldswithin a preformatted text area using the PRE container. Unfortunately, while that solves the spacing problem, it also generates a problem of its own—the change from the default page font to the monospaced font for the field labels, as seen here.

Please provide the following:

Name:

Email:

Telephone:

A better solution would be to create a two column table.

```
<TABLE BORDER="0">
<TR>
<TD>Name:</TD>
<TD><INPUT TYPE="text" NAME="name" SIZE="30"></TD>
</TR>
<TR>
<TD>Email:</TD>
<TD><INPUT TYPE="text" NAME="email" SIZE="30"></TD>
</TR>
<TR>
<TD>Telephone:</TD>
<TD><INPUT TYPE="text" NAME="phone" SIZE="15"></TD>
</TR>
</TABLE>
```

As you can see here, the alignment looks the same as with the preformatted text solution, but the table doesn't tamper with the font display.

Please provide the following:

Name:

Email:

Telephone:

The next area that could use some work is the group of checkboxes. The current presentation has them all on a single line:

```
<P><INPUT TYPE="checkbox" NAME="hardware" VALUE="sound"> Sound Card
<INPUT TYPE="checkbox" NAME="hardware" VALUE="mouse"> Mouse
<INPUT TYPE="checkbox" NAME="hardware" VALUE="trackball"> Trackball
<INPUT TYPE="checkbox" NAME="hardware" VALUE="scanner"> Scanner
<INPUT TYPE="checkbox" NAME="hardware" VALUE="printer"> Printer
<INPUT TYPE="checkbox" NAME="hardware" VALUE="CDROM"> CDROM
<INPUT TYPE="checkbox" NAME="hardware" VALUE="tape"> Tape Back-up device
```

NOTE

> The checkboxes display on a single line because the INPUT tag does not inherently generate a line or paragraph break. Until the browser reaches a new P or BR tag (or a tag that implies one), it will continue to place the elements inline until it's forced to wrap at the right edge of the available window.

Two columns of boxes would present a more traditional grouping of items. A table works best in this instance as well.

```
<TABLE BORDER=0>
<TR>
<TD><INPUT TYPE="checkbox" NAME="hardware" VALUE="sound"> Sound
    Card<BR>
<INPUT TYPE="checkbox" NAME="hardware" VALUE="mouse"> Mouse<BR>
<INPUT TYPE="checkbox" NAME="hardware" VALUE="trackball"> Trackball<BR>
<INPUT TYPE="checkbox" NAME="hardware" VALUE="scanner"> Scanner
</TD>
<TR>
<TD VALIGN=TOP><INPUT TYPE="checkbox" NAME="hardware" VALUE="printer">
    Printer<BR>
<INPUT TYPE="checkbox" NAME="hardware" VALUE="CDROM"> CDROM<BR>
<INPUT TYPE="checkbox" NAME="hardware" VALUE="tape"> Tape Back-up
    device
</TD>
</TR>
</TABLE>
```

The output will be two columns of checkboxes, four on the left and three on the right, as shown here. Notice that the attribute VALIGN="top" was used in the second <TD> cell. This attribute assures that the top of the two columns will be aligned, rather than leaving the smaller right-hand column aligned to the middle of the left-hand column (the default behavior).

☐ Sound Card ☐ Printer
☐ Mouse ☐ CDROM
☐ Trackball ☐ Tape Back-up device
☐ Scanner

Skill 8

Processing the Responses

So far one key instruction has been missing from our form examples—how to actually process the form. There are two basic options: a process using the user's mail client and a server-based process. These two options are commonly known as *mailto forms* and *CGI scripts*.

In either case, when the submit button is pressed, the browser gathers the information entered by the user, joins it into *key=value* pairs, and then converts it into *URL encoded format*. URL encoding takes the *key=value* pairs and *concantenates* them— joins them together— into one long string of characters. Spaces, carriage returns, and line feeds are replaced by their ASCII character codes. This big long string is then transferred to the form processor.

Using Mailto Forms

The first process, a mailto form, is the easiest for the novice Web designer to implement, but it's the poorer of the two choices. A mailto form takes the URL encoded data string and sends it to a designated e-mail address through the visitor's e-mail program. The catch with this is that the visitor's Web browser must be "aware" of their e-mail program. While Navigator has long had an e-mail client integrated right into the product, not all Web browsers have one—not even IE. Visitors using those browsers may have difficulty completing this type of form. An alternative contact method such as a telephone number or e-mail address should be plainly available.

Adding the Form Action

To initiate mailto handling, two new attributes need to be inserted in the opening FORM tag: METHOD and ACTION.

METHOD   tells the browser how to pass off the URL encoded string of data. For most purposes, you will use the value post here.

ACTION   defines what process will "act" upon the string. In this example, that's an e-mail link, as shown here:

```
<FORM METHOD="post" ACTION="mailto:you@yourcompany.com">
```

The instruction mailto: tells the browser to activate the e-mail client and send the data (the URL encoded string that's being passed off) to the address specified.

 **WARNING**   What happens when a Web browser doesn't understand how to handle a mailto form can't always be predicted. One of the most common scenarios is that the data simply falls into the "bit bucket" and is never sent to you. Not a good thing!

What Arrives in the Mail

Adding the processing instructions to the form was the easy part. The downside to mailto forms, outside of not all browsers being able to handle them properly, is that the responses arrive in e-mail—often as an attachment instead of in the body of the message—in that same URL encoded format in which the browser passed them off.

Filling out the form pictured in Figure 8.7 with mailto processing, the following data came back:

```
Form=Tech+Support+Request+Form&name=Ann+Navarro&email=ann@webgeek.com
    ➥ &phone=&OS=Windows&hardware=sound&hardware=trackball&hardware=
    ➥ scanner&hardware=printer&hardware=CDROM&hardware=tape&problem=
    ➥ My+computer+crashed%21
```

Yikes! If you look closely you can see the *name=value* pairs: Form=Tech Support Request Form, OS=Windows, etc. But it's far from easy reading in this state.

A far better solution is to employ a few lines of code in one of many programming languages that can handle information passed in the URL encoded state.

Processing with CGI Scripts

CGI stands for *Common Gateway Interface*. Ordinarily, the Web browser communicates directly with the Web server. Requests for HTML and graphic files go from browser to server, and the actual files are passed back in response. When the browser needs something to be processed, rather than having a file handed back, the request passes through the CGI.

A CGI script is a small program—a script—that runs on the server based on a request that's come through the gateway. For Web purposes, they're most often written in Perl or C, though with the rise in popularity of Windows NT–based servers, more and more are cropping up in other languages. At the most basic level, all that's required is that the language be able to create an executable file that runs on the same platform as the server.

In order to run CGI scripts on your Web site, you need to have access to a *cgi-bin*. A cgi-bin is a special directory on the site that holds scripts and executable programs. If you are working in a virtual Web hosting environment—that is if you pay an Internet Service Provider for Web site space—you'll need to find out whether or not you have access to your own cgi-bin. Some ISPs won't allow them or will allow use of only the special scripts that they've made available to all their customers.

The opening FORM tag on the HTML file takes the new attributes of METHOD and ACTION as it did with mailto: forms. This time, the ACTION is the URL that leads to the Perl script, as seen here:

```
<FORM METHOD="post" ACTION="http://www.yourcompany.com/cgi-bin/
   formhandler.cgi">
```

The file formhandler.cgi shown below is one such script. The numbers to the right of many lines are the line numbers, which will be referred to in a moment.

formhandler.cgi

```
#!/usr/bin/perl                                                      #0
# enter the email address the data should be sent to
# don't forget to use the format name\@company.com

# Next edit the subject line appropriately

# Edit the return variable to hold the URL for the page you want
# your visitor to go to next

# Title is the name of the page they'll go to

# Ask your system administrator for the 'the path to sendmail' on your system
# edit below if necessary


# --- edit only these variables. Do not remove quotes ------#

$email = "you\@yourcompany.com";                                     #1

$subject = "Form Responses";
#2

$return = "http://www.yourcompany.com";                              #3

$title = "The Widget Home Page";                                     #4

$SENDMAIL = "/usr/sbin/sendmail -t";                                 #5



# -------- do not edit below this line --------- #

read(STDIN, $data, $ENV{'CONTENT_LENGTH'});                          #6
open (MAILOUT, "| $SENDMAIL") || die "Error, where's your sendmail?"; #7
```

```
@response = split(/&/,$data);                                    #8
foreach (@response) {                                            #9
    tr/+/ /;                                                     #10
    s/=/ = /;                                                    #11
    s/%(..)/pack("C",hex($1))/ge;                                #12
    print MAILOUT "$_\n";                                        #13
}                                                                #14
close(MAILOUT);                                                  #15

print "Content-type: text/html\n\n";                             #16
print "<HTML><HEAD>\n";                                          #17
print "<TITLE>Form Sent!</TITLE>\n";                             #18
print "</HEAD><BODY>\n";                                         #19
print "<H3>Form Sent!</H3>\n";                                   #20
print "<P>Follow this link back to <A HREF=\"$return\">$title;</A>.\n"; #21
print "</BODY>\n</HTML>\n";                                      #22
# end                                                            #23
```

While this book isn't intended to be a comprehensive resource for CGI scripting, understanding how a script that's as frequently used as this one can truly add to your marketable skills.

To use this script, you need only to edit the six lines marked #0 through #5 in the following manner:

Line 0: Path to Perl   The first of two bits of information you'll need to obtain from your system administrator. The *path* is the route that a computer would travel through the directory structure to get to the exact location of the Perl language interpreter on the server. This line will always begin with the #! symbols immediately preceding the path statement and should always be the first line in any Perl script.

Line 1: E-mail address   This line holds the e-mail address that you want the responses sent to. The @ symbol is always *escaped* by inserting a backslash (\) immediately preceding it in the e-mail address. An @ symbol is a special character in the Perl language; by using the backslash, you tell the server to interpret the @ as text rather than with its assigned programmatic behavior.

Line 2: Subject   This line holds the text that will show up as the subject line in the e-mail message being generated.

Line 3: Return URL   After the form is processed, your visitor is taken to an HTML page that informs them of the successful submission. This line holds a URL that will be provided as a link. Enter the URL of the page you want them to move to next.

Line 4: URL title What do you want to call the URL you're sending them to? The text will tell them "Follow this link back to *Your Title.*"

Line 5: Path to sendmail This is the second bit of information you'll need from your system administrator. Enter the information exactly as they give it to you.

That's it! The rest of the script doesn't change. Upload the file to your `cgi-bin` directory and set any required file permissions before trying to use it. Unix users will want to set permissions to 755. Others will want to consult their system administrator for any special instructions.

 NOTE

Not every Web server will require you to set file permissions. This is a setting found within Unix and Unix-like servers that grants specific permission for various events to occur—including the execution of a CGI script. The actual process of setting file permissions goes beyond the scope of this text. Your system administrator is the best source of assistance for ISP-specific information.

The differences in how the browser handles the form are immediately apparent. With a mailto form, it was hard to tell that anything actually happened. With this script, the user is taken to a whole new page that confirms the success of the process, as seen in Figure 8.8.

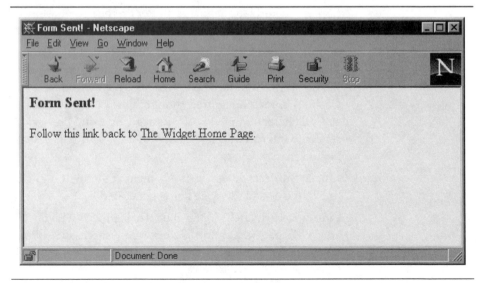

FIGURE 8.8: The HTML page displayed upon successful submission of the form processed by the script `formhandler.cgi`.

There's a marked difference in the e-mail that you receive from a form submission processed with the above CGI script. The following is the entire contents of the message created by the script:

```
From: httpd <httpd@mail.yourcompany.com>
Date: Fri, 26 Sep 1997 15:39:03 -0700
To: you@yourcompany.com
Subject: Tech Support Form Response

Form = Tech Support Request Form
name = Maggie Thomas
email = mt@widgets.com
phone = 555-1234
OS = Windows
hardware = sound
hardware = mouse
hardware = printer
problem = Can you help me upgrade to Windows NT?
```

Much easier to read, isn't it? The lines of Perl code between lines 8 and 14 are what's responsible for reverting the information back into a much more legible format.

 WARNING   When you are using this particular script, the From header on this message is the name of the Web server process—httpd. More advanced forms can capture the e-mail address that the user enters and insert it into the headers so you can use your e-mail program's reply function normally. If you were to respond to this message from Ms. Thomas, you'd need to be sure to edit her e-mail address to replace the httpd daemon address.

Skill 8

Have You Mastered the Essentials?

Now you can. . .

- ☑ **Create a form to retrieve information from your Web site visitors.**

- ☑ **Choose a response format from ten commonly used input controls.**

- ☑ **Integrate a form into the existing "look and feel" of your site.**

- ☑ **Send form data directly to an e-mail address.**

- ☑ **Edit a basic form-handling CGI script for your own use.**

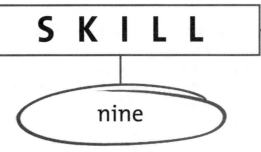

Navigating Your Site

❑ Pre-production planning

❑ Basic site organization

❑ Navigational menus

❑ Site maps

❑ Navigating with image maps

The site elements that are among the easiest for the novice Web designer to overlook are the navigation tools. How does the user move around your site? Can they jump to unrelated sections of the site from any page? Must they use the browser's back button to trace their steps through half a dozen pages before they can move off in another direction?

Imagine you are walking down an avenue window shopping and decide to stop in a store that had a few interesting items in the display window. You step through the door and are immediately faced with five different pathways to choose through the merchandise. There are no signs and no friendly sales staff available to give directions. You set off down one of the most promising aisles and instead of finding the lamp you wanted to look at up close, you find yourself in men's clothing. How many times will you trace your steps back to the beginning and try again before you give up and walk out the door?

Providing easily accessible and intuitive means of navigating your site will exponentially increase your chances of having your visitors find what they want and stick around to explore some more. How the user moves around the site should be a topic of discussion from the earliest planning stages of your site's development.

Pre-Production Planning

In Skill 13 you'll step through the process of identifying your site's purpose, what response you want your users to have (do you want to inform? to sell? to persuade?), determine design constraints placed on you by an existing trade dress, and gathering your existing materials to be converted to use on your Web site. It's important to keep navigation in mind while you work through those processes. A solid plan for site construction will go a long way toward saving time in the actual HTML production process.

Every Web design studio and individual Web developer seems to have their own methods for laying out and keeping track of how each document fits into the grand scheme of a new Web site. They range from the "crayon-on-napkin" crowd all the way up to those who use powerful database tools or professional flow charting systems. The most important thing is to choose what works best for *you*. If you're constantly digging for Post-It notes or searching your hard drive for that image file you worked on last week, you'll lose valuable productivity time.

Several ideas that can help you plan a Web site more efficiently include:

> **Make a basic site map.** This can be as simple as an outline or hand-drawn flow-chart. Visualizing the site helps determine how many sub-directories you'll need and where each file should go.

Keep images in one place. If you have a single image directory, graphics can be readily located and easily called from any directory within the site.

Keep a "mirror image" of the site locally. When producing your documents, save them in a directory structure that's a duplicate of what will be found on the live Web site. This system makes uploading and maintenance a breeze.

Once you have your basic layout determined, it's time to think about how your visitors will get around your site. Just like in real life, when someone visits some place new, they'll often need directions on how to get where they want to go.

Navigational Menus

Most every computer user is familiar with the concept of a *menu*. Just under the title bar of most programs you'll find the menu bar, a collection of words or phrases that when activated with a pointing device or a keyboard combination reveal a list of options—the menu. A menu bar and menu are shown below:

File   Edit   View   Go   Window   Help

Web sites need menus of their own. Because the look and feel vary so much from site to site, the visitor doesn't always find a familiar navigational model. It's your job as the Web designer to make sure the visitor recognizes the tools that you provide as navigation aides and to present them in a logical and attractive manner.

Visual Cues

Figure 9.1 is a screen shot of the Brea Chamber of Commerce Web site. The designer has chosen to provide navigation links in a column down the left side of the page. This treatment has become very popular with designers. It allows you to set off a relatively small portion of the available screen for hyperlinks, while making the "nav bar", as it's often called, immediately visible to the site users.

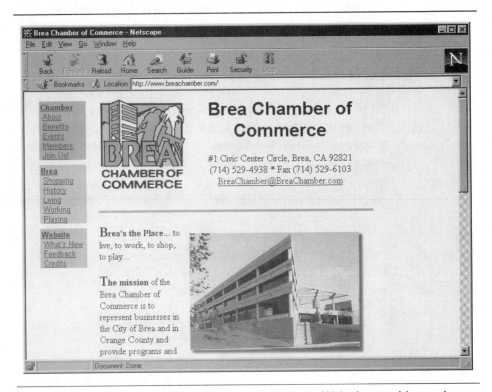

FIGURE 9.1:   The Brea Chamber of Commerce Web site provides navigational tools set off visually in more than one way.

On this site, the hyperlinks are not only arranged in a left-hand column but also separated into three groups set off in individually colored boxes. Each group of links is topically related—information about the Chamber of Commerce, about the city of Brea, and about the Web site itself. The colors chosen for the boxes were pulled from the organization's logo, creating a complementary visual effect.

The vernacular of Web design has embraced the term "buttons" for graphics that represent links. From very early on, the metaphor originated from the use of images that, well, looked like buttons—something that you'd push if they were activated by touch.

In Figure 9.2, the Working Solo Online site—located at `http://www.workingsolo`
`.com/`—provides two sets of navigation aides. The three images in the dark shaded area of the main graphic are sections of the Web site that the designer felt needed special attention. The remaining six sections are accessed from the row of six buttons near the bottom of the screen. Additionally, this layout succeeds on several other fronts. The nav bar serves as a visual break between the large logo graphic and the text below. It balances well in relation to the width of the rest of the page and fits with the primary color design theme.

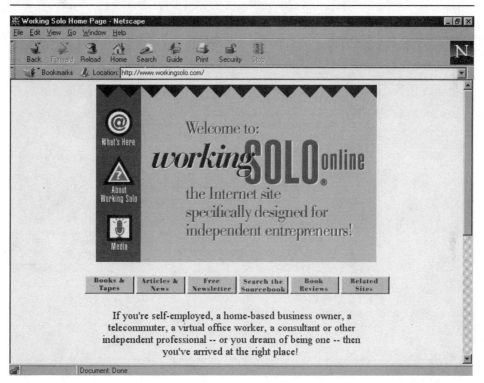

FIGURE 9.2:   Working Solo: navigational buttons that really do look like buttons

Beyond the button metaphor, designers often opt to create graphical representations of a site's subsections. The HTML Writers Guild site—found online at `http://www.hwg.org/`—takes this approach (see Figure 9.3). The icon on the bottom left of the screen is a pair of binoculars with the label "search," giving the user the mental picture of gazing through field glasses in order to locate the hunted item. The membership services icon is made up of four silhouettes, representing the individuals that make up the organization's membership. Each image has a visual tie-in with the section it identifies.

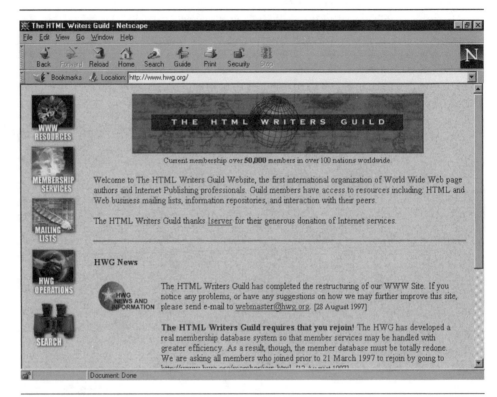

FIGURE 9.3:   The HTML Writers Guild uses representational icons for navigation.

 **WARNING**   Notice that a text label accompanies each graphical icon. No matter how obvious you may think a visual representation is, you should provide the written meaning to prevent confusion or misunderstanding. For example, U.S. residents have little trouble identifying the purpose of the red flag on the side of a mailbox. When it's up, it's alerting someone (the mail carrier, in "real life"), that there is mail in the box ready to be picked up. When some online services began using that metaphor to alert users to waiting e-mail, many non-U.S. residents were perplexed by the imagery. Their postal delivery systems are handled differently, and many of them had never seen mailboxes with red flags.

A well-designed navigational system will not only inform your site visitors of where they *may* go but also where they *are*. An often frustrating reality of the hyperlinked state of the Web is that your visitors won't always come in to your site through the "front door." People often bookmark and link in to pages that are several levels deep into your Web site, or they may come in from a search engine where they could wind up entering from any individual page (search engines such as AltaVista may provide direct references deep into your site). Providing a visual cue of the visitor's current location as a function of your navigational tools takes care of two issues with the same design element.

Table 9.1 lists six features that you should consider incorporating into your Web site's navigational tools.

TABLE 9.1:   Features that enhance navigation

Feature	How It Helps
Use the Button metaphor.	Even novice Web users are familiar with buttons from the Windows and Macintosh user interfaces. Carrying that metaphor into your site design creates a natural association for the links with your user.
Emphasize with bullets.	Bullets or other small geometric images help draw attention to lists. A row or column of items set off by bullets grabs the user's focus, helping them immediately notice the navigation area.
Reserve a distinct visual space.	Setting off the links by using a border, an identifiable column, or other visually separating characteristic helps identify the panel as the navigation tools.
Label all images.	Don't assume every visitor will understand pictorial representations. Provide them with clear labels for each link in addition to the images.
Keep a consistent interface.	If you use the same design and location for your navigation tools, the user will know just where to look in each section in order to move on. The individual items in the group can change, but the successful site keeps the look and placement across all pages.
You are here.	Provide users with cues as to their current location. Not everyone comes in the "front door" of your site. Let them know where they are as well as where they can go.

Skill 9

Site Maps

Back in the pre-production planning phase, we encouraged you to create a basic site map or flow chart that described your site's structure. On large or complex sites, this can be expanded into a navigational tool for your visitors as well.

Ziff-Davis Publishing Company produces dozens of magazines covering almost every aspect of the world of computing and the Internet. Their Site Guide at `http://www.zdnet.com/findit/guide.html` makes use of many of the features discussed in the previous section: a left-side navigation bar with small, readily identifiable buttons, a clear indication that "you are here," along with graphical links with descriptions of each section.

One of the difficulties of navigating through a large site is that to keep navigational cues intuitive, the amount of information provided in each content page may need to be limited. If you provide a single comprehensive catalog of all the destinations available to your visitors, they'll always know where to turn if they find themselves wanting to jump to a new area quickly.

Non-Visual Alternatives

All of the sites we've discussed so far have made use of graphical elements in order to bring attention to navigational tools. Thinking back to Skill 2, you'll remember that some browsers, such as Lynx or adaptive programs for individuals with certain handicaps, do not have graphical interfaces. Also, many busy Web surfers will turn off the automatic loading of images option in their browsers when they want to be able to skim sites quickly.

In these instances, providing a non-visual, or *text-based,* alternative for navigation will accommodate both types of users.

At the bottom of each page on the public Web site, the HTML Writers Guild makes use of a text-based nav bar, as seen in Figure 9.4. It's simply a set of hyperlinks divided by the pipe character (|), centered on the page in two rows. There are links to each major component of the site, allowing visitors with images turned off or with text-based browsers to navigate with ease. In fact, there are links to more sections in this text-based bar than there are in the graphical column of icons on the left side of the page. Because only text is used to build the bar, more links can be included in a smaller space without sacrificing readability.

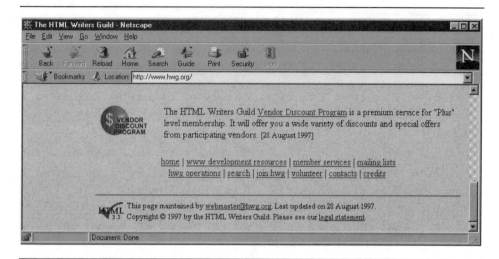

FIGURE 9.4:   A text menu at the bottom of the HTML Writers Guild site

Image Maps

An image map has three components: the *image*, the *map definition*, and the *supporting HTML*. The image component is something you're already familiar with. Almost any image—a line drawing, simple shapes, and even photographs—can be turned into an image map.

In Figure 9.5, we see the opening screen of the Monterey Bay Aquarium's Web site, fondly known as the E-Quarium. At first glance, it's not very different from the other sites we've visited in this skill. There are three buttons in a row at the bottom of the page, which were created with the traditional image and anchor tags. However, the image in the middle also seems to be one big link! If you look closely at the status bar—the gray bar at the bottom of the browser window—when you run your mouse pointer over the image, you'll see a pair of numbers changing in response to where your mouse is.

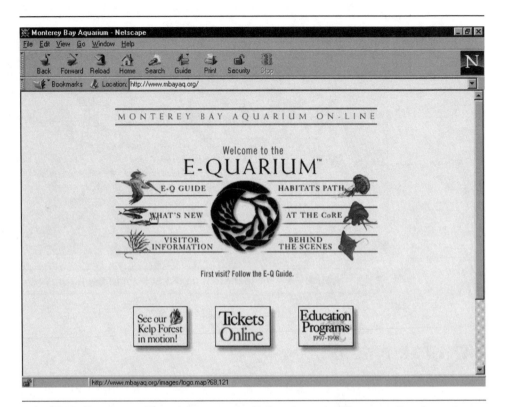

FIGURE 9.5:   The entrance to the E-Quarium, the Monterey Bay Aquarium Web site. The mouse pointer over a hot spot produces the x,y coordinates shown in the status bar.

That pair of numbers represents the *x,y coordinates* for the location of your mouse. If you'll think back to geometry class for a moment, you'll remember that a two-dimensional object set within two planes can be measured in distances from the x and y axes. With image maps, the concept is similar, with the unit of measure being the pixel. The starting point, where x and y are both equal to zero (0), is the upper left-hand corner of the image. The x value (the width) grows as the user moves to the right, and the y value (the height) increases as the user moves down. The value of 68,121 seen in Figure 9.5 corresponds to the point 68 pixels to the right of the image's left border and 121 pixels down from the top.

When a user clicks on a *hot spot*, the image map system reads the pixel coordinates of their mouse pointer and the browser undertakes the action that's specified in the hyperlink anchor for that area. Hot spots are the "clickable" areas within an image map. They can take three shapes: a circle, a rectangle, or a polygon. Each hot spot is hyperlinked to another file using the standard anchor tag you learned back in Skill 4.

To create an image map, you'll need one new tag and a new attribute for the IMAGE tag.

Creating an Image Map

We'll step through the process of creating an image map by using an image that best fits this metaphor—a geographical map. Figure 9.6 is a rudimentary map of the state of Hawaii. We'll create an image map with hot spots over the major islands, which will be linked to pages detailing resorts on each island.

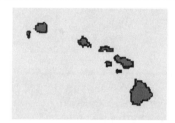

FIGURE 9.6:   We'll use this image to create an image map.

 By their nature, image maps tend to be large images. Be sure that you've chosen an image that can be optimized for as small a file size as possible to help decrease download time. File size optimization will be covered in detail in Skill 17.

The HTML for your map begins with the familiar IMAGE tag.

```
<IMG SRC="hawaii.gif" WIDTH="200" HEIGHT="140" ALT="Image map of
   Hawaii" USEMAP="#MyMap">
```

The last attribute, USEMAP, is new. Its name identifies its function—it tells the browser that there is an image map definition associated with the image and that the browser should *use* the *map* definition named MyMap to process it. The object name—in this case the map's name—must always be preceded by the hash mark #, as seen here. Next is the MAP container.

The *MAP* Container

The MAP container is the object that the USEMAP attribute makes reference to. It holds the x,y coordinates of the hot spots that the browser will interpret to process the hyperlinks. The tag opens with the NAME attribute:

```
<MAP NAME="MyMap">
```

This is the name previously referenced in the USEMAP attribute from the IMG tag, minus the hash mark.

Within the MAP container is a set of AREA tags that define each hot spot. We'll start with the AREA tag for the hyperlink over the island of Hawaii.

```
<AREA HREF="hawaii.html"
      ALT="Hawaii, The Big Island"
      SHAPE="circle"
      COORDS="167,108,24">
```

WARNING In this example, each attribute of the AREA tag is shown on a new line. This was done for enhanced readability. You do not have to format your AREA containers in this manner.

The SHAPE attribute is self-explanatory; the value can be circle; rect, for rectangle; or poly, for a polygon. The COORDS attribute defines the coordinates for the circle (represented by the x,y coordinates of the circle's center point, measured in pixels from the upper left-hand corner of the image) and the radius (also measured in pixels).

Determining the coordinate values can be done by hand, as was done here, or by using one of several handy image mapping software products available on the market. (See *Downloadable Image Map Tools*.) In this case, the information was retrieved using Corel Photo-Paint 7. The process is described in the steps below. If you're using a different graphics package, the tool names and menu choices may not be the same.

1. With the image open in the program workspace, click the Circle Mask tool from the toolbar.

2. A circle is actually created within a perfect square. Click your mouse at the upper-left corner of the square that will contain your circle and drag down and to the right.

3. Watch the radius values on the status bar as you drag. When they match, you've created a perfect circle. Note the center value and the radius values, as seen on the status bar in Figure 9.7, then release your mouse.

4. Right click within the image and select Undo Mask Circle from the pop-up menu to clear the selection.

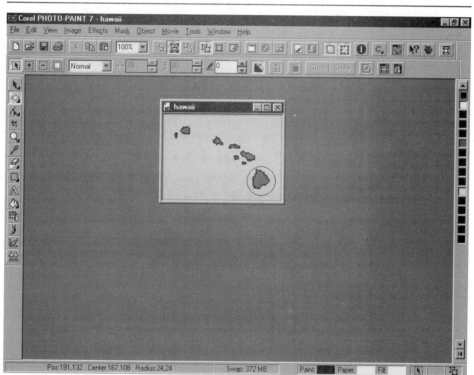

FIGURE 9.7:   The circle's center and radius are displayed on Photo-Paint's status bar.

Now you're ready to find the coordinates for the next AREA tag.

DOWNLOADABLE IMAGE MAP TOOLS

Calculating hot spot coordinates by hand can be a drag, especially when you have a considerable number of active areas on the map. Luckily, there are some software tools available that help you through the process.

Some of the favorites for Windows 95/NT include:

Live Image   From LiveImage Corporation. This shareware tool, an extension of the product well known as Map THIS!, can be found at `http://www.mediatec.com/`. Version 1.26 was a winner in PC Magazine's 1997 Shareware Awards.

Mapedit   By Boutell.Com, Inc. The shareware version of this product is included on the CD that comes with this book.

For the Macintosh:

Mapper   Produced by Nisseb Softwares. A fully WYSIWYG (What You See Is What You Get) mapping tool for the Mac. Download at `http://www.calles.pp.se/nisseb/mapper.html`.

MapMaker   From Twin Moon Development and Design. This shareware tool produces code for client-side and server-side maps and can be found at `http://www.kickinit.net/mapmaker/`.

The island of Maui, the next island up the chain from the Big Island, is near two smaller islands that are "in the way" of using a circle for a hot spot. Since the island is also tilted at an angle, a polygon would be the best choice here.

The coordinates for a polygon are listed in pairs of x,y values. Our polygon will have four corners, so there will be four pairs of numbers listed as the COORDS attribute value, in x1, y1, x2, y2, order. The values seen below were retrieved again in Photo-Paint 7, using the Freehand Mask Tool and noting the coordinates of each corner point.

```
<AREA HREF="maui.html"
        ALT="Maui"
        SHAPE="poly"
        COORDS="122,60,149,87,165,68,143,54">
```

Lanai can be easily covered with a rectangle. The COORDS attribute value is
noted by two pairs; the x,y coordinates of the upper-left corner and the x,y coordinates of the bottom-right corner, as seen here.

```
<AREA HREF="lanai.html"
            ALT="Lanai"
            SHAPE="rect"
            COORDS="110,55,129,45">
```

 WARNING

Be sure when working in tight spaces not to overlap any of the hot spot
boundaries. The map won't function properly if you do.

Adding in the AREA tags for Oahu and Kauai, the final MAP container appears here:

imagemap.html

```
<IMG SRC="hawaii.gif" USEMAP="#MyMap">

  <MAP NAME="MyMap">
  <AREA HREF="hawaii.html"
          ALT="Hawaii, The Big Island"
          SHAPE="circle"
          COORDS="167,108,24">
  <AREA HREF="maui.html"
          ALT="Maui"
          SHAPE="poly"
          COORDS="122,60,149,87,165,68,143,54">
  <AREA HREF="lanai.html"
          ALT="Lanai"
          SHAPE="rect"
          COORDS="110,55,129,45">
  <AREA HREF="oahu.html"
          ALT="Oahu"
          SHAPE="rect"
          COORDS="76,30,104,54">
  <AREA HREF="kauai.html">
          ATL="Kauai"
          SHAPE="circle"
          COORDS="35,27,13">
  </MAP>
```

Figure 9.8 shows the finished image map displayed in a Web browser. When the mouse pointer is over a hot spot, the ALT attribute for that <AREA> is displayed as a tool tip in newer browsers like Navigator 4.03 shown here.

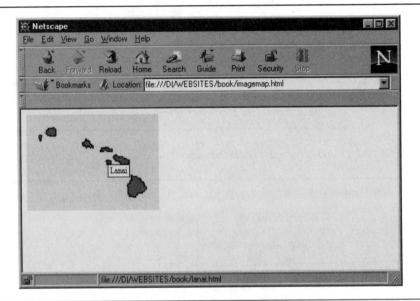

FIGURE 9.8:   The finished image map with the pointer over the hot spot for Lanai

The HTML seen here in the `imagemap.html` listing is known as a *client-side* image map. Client-side means that the image map is processed by the client program, in this case, the browser. Other image map processes are available that are processed by the Web server. Those are known as *server-side* image maps. Server-side processing is generally done with a CGI script. The map data is defined in a file that also resides on the server, instead of with the MAP container as was done in `imagemap.html`. That file is formatted specifically for the type of Web server software that is running on the server where it will be placed. Server-side maps are generally considered the "older way" of handling image maps, though you may wish to include them if you're concerned about accomodating a portion of your audience that uses older browsers that can't support client-side maps. Creating these files goes beyond the scope of this text. Pointers to information found online is located in the section *Online Resources for Server-Side Image Maps*.

ONLINE RESOURCES FOR SERVER-SIDE IMAGE MAPS

Image map configuration files come in two major types, NCSA or CERN. Your ISP will be able to tell you which one you should use or will provide you with alternate instructions.

A tutorial for image maps created for NCSA servers can be found at `http://hoohoo.ncsa.uiuc.edu/docs/tutorials/imagemapping.html`.

A reference for the CERN format, including the CGI script to go with it can be found at `http://www.w3.org/Daemon/User/CGI/HTImageDoc.html`.

Wandering Italy: The Introduction of Intelligent Navigation

The truly effective Web developer blends traditional metaphors with new and unexpected features, all the while staying within the bounds of an intuitive presentation. The Web site featured in this section takes technologies and ideas that we're already comfortable with and puts them on the Web. The idea that the Web crosses boundaries is alive and well in the projects created by these talented people.

If you think of travel writing, you probably think of the thick glossy pages of magazines like *Conde Nast Traveller*, the "adventure" feature in your weekend paper's travel section, or cruise line brochures with center-fold spreads featuring sumptuous buffet tables topped with ice sculptures.

Imagine travel photos, and you may envision videotapes captured by friends and family, the shoebox of snapshots you keep meaning to put into albums, or the ubiquitous home slide show.

What you probably *don't* immediately think of is a Web site that combines the story telling of the newspaper feature; the enticing photographs of the glossy monthlies; and enhancements such as music, native language pronunciation guides, and 360 degree views available only through the virtual reality experience.

Skill 9

Wandering Italy—http://www.wandering.com/—produced by Spotted Antelope Multimedia (http://www.spottedantelope.com/), a San Mateo, California based Web development firm, does just that (see Figure 9.9).

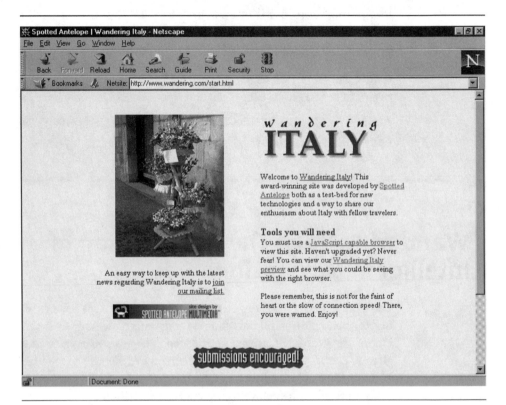

FIGURE 9.9:   The Wandering Italy entrance

The site makes use of JavaScript technology compliant with Navigator 3.0+ and Internet Explorer 3.0+ browsers. The interface mimics the designs frequently seen in CD-ROM presentations: a collection of buttons that provide "intelligent" access to the content available for each city detailed on the site.

In fact, the site grew out of a CD-ROM that Spotted Antelope developed several years ago. As they worked on a Web project that took advantage of the significant multimedia capabilities of Navigator 3.0, they put a high priority on their plans to port the CD-ROM into a Web site.

COMPATIBILITY NOTE   Wandering Italy developer Bill Womack noted that the primary reason that Netscape 2.0 versions aren't compatible with the site is a little known bug in that implementation of JavaScript 1.0. In those versions, JavaScript can only handle reading a file that's 32K or smaller. Wandering Italy's navigation system, without content, came in at 34K—still a very small file size. With browsers currently in production at versions 4.0 and higher, they're comfortable with the choice to continue development while supporting browsers with capabilities equivalent to Navigator and IE 3.0 and higher.

Wandering Italy is the result of merging audio, video, and virtual reality scenes into a Web site without the clutter and anti-intuitive interfaces that has plagued other sites that made the attempt. Tallying all the components they had to include made it pretty obvious that a traditional catalog interface would be a daunting prospect, both from a design and user standpoint.

The developers then tried to figure out how many different ways a viewer might like to "get lost" in Italy. Many visitors enjoy reading through all the stories, others are more interested in information that will help them plan a trip or are fascinated by the 360-degree panoramas that the virtual reality scenes provide. These varying needs provided the spark for creating the context-sensitive or "intelligent" navigation that's now a hallmark of the site.

In Figure 9.10, the user has just clicked on the button for the city of Firenze (a.k.a. Florence). The left pane loads two new panels: a photo of a city attraction and a short description of what can be found in that section. The buttons along the bottom of the screen are now all set to the Firenze offerings. The authors use JavaScript to track the city that was selected, which allows them to dynamically set the hyperlinks on the buttons to those Firenze options.

The virtual reality scenes make use of the RealSpace Viewer *plug-in*. A plug-in is a small application that, once installed, can enhance the capabilities of the Web browser. The 360-degree panoramas are created using the Photo Vista software from Live Image, Inc. (http://www.livepicture.com/). Some of the music files that are served using Apple's QuickTime plug-in were composed by Thomas Dolby, a well-known musician who's also a Wandering Italy fan.

Travel stories from the Wandering Italy developers, as well as those submitted by site visitors, are sprinkled throughout the cities. Each has hyperlinks to short audio files that provide pronunciation cues for the Italian words and phrases highlighted in the text, and some even have video files that really help bring the vision of Italy to life.

FIGURE 9.10:   The menu buttons across the bottom of the screen are "aware" of the content available for each city.

The technologies incorporated in this site represent the talents of individuals with years of experience in Web and multimedia development. The site has been presented here not to intimidate you but to inspire you into new ways of thinking in your designs and to encourage you to explore bringing ideas found in other media to the Web!

Have You Mastered the Essentials?

Now you can...

☑ **Plan your site's structure using a variety of tools.**

☑ **Mirror your site's organization on your local computer.**

☑ **Identify your navigational system for your visitors.**

☑ **Create a client-side image map.**

☑ **Imagine the possibilities of bringing user interfaces from other media to the Web.**

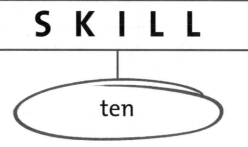

Search Engines

- ❑ Entering Web sites into search engines

- ❑ Getting to know robots

- ❑ Limiting robot access to your site

- ❑ Searching with Yahoo! and AltaVista

Any time large amounts of information are gathered in one place, supporting documents such as a table of contents and an index are needed for people to be able to find the most relevant data quickly. The same thing applies to the World Wide Web. There are several million Web pages out there, and users need to find the information of specific interest to them.

The Internet version of a table of contents is known as a *search engine*. A search engine is a site that provides a collection of links to other Web sites and a method of searching through those links in some logical manner. They can be directory style services—think of the yellow pages in your telephone book—or they can be details stored in indexes or databases that respond to keyword searches.

The *PC Webopaedia* (`http://www.pcwebopaedia.com`) defines a search engine as "A program that searches documents for specified keywords and returns a list of the documents where the keywords were found. Although search engine is really a general class of programs, the term is often used to specifically describe systems like AltaVista and Excite that enable users to search for documents on the World Wide Web and USENET newsgroups."

How Sites Get Indexed

There are two ways for a Web site to be entered into a search engine's database or index: through user submission or by being discovered by the search engine's Web robot.

The majority of search engines rely primarily on user submission for the acquisition of new sites. The process is pretty self-explanatory: the Web developer will visit the search engine Web site and enter the data requested by that particular service. The developer may be asked for a site description, a list of keywords, the name and e-mail address of a contact person, and sometimes even a mailing address and telephone number. Once the data has been reviewed or merged into the existing service, the site will begin appearing in search results.

 TIP Some services are faster than others when incorporating new submissions. Yahoo has surfers that check all submissions, so there's a human factor. Others are automated; for example, Alta Vista gets your index page as soon as you submit it and includes it within 24 hours. Anywhere from two days to three weeks can be considered a "normal" turnaround time.

Robots

World Wide Web robots (also called *spiders*) are programs that have been instructed to visit and *parse* Web sites. Parsing is the process of breaking something down into individual pieces. For example, a sentence can be parsed into individual grammatical objects. A Web site is parsed into individual pages and links. What the robot does with the parsed information depends on its programming. Most will, at a minimum, keep a record of the content of the page and note any links contained within it, queuing them into the list of pages to visit next. The result of all of this link following and content recording is a huge database of information that is compiled into the search engines.

But is having *everything* on the Web catalogued and indexed really a good idea? For the most part, it's an invaluable tool. How else could just a few keystrokes bring thousands of documents on subjects as varied as biochemistry and classical music right to your fingertips?

There will be times, however, when portions of Web sites shouldn't be included in the databases of these search engines. Common situations include the contents of a site's `cgi-bin` directory—where CGI scripts are stored and run—or data and log files that are available to the Web server software but aren't intended for direct display to the user.

In 1994 a group of Web robot authors realized that a standard set of behaviors for robots would help all site owners to control the robots' access to their sites as well as to protect them from being overwhelmed by an overly enthusiastic robot nudging aside human users on limited-bandwidth sites. The discussions evolved into what is today known as the *Robots Exclusion Standard*. This standard allows site owners to control access by robots, keeping them out of binary directories, such as the cgi-bin, and blocking access to private data. This agreement isn't the result of work within a standards body such as the W3C, nor is it enforced or guaranteed in any manner. However, in the cooperative environment that exists in many quarters of the Internet, the authors of most robots have supported the effort and will likely to continue to do so.

Skill 10

The Robots Exclusion Standard

Robots that honor the exclusion standards are all programmed to look for a file named `robots.txt` in the root directory of every Web site they visit.

NOTE The requirement that the `robots.txt` file reside in the root directory of a Web site does present some difficulties for sites that aren't housed on their own servers or on virtual servers. If this applies to you, ask your provider if they will include information in their `robots.txt` file that pertains to your site. If not, take heart—the methods discussed in the upcoming section, *META tags and Robots,* can help you.

Your `robots.txt` file needs to contain, at a minimum, two statements that might look like this:

```
User-agent: *
Disallow: /cgi-bin/
```

The first line addresses a specific *user-agent*; in this context, that's another name for a robot. The asterisk character * holds special meaning here, similar to the use of the asterisk as a wildcard in DOS and Windows environments. When present, it tells any compliant robot that unless it is named specifically in another section, that it must follow the directions stated here. So, if the two lines above were the entire contents of a site's `robots.txt` file, all compliant robots would know to stay out of the /cgi-bin/ directory.

More than one disallow statement can be made per user-agent group. For example, if a site wanted to keep robots not only out of the /cgi-bin/ directory, but also out of directories named /internal/ and /private/rawdata/, their `robots.txt` file would look like this:

```
User-agent: *
Disallow: /cgi-bin/
Disallow: /internal/
Disallow: /private/rawdata/
```

More than one user-agent group or individual agent can be specified as well. Each requires its own set of disallow statements. For instance, one of the known robots is the CACTVS Chemistry Spider. It searches the Web and FTP servers for chemical structures in chemical MIME formats. A site that doesn't deal with chemistry could choose to exclude this spider from all areas yet allow all other known spiders access to everything but the /cgi-bin/ directory. The `robots.txt` file would appear as follows:

```
User-agent: cactvschemistryspider
Disallow: /
User-agent: *
Disallow: /cgi-bin/
```

In the first set, the single forward slash tells the CACTVS Chemistry Spider that it's not allowed to enter the site at all. Other robots skip that instruction and move on to the next set that tells them they may look at anything but the CGI scripts.

 TIP   Webcrawler maintains *The Web Robots Database*, a collection of known robot names, contact information for their owners, and descriptions of their activities. It can be found online at `http://info.webcrawler.com/mak/projects/robots/active.html`.

You can't always wait for the Robots to find you. There has been an explosion of search engines on the net in the past few years, and being listed in a search engine is an important factor in visitors being able to find your site! Two of the most popular search engines are covered here; including details about submitting your sites, how the engines index or categorize sites, and whether or not they follow the Robots Exclusion Standard.

Yahoo!

Yahoo! (`http://www.yahoo.com`) is one of the Internet's great success stories. What started as a public copy of two Stanford University Electrical Engineering graduate student's browser bookmarks has turned into a multi-million dollar enterprise. The site now list tens of thousands of sites in hundreds of categories. The company classifies their site as "A hierarchical subject-oriented guide for the World Wide Web and Internet."

Yahoo! Site Details

Submission method	Via form from within the desired Yahoo! category.
Robot name	None.
Indexing method	User provided descriptions of 200 characters or less. Entry within multiple categories at Yahoo! staff discretion.
Adherence to Robots Exclusion Standard	N/A
Search Methods	Searches for keywords. A site is returned if the keyword is found in category headings, listing titles, or individual site descriptions.

Skill 10

Yahoo! Organization

The primary Yahoo! site is divided into fourteen main categories, as seen in Figure 10.1:

Arts and Humanities	News and Media
Business and Economy	Recreation and Sports
Computers and Internet	Reference
Education	Regional
Entertainment	Science
Government	Social Science
Health	Society and Culture

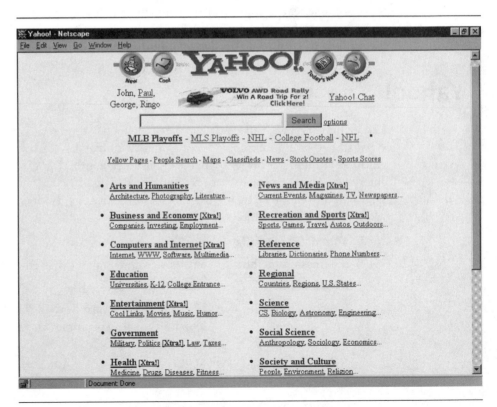

FIGURE 10.1:   The Yahoo! Web site (http://www.yahoo.com)

Each major category forks out into dozens of additional categories and sub-categories, some more than half a dozen levels deep. One quirk of their system is that all commercial sites—defined in their help files as a site that "sells something, promotes goods and services, or promotes a company that sells goods and services"—are listed under the Business and Economy section.

Early on, Yahoo! made this decision to keep a clear division between the commercial and non-commercial Web sites. However, cross-references to the commercial sites are available in the other areas. When this occurs, you'll see a subcategory title called "Companies@", as seen in Figure 10.2.

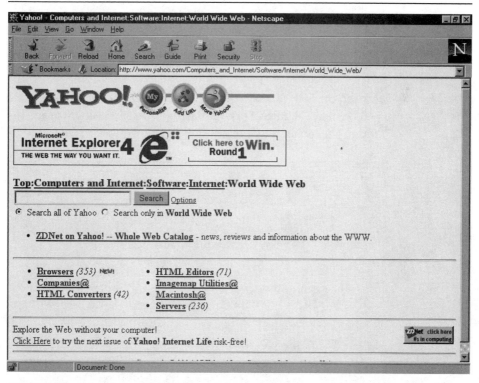

FIGURE 10.2: Commercial sites are cross-referenced in other major categories under the Companies@ heading. Copyright © 1994-98 Yahoo! Inc.

Searching on Yahoo!

Yahoo! offers several search methods:

Intelligent Default   A standard keyword search. If more than one key is entered, sites that include multiple matches will be presented first. For example, if the words **Western United States** were entered, categories or sites that include both "Western" and "United States" would be presented before categories or sites that only matched on "United States."

Exact Phrase Match   Only categories and sites that match the keyword exactly will be returned. For example, an exact phrase entry of **art** would not return "arts" or "artistic" as would happen in a default keyword search.

Matches on All Words   Returns must include all words entered. This is equivalent to the boolean AND statement.

Match on Any Word   A category or site will be returned if it matches on any one word entered. **United States** entered as a match on any word search could possibly return sites about the "United Arab Emirates," the "United Auto Workers," etc.

FUN YAHOO! FEATURES

Looking for something new or nifty on the Web? Yahoo! has a handful of collections that can point you on your way:

Today's Web Events `http://events.yahoo.com/`. Almost anything live on the Net is listed here! Events can be as varied as professional sports broadcasts via RealAudio, celebrity interviews in text-based chat rooms, and concerts in full video.

Weekly Picks `http://www.yahoo.com/picks/`. The Yahoo! Surfers see a lot of sites during the course of their workdays. Each week they pick a handful or two to shine the spotlight on. Want to have them delivered right to you? Subscribe to their pick of the week e-mail newsletter!

Random Yahoo! Link `http://random.yahoo.com/bin/ryl`. Don't care where you end up? Enter this URL and be swept away to a site randomly selected from the entire Yahoo! database.

continued ▶

My Yahoo! `http://edit.my.yahoo.com/config/login`. Want to build your own custom Web directory, get headlines, stock updates and weather reports? Create your own Yahoo! here.

Yahooligans! `http://www.yahooligans.com`. Yahoo! for the pre-teen set. A collection of sites intended for Web surfers 7 to 12 years old.

 TIP

Keywords can be specifically excluded as well. A search on California could be entered as **California –Southern** to exclude entries for Southern California. The minus sign (–) should be typed immediately preceding the word to be excluded.

To select a search option other than the intelligent default, click on the Options link immediately to the right of the search submit button. An expanded search interface will be presented to you, with radio buttons for each search type and select controls that allow you to narrow your search by when a site was added to the database and to adjust the number of returns presented per page.

Submitting to Yahoo!

The process of adding a site to the Yahoo! database begins with a submission from a user, most often the Webmaster or an individual associated with the new site. To submit your site to Yahoo!:

1. Locate the most appropriate subcategory for your site within the existing Yahoo! categories. Remember that commercial sites must be placed within the Business and Economy section.

2. When you've located the subcategory that best matches your site, click on the Add URL icon at the top of the page. You'll be taken to a Web page that asks you to confirm that you've selected the most appropriate category for a site that isn't currently in their database.

3. Click on the Proceed To Step One button to begin the submission process.

4. Enter a title for your site, such as Widgets, Inc.; the URL; and a brief description of the site. Yahoo! requests that your description use 25 words or less, avoids repeating the title or URL, and is as informative as possible. Use the Submit button to proceed.

5. The next step allows you to suggest additional categories that would be appropriate for your site or even new categories that you feel would better serve sites like yours. Entries here are not required. When you are finished here, click submit.

6. Provide contact information as requested. Use the submit button to proceed to the final step in the process.

7. Fill in the blanks to describe whether your site deals with time-sensitive information. Examples are a Web site dedicated to a governmental election, an annual arts festival, or other activities that won't continue to be supported past a given date. You're also given the opportunity to make additional comments to the Yahoo! staff. Click this last submit button, and you're done!

Now the process continues at Yahoo! Their staff of Yahoo! Surfers will visit the site to confirm your choice of categories and to determine if additional placements are warranted. Because a real human reviews each submission, it can take some time before new sites appear in the database. Turnaround times of several weeks are not uncommon.

 NOTE You should be aware that Yahoo! reserves the right to decline submissions as well as the right to edit descriptions or change categories. Web designers should not guarantee a listing with a client or supervisor.

AltaVista

AltaVista, found at `http://www.altavista.digital.com/`, originated in 1995 as a project at Digital Equipment Corporation's Palo Alto Research Lab to index the entire Internet. An integral part of the success of the experiment was the development of *Scooter*, AltaVista's souped-up spider. More than just a robot following a single trail of links across the Web, Scooter was programmed to be *multi-threaded*. Multi-threading allows a computer program to tackle more than one task at a single time. Scooter's talents made AltaVista's collection of information about millions of individual Web pages possible in very short amount of time. The AltaVista index now consists of over 60 gigabytes of data connected to the Web via powerful Digital AlphaServers.

AltaVista Site Details

Submission method	Via the form located at `http://www.altavista` `.digital.com/av/content/addurl.htm`.
Robot name	Scooter.
Indexing method	Indexes page titles, keywords, and descriptions provided through META tags or the content of the page itself.
Adherence to Robots Exclusion Standard	Yes.
Search Methods	Natural language queries, keywords, special search functions.

Searching on AltaVista

AltaVista's index allows you to search through documents found on the Web or in Usenet newsgroup archives by using keywords from over twenty different languages. They recommend you begin with what they call *natural language queries*. A natural language query is performed by simply typing in exactly what you're looking for. If you want to answer the question "What is the population of the United States," just type that in and click the search button. If your question was phrased succinctly, the Web pages returned will likely be relevant.

A query using just the keywords "population" and "United States" produced identical results on the first page of returns.

Excluding or Including Search Criteria

You can require or exclude specific words by using the plus (+) and minus (–) signs. For example, if you wanted to search for information about World War II and specifically about the war as it pertained to France, you could enter **World War II +France** which would require all returns to include France in the results.

Exclusion works the same way. To search for Web pages about dogs but not Chihuahuas, you would enter **dogs –Chihuahua** to exclude those short, nervous-looking animals.

Specialized Search Syntax

Just over a dozen special functions are available for searches. Sites can be located based on domain name, titles, pages that have *linked in* to a specific domain, and much more. Table 10.1 outlines the more commonly used functions.

TABLE 10.1:   Special Functions for AltaVista Searches

Function	What It Does
link:*URL*	Compiles all sites that contain hyperlinks to the specified URL. For example link:http://www.foo.com displays all sites linking to http://www.foo.com or any subdirectories and individual pages.
image:*filename*	Search for images by complete file name (logo.gif, etc) or search for characters included in a file name. image:logo would return matches on logo.gif, logo.jpg, or any other image file name containing the string logo.
anchor:*text*	Searches for instances of the specified string being wrapped in a hyperlink anchor. A search on anchor:Click here produces over 130,000 matches!
domain:*domainname*	Locates Web sites within the desired domain. A search of domain:fr would return all French sites.
title:*text*	Hunts for Web pages with the specified text contained within their TITLE tags.

A Few Peculiarities

A few practices peculiar to AltaVista:

- Keywords containing upper-case letters will be *case sensitive*. If you want case *insensitive* searching, use all lower case letters.

- To return all forms of a keyword (discuss, discussion, discussed, etc), use the asterisk symbol (*) as a wildcard entry: discuss*.

- Enclose phrases in quotation marks if you want the phrase evaluated as a single word. For example, you could enter **"United States"** instead of **United States**.

Additional help on advanced AltaVista search topics can be found online at http://www.altavista.digital.com/av/content/help_advanced.htm.

Submitting to AltaVista

All submissions to the AltaVista index can be made from one location: `http://www.altavista.digital.com/av/content/addurl.htm`. The staff asks that you submit only one URL. Because Scooter the spider will be sent out to index your site and follow all the hyperlinks contained within it, it's not necessary to submit each individual page—Scooter will find them on its own.

More Popular Search Engines

There are literally hundreds of search engines available on the Web. Many strive to cover much of the entire Web as Yahoo! and AltaVista do, while others, such as the Internet for the Fine Arts directory or EuroSeek, concentrate on specific fields of interest or geographical collections.

To find the best places to list your new site, consider searching for additional search engines!

TIP   Want to see how five of the top search engines rated against each other in a test designed to count relevant search returns? Visit `http://neal.ctstateu.edu:2001/htdocs/websearch.html` and look at the results gathered by reference librarians at Central Connecticut State University.

PAID SUBMISSION SERVICES

With the explosive growth of Web based search engines, submission "services" have sprung up all over the world. These companies, for a fee, will submit your site to a number of search engines for you, relieving you of what can be a time consuming task.

Sounds great, doesn't it?

There are a number of legitimate businesses offering these services. Whether the cost of those services represents a value to you is an individual decision. However, there are companies out there that make claims that would be very hard—nay, impossible—to accomplish, at any price.

continued ▶

Skill 10

Beware the company that claims to guarantee placement within a search engine or directory. As you've learned, some services have staff review all submissions and reserve the right *not* to include sites. No company can guarantee inclusion in such instances.

Also hesitate if a firm claims to be able to guarantee a high placement within a search engine. Web developers can increase their chances of being located and returned in relevant searches through the proper use of META tags, carefully constructed site descriptions, and well-written HTML. But No company can guarantee that its customers will always come up in the top 10 or even top 100 sites returned on searches.

Have You Mastered the Essentials?

Now you can...

- ☑ Explain what a search engine is.
- ☑ Create a *robots.txt* file to control robot access to your site.
- ☑ Perform searches using Yahoo! and AltaVista.
- ☑ Submit your site to search engines.

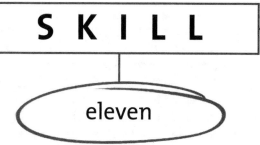

SKILL

eleven

Validating Your Work

- ❏ What is a validator?

- ❏ Using the Kinder, Gentler Validator

- ❏ Using Weblint

- ❏ Interpreting the results

One of the most important concepts you could take away from this book is the understanding of what makes HTML *valid*. In Skill 3 you learned about the DTD—document type definition—that sets the "grammar" rules for HTML. The process of validation ensures that your markup hasn't broken any of those rules. Rather than simply being nit-picky, following all the rules for your selected DTD greatly increases your chances of the Web page being seen exactly how you intended by *as many* users on *as many* different platforms in *as many* different Web browsers as possible.

Remember the cross-browser cross-compatibility concept introduced back in Skill 1? Validation is compatibility in action. HTML markup that doesn't conform to the rules set down in the DTD introduces an element of uncertainty into the display equation. That equation takes your markup, adds the Web browser's programmed response to expected markup syntax, and results in the final display. Factor in unexpected markup—the element of uncertainty— and the browser doesn't necessarily have a preprogrammed response ready. It must begin to "think" on its own and alter the display to how it has decided you really intended it. Consider the success that spell-checkers have within word processing programs. Sometimes they suggest the word that you meant— and sometimes it seems they pull the suggestion out of a hat. Validation virtually eliminates the chance that the browser will need to guess in this manner.

There are two major types of validation services: *heuristic* validators and SGML-based validators. In this context, heuristic means that the validator searches through your HTML files looking for errors and for constructs that are valid but are considered poor form. SGML-based validators parse the files according to the strict rules of SGML (refer back to Skill 1 for a discussion of SGML and its impact on HTML).

Both types of validators have their advantages. Heuristic scanning can pick up omissions such as the lack of HEIGHT and WIDTH attributes within an IMG tag or skipping from a level 1 heading <H1> to a level three heading <H3>. SGML-based validators don't make assumptions about your stylistic choices but do strictly interpret the structural integrity of your documents. In the next sections we'll take a look at two validators: the SGML based Kinder, Gentler Validator and the heuristic validator, Weblint.

Submitting an Error-Free Page for Validation

Of course, we all hope that our HTML is error-free from the start. Let's take a look at the messages our two validators return for an HTML page that's been written correctly.

The Kinder, Gentler Validator

The Kinder, Gentler Validator—or KGV, located at `http://ugweb.cs.ualberta .ca/~gerald/validate/`—was created by Gerald Oskoboiny in August of 1995 as a means for the lay HTML author to be able to validate their markup and understand the results of the analysis provided. Previous tools based on SGML parsers provided error reports, but most of them did not have user-friendly interfaces.

Let's revisit a complete HTML file that we saw in Skill 8:

form3.html

```
<!DOCTYPE HTML PUBLIC "-//W3C//DTD HTML 4.0 Draft//EN">
<HTML>
<HEAD>
<TITLE>Tech Support Request Form</TITLE>
</HEAD>
<BODY BGCOLOR="#FFFFFF" TEXT="#000000">

<FORM METHOD="post" ACTION="http://www.webgeek.com/webgeek-cgi/formhandler.cgi">

<INPUT TYPE="hidden" NAME="Form" VALUE="Tech Support Request Form">

<P>Please provide the following:
<P>
<TABLE BORDER="0">
<TR>
<TD>Name:</TD>
<TD><INPUT TYPE="text" NAME="name" SIZE="30"></TD>
</TR>
<TR>
<TD>Email:</TD>
<TD><INPUT TYPE="text" NAME="email" SIZE="30"></TD>
</TR>
<TR>
<TD>Telephone:</TD>
<TD><INPUT TYPE="text" NAME="phone" SIZE="15"></TD>
</TR>
</TABLE>
```

Skill 11

```
<P>Please describe your computer system:

<P>Which platform do you use?

<INPUT TYPE="radio" NAME="OS" VALUE="Windows"> Windows
<INPUT TYPE="radio" NAME="OS" VALUE="Mac"> Mac
<INPUT TYPE="radio" NAME="OS" VALUE="Unix"> Unix

<P>Hardware (please mark all components present on your machine)

<P><table border=0>
<tr>
<td>
<INPUT TYPE="checkbox" NAME="hardware" VALUE="sound"> Sound Card<BR>
<INPUT TYPE="checkbox" NAME="hardware" VALUE="mouse"> Mouse<BR>
<INPUT TYPE="checkbox" NAME="hardware" VALUE="trackball"> Trackball<BR>
<INPUT TYPE="checkbox" NAME="hardware" VALUE="scanner"> Scanner
<td valign=top>
<INPUT TYPE="checkbox" NAME="hardware" VALUE="printer"> Printer<br>
<INPUT TYPE="checkbox" NAME="hardware" VALUE="CDROM"> CDROM<BR>
<INPUT TYPE="checkbox" NAME="hardware" VALUE="tape"> Tape Back-up device
</td>
</tr>
</table>

<P>How much RAM is installed?

<SELECT NAME="ram">
<OPTION VALUE="8mb"> 8 MB
<OPTION VALUE="16mb">16 MB
<OPTION VALUE="32mb">32 MB
<OPTION VALUE="64mb">64 MB
<OPTION VALUE="128mb">128 MB
</SELECT>

<P>Please describe the problem thoroughly:

<P><TEXTAREA NAME="problem" ROWS=6 COLS=70></TEXTAREA>

<P><INPUT TYPE="submit" VALUE="Submit"> <INPUT TYPE="reset" VALUE="Reset">

</FORM>

</BODY>
</HTML>
```

In order to validate a Web page using the KGV, the page must be available online so that the Validator's CGI scripts can retrieve it. We placed `form3.html` online and submitted it for validation using the form found on the main KGV Web site (see Figure 11.1).

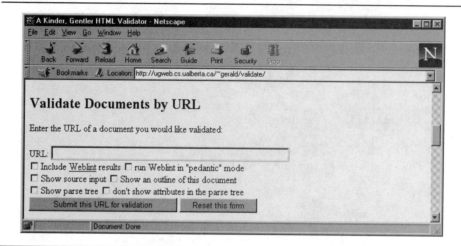

FIGURE 11.1:   The Kinder, Gentler Validator interface

This file does indeed validate to the HTML 4.0 DTD. If you submit the file for validation, KGV will present you with a page similar to the one seen in Figure 11.2, announcing that no errors are found on the page and congratulating you on the successful validation of the file. KGV will also give you instructions for including the HTML 4.0 Checked! icon that KGV makes available to sites that have validated their pages.

Weblint

The heuristic system known as Weblint—found at `http://www.cre.canon.co`
`.uk/~neilb/weblint/`—can be accessed through one of several Web based interfaces or installed locally if you're running one of the supported platforms. Details on compatibility and installation can be found on the main Weblint Web site.

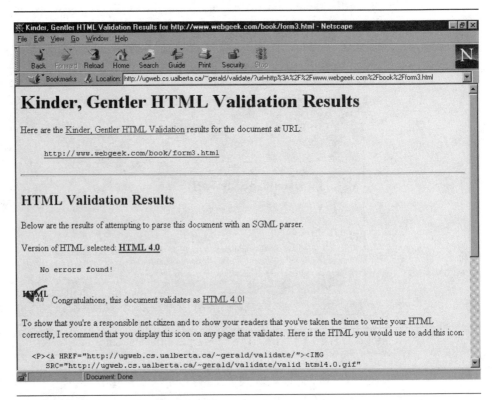

FIGURE 11.2:   A successful validation

Interpreting Reports of Errors

In order to see the validators in action, let's take a look at a file that contains a few basic errors.

error.html

```
<!DOCTYPE HTML PUBLIC "-//W3C//DTD HTML 4.0 Draft//EN">
<HTML>
<HEAD>
<TITLE>Validation Test Page
</HEAD>
<BODY BGCOLOR=FFFFFF TEXT="#000000">
```

```
<H2>This is a test</H2>

<P>This is <I>only</I> a test.

<H3>Had this been an actual HTML emergency</H3>

<P>Would <FONT COLOR="blue">YOU</FONT> be able to fix it?

<BODY>
</HTML>
```

The Kinder, Gentler Validator

When this file is uploaded to the Web and submitted to the KGV, it returns the results seen in Figure 11.3.

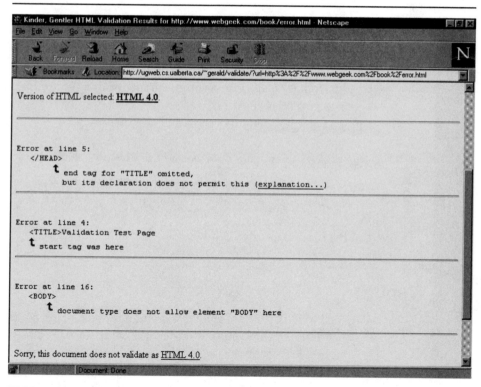

FIGURE 11.3:   Error output produced by the KGV

The first error reported by KGV is a reminder that the closing tag is required for the TITLE element:

```
"Error at line 5:
    </HEAD>
           end tag for "TITLE" omitted but its declaration does not
  permit this"
```

If you look down at the next entry, which points us back to where we opened the tag, the problem becomes even clearer:

```
"Error at line 4:
    <TITLE>Validation Test Page
    start tag was here"
```

Compare these two error statements with lines 4 and 5 of the source file:

```
<TITLE>Validation Test Page
</HEAD>
```

With the TITLE element, it's pretty easy to see where you began something. However, in complex HTML documents, such as those with nested tables, it could be difficult to immediately pick out which tag wasn't closed properly. That extra hint from the validator becomes very helpful in those situations!

The final error reported says:

```
"Error at line 16:
    <BODY>
           document type does not allow element 'BODY' here"
```

If you look back at line 16 of the error.html file, you can see that what *should* be there is a closing tag, </BODY>, not the opening tag, <BODY> that was typed instead.

Did the Kinder, Gentler Validator pick out all the mistakes in error.html? Let's take a look at what Weblint has to say about it.

Weblint

Using the Weblint interface available on the Kinder, Gentler Validator site, we can get additional comments on the error.html file. Figure 11.4 and Table 11.1 show the results.

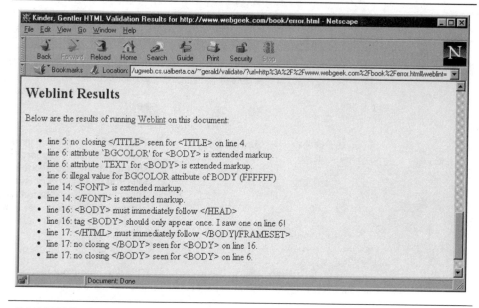

FIGURE 11.4:   The report compiled by Weblint for error.html.

TABLE 11.1:   Error messages returned by Weblint for the file error.html

Error Message	Meaning
line 5: no closing </TITLE> seen for <TITLE> on line 4.	This is a more concise reporting of the error that KGV caught: the closing TITLE tag is missing in the error.html file.
line 6: attribute `BGCOLOR' for <BODY> is extended markup. line 6: attribute `TEXT' for <BODY> is extended markup.	When Weblint says something is *extended markup*, it's warning you that the tags may include "browserisms" or markup that won't be supported by all browsers. Both of these attributes are supported in the HTML 4.0 Draft DTD, so they can be safely ignored.
line 6: illegal value for BGCOLOR attribute of BODY (FFFFFF)	This is a catch that KGV didn't make. Do you remember how hex colors are supposed to be handled? They must have the hash mark "#" preceding them and be contained within quotes. "#FFFFFF" would be correct.

Skill 11

TABLE 11.1 CONTINUED: Error messages returned by Weblint for the file error.html

Error Message	Meaning
line 14: <FONT> is extended markup. line 14: </FONT> is extended markup.	The FONT tag is allowed in HTML 4.0, though stylesheets are encouraged instead. This is worthy of a mental note, but it's not truly an error.
line 16: <BODY> must immediately follow </HEAD>	The last five lines were generated by the same error, that <BODY> appeared where </BODY> should on line 16 of the file. The first message tells you that <BODY> must come immediately after closing the HEAD container. Because the error message references line 16, you can tell immediately that you have a stray BODY tag in your markup.
line 16: tag <BODY> should only appear once. I saw one on line 6!	This line points out that only one BODY tag is allowed, and it tells you where the first one was located—on line 6.
line 17: </HTML> must immediately follow </BODY|/FRAMESET>	This message reminds you that a closing </HTML> must immediately follow the closing tag, </BODY>. The </HTML> in our file was found before a closing </BODY>.
line 17: no closing </BODY> seen for <BODY> on line 16. line 17: no closing </BODY> seen for <BODY> on line 6.	The next two messages alert you to the fact that a closing BODY tag is missing for not one but two instances of an opening BODY tag. These messages are a double alert that something is wrong.

Strategies for Success

From the results seen using both the Kinder, Gentler Validator and Weblint, it's clear that a single tool won't always be the best way to look after your work. The heuristic tools such as Weblint can pick up the stylistic issues regarding markup that, while technically valid, will create problems for some browsers.

Most Web designers make use of at least two validation tools to give themselves the most assurance possible that they've constructed quality Web pages. In addition to the two validators described in this skill, quite a few more online and offline validators are available for your use. A few more include:

Validator	Where to Get It
Doctor HTML	`http://www2.imagiware.com/RxHTML/`
WebTechs HTML Validation Service	`http://www.webtechs.com/html-val-svc/`
CSEE 3310 HTML Validator	`http://htmlvalidator.com/`
Dr. Watson	`http://www.addy.com/watson/`

Have You Mastered the Essentials?

Now you can. . .

☑ **Decide what kind of validator to use.**

☑ **Use KGV or Weblint to review your work.**

☑ **Interpret the results of the validation process.**

Skill 11

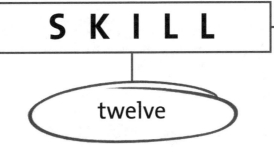

SKILL

twelve

Using Server Log Analysis, Cookies, and Surveys to Learn About Your Audience

❑ Why learn about the audience?

❑ Deciding whether to purchase additional software

❑ How Web servers work

❑ Understanding log analysis

❑ Creating state with cookies

❑ Using surveys

There are many reasons to know more about the people using your Web site and how they are using it. In this skill, we'll go over some ways you can gather useful information and some reasons you might want to. Information about attracting and retaining visitors is contained in Skill 21.

Reasons to Know Your Audience

It's important that you think of your Web site as a valuable resource for distributing information to your audience. For this reason, it is important that your Web site targets the people you want, especially if you are using your Web site to promote a business. Skill 21 goes over a lot of information about how to get the audience you want. However, there is a whole other side to the coin—finding information about your audience and how they use your site. This information can range from the impersonal, such as whether a particular page is ever looked at, to the much more personal, such as shoe size. As you'll see, there are different ways to gather information: some are automatic, and some require audience participation.

Knowing your audience as well as possible benefits both you and the audience:

- You can target your Web site toward the demographic you want.

- You can learn how people navigate your site and move pages accordingly.

- You can find out when your site is most and least busy.

- You can get valuable comments from people browsing your site, which allows you to correct confusing elements or update outdated information.

- You can ask your customers if they are interested in receiving further information, for example from a mailing list. You can use the mailing list to send out further announcements.

- You can keep track of which Web pages browsers come from. This means you know which links and banner ads are most useful. (You can see a banner ad in Figure 12.1. In this ad, US Robotics has put a banner on CNET's Web site. As customers click the banner and go to the US Robotics site, the US Robotics server tracks who came from CNET.)

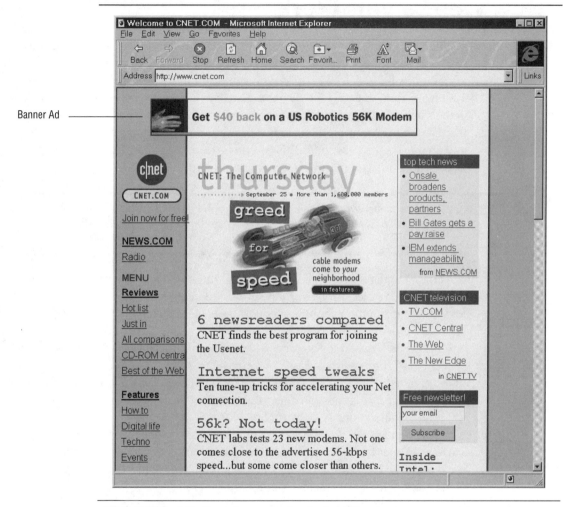

Banner Ad

FIGURE 12.1:   An example of a banner ad

Additional Software

Much of the Web server log analysis and automatic data entry of information into databases requires additional software, most of which must be run on the servers that are actually serving your Web pages to the world. Therefore, your ability to get the information depends on whether your systems administrator or your ISP will allow you to run additional software.

How Web Servers Work

When you request a page by typing a URL or following a hyperlink, a message gets sent to the Web server telling it which page to send back. In the case of dynamically generated pages (you can think of these as pages that are generated from a database on the fly), there are extra steps involved, but the concept is the same: The browser tells the server what to send back so the browser can display the information the user has requested, whether it's text, images, Java, and so on. The browser does this by converting your action (clicking or typing a URL) into a GET command—a type of command that tells the server to get data.

 NOTE   Browsers and servers "talk" to each other by using a common protocol (you can think of it as a language). The protocol used is *hypertext transfer protocol* (HTTP). URLs that begin with http:// use hypertext transfer protocol.

At the time the server receives the GET command, it logs the request in one or more server log files. Along with the information about what it sent out, the server logs other information about the request (see *Log Analysis*). Each GET command is recorded as a *hit* to the server.

Servers can be used to forward information to other programs; for example, a server could forward the results of a survey to a database. Servers can write bits of data, called *cookies*, to a user's hard disk (see *Using Cookies to Create State* later in this skill). Servers can also perform other functions, such as providing encrypted connections and restricting access to documents.

In addition to serving data and logging requests, Web servers can perform a variety of other tasks. They can forward information to other programs such as databases and they can write bits of data, called *cookies*, to a user's hard disk (see *Using Cookies to Create State* later in this skill). Web servers can also provide encrypted connections and can restrict access to documents.

Log Analysis

Web servers generate logs that contain records of server activity. A limited amount of information is contained in these logs, but more information can be mined by using additional (often commercial) software on the server. These software products work closely with the server and keep track of infomation and statistics that are not normally recorded in the server log files. They can also be used to analyze the large amounts of data contained within the log files themselves for easier analysis by people.

The information you can find out will depend on which type of software you decide to use and also what your server is configured to log by itself. First we'll take a look at a typical server log, and then we'll examine other possibilities for gathering data using analysis software.

 NOTE   Most log analysis is done using software. It would be difficult to analyze more than a very small sample by hand.

Server Logs

Remember W3, the folks who brought us HTML standards? They also set other types of standards, including a common log format for servers that use HTTP (Web servers). A server log is simply a text file, and the server adds data to it as it serves pages. The location of the text file on the server will depend on the server being used. Once it has been located, it can usually be read using a text editor. The log file consists of lines and lines of data, and they can be very tedious to read through. Every time there is a GET request to the server, it records a line of data in the log file. For this reason, many people never look at the server log files themselves. Instead, they use software that either reads the log files and enters the data into a more useable format such as a database, or they purchase software that never looks at the server log but instead records the same data as the log, but in a more useable format.

 NOTE   Remember, servers can be configured to record different types of data.

Below is a generic line of data from a common format server log. It is important to note that this line of data represents a hit to the server. Remember, while most people use software to sort this type of information rather than reading it directly, this example shows you how to understand a server log if you want to get the data it contains without any additional software. The generic log below shows the order in which items appear in an entry in an example log file. That is, the first item in a line from the file is the remotehost.

remotehost rfc931 *authuser* [date] "*request*" *status bytes*

Here is a line that contains sample data:

```
home.netscape.com rfc931 acorn [01/Sep/1995:16:29:02 -0400] "GET /
    contact.html HTTP/1.0" 200 1765
```

It is possible to make a direct correlation between the generic line and the sample line, as shown in Table 12.1.

TABLE 12.1:   Server logs

Generic Server Log	Example Server Log	Meaning
remotehost	home.netscape.com	Remote hostname (or IP number if DNS hostname is not available or if DNSLookup is Off. DNSLookup is a way of looking up IP addresses to find out which domain they are associated with). This data can be used to find out the domain names of visitors.
rfc931	rfc931	RFC931 is a protocol for identifying users. In this case, the RFC931 protocol has been used to specify the fomat of this field.
authuser	acorn	The username with which the user has authenticated himself if the server has been configured to ask for a username and password.
[*date*]	[01/Sep/1995:16:29:02 -0400]	Date and time of the request. (The 0400 is the timezone of the server, as an offset from GMT.)
"*request*"	"GET /contact.html HTTP/1.0"	The request line exactly as it came from the client. This is an HTTP command, as indicated by the HTTP/1.0 note.
status	200	The HTTP status code returned to the clients. Status 200 simply means the file was sent successfully to the requestor.
bytes	1765	The content-length of the document transferred, in bytes.

MORE ABOUT HTTP COMMANDS

The "request" sent to the server from the user's browser is an HTTP command, meaning that it uses the hypertext transfer protocol to communicate with the server. The three types of commands commonly logged by servers are "GET", "HEAD", and "POST".

"GET" is the one we have been talking about—it's what the server logs when a browser "gets" a page from the server. A "HEAD" request is commonly logged when a robot from a search engine checks to see if a Web page still exists. We'll go over this more in Skill 21. A "POST" command is usually logged when someone submits information by filling out a form on the Web site.

Here are some types of data about your audience that that can be gleaned from server logs.

- Type of browser
- Operating system
- CPU type
- Service provider
- What Web site a visitor came from
- IP address of a visitor

NOTE   An IP address is a numerical representation of a machine's address on the Internet. When you are on the Internet, your machine automatically has an IP address. Depending on your method of accessing the Internet, this number may be the same every time you log on (a static IP address) or different (a dynamic IP address). Domain names such as sybex.com are really just representations of IP addresses and are used because people deal better with domain names than with long strings of numbers.

Log Analysis Software

The server log example and the bulleted list above show many of the types of data servers track automatically and include in their log files. Most of the time, people want additional statistics, and that's where other pieces of software enter the picture. As mentioned before, these programs can be used not only to gain additional statistics, but also to analyze the data automatically stored in the server logs so it is more useful for people. There are literally hundreds of these packages designed to analyze traffic on your Web site, and many of them have features such as:

- How many pages were looked at by each user (average)

- When someone comes from a new domain that's never been to your site before

- The times when your site is most and least busy

- An estimate of the number of unique visitors

- The path people follow through your site

- Which pages are most and least viewed

- How many registered users

- How much time people spend reading each page

These programs vary greatly in complexity and cost. If you are in a position to have the server administrator install software for traffic analysis, by all means consult with him or her when deciding what to use. You can see a sample interface for Accrue's analysis software in Figure 12.2.

When deciding whether or not to purchase log file analysis software, there are a few key factors to consider. The first thing to do is to determine which statistics you are interested in measuring. In larger companies, there are often two main categories of statistics: those needed for marketing purposes and those needed for technical purposes. Statistics for marketing purposes might include information about site traffic, how visitors navigate through the site, and whether or not a new image makes more people follow a particular link. More technically oriented statistics might include information about server speed, slow scripts, and how much load the server can handle.

Once you have determined the types of data you would like to have, the process differs, depending on whether you (or your company) maintain your own server or whether an ISP hosts your Web site.

You Have Access to the Server

If you or your company maintains the Web server, the next step is to examine its capabilities. Earlier in this skill, you reviewed a list of the items most server log files contain for each hit on the server. Many servers also keep track of other data. These server functions vary between servers and are added as additional features to provide incentive for purchasing the server.

Once you have determined the difference between what you would like to measure and what the server automatically measures, you have a list of what performance you need from additional software. The idea is to not purchase software that duplicates the functionality of the server.

For example, Netscape's Enterprise Server, in addition to handling the basic statistics, also provides a summary analysis of which browsers visitors are using. So, if you wanted that information and you were using the Enterprise Server, it would be pointless to purchase additional software.

The Web Site Is Hosted by Someone Else

If the Web site is being hosted at an ISP, they will often provide statistics for it. However, these are generally pretty basic statistics, such as the number of hits that the site has received. A better option, and one that you should look for in an ISP if detailed statistics are important, is to be able to download the logs to a local computer and run log analysis software there.

If you plan to do this, make sure to purchase log analysis software that does not need to be installed on the server in order to work. This also applies even if the server is not hosted on an ISP's server but is hosted on a company server that you do not have access to. In this case, a request should be made to the Webmaster for the log files.

There are several popular programs for Web site analysis. Accrue, from Accrue Software (http://www.accrue.com) is shown in Figure 12.2. Another popular program is Analog, from the University of Cambridge Statistical Laboratory (http://www.statslab.cam.ac.uk/~sret1/analog/). Analog is popular, fast, and is available on many platforms. Another popular program is NetIntellect (http://www.webmanage.com/netintl.html). If the Web server is a Macintosh, a good tool to try is LogDoor (http://www2.opendoor.com/logdoor/).

Skill 12

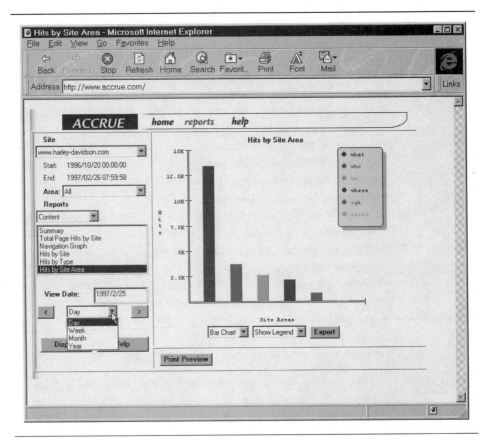

FIGURE 12.2:   An example of server analysis software

Limitations

Despite all of the information that can be gathered about Web site visitors, there are many limitations to what you can definitively know. Here are some issues you should be aware of.

Number of Hits versus Unique Visitors

The easiest way to think of hits is to think of them as the number of items a server sends anything out. So, if the server sends out a page which has two graphics on it, then the server sends out three items—the HTML page and the two images—

and logs 3 hits. The number of hits to a Web site can be misleading if it is interpreted as the number of pages served. Rather, it is a representation of the number of *files* served, including image files.

This can be contrasted with the number of distinct users, another measurement which tracks the actual number of people coming to the Web site. This number, while it can be more difficult to obtain, is a more accurate representation of the actual number of people who visit your site. The number of unique visitors to a Web site is best determined using analysis software, whether this is additional software or is a feature of the server. The software will look at duplicate IP addresses and remove the duplicates for all the hits in order to arrive at a unique number of visitors. Remember, IP addresses are the unique numbers associated with a machine at the time it is connected to the Internet. For a server that is even slightly busy, removing all duplicate IP addresses is a task impossible to do efficiently by hand. Even with software analysis, it is possible to get only an estimate of the number of unique visitors, for the reasons explained below in *IP Mix and Match* and *Caching*.

IP Mix and Match

There are problems with IP numbers, which is the main way servers keep track of the comings and goings on Web sites. For each hit, the server also keeps track of the IP address to which the data was sent.

Many service providers have a pool of IP addresses assigned to them. What this means is that as users log on, the system assigns their computers IP addresses, which identify them for that particular session. When they log off, someone else gets the IP address. The next time a user logs on, they will be assigned a different one. This makes it difficult for you in a couple of ways. First, if a particular IP address returns to your site, it may not be the same user—it could be a different person who uses the same online service provider. That would mean that while you thought one person had visited your site, there were actually two.

The opposite can also occur. A person who has come to your Web site using one particular IP address may return the next time with a different one. In this case, you thought that two people have visited your site, when actually it was only one. While this may not seem like a big deal, if you have a fairly popular Web site, this system of dynamic IP address assignment can affect the calculated numbers of unique visitors and return visitors to a Web site.

However, having static IP addresses is not a guarantee of accurate audience data either. Consider the problem of people who use more than one machine, and the machines that are used by more than one person. Many people now have Internet-connected computers both at work and at home. They may come to your

Skill 12

site from work and then again once they get home, resulting in skewed data because, based on the different IP addresses, it appears two different people have come to your site. Or consider a machine which is shared by members of a family, a workgroup, or students in a computer lab. While you're thinking that the same person keeps returning to your site, they are actually all different people. Crazy, huh?

This is one of the big reasons that some Web sites have begun using registration for users. Registering for a Web site usually involves choosing a user name and a password and then using those to gain access to the site whenever you return. Usually, when you try to follow a link that requires registration, a dialog box asking for the username and password pops up on the screen. Once the correct username and password have been entered, access to the site is granted.

Registration is usually free to the user and provides a huge advantage to the publishers of the Web site—they can keep track of users much more easily. Of course there will be the occasional people sharing logins and passwords, but if the site makes it easy to register, people will likely get their own. The only drawback is that the site may lose the users who are reluctant to register, even though they can use any name.

If your server logs only IP addresses, then you will have to do a lookup to be able to correlate the IP addresses with a domain name. This can be somewhat helpful, but keep in mind that you may not get too much information if you find out that the domain is a large service provider. It might be helpful if you notice a lot of hits from a particular company, though, or if you are interested in knowing if your competitors are coming to your site.

Caching

You may or may not be aware of caching. Broadly defined, caching is the process of storing files on a computer so that they do not have to be retrieved from the original server every time they are viewed. Often files are cached on your own computer. Suppose that you visit a page and the contents of the page get stored on your computer. You click a hyperlink and go to another page. When you use the Back button on your browser to return to the original page, it is loaded from the cache on your hard disk, not from the server. This saves time because accessing a file from a local hard drive is faster than retreiving it again from the Web.

 TIP   You can set the size of the cache on your hard disk. Once the cache is full, the browser will remove data from the cache to make room for the new ones. In Navigator, you can do this in the Network Preferences section under the Options menu. In IE, you can go into the Preferences under the Edit menu and set the cache size under the Web Browser Advanced options.

There's a second type of caching where the pages are stored not on your hard disk but on an intermediate computer, usually belonging to the service provider. This intermediate server is called a *proxy server*. Service providers such as AOL use proxy servers to provide a faster turnaround time for requests. So, in this case, if another user requested a page earlier in the day, the page is stored on the service provider's proxy server. When you request the page later in the day, the page is served from the proxy server—the service provider's computer does *not* send an HTTP GET command to the original server.

Caching can result in inaccurate server statistics. You don't know how many people would have hit your server to get information but got it served from their service provider's computer instead. You also don't know if someone has come back to your home page repeatedly if the page is being served from a cache on their computer.

 NOTE Caching is not necessarily a bad thing. It allows users to download data such as graphics and to use them over and over again without having to request them every time they are used. It allows faster access and takes up less bandwidth on the Internet. But, it does affect your ability to get accurate numbers.

Using Cookies to Create State

You've seen some of the factors that can make it difficult to know your Web site audience. Some factors you really have no control over, such as numerous people using one machine. Another factor over which you have no control is the fact that HTTP is inherently stateless. This means that each time a computer makes a request to a server, the server fulfills the request by sending data and then closes the connection between the computer and the server.

For example, when a visitor comes to a page, the server sends the requested files to the visiting computer and then closes the connection. When the visitor follows a links to another page, a new connection is opened and the new files are sent through that connection. To the visitor, it appears that the connection to the server is always open, but in reality this is not the case. This method of delivering files allows Web servers to handle a greater number of requests since they don't have to keep connections to other computers open while no data is being sent. The disadvantage is that the server does not really remember anything between

Skill 12

the connections. If the situation was applied to two people talking back and forth in turn, the problem would be that each remembered talking to the other, but could not remember the last sentence. It would be pretty difficult to talk that way, because there would be no state, or continuity. Another way to think of state is to think of it as persistence. State can be a desirable thing for a Web site manager. By providing state, a server can keep track of a user, whether it is the same visit or a return one. Reasons to use state are numerous, and examples include having the ability to place the user where they last left the Web site, and keeping track of items they order from a company. You may have seen the Web sites where customers can browse the site, choosing items to purchase before proceeding to an area to pay for all the purchases at once—the ubiquitous "shopping cart" metaphor. This is possible only because a state has been provided—otherwise, the server would forget the items chosen on one page when the next page was requested. Basically, state is helpful anywhere continuity between server requests is needed on the Web.

Cookies are used to allow the server to store information about the connection between the server and the visitor's computer. This information is stored on the user's hard disk in a plain text file. Simply put, cookies are small amounts of data written to the cookies file by the server. The cookies file is not the cookie itself—the bits of data written to the cookies file are the cookies. The contents of the cookie depend on the server and the circumstance, as does the length that they stay in the file. Sometimes the data stored in the cookie is returned to the server that wrote it.

 TIP   The name of the file depends on the browser and the platform you are using. If you'd like to see your own cookies file, do a search on your hard disk for "cookie" and view the file in a text editor such as Notepad or BBEdit.

The Information Stored in Cookies

Cookies can store all kinds of information. Sometimes, the cookie is just a reference, and the actual data is stored in a database on the server side. Examples of information could include login, shirt color preference, last page viewed on the site, and so on. Figure 12.3 shows a sample cookies file.

Let's take a look at the second line from the sample cookie file. Table 12.2 analyzes what is meant by each field of the cookie. Fields within a cookie are separated by Tabs.

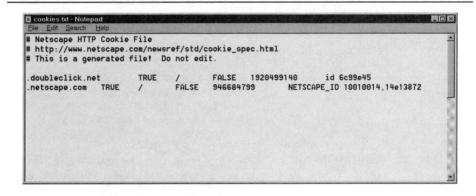

FIGURE 12.3: A sample cookie file

TABLE 12.2: Understanding cookies

Value in the Example	What It Means	Field
.netscape.com	The domain name of the site which created the variable defined in the cookie. This is also the only site which can read the variable.	domain
TRUE	This true false means whether or not all the machines that are within the domain can access the variable. This means that www.netscape.com and home.netscape.com, for example, can both access the cookie.	flag (TRUE/FALSE)
/	This is the path for which the variable is valid. Try thinking of it as a directory structure. / means that the cookie is valid for all the pages in the domain.	path
FALSE	This is another flag. It represents whether or not the connection needs to be secure in order to access the variable. An example might be if the variable is a credit card number.	secure (TRUE/FALSE)

Skill 12

TABLE 12.2: Dissection of a cookie

Value in the Example	What It Means	Field
946684799	The server can set the expiration date for the cookie. It is later converted from GMT into Unix time. Unix time is the number of seconds since 12:00 am on 1/1/70. Using Unix time, this cookie will expire in the year 2000.	expiration
NETSCAPE_ID	This is the name of the variable. This is set by the programmer and is hopefully descriptive. In another example, it might be something like SHIRT_COLOR.	name
10010014.14e13872	This is the actual value of the variable. If the variable were SHIRT_COLOR, the value might be BLUE.	value

Cookies can be used to enhance the user's Web experience. Using the shopping cart metaphor, it is much more convenient for the user to not have to purchase each item separately, but instead select all of the items and then purchase them all together at the end. Some companies currently have Web sites that can be customized so that when the user comes to the site, they see information like the weather in their current area and stock market quotes for their favorite stocks. Certain banking institutions allow banking online, and a lot of the customized information is stored in cookies. Cookies can also store information so that users don't have to fill out an address everytime they want to order new products from a site. Their use is only limited by your imagination.

Cookie Security

There has been a lot of concern in the past about cookies, mostly because they are made by writing data to the user's hard disk. There have also been concerns about whether cookies can grab data from a user's hard disk and send it back to the server.

First, let's take a look at the aspect of writing to the user's hard disk. Servers can only write to the cookie file. While there may be more than one file associated with cookies, they are all text files. Text files are harmless to computers—they cannot contain viruses. The only information servers can write to the cookie file is either supplied by the server (such as the expiration date of the cookie) or by the user (such as their favorite shirt color). In most cases, if the user supplies any information, it is the value of the variables. The cookie cannot contain any personal information unless it is supplied by the user.

Next, let's examine the sending of data from the hard disk back to the server. Only data that is in the cookies files can be sent back to the server. Not only that, but a server can only get data that it has written. All in all, some users may find that they are uncomfortable with having their movements tracked on a Web site or with recording their personal preferences. While this is a valid viewpoint, it is important to realize that cookies are not inherently *insecure*.

Why Use Cookies?

There are many reasons to use cookies on your Web site. As mentioned above, they allow you to create a state so you can find out more about your audience.

One of the most common examples of the use of cookies is the "shopping cart" metaphor mentioned previously. If you are not familiar with the metaphor, the idea is that a user can browse through a Web site, going from page to page while adding items to a shopping cart. The mechanism for adding items to a shopping cart is usually via a shopping cart button. Finally, when the user is ready, they can "check out" and pay for the items all at once. Without cookies, there would be no state, and there would be no way for the server to "remember" what the user had chosen while moving around the site. If a cookie is set, though, the cookie can be used to associate data—the cookie is the common element that is used as a reference as the user moves throughout the site.

Another commonly used example is that of product preferences. For example, a user might go to a site to purchase software. The cookies for the site could keep track of what type of computer the user has, the operating system, the amount of RAM in the computer, and the user's credit card number. Next time the user goes to order software, that information is already there. The credit card number is sent over a secure connection. Note, though, that the server did not just grab this information—the user had to deliberately enter it.

Using cookies can enhance your users' experiences, in addition to allowing you to keep better track of them. Depending on the data the cookies contain and how much data a Web site manager is willing to gather, it is possible to a lot about visitor preferences. Provided the user gives this information, it is possible to correlate demographic data such as region with color preferences, or age with musical tastes.

Writing Cookies

Writing cookies generally takes some knowledge of programming that is beyond the scope of this book. Cookies may be written in many ways—for example, the shopping cart can be written in Java, JavaScript, C, or other languages such as Perl.

Cookies can be written by either the visitor's computer (the client) or the server. Clients cannot write cookies to the server, but they can write cookies to their own cookies file that can be read by servers. Servers on the other hand, can write cookies to clients and to servers. The most common scenario is to have the server write a cookie in the client's cookies file. The most common way to do this is to insert a *Set-Cookie header*, which means that the server sends additonal information to the client when the client makes a GET request. A generic Set-Cookie header would look like this:

```
Set-Cookie: NAME=VALUE; expires=DATE; path-PATH; domain=DOMAIN_NAME;
    secure
```

The programming part comes in when this information is sent to the client, because it is not sent manually. Usually, a program is written (like a CGI script) which autmomatically gathers the information and sends it. For example, a Set-Cookie header from Microsoft might be:

```
Set-Cookie: NAME=msuser; expires=Friday, 30-Jan-98 12:00:00 GMT; path-/;
    domain=microsoft.com; secure
```

A program is used to get the information about the username, the domain, and so on.

A separate program is used to handle the cookie when the user returns to the site. When a browser comes to the Microsoft site, the browser checks the URL that the user has chosen (microsoft.com) and tries to match it to the different URLs in the cookies file. If the user has come to the site before, and a cookie was set, then the browser will locate that cookie and send it to the server so that the server now has the cookie information readily available. How the server uses the cookie information depends on the contents of the cookie.

Browser Support for Cookies

Navigator began supporting cookies with 1.0, and they are supported in all subsequent versions. The same is true for IE. Lynx has some limited support of cookies. The browsers do differ in their support of cookies, which is why you should be careful not to rely on them more than you have to.

As newer versions of browsers have been released, the user has been given more and more control over the treatment of cookies. For example, the earliest versions of Navigator did not give the user any choice—all cookies were accepted. In the latest version, users can decide if they want to be warned before accepting a cookie, if they want to reject all cookies, or if they want to accept all cookies. They can even decide if they only want to accept cookies which are sent back to the original server. The latest version of IE offers users a similar choice.

SENDING COOKIE DATA TO OTHER SERVERS

Sometimes a server other than the one that originated the cookie is sent the cookie data. Only a server that has written a particular cookie or a server *specified by the server* that has written the cookie can read the cookie data.

Cookies are still very secure because most Web sites do not want other sites to know the data of cookies set by them. This feature is almost exclusively used for marketing purposes, where a Web site might collect cookie data and send it to a marketing firm rather than analyze it themselves.

Users were becoming annoyed with the idea that their cookie data was being sent directly to marketing firms, so Netscape added this option of only accepting cookies which were set to be returned to the originating server. This hasn't really fixed the problem from the user's point of view because now marketing firms simply set up their servers to have the same domain name as the site the user is on. That is, the user may visit the domain foo.com, and the server which gathers the cookie data for the marketing firm might be marketing.foo.com, even though the people at foo.com don't really have anything to do with that machine—they have simply given permission to the marketing firm to use that name. Provided that the cookie is set up to be valid for the path /, the user's machine will accept all of the cookies as if they were returning data to the original server. (See Table 12.2 if you don't remember how the path works.) Cookies can be disabled in ways other than simply turning off the preferences. Deleting the cookies file or making it "read-only" will also work.

Skill 12

The important thing to realize here is that users may choose to browse your Web site without cookies. Other users may have browsers that do not support cookies. It is in everyone's best interest if you rely on cookies as little as possible. That is, you should feel free to use cookies, but you should provide alternatives for those users who are not enabling cookies in their browsers. This may mean that the user has to re-enter credit card information every time they make a purchase, or they may have to purchase items one at a time. Be sure to make this as easy as possible for them.

Surveys

Just as they work in more traditional marketing practices, Web surveys can be an effective way to get to know your audience. They have some of the same problems as traditional surveys, along with some new twists. But, they also have advantages. We'll look at the different aspects first, before we move on to the actual implementation of surveys.

Online Surveys versus Offline Surveys

In a lot of ways, online surveys are the same as offline ones. Mainly, they are both used to gather customer/user data. This can include information about who they are, their preferences, comments about your Web site or your product.

You want to motivate people to take them. This doesn't change simply because the survey is online. Perhaps people want to feel that they have input, or maybe they will receive a discount for filling out your survey. You may not have to provide a lot of motivation, as most people will automatically fill out forms if they are given. You also need to be concerned with your sample—how representative is it of your audience?

One of the best differences between online and offline surveys is that the user inputs the data electronically. This not only saves paper, it also saves you from entering all of the data from a paper form into a database. It can be a huge savings in data entry expenditures, both in terms of time and money. Users are also more likely to respond to questions when you make it easy for them, and many times, there is no easier way for people to provide feedback than by just clicking some buttons. Online surveys often have higher response rates than more traditional ones in which people have to use traditional mail to send in their responses.

You can also have the data almost immediately, rather than waiting for the user to fill out the paper form, drop it in the mail, and then for someone to enter the data electronically. Depending on the software (more on this in *How to Make a*

Survey, below), the user may be able to get instant feedback. For example, a survey respondent might choose his favorite soft drink, and after submitting the results, find out which percentage of people chose the same drink.

One of the challenges of conducting an online survey is that people do not always behave the way we expect them to, and computers are not often smart enough to understand what a person actually means if they do something other than what the computer expects. When data is collected by people, they can handle problems such as missing data, extra comments, and misspelled words. If the data is entered by the user, is submitted electronically, and is parsed into a database without ever being seen, there can be problems with data integrity. If you as for a person's occupation, for example, and they accidentally type **cemist** instead of **chemist**, they will not turn up later when you do a search for "chemist." If the data had been seen by a person, they would have had the opportunity to correct the error when the data was entered.

There are some things you can do to make the data as sound as possible. First, you can show the user the data before it is submitted. Forms can be set up so that after the user fills in the information and clicks a button, a new Web page comes up which shows the exact information about to be submitted. The user can return to the previous page and make corrections in the form if there is an error. Once everything is correct, the survey can be submitted.

There is another method for increasing the likelihood that the data will have as much integrity as possible. When the user submits information from a survey, the Web server doesn't actually deal with it. It passes it to another program, called a Common Gateway Interface, which deals with the data. Although the program will be different, this is the same concept as the CGI needed to write cookies. The server can "contract out" work it can't handle, such as writing cookie data and inputting data from forms. It sends them to a CGI. CGIs can be written in many different programming languages. This is covered in greater detail in Skill 8. The important thing to note here is that the better (read: more complicated to write) the CGI is, the more errors it can catch. For example, in order to show your audience what they are about to submit once they have filled out the form, you would use a CGI.

Another option is to have the only available answers to questions provided for a user. If you're not careful, though, you can end up with some pretty vague data. Following our occupation model, you might have a pulldown menu or buttons which say Chemist, Physicist, and Mathematician. You might provide an option labeled Other for people who do not fall under any of these categories. This is where you have to be careful, though. If a lot of your users select Other, you're not going to know what a lot of them do. This type of option works best when you know you have a limited number of correct answers, such as age ranges or state of residence. Providing as many of the possible answers for your audience cuts down on data entry errors. After making the survey available, if you find that you have too many "Other" responses, you might want to go through those responses and make the most popular "Other" answers into real survey answers. This is another example of the benefits of online surveys—they are much easier to change than paper ones.

A common survey format is to have all of the questions be answered by check-boxes or radio buttons, and then at the end allow one area for the user to write any additional items.

How to Make a Survey

So surveys are great, and you want to make one and get to know your audience a bit better. There are a couple of ways you can go about it, so read on!

Forms

Using forms is probably the most common method of conducting an online survey. If you need more information about setting up forms, you should read Skill 8. Once the survey is filled out, the information is submitted when the user takes an action, usually clicking a button labeled something like Submit or I'm Done. The information is submitted to the server, which passes it to a CGI script.

Depending on the sophistication and features of the CGI script, a lot of different things can happen to the data from there. The data might be checked for errors, or it might be put into a database. It might also be sent in an email to someone who reads it and then maybe enters it into a database. There are many possibilities—they just depend on what your CGI is written to do. CGI programming is beyond the scope of this introductory book, but it is possible to have someone else write a CGI, or to purchase one. There are even free ones.

 TIP   Even if you get a CGI script, you still need access to the server in order to have them running. If your Web site is hosted by an Internet service provider, check with them—ISPs will often let you use their prewritten CGI scripts which perform common functions. Most ISPs will not let you run your own scripts for security reasons.

Online Survey Services

One of the newer ideas to come along is the online survey provider. An online survey provider lets you set up surveys on the provider's site and takes care of all of the CGI scripting necessary. To your audience, it appears that they are still on your Web site, but they are submitting their survey results to the online survey provider. You can view the results of the survey by logging onto the survey provider's Web site with a login and password. The advantage, of course, is that you can set up more sophisticated CGI-based surveys without needing to program everything. This is a pretty new idea, so you may not have seen it before. For an example, you can check out SurveySez! at http://www.surveysez.com/, also shown in Figure 12.4 below.

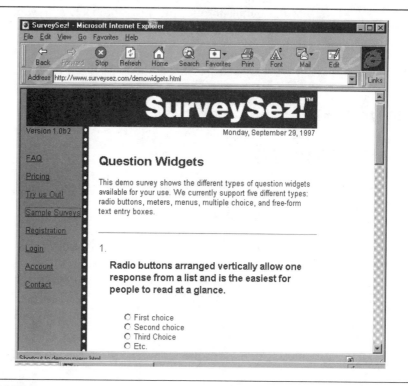

FIGURE 12.4: SurveySez!, an online survey provider

E-Mail

For various reasons, you may decide that you don't want to deal with forms at all. In that case, it's best if you provide at least an e-mail link so that users can provide feedback to you that way. When they click the link, they will be able to send an e-mail to the address you specify. You can use the following HTML to make a mailto link to *you@yoursite.yourdomain*:

```
If you have comments, please send mail to
<a href="mailto:you@yoursite.yourdomain"> you@yoursite.yourdomain</a>.
```

Of course, you should replace *you@yoursite.yourdomain* with the real e-mail address you'd like your audience to send email to. It's good to provide this e-mail link on every page, probably at the bottom. People appreciate the ability to give feedback easily.

All browsers support forms and mailto links.

Have You Mastered the Essentials?

Now you can. . .

- ☑ Plan your use of log analysis, cookies, and surveys.

- ☑ Analyze information from server logs.

- ☑ Use cookies to enhance the user experience.

S K I L L

thirteen

Planning the Design of Your Web Site

❑ Identify, identify, and identify some more!

❑ Developing a look and feel

❑ Establishing design constraints

❑ Planning your Web site

❑ Tying it all together

With your HTML skills honed to a fine edge, you're anxious to get started building your Web site. But, where do you start? In this skill, you will learn the steps necessary to design an effective Web site.

It's time to push back from the computer, pull out a pad of paper and a pen, find yourself a comfortable chair, and roll up your sleeves for a serious analysis and planning session. Design is a step-by-step process guides you through choosing what materials to present, how they should look, and how to structure your Web site.

Identify, Identify, Identify!

Effective design results in the successful communication of your message to your intended audience.

While this sounds simple, consider that your message will be one of many messages available on the Web. People are saturated with information from the Web, e-mail, postal mail, newspapers, commercials, billboards along the side of the road, and even the back of the morning milk carton! How do you make your message the one that will get your audience's attention and response?

The first step to an effective design is to identify three things:

- What do you want to say?

- Why is your information needed?

- What do you want people to do as a result of what you have told them?

With these questions answered, you are well on your way to developing an effective design that will accomplish your mission—to communicate your message.

What Do You Want to Say?

Identifying your message may sound obvious, but this is where many Web sites fail. How often have you visited a Web site that was confusing in its message? You weren't sure if the site was promoting a product, trying to inform you, or just wasting your time. How long were you willing to stay and figure out what the author was trying to communicate? Did you ever go back to that site again? And the most important questions: Did you respond to the Web site in any tangible way? Did you e-mail or phone for more information? Did you take out your credit card and buy anything?

When people visit your Web site, they need to be able to quickly recognize your message and be interested enough to stay and learn more and respond to your message. By identifying what you want to say, you're on the way to getting your message delivered.

Web sites usually serve one or more of the following purposes. Use this list as a guide to help identify your purpose, step one in developing your Web site plan.

Purpose	Common for This Type of Organization
To inform or educate	universities
	schools
	charitable foundations
	non-profit organizations
	government
	businesses
	political organizations
	personal homepages
To entertain	magazines
	e-zines
	galleries
	museums
	media clubs
	organizations
	personal homepages
To market, sell, or persuade	businesses
	political organizations
	non-profit organizations
	universities
	schools
	personal resumes

It's very likely that you will have several purposes. In fact most Web sites serve a couple of purposes: "To inform people about my company and to persuade them to purchase my services and products," is a typical statement of purpose.

Now it's time for that pad of paper. Jot down just what it is that you want to tell your audience. This doesn't have to be a lengthy description; in fact, a simple sentence describing your purpose would be ideal. If you need to write multiple sentences, that's fine.

Skill 13

NOTE Not For Profit organizations usually have multipurpose Web sites. Typically, an NFP has a multipurpose mission statement that includes a requirement to disseminate information about their purpose, as well as soliciting memberships, donations, and offering other opportunities to their membership and the public. While this makes for a complex site plan, prioritization of the Web site's purpose will simplify your project.

Why Is Your Information Needed?

The key to capturing your audience's attention is to understand why they need or want to know the information you are presenting to them. By focusing on the audience's needs, you make the planning process easier for yourself and make the resulting Web site more likely to interest your audience.

Make a list of all of the reasons that someone would want to learn more about your message. For example, will it:

- Solve a problem?

- Make them feel good?

- Get them involved?

- Tell them something they don't already know?

- Save their life or their families' lives?

- Give them an opportunity to realize a dream?

- Show them a new way to do something?

- Raise their consciousness?

- Expand their horizons?

The list above isn't meant to be all-inclusive but a starting point for your own list. Remember, your audience is being bombarded with demands for their attention and at best is indifferent to your message. Recognize their indifference and analyze their need for your message.

TIP If it's possible, prioritize the reasons your audience needs to know your message as you jot them down. Perhaps your product will solve a problem, is good for their health, and also costs substantially less than your competitor? Which selling point is more likely to get your audience's attention? Prioritization now will make your job easier later when you develop a site structure.

Now that you have identified what you want to say and why it is important to your audience, you're ready to get to the next step of determining just what you want your audience to do when they receive your message.

What Do You Want People to Do?

So, for a moment, let's assume that you have designed this great Web site and that people are flocking to it and getting excited about your message. Quick! They are focused on your message, here's the opportunity to have them act, but you need to decide what you want them to do. Grab that pad of paper again for making more lists.

Some of the possible actions your audience could take:

- Send you e-mail for more information.
- Fill out an order form.
- Phone you to purchase a product or service.
- Complete a survey or application form.
- Write a letter.
- Call their political representative.
- Vote.
- Volunteer.
- Join a mailing list.
- Send fan mail.
- Return to your Web site on a periodic basis.

It's extremely important to identify what you want your audience to do as a result of your message. It's likely that you want people to take several of the above actions as well as others not listed. Be sure to note all desired outcomes and, if possible, prioritize them in your list.

 TIP   Feedback from your Web site is often very useful. While a Web site statistics program can tell you the number of hits and how much time visitors spend viewing your site, nothing provides you with better perspective than the quick e-mail from a visitor. Be sure to make it easy for people to drop you a note to let you know what they think of the site and perhaps make suggestions for improvements. This topic is covered more fully in Skill 21.

Develop a Look and Feel

Now we get to the exciting part: designing the look and feel of your Web site. Your online image should support your message and invite your audience to receive that message. Without the appropriate image, your message may never be read, your visitor may glance at the site and move on to the next. Finding your "look and feel" is a matter of creativity and (yes, you guessed it) planning.

Portraying an Appropriate Image

We're not talking about political correctness here, rather the appropriate match between message, image, and audience. You encounter messages every day that strive to get your attention via a look and feel. Consider the hard edge feel of many blue jeans commercials on TV; the escapist images presented by a bubble bath; the fast-paced, party themes of soft drink commercials. Each of these advertisements sets a strong mood.

Figure 13.1 shows The Beer Info Source, a Web site devoted to "the seekers of fine brews." This site is informational and offers the visitor comprehensive information about beer and the brewing industry.

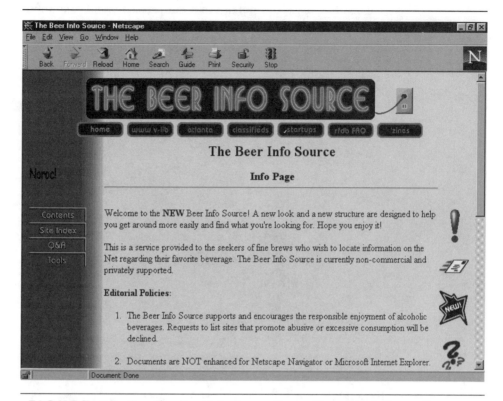

FIGURE 13.1:   The Beer Info Source (http://www.beerinfo.com/)

The designer has chosen to present the information by using a neon signs theme to evoke the feeling of a bar and nightlife. The site's logo is "plugged in" a reference to the electronic nature of the information. Icons and navigation buttons continue the fun theme of the site using the neon look and bright colors, while providing an intuitive menu for the audience to explore the more than 100 page site. An animated text line—the common toast, "Cheers!" in various languages—appears on every page, again complementing the theme of fun and celebration.

Figure 13.2 presents Northwestern University's Web site which offers the visitor a wide variety of information, from admissions to concert schedules. The designer has selected a photograph of landmark buildings on campus viewed against a blue sky, implying "the sky is the limit at Northwestern." The conservative rugged brick spires evoke a feeling of stability, age, and achievement. A graphical text menu encourages the audience to visit the various sections of the site. The site feels well organized, conservative, and hints at upward mobility, an image universities typically portray.

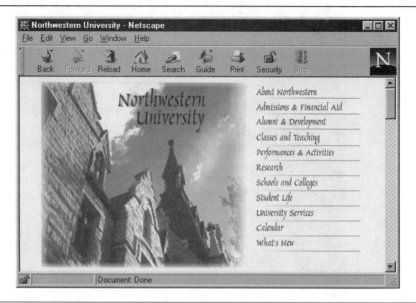

FIGURE 13.2:   Northwestern University (http://www.nwu.edu/)

W. D. Little Mortgage Corporation's Web site is presented in Figure 13.3. This is a commercial site representing a mortgage brokerage in Metro Atlanta. The site uses a gas lamp and navigation buttons disguised as street signs to give a period feeling to the site evoking longevity, stability, and old-fashioned good service. The marble logo implies affluence, desirable in a financial institution. On the *splash page*—the term often given to a short concise entry point to a Web site— the audience is invited to contact the mortgage brokerage by e-mail, telephone, or fax to discuss their service needs.

Presenting your information with a look and feel complementing your message is essential to evoke a mood to engage your audience. People make decisions both consciously and unconsciously based upon their emotions. One of your jobs as a designer is to create an image for your Web site to evoke the appropriate emotion in your audience to best communicate your message.

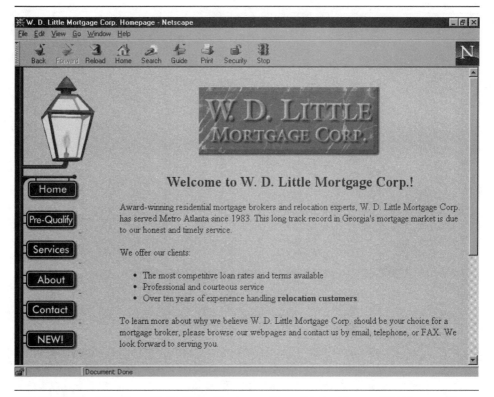

FIGURE 13.3: W. D. Little Mortgage Corp (`http://www.wdlittle.com/`)

WHAT *IS* INAPPROPRIATE?

Inappropriate can't really be defined by a hard and fast rule—it's subjective and based upon your message. The easiest way to illustrate an inappropriate image for the message is by example:

A travel agency promoting island vacation getaways is unlikely to publish full color photographs of run-down neighborhoods or communities. These photographs would be inappropriate to a message of tropical relaxation.

continued on next page ▶

Skill 13

A financial institution offering investment opportunities is probably not going to use the phrase "Go For It!" to encourage people to invest in a high-risk fund. Financial organizations usually use conservative images, fonts, and words to promote a feeling of security and deliberate decision-making. A whimsical approach is unlikely to encourage investment.

Another inappropriate image would be a governmental Web site using a photograph of their chief executive standing in front of a limousine or yacht purchased at taxpayer expense. This would be a negative message to the site's audience.

Visioning and Free Association

Is there a way to get that message across to them quickly? Does your company name say it? Can you say it in a headline? How about one word? One image? It's time to do some free association to find the best ways to deliver your message.

Visioning isn't difficult, you do it unconsciously all the time. When you're driving home from work and imagining dinner on the table, when you make your holiday gift list, when you think about your vacation plans: these are all examples of visioning. You think about the event or the subject and develop images in your mind related to the topic. You can almost smell the dinner, see the smiles of loved ones opening presents, and feel the wind in your hair and the freedom from regular routine. Now it's time to apply this daydreaming to designing your Web site.

For example, pretend you are designing a Web site for a travel agency specializing in tropical vacations. What images and feelings come to mind?

Blue oceans, tropical flowers, sailboats, relaxation, parrots in trees, palm trees, adventure, hot sun, white beaches, water rushing up to shore, shells on the beach, romance, tropical punch, exotic food, outdoor torches at parties....

The above list provides many ideas for selling travel services. You can appeal to people both emotionally and visually by using the images conjured up by that list. Imagine the colors involved for a tropical vacation: the hot pinks and oranges of the flowers, the cool greens in the palms, and the serene blue of the ocean.

There are a number of images that could be used as graphical elements throughout the Web site: perhaps a parrot as a guide to various destinations? A conch shell as a bullet point?

Photographs of sailboats against an azure sky generate a feeling of adventure. The romantic would identify with a photo of a candlelit table set with a bowl of exotic fruit and a bottle of wine. And what is more enticing than the image of people relaxing in the sun on an endless white beach?

ANALYSIS OF TROPICAL ESCAPES WEB SITE

In the graphic below, some of the ideas we listed in this section are turned into a design concept for a hypothetical Tropical Escapes Web site. While much remains to be done to improve this Web site for actual publication on the Web, you can already see that a theme is established.

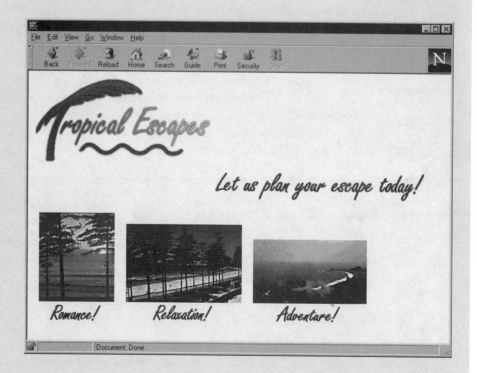

continued on next page ▶

Skill 13

It didn't take much to set the theme. The palm tree used as the letter "T" in the logo enhances the feeling of the tropics in the company name. The blue curvy line below the company name evokes water. The blue text "Let us plan your escape today!" triggers an emotional response of "Yeah!" (We all want to escape.) The photographs of tropical scenes enhance the emotional appeals printed below them: Romance, Relaxation, Adventure. If a tropical vacation is a likely possibility for the Web site visitor it will be hard to resist exploring this site further.

We will return to this site in Skill 14 to make some improvements and additions to this Web site draft.

Visioning is an excellent way to gather impressions, ideas, and feelings about your subject. As you vision, take notes and don't be analytical about your ideas. The analysis comes later after you've captured all of those free-flowing ideas on paper. First jot down as many as possible, then go back to some of those notes and expand on them individually with more free-associating. This is an effective way to come up with some excellent ideas for your look and feel.

Once you have your list, analyze it for common themes. Are there strong emotional concepts? Do clear images come to mind to illustrate these? Can you translate these concepts into a headline or copy for your Web site? You're on your way to finding the right image for your site.

NOT ALL IDEAS ARE POSITIVE

In your list of ideas were there some negatives that you came across as well? Are these negative concepts something that is likely to occur to other people as well? If you can answer "yes" to this, you may have found a "feature" to add to your Web site to help distinguish yourself from the competition!

continued on next page ▶

For example, in the previous travel agency example, you could have also thought about the hassle of organizing travel visas and passports. No one likes to deal with red tape, especially when they are dreaming of their vacation!

One option for the hypothetical travel agency would be to provide a service to help solve red tape easily. They could offer a list of phone numbers and addresses on the Web site, the same list could be offered via e-mail if the visitor submits their e-mail address, or perhaps an agent could call with advice in exchange for a phone number being sent via e-mail. Each of these are excellent "hooks" to make your audience feel welcome and bring them back again!

Review Your Competition

Another way to help identify an effective image for your Web site is to visit your competition's site and do a little market research. Knowing how they present themselves on the Web is an excellent way to learn from both their successes and their failures. After all, your competition is vying for the same audience that you are.

So, get yourself to a search engine (you learned about some of these in Skill 10) and track down your competition. Grab your pad of paper and get ready to make some notes.

When you visit each site, note the following:

- What is the message?

- What look and feel is being used? Is it appropriate to the message?

- What action do you feel compelled to take, if any?

- Is their message the same as yours? Does it have a different twist? Is there a negative to their message? Are they attempting to make themselves different from their competition?

- What tools or features are they using at the Web site? Graphics? Animation? Plug-ins? Sound?

- Are the features professionally executed? Do they support the site's message or do they confuse and distract?

Skill 13

- Are you still waiting for images to load after five minutes?

- Does the site offer anything unique? Is it useful? Were you interested enough to go deeper into the Web site to take a look?

- Is the overall presentation effective? Why or why not?

If your project isn't too obscure, there will likely be a variety of sites where you can see the different ways that your message has been handled previously. You can compare the different sites to each other and to the ideas that you have for your own Web site. Analyze sites that work and sites that don't work; both types have valuable information that you can use.

 TIP   As you visit each site, be sure to take note of commonalties in your competitors' sites. For example, are there always links to outside data, graphs illustrating some aspect of the information presented, testimonials, or whatever? If you notice common themes or presentation of information, you may have encountered an industry standard, formal or informal. This is especially valuable to know when planning your own site. If most of your competition presents information in a particular way, you need to understand why—even if you choose not to follow the convention.

Determine Design Constraints

Before launching into a detailed plan of your Web site design, it's important to define any constraints that you may have for your design. Developing your design while knowing any constraints will save you grief, time, and money later on.

Corporate Presentation Rules

Many business, especially large corporations, have a graphics standards manual or specification sheet which describes how their corporate logo, trademarks, and other proprietary marks may be displayed in print or other media. Typically, these specifications or rules are used to make it easy for people in different departments or even countries to provide consistent advertising and other corporate communications.

Obviously, not all businesses or organizations have this level of documentation or formality. However, there are often undocumented rules that smaller organizations adhere to by convention. Before you develop a design, it's a good policy to check existing materials for rules or conventions. In Skill 14 you will learn more about how to ensure conformity in your Web site design.

The following is a brief list of some questions you may want to ask:

Corporate colors   Does the business use a specific color? Often businesses have adopted a particular color, usually described as Pantone *XXX*, for the printing of all of their materials. Unfortunately, the color used by the business for print may not have a corresponding safe palette color. (You will learn more about this in Skill 16.)

Logo specifications   Does the corporate logo require a particular layout such as always appearing to the left of the page? Is it always sized proportionately to other graphical or text elements?

Trademarks   Are particular phrases always capitalized? Are product names trademarked? Are you using trademarks of other companies on the site?

Does the organization use a style manual such as the *Chicago Manual of Style*? The style manual will affect any copy you write by dictating grammatical structures, so be sure to check this one!

No existing image   Is the company brand new or do they desire a revised image for their Web efforts? Be sure to look over the previous section *Visioning and Free Association* for design ideas.

COPYRIGHT ISSUES

Copyright protects intellectual property created by a person or entity such as a corporation. This can include written materials, artwork, music, software, choreography, and other forms of expression. The concept of copyright is to protect the creator's or publisher's rights to ownership of their creation and from theft of those rights by others. This means that someone cannot use something that you created without your permission.

Web pages are copyrighted as soon as you save the text or the image to disk. While it isn't required by United States law, it is generally a good idea to actually mark your materials with a copyright statement. Typically, you would include at the bottom of your page the standard copyright symbol (©) along with the year of the publication, the name of the copyright holder, and the phrase "All Rights Reserved."

continued on next page ▶

Skill 13

If you are considering using artwork, an article, software, or other materials that you did not originate be sure to ask the copyright holder for permission to use the property. Publishing or using copyrighted materials without the author's permission can result in a lawsuit.

Additional information about copyright can be found at the following URLs:

The Copyright Web site (`http://www.benedict.com/`) This site is maintained by Benedict O'Mahoney and provides some excellent plain English information about copyrights, their use, abuse, and some sample case histories. There are especially good links to Web specific copyright issues.

10 Big Myths About Copyright Explained (`http://www.clari.net/ brad/copymyths.html`) This site is maintained by Brad Templeton of Clarinet and provides a good list of urban myths regarding copyright.

Copyright FAQ (`http://www.aimnet.com/~carroll/copyright/ faq-home.html`) Terry Carroll maintains what may be the most comprehensive document on the Net regarding copyright issues.

Budget Issues: Time and Money

Time or money constrain everything, including just how cool your Web site can be. Your Web site plan needs to include some budget considerations even if you are a volunteer site designer. After all, you really want to have time to do something else besides working on this Web site right?

While it's difficult to predict just how long it will take for you to design your first Web site, you can make some estimates of the time required to gather your materials, have images scanned, and other chores. If you are working with a client or for a large organization that needs to be involved in site review and approval, be sure to build some time into your development schedule to accommodate this process.

Also, try to make some assumptions regarding the long-term maintenance and updates of your Web site. If you are contemplating building a site that requires daily updates that cannot be automated, be sure to realistically estimate how much time you can allot for this and how you will handle sick days or vacations.

Few things look worse on the Web than a site that was designed for daily updates but hasn't seen an addition in three months.

Consider your Web site design from a financial perspective. What is it likely to cost you to keep your site up to date? Is your design sufficiently general that you won't need to redesign pages as you add information? Is your HTML so complex that it is difficult to make changes easily? Be sure to consider each of those questions before you write a single page: it's always far more expensive (and tedious) to have to rethink a design when you are fairly far into your project and perhaps very close to deadline.

If you are building a complex Web site and you're like most designers, you cannot personally create all features of your site. Perhaps you are a whiz at writing HTML but couldn't write a script or draw an icon if your life depended on it. You have a few choices:

- Use public domain graphics and scripts.

- Purchase the rights to use copyrighted images or software.

- Hire a subcontractor to provide you with original graphics or custom software.

Subcontracting is an excellent way to get high quality materials designed specifically for your needs, and it usually will save you time. If you choose to use a subcontractor or purchase rights to use copyrighted materials, be sure to include this in your budget planning.

RESOURCES FOR SCRIPTS AND IMAGES

There are excellent sources on the Web for scripts and graphics that are either in the public domain or available for a fee. Check out the following URLs:

- The CGI Resource Index (`http://cgi-resources.com/`)
- Matt's Script Archive (`http://www.worldwidemart.com/scripts/`)
- Realm Graphics (`http://www.ender-design.com/rg/index.html`)
- Rainfrog's Web Art (`http://www.rainfrog.com/webart/`)

Skill 13

Gather Your Existing Materials

OK, roll up your sleeves and get ready to dig into the serious business of planning. Here's where you get to see the shape of your site emerge from the lists you have made.

With your message defined, you will now determine the details of the information you will present to your audience. Remember: no matter how good your idea is, if it is poorly presented it won't communicate your message and may even be worse than having presented nothing at all. The key to successful communication is in the delivery.

Your mission is to locate all pertinent materials that will help deliver your message. This includes written materials, photos, artwork, videos, URLs for other Web sites, and anything else you may find helpful. Your goal is to assess your existing materials that could be used for the Web site.

Is there a brochure that tells your story well? Perhaps you could use the copy in the brochure as a draft of a company history page? With a little rethinking and copy changes, much of the copy in corporate brochures provides an excellent starting point for Web pages.

What about your organization's artwork? How much of it is already available electronically? And are existing photos or graphics appropriate for your site's message?

Examples of written content:

- Marketing materials (sales brochures, prospectuses)

- Fact sheets (parts lists, rate cards)

- Advertisements

- Press releases (flyers, posters, invitations)

- Curriculum guides

- Training materials (manuals, guides)

- Periodicals (newsletters, magazines, bulletins)

- Forms (order forms, surveys, applications)

Examples of images:

- Photographs (original images when possible))

- Artwork (logos, illustrations, icons, nameplates)

TIP

It is best to use original art, whether photos or artwork, whenever possible. Most images reproduced for printing, such as in a magazine or newsletter, have been *halftoned* (sometimes referred to as "screened"), a process that optimizes an image for viewing on paper.. The process of halftoning creates beautiful printed output; however, if you scan this printed piece to use as a Web image, you will see an ugly pattern of dots. This dot pattern is known as a *moire pattern* and is very difficult to remove without sophisticated image editing software.

Examples of other materials you could gather:

- Videos (a commercial, the company picnic)

- News articles (print, voice, Web, or video)

- URLs

- Reference materials

Get Selective

Now that you have your materials together, you can start the selection process. Review your collection keeping in mind your site's statement of purpose and your visioning exercise.

In some cases, existing materials aren't appropriate for the Web. For example local advertising flyers don't usually translate smoothly to the Web. However, there are likely elements in those flyers that could be used with some modification for the world-wide nature of the Web.

If you are designing a typical business Web site, you will likely have redundant information in your traditional materials. For example, your corporate brochure and product sales sheets may contain similar information about company history and background. In designing a Web site, you will want to provide this information only once. Hyperlinks make this very easy to accomplish.

Skill 13

 TIP

Less is more. These magic words will help you time and time again in the design process. Consider writing them on a sticky note and attaching it to your monitor. You need to walk a tightrope between providing your audience with sufficient information to make your point and boring them by repeating yourself. Web site visitors have a limited amount of time they are willing to spend reading your message. Take advantage of every second that your visitor is willing to give you!

Marketing on the Web is different from traditional marketing. You have limited real estate on your splash page to present your message. You don't have to say everything on your splash page; use hyperlinks to provide detailed information on subsequent pages. Think of your splash page as the storefront to your Web site. Use that storefront to encourage people to come inside your Web site. Your splash page should pique their interest and make them want to learn more about what you offer. Plan now to use that real estate effectively.

Do You Need to Do Research?

Is there anything missing from your materials that would strengthen your presentation? Perhaps it would be helpful to provide some basic data about your topic from an independent source? Do you need to do some market research on the people that purchase your product or service? Would it be useful to offer your audience testimonials about your product?

There are a variety of resources for obtaining research: industry publications, market research firms, your own customer service department, and of course the Web. Don't forget to check out the search engines as an excellent source for supporting information.

Do You Need to Provide Off-Site Links?

There are both advantages and disadvantages to providing off-site links. The disadvantage of having off-site links is that your visitor may leave your site before completely absorbing your message and acting on that message. The advantage of off-site links is that you can provide your visitor with backup information related to your topic without having to duplicate information that it is already available elsewhere on the Web.

It's a tough balance to choose which way to go or whether to compromise. This decision needs to be made carefully and is very dependent on your Web site's purpose.

Two common compromises on this issue:

- Provides off-site links only when the page linked to offers some bit of detail to assist in understanding the material you have provided. This compromise would include defining some rules such as "Never offer off-site links on pages that require the visitor to take some action such as filling out an order form." After all, you don't want to lose your customer!

- Provide a Links page with links to additional information. This assumes that your visitor has browsed your entire site and is still looking for more information and will leave anyway. Providing a collection of links at this point is a friendly assist.

Tying It All Together: A Case Study

The following is a short case study of developing the Oxalosis and Hyperoxaluria Foundation's (OHF) Web site. The foundation's mission statement reads: "OHF is committed to providing information, service, and support to patients and to families of those with oxalosis and hyperoxaluria and to the medical professionals who treat them." The foundation was formed in 1989 by parents of children affected with the rare disease hyperoxaluria. OHF has an international membership base and provides information and support to its members in a variety of ways: a quarterly newsletter, informational brochures, a support network of physicians, supportive people dealing with the same issues, and a toll-free phone number.

Most people learn about OHF when they are in crisis: their child (or, in the case of physicians, their patient) has been diagnosed with a life-threatening rare disease, and they need help immediately.

Site Planning Process

The OHF Web site must provide information to three general groups of people: laypersons who are often frantic and in need of immediate support, medical professionals seeking information about research and treatment methods, and medical researchers seeking information and grant funds.

A great deal of thought went into the planning of the OHF Web site. A previous volunteer Web site had been successful at attracting new members to the organization and providing people with much needed information; however it was out of date and needed additional data and services.

Site Purpose and Goal

OHF's mission statement served as a pretty clear site purpose: "To provide information and support to the people affected by the rare disease." OHF had some subsidiary goals that they also hoped to accomplish with the Web site: "To encourage financial support of the organization through a membership program and fundraisers and to solicit information from medical professionals via various surveys and grant applications."

Skill 13

Special Considerations

When the site planning process was conducted, OHF's past experience with a small volunteer Web site was considered. Analysis of the organization's membership indicated that the membership wasn't very Web savvy and that it tended to use older equipment and slow modems. Past e-mail to the Webmaster indicated that users were relatively new to the Internet and needed information presented simply with few bells and whistles.

Development of a Look and Feel

Producing a look and feel for the OHF Web site was a challenge. The information that they needed to provide to visitors wasn't especially visual. There are few appropriate images that come to mind to describe a rare disease. However, the site's purpose was to provide information, so the visioning process focused on images connected to presenting organized information to an audience unfamiliar with the Web.

A file cabinet metaphor was chosen for site navigation and graphical elements because most people are familiar with a typical office filing system for organizing information. The concept of each drawer being dedicated to a specific subject and containing related files is intuitive and easy to remember. The metaphor of adding "files" to the collection of information is easy to extend and therefore makes site maintenance relatively simple.

Implementation

The file cabinet metaphor was implemented by creating pictures of file cabinet drawers labeled with the name of each second level page of the Web site. These drawers appear on the left side of every page.

Figure 13.4 shows the Oxalosis and Hyperoxaluria Foundation's (OHF) splash-page. The non-profit's mission statement, displayed beneath the logo, clearly defines the site's purpose. On the left side of each Web page, a set of drawers present you with links to information that answer the following questions:

File Drawer	Questions It Answers
OHF Info	Who is this organization? What do they do?
Medical Info	What kind of disease is this? How does it affect people?

File Drawer	Questions It Answers
Member Services	What benefits are there in joining this organization?
Vision 2000	Why is the organization fundraising? How can I help? Do they have research grants?
Contact Us	Where are they located? Who can I ask a question?
What's New	I've been to this site before - is there anything new here?

File Drawers—

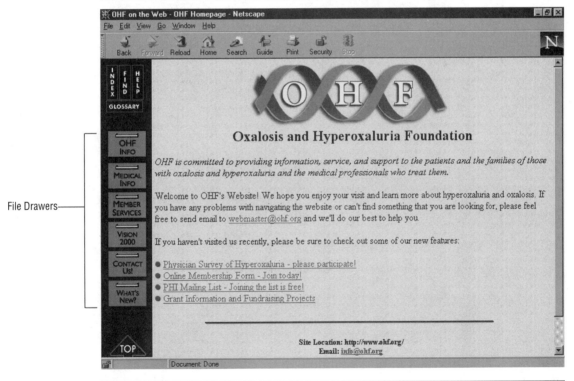

FIGURE 13.4:   OHF Website (http://www.ohf.org/)

The copy on the splash page welcomes visitors, encourages them to explore the site, and invites their questions via e-mail. Also provided are text links to pages contained within the site that may address a visitor's special interests that are not targeted on the navigation graphics. This area is designed to be easy for the Webmaster to change as the organization's needs change. One of the text links is to a physicians' survey. This online survey has been publicized in various medical journals and its placement on the splash page makes it easier for busy people to find.

Figure 13.5 illustrates the About OHF page, a second level page in the Web site. The file cabinet continues with a tabbed folder image at the top of the page. The navigation bar at the top of the page also offers graphical links to sections within the existing page. There are also separate folders that are links to third level pages within the site.

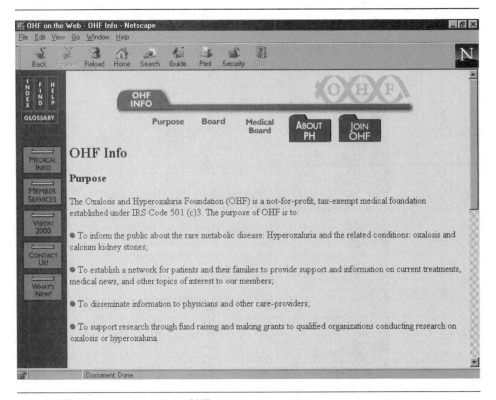

FIGURE 13.5:   About OHF

The file cabinet drawers on the left side of every page give the visitor the ability to jump to another section of the site, thus reducing confusion for inexperienced visitors. Additional navigational tools always appear in the upper left corner of each page. These tools lead to a site index page, a search page, a glossary, and a help page.

Conclusions

To meet the design goals of accommodating older equipment and slow modems, Alt text was generously used on all images so that non-graphical browsers and regular browsers running with images turned off still displayed links clearly. The site does not use animations, JavaScript, or other sophisticated plug-ins. A Perl script and a search engine are used on subsidiary pages.

To provide the quick support needed by patients and their families in crisis, the site offers the navigation graphics with links to medical information, member services, and the contact page. The needs of physicians and researchers are met with the same navigation graphics with the links to medical information and the contact page.

OHF's subsidiary goal of increasing their fundraising is accomplished by providing a page titled "Vision 2000". This page (still in development) offers a calendar of fundraising events and other ways for people to donate time, funds, and materials to support OHF's goals of research.

The OHF Web site design has been quite successful to date. The original design goals of providing information for patients and professionals has been accomplished. Traffic to the site has been steadily increasing, questions regarding location of information are negligible, and the interactive forms are being used by site visitors.

Have You Mastered the Essentials?

Now you can. . .

- ☑ **Write a statement of purpose for your Web site.**
- ☑ **Determine an appropriate image for your Web site.**
- ☑ **Use visioning to develop ideas for your Web site's look and feel.**
- ☑ **Analyze your competition's message and site design.**
- ☑ **Plan your Web site within budget and other design constraints.**
- ☑ **Evaluate a Web site design to determine if it meets the original design goals.**

Skill 13

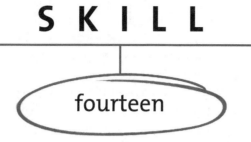

Effective Visual Presentation

- ❑ Applying basic art principles

- ❑ Designing images, graphics, and text

- ❑ Using grids

- ❑ Putting it all together

You've identified your message, developed your Web site's look and feel, and selected the materials you are going to use. Now, how do you decide where to place text and graphics for the best effect?

This skill will teach you how to achieve a unified layout and structure for your Web site. You will learn some basic art principles for presenting information visually, how to use a grid to simplify your layout decisions, how to maintain a consistent presentation throughout your site, and have a chance to look at some examples of Web sites that have "done it right."

Basic Art Principles: Art 101

Effective visual presentation doesn't just happen—it results from the designer's decisions about placing specific elements on a page. Whether you are designing a newsletter, an advertisement, or a Web page, you need to decide how to organize graphics and text to deliver your message in a logical and understandable manner. Although an experienced designer often makes these decisions unconsciously, the decisions are actually based on an understanding of how the human eye perceives elements and organizes them into information that the brain can understand.

In this skill, you will learn some art principles that you can use as a basis for making decisions about placement of elements on your Web pages—whether copy or graphical elements. These principles will help you develop an eye for analyzing the best way to present information visually for maximum effect and understanding.

Visual Unity

To understand visual information represented by a collection of graphical elements, you must be able to recognize a relationship among those elements— that is, some sort of whole pattern.

In Figure 14.1, you can see a collection of elements that at first glance appear to have no relationship. Your eye looks at each element, enjoys it, and then moves to the next element, much as you would view images in a scrapbook.

 NOTE   Several of the graphics from this skill are provided in color on this book's CD. You'll know which ones they are because we've included their filenames along with the figure captions. You can open the graphics using Navigator or IE (both are included on the CD)—just enter the file's path name in the place where you usually enter the URL. The figures for this skill are located in the graphics\Skill14 folder.

FIGURE 14.1: A scattered arrangement of shapes

After studying these elements briefly, you may notice that they are all geometric shapes—a square, a rectangle, a circle, and a triangle. But the relationship of geometric objects is an intellectual relationship—not a visual relationship. Your eye sees elements on a page, and your brain interprets them and defines them as shapes. There is no visual unity in this example, only intellectual unity.

Unity by Proximity

In Figure 14.2, the same shapes are visually related by proximity. Visual unity is achieved because your eye first sees the elements as a group rather than as a series of elements. The intellectual unity is still there, but the whole image is now more obvious than the individual elements.

FIGURE 14.2: A more unified arrangement of the objects in Figure 14.1

Unity by Repetition

Another device for achieving visual unity is repetition. The repeating factor could be anything—a shape, a color, a line, an angle, nearly anything that the eye will see and recognize as a repeated element. In Figure 14.3, you can see a variety of shapes enclosed by circles all in a row. The repeated circle provides a sense of visual unity—the eye is drawn to the pattern and sees the series as a pattern. Also note that the shapes contained within each circle are approximately the same size in relation to the circle—another repeat factor that helps unify the images.

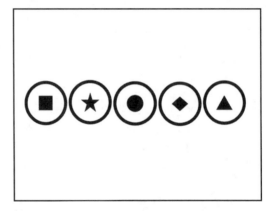

FIGURE 14.3: Repetition of the circles provides unity.

Figure 14.4 illustrates a common table of contents design that uses repetition of text and graphic elements. Your eye recognizes the pattern of repetition in the triangles and circles. Your brain recognizes the information contained within this pattern. These things clearly belong together; thus, visual unity and, again, intellectual unity are achieved.

Creating Balance

We learn our sense of balance as infants—if you hold young babies uncertainly, they feel "off-balance" and startled. Children learn to feel balance in their bodies as they play on gym equipment and learn to ride a bicycle. People desire balance in their environments: they straighten a crooked picture frame on the wall unconsciously, they rearrange books stacked on a table until the stack looks stable, and they feel uncomfortable in a room with a sloping floor. This urge for balance even shows up in our language in phrases like "feeling off-balance" to describe a feeling of disturbance.

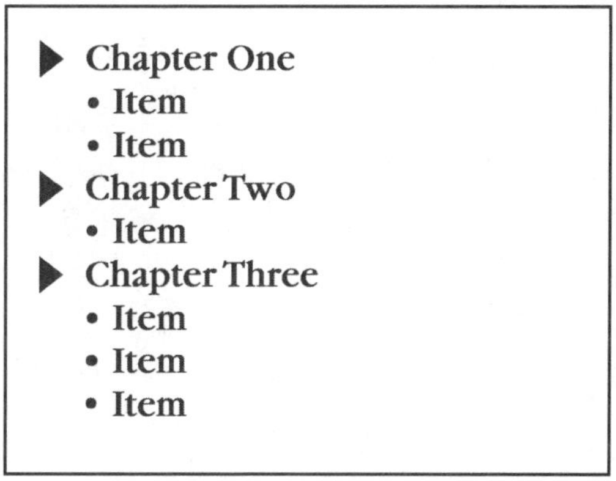

▶ **Chapter One**
  • Item
  • Item
▶ **Chapter Two**
  • Item
▶ **Chapter Three**
  • Item
  • Item
  • Item

FIGURE 14.4:   You can unify a table of contents through the use of bullets.

This strong human need for balance is demonstrated in people's reactions to graphic design. Look at Figure 14.5. What is your immediate reaction? Do you feel a need to rearrange the circles on the page? Most people do. Your eye perceives the image as if it is divided in half with many circles appearing on the left of the imaginary line and only three circles on the right. This image feels "out of balance" and is visually uncomfortable for most people.

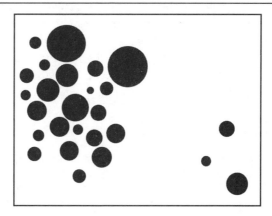

FIGURE 14.5:   Are these circles balanced within the image?

BREAKING DESIGN RULES—BALANCE

As a designer, you can use the sense of discomfort generated by an out-of-balance composition to your advantage. You can use the viewer's sense of "out of balance" to draw attention to the element that is out of balance. The viewer will look at this item carefully, trying to make sense of it and searching for a way to integrate it into an overall feeling of balance.

Experiment with this kind of idea and test it with some sincere critics before integrating it into your final design. This is a powerful tool and can be very successful if you employ it appropriately. If you use it improperly, it will unsettle your viewer and perhaps frustrate him or her sufficiently to stop reading your message.

Symmetrical Balance

You can use balance in a number of ways to arrange elements on a page. The simplest is symmetrical balance, which is best described as like elements repeated on either side of a center line. In effect, the image is mirrored.

Figure 14.6 illustrates symmetrical balance. Two circles appear on either side of a central triangle. Although this is a simple example, you can see examples of symmetrical balance all around you, particularly in architecture and interior design. Symmetrical balance feels formal and rather static, but it's also comfortable and predictable.

Asymmetrical Balance

Asymmetrical balance has a more casual feeling than symmetrical balance and is typically more interesting to the eye than symmetrical balance. In asymmetrical balance, different elements are balanced by having a similar visual weight or eye attraction.

In Figure 14.7, asymmetrical balance is provided by similar weight on either side of the imaginary vertical line bisecting the large box and the eight smaller boxes. Although the elements are different, the image feels balanced to the viewer.

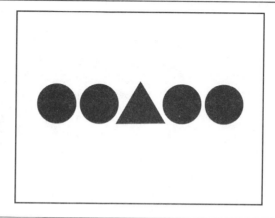

FIGURE 14.6:   Symmetrical balance gives a feeling of "fit," like puzzle pieces properly in place.

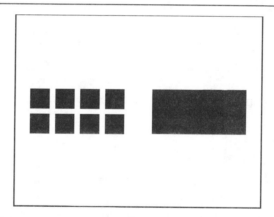

FIGURE 14.7:   The group of smaller boxes on the left has the same total area as the single larger box on the right, giving the appearance of balance.

Figure 14.8 illustrates differing textures that accomplish asymmetrical balance. Your eye sees the text on the left side of the image as a visual gray texture, even though it also contains symbols with their own meaning. (Remember the difference between visual and intellectual information?) The gray texture of the text balances the solid smooth graphic because, although the text is lighter in weight than the solid graphic, a texture is naturally more interesting to the eye.

Skill 14

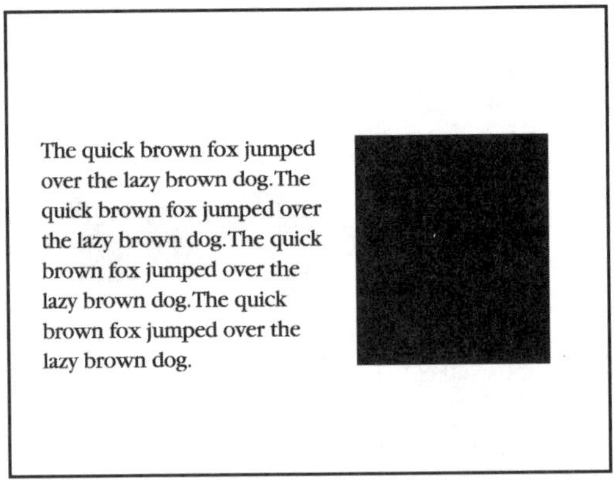

The quick brown fox jumped over the lazy brown dog. The quick brown fox jumped over the lazy brown dog. The quick brown fox jumped over the lazy brown dog. The quick brown fox jumped over the lazy brown dog.

FIGURE 14.8:   Balance can be achieved with different textures.

Providing a Focus

You use a point of emphasis, or visual *focus,* to grab the viewer's attention and direct it to a specific element in a design to consider it more carefully than the surrounding elements. Although not all designs use a focal point, it is typical to use this device when delivering a message. You can provide a focal point in any number of ways; some are subtle, and others are as strident as a flashing neon sign.

Using Contrast

One of the more common ways to the viewer's eye to a particular focal point is to use contrast. The contrast can be one of color, value, shape, texture, size, angle, or pattern. Figure 14.9 illustrates the use of sizing one element larger to create a focal point among a collection of small rectangles.

Figure 14.10 uses a variant of the graphic in Figure 14.9 to illustrate using color as the contrast to create a focal point. The rectangle on the right is gray, and the other rectangles are black. The drama of the gray against the series of black rectangles is rather startling and draws the eye much quicker than the size difference shown above. In the image provided on the CD, the rectangle on the right is bright red—even more dramatic!

FIGURE 14.9:   A designer can purposefully draw the viewer's eye to an object of dissimilar size.

FIGURE 14.10:   You can use color to produce contrast. (f1410.jpg)

Isolating an Important Element

Another effective way to create a focal point is to isolate an element. Figure 14.11 shows an assortment of circles; one circle stands alone and isolated from the others. Your eye is drawn to that lone circle, and you can't help but wonder why this circle is different from the rest.

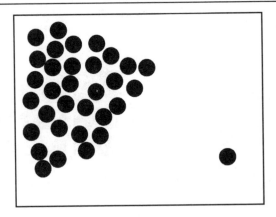

FIGURE 14.11: Which circle are your eyes drawn to?

Radial Placement

Figure 14.12 illustrates the common bull's eye—a simple focal point achieved by radial placement. The concentric circles surrounding the solid circle draw your eye to the center of the image, almost irresistibly. Imagine a photograph of a tunnel with something emerging from the tunnel or a crossroads with a person in the crosswalk.

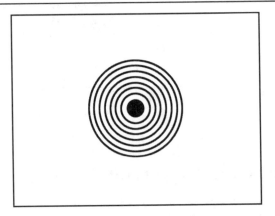

FIGURE 14.12:   The bull's eye draws your eyes toward its center.

Achieving Depth

Although the Web is a two-dimensional medium, you can use many tools to give your presentation a feeling of depth and dimension, and you can achieve the illusion of depth in a number of ways.

Working with Size

Size is an easy way to imply depth; objects appear smaller as they recede into the distance. Figure 14.13 shows a series of rectangles that start tall at the right and left margins of the page and grow smaller as they approach the center. Your eye is fooled into believing that the images are receding into the distance, creating an illusion of depth.

FIGURE 14.13:   Shorter and thinner lines introduce the visual trick of depth perception.

Add Layering

Another way to imply depth is through layering or overlapping elements. As you view a layered image, your eye perceives the top element to be "hiding" the partially covered element. As a result, you believe that you are viewing a three-dimensional image. Figure 14.14 illustrates this principle with a series of rectangles that appear to be stacked.

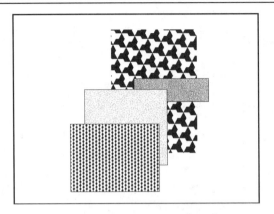

FIGURE 14.14: Is one image really on top of the other?

 TIP By layering elements and decreasing their size, as shown in Figures 14.13 and 14.14, you can greatly exaggerate the illusion of depth. This technique is especially effective for implying three-dimensional images.

Creating Shadows

Adding a shadow to an element is another way to create an illusion of depth. Figure 14.15 illustrates several common shadow techniques used in desktop publishing and on the Web.

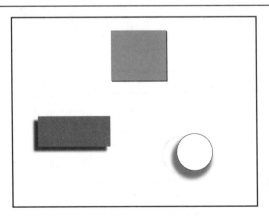

FIGURE 14.15: The different types of drop shadows

Images and Text

You can have the best copy, photos, and graphics and an exciting image for your Web site, but if they are not presented effectively, your audience won't give them a second glance. Effective presentation requires applying the basic art principles to your images and text in your Web designs. In the following sections, we have provided some specific examples that will help you present your Web site effectively.

Using Images

The liberal use of images is much of what makes the Web an appealing medium for providing information to the world. Full-color images have never been so easy! But presenting graphics and photographs in an appealing and accessible way requires some planning and an eye for detail.

Relevance to Copy

Illustrating copy isn't difficult. Many illustration resources are available to you, from do-it-yourself to professionally designed images. The key to effective illustration lies in determining the purpose of the illustration and achieving that purpose in your selection of images.

You might choose to provide illustration for your Web page to provide support or additional information for the copy, for decoration, to break up a dense text-oriented page, or to promote a mood or feeling. Whatever your reason, you will need to identify it and be sure that the image you provide achieves your goal.

For example, if your copy is a step-by-step description of how to put together a technical device, placing a photograph of Monet's water lilies on the page won't contribute to your message and will almost certainly confuse and distract your visitor. This is an inappropriate use of illustration.

Illustrating a stock prospectus with a chart showing the performance of the stock over several years is an excellent use of an illustration. People grasp a well-designed information graphic much more quickly than a textual description.

Adjusting Sizing

Sizing your illustrations appropriately helps their overall effectiveness on your Web page. Pay careful attention to the balance of your illustration against your copy. A too large or too small image will unsettle your audience. Figure 14.16 shows an illustration that is too large for the copy.

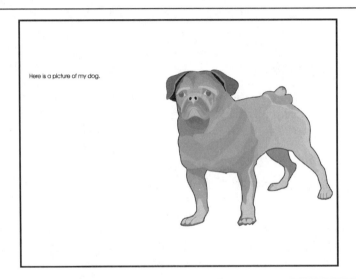

Here is a picture of my dog.

FIGURE 14.16: This text gets lost next to the large dog. (f1416.jpg)

Incorporating Photographs

Photographs are an excellent way to illustrate your Web page; however, photographs often need some attention prior to placement in your pages. Step back and look at the photograph to be sure that it is sharp, that the light and dark levels are correct, and that extraneous parts of the image have been cropped.

Figure 14.17 shows a good photograph of an Egyptian museum. Although the photograph has plenty of interesting features, there are a few problems. The original photo is a bit blurry and dark. Using photograph-retouching software, we were able to sharpen the image a bit and lighten some of the darker tones, bringing out some of the details in the shadows, as you can see in Figure 14.18.

FIGURE 14.17: The original photograph (f1417.jpg)

FIGURE 14.18: A sharper image, with more detail visible (f1418.jpg)

The image isn't yet ideal. The far left side of the image shows steps and a handrail leading into a dark corridor, and instead of adding to the overall atmosphere of "Egypt," it distracts the viewer into wondering where the steps lead—not the intended effect. By cropping the extraneous stairs and rails, the photograph is much improved, as you can see in Figure 14.19. The photograph could be improved further with a bit of retouching and removal of the trash can in the approximate center of the image.

NOTE   We'll take a look at some popular photograph-retouching software in Skill 17.

FIGURE 14.19: The cropped version removes the "modern" amenities of the steps and handrails. (f1419.jpg)

Styling Issues

Once you decide on a look and feel, maintain consistency throughout the images on your Web site. This doesn't mean that you can't use a variety of images—both graphics and photographs, but be sure that things go together stylistically.

For example, it would be confusing to use the currently popular '50s retro black and white photographs next to Renaissance paintings and icons. Radical changes in style are distracting and often leave your audience feeling puzzled and unsettled. Worse yet, if the changes occur between pages on your Web site, the level of confusion can increase, leaving visitors wondering if they have somehow left your site and are now lost.

If your site has a great deal of variety in the images you are using, experiment with ways to create a feeling of repetition. Sometimes you can help tie together your images by using a common theme for presenting images such as a consistent way of bordering photographs, a consistent style of shadow or spacing around graphic images, or a repeating color theme. In the sample sites at the end of this skill, you will see some examples of how you can maintain the continuity of images throughout a Web site.

Effective Styling of Text

Of course your copy is well written, it's exciting to read, has no spelling or grammatical errors, and is all ready to be pasted into your Web page—right? Well, maybe. You can use a few design principles for working with text to help your page go from good to great!

Tones of Type

When you look at a document, your eye takes in information about that page long before your actually read a single word. First you notice the tone, or value, of the page. Is the page covered with lots and lots of text, unrelieved by headlines, images, or white space? Your eye is evaluating the "tone" of the page. The quick look at a document sets the reader's expectations for that page: Will it be interesting? Dreary and dull? Short? Long?

Black Space   Black space refers to any graphical information on the page, regardless of color. This includes photographs, illustrations, or anything else that is neither text nor empty space. Your eye is naturally attracted to black space to avoid doing the work of reading. Have you ever decided to put down a document to read later because it looked like "work"? The document would have looked more appealing with more black space.

White Space   This is your eye's second favorite thing to look at on a page. White space is empty space on a page—margins, breaks between paragraphs, and space around graphics. White space breaks up long columns of text, giving your eyes a rest from the work it will need to do in reading the copy on the page.

Gray Space   This is the actual text on the page—your carefully written copy. The eye is least interested in looking at this information. It's hard work; all that text has to be processed. Consider your reaction to reading the fine print in a contract or reading classified ads in the newspaper. You don't want to do it, right?

Balancing Tone

Presenting text effectively requires balancing of the tone of text—providing sufficient black space and white space to offset the gray space of the text. By judicious placement of white and black space, you can provide your visitors with copy in the smaller doses their eyes crave, thus ensuring that your message gets read.

Using Grids

The basic grid is an invaluable tool to help simplify your layout decisions. A grid provides structure, defining where you will place elements on your page—both text and graphics. A grid assists you with balancing tone and elements on your page thus increasing interest and readability.

Perhaps most importantly, a grid provides a strong feeling of continuity for your Web site. Your layout can provide your visitors with important clues on where to find information. If content always appears in a particular column and if your links and navigation graphics always appear in another, your visitors will naturally understand your design. That understanding makes them feel comfortable and reduces the possibility of their "getting lost" on your Web site.

If you analyze printed materials, you will discover an underlying grid in most cases. Business letters, invoices, tax forms, resumés, and even this book all use some variant of a grid for organizing information and helping lead your eye through the document. Even when the grid's lines are not apparent on the page, most documents use a series of columns and rows to format visual information.

One-Column Grids

A one-column grid is the simplest HTML page layout you can use. Text and graphics are laid out horizontally with or without wrapping text around graphics, as shown in the examples in Figure 14.20. Text and images can be centered, aligned left or right, or allowed to fit to the page without any formatting.

FIGURE 14.20:   Four possible one-column grid layouts

This grid works well for a variety of Web pages, particularly those that don't require elaborate formatting or presentation of complex graphics. This format is especially good for the beginning designer. No complex formatting or tables are required. Simple HTML is all that you need.

Long documents with sequential pages organized by chapter or section are particularly well served by a one-column layout. With the addition of a table of contents page linked to each section or chapter page, and providing navigation tools such as a home, forward, and back button for moving through the document a page at a time, this becomes the ideal design for manuals or other long documents that people are likely to read sequentially.

This layout, a variant of the one-column grid, uses one wide column for presenting most of the content and a narrow column for links or other navigation content. It is a commonly used both on the Web and in traditioal paper publishing. For the Web, the narrow column most typically appears on the left side of the page.

TIP   The one-column grid tends to create very "gray" pages. Long uninterrupted paragraphs of text can create a dense and complicated look, making the viewer feel as if all that text may be tedious to read. You can break up the gray look by adding graphics, lines, and section headers where appropriate.

In the examples in Figure 14.21, you can see that a single column is used for the content of the document, while the narrow column can be used for locating graphics, subheads, links, navigation buttons, or even small amounts of text. Formatting can be carefully aligned left, right, or center or can flow naturally, depending on the choice of the designer.

Skill 14

FIGURE 14.21: Several examples of a modified one-column grid

Although this grid design requires using tables, it is a sophisticated look for a Web site that isn't too complex for the beginning Web designer to produce. (Refer to Skill 6 for more information on HTML tables.) This design naturally incorporates white space, which sets off the elements in the narrow column and gives your pages a lively feeling.

Another variant of the one column grid uses two narrow columns for presenting links and images while continuing to restrict content to the wide column. Figure 14.22 shows several versions of this layout.

FIGURE 14.22: Additional variants of the one-column grid method

With the addition of a second narrow column, the flexibility of your design increases; however, the complexity of writing the HTML to format this design also increases. Although the design is not complicated, planning becomes more important. Balancing this layout is more of a challenge than it is with the previous designs.

The grid design shown in Figure 14.22 works especially well for complex Web sites containing several sections or areas that your visitors might want to view in an unpredictable (rather than sequential) manner. You might use one narrow column for section navigation and then use the other narrow column for overall site tools such as search page links, glossaries, and other links that are supportive of the overall site. When used consistently throughout your Web site, this structure is easy for your audience to understand.

Putting It All Together: A Gallery

We've presented you with a great deal of information, and you're trying to figure out just how you integrate all of it—right? Well, don't despair; it's really not as difficult as it seems. Once you make some of the basic decisions about your look and feel and the grid you will use, many decisions will fall naturally into place. To help you see the integrated product, here's a quick tour of a couple of Web sites. We'll point out where some of the principles we described are actually being used.

Career Sources Unlimited

Career Sources Unlimited, Inc. (CSU) provides job placement services in the Chicago area. The Web site (at `http://www.careersources.com/`) is professional but has a personal touch, demonstrated in the photographs and the personal contact information and e-mail address that is apparent all through the site.

Art Principles

As you can see in Figure 14.23, the splash page of the CSU Web site, the corporate logo and the corporate contact information use asymmetrical balance to give a professional but informal look to the page. The navigation graphics at the bottom of every page use simple shapes, symmetrically balanced. The shapes are the same maroon color as the corporate logo to repeat the corporate color and to help unify the site's look. The soft drop shadow behind the navigation graphics gives the illusion of depth and helps dress up the simple shapes. To get the full effect, visit their site at `http://www.careersources.com/`.

Skill 14

FIGURE 14.23: Career Sources Unlimited

Using a Grid

The CSU site primarily utilizes a one-column grid throughout the pages. Because one-column grids tend to look somewhat "gray," the site designer broke up the copy with plenty of white space and custom-designed maroon bullets for lists. Contact information is aligned center, providing additional white space on each side of the text (see Figure 14.24).

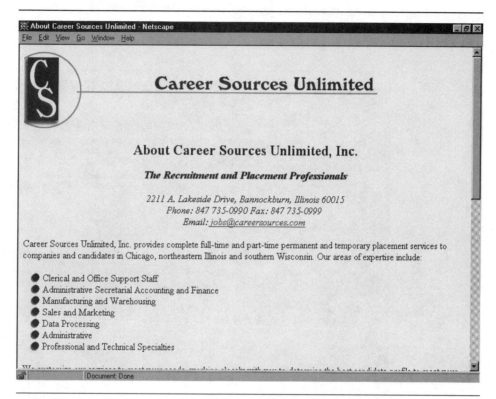

FIGURE 14.24:   White space and bullets help break up the text.

Beer Info Source

We introduced you to the Beer Info Source site (at http://www.beerinfo.com/) in Skill 12. It is a large Web site with more than 100 pages of information. The complexity of the site and the need for easy navigation mandated careful attention to structure and design.

Art Principles

As Figure 14.25 shows, the site's look and feel are unified by the neon signs, which are used consistently throughout the site. The large logo's rounded corner rectangle shape is repeated in the site navigation buttons shown just below the logo. The

Home button is animated, providing visitors with a clue to their location within the site. The neon and type styling are repeated throughout the site, maintaining a strong sense of consistency and site identity.

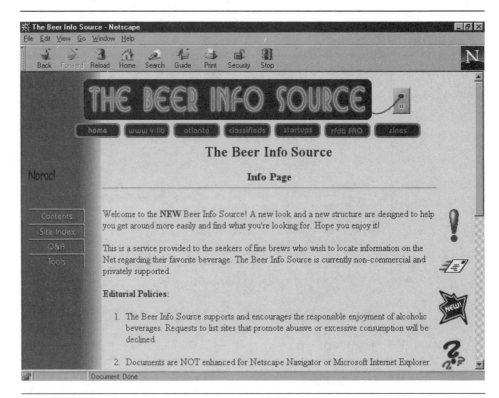

FIGURE 14.25: The Beer Info Source splash page

At the far right of the logo, you can see an electrical cord and plug going into an "electrical outlet." This "plugged-in" reference particularly entertained visitors and raised a number of questions, such as, "What happens if I try to unplug the sign?" The site owner was so amused that he chose to add a hidden link—an "Easter egg"—to amuse the curious.

Figure 14.26 shows what happens if a visitor "unplugs" the electrical cord. The fun aspect of design at this site led to visitors actually having an impact on Web site design.

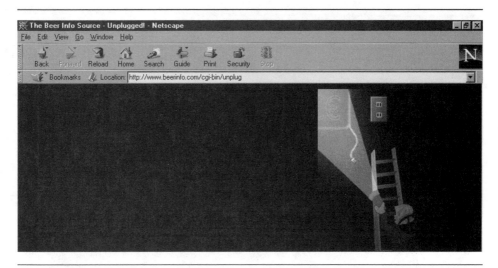

FIGURE 14.26: The Easter egg

Using a Grid

Beer Info Source uses a modified one-column grid consistently throughout the Web site. As you can see in the diagram in Figure 14.27, the structure is formal and consistent, despite the variety of sections. The visitor quickly learns the navigation scheme and can travel the site with ease. This design never requires the visitor to go backward in order to jump to a new section. All sections are available from all pages.

One page at Beer Info Source does use a somewhat different format, as you can see in Figure 14.28. The same basic structure of the site is used with the navigation buttons and tools; however, a calendar created by a separate table with the borders turned on is displayed in the area normally used by textual content.

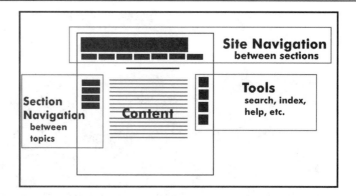

FIGURE 14.27:   A consistent structure helps your visitors with navigation.

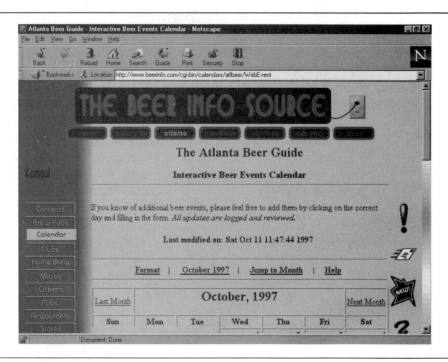

FIGURE 14.28:   The table structure used at http://beerinfo.com/
cgi-bin/calendars/atlbeer/WebEvent helps offset the calendar information.

Have You Mastered the Essentials?

Now you can. . .

☑ Apply basic art principles to your draft Web design.

☑ Produce effective graphics and photographs for your pages.

☑ Balance white space, gray space, and black space.

☑ Develop a layout using a grid.

Skill 14

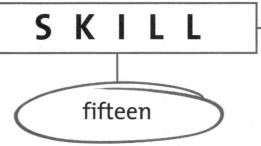

fifteen

Making a Statement with Fonts

❏ Understanding fonts, typefaces, and typography

❏ Using HTML to specify fonts

❏ Fonts and browser support

As you know from working with regular, paper documents, fonts can make a really big difference in the way your documents look. You can use fonts on the Web, as long as you keep certain limitations in mind. We'll cover the techniques and challenges of fonts on the Web in this skill.

What Are Fonts, Really?

A *font* is usually a part of a *typeface* family. One example of a font would be Courier, 14 point bold. Courier is the name of a typeface, and 14 point bold is a font within that typeface.

Fonts can be divided into two broad categories: fixed-width fonts (also called monospaced fonts) and proportional fonts. A fixed-width gives the same amount of space to each letter, whereas a proportional font gives different amounts of space to different letters.

```
This sentence is written in Courier, which is a
fixed font.
```

The font for this sentence, Times New Roman, allocates more space for the letter M than it does for the letter I.

Many people consider fonts the basis of graphic design. Well chosen and well placed fonts are a key factor in whether documents communicate effectively to the intended audience. *Typography* is the study of the selection, combination, and placement of fonts.

Fonts have been around for a long time, but before the advent of personal computers, they were used mostly by people who ran printing presses. Now that more people have personal computers, and countless fonts are available in electronic versions, fonts are much more accessible. Computer users are able to choose which typeface to use, along with its style (*italic*, anyone?) and size. But being able to choose fonts on the computer is not the same as knowing what they actually are, or *how* to choose and mix them.

Default Fonts

You can assign fonts to the text in your Web pages. Any text you do not assign a font to will appear in the browser's default font. Visitors to the Web can set their default fonts in the preferences for their browser. The default font cannot be changed in a browser (such as Lynx) that does not support different fonts.

Most people never change their default fonts. Occasionally, though people change fonts simply due to personal preference. Default fonts are also sometimes changed to get more words on a page, either for printing or because of screen issues. People who have trouble seeing small type often make the font sizes larger so text is more readable.

Changing the Default in Internet Explorer and AOL

In IE 3.0 and I.E. 4.0 the user goes to View ➣ Options ➣ General and clicks the Font Settings button in the lower right hand corner. The screen shown in Figure 15.1 appears. The user can choose their fonts from the Fixed-Width and Proportional menus.

You can see that IE gives two options for the choice of font: a fixed-width font and a proportional font. The fixed-width font is what shows up in a for text which is surrounded by the TT or PRE container tags.

The current AOL browser is IE 3.0. Prior to forming an alliance with Microsoft, AOL was using a browser from a previous acquisition. Some people still use the old AOL browsers, although they don't have too many capabilities. Even if people are using the old AOL 3.0 browser, when they go into the preferences menu, the old browser calls up the IE 3.0 preferences.

In order to change the size of the fonts used to view Web pages, the user can go to View ➣ Fonts and choose the preferred font size. The font sizes are not specified by point size, as in other applications. Font size can also be changed from the toolbar. Simply choose Larger or Smaller or the larger or smaller A icon.

Changing the Default in Navigator

Similarly, a user can also specify the default fonts used to view pages in Navigator. To do so, they choose Options ➣ General Preferences ➣ Fonts. The screen shown in Figure 15.2 appears.

In this screen, the user clicks the Choose Font buttons to set the fixed and proportional fonts. One difference here is that Navigator will allow the user to set the font size in the same screen used to set the font. Also, Navigator allows the user to choose the font size by point size (such as 12 point), rather than by descriptive terms (such as Large or Medium).

FIGURE 15.1:   The IE 3.0 Font Options

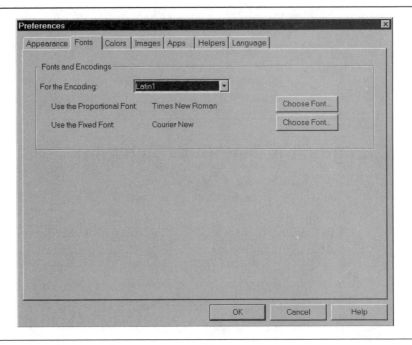

FIGURE 15.2:   The Navigator 3.01 Font Preferences

Using HTML to Specify Fonts

Web designers can specify the font that visitors to see, provided that:

- The correct HTML font specification is used.

- The user's browser version supports the version of HTML that allows font specification (generally 3.0 generation browsers or higher).

- The user's machine has the specified font installed.

There are three main ways of using HTML to specify the fonts for your Web site. The first way, which uses stylesheets to specify fonts for multiple pages, is covered in Skill 7. The second way is to specify a font for each entire page, and the third way is to specify fonts for selected words on the page. The differences in how each method works will become clearer as we go on.

Using the *BASEFONT* Tag

You can specify the font color and size, but not the typeface, for an entire HTML page by using the BASEFONT HTML tag. This tag traditionally goes at the top of the HTML page, after the BODY tag. The important thing to remember about <BASEFONT> is that the font it specifies is the default font for the entire page—in order to specify fonts for certain words within a page, the FONT tag must be used within the page. This tag is a Netscape extension, which is supported by all versions of Navigator, by IE 2.0 and later, and by WebTV 0.9 and 1.2.

Here's an example of HTML without the BASEFONT tag:

```
<HTML>
<HEAD>
<TITLE>Web design is fun!</TITLE>
</HEAD>
<BODY BGCOLOR="#FFFFFF">
Web design is fun!
</BODY>
</HTML>
```

Figure 15.3 shows what this HTML looks like in Navigator 3.01.
Now, take a look at HTML that uses the BASEFONT tag:

```
<HTML>
<HEAD>
<TITLE> Web design is fun!</TITLE>
</HEAD>
<BODY BGCOLOR="FFFFFF">
<BASEFONT SIZE="+5">
```

```
Web design is fun!
</BODY>
</HTML>
```

Figure 15.4 shows what this HTML looks like in Navigator 3.01.

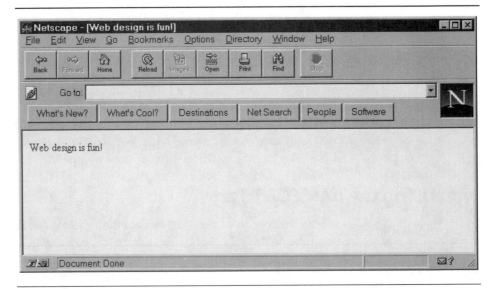

FIGURE 15.3:   The Web page without the BASEFONT tag

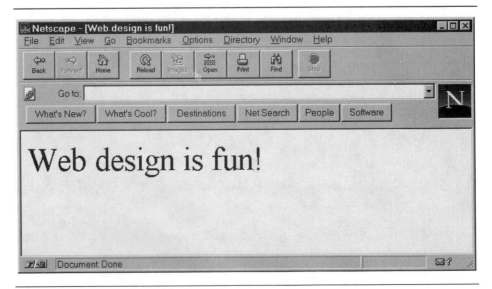

FIGURE 15.4:   The Web page with the BASEFONT tag

You can see from the sample HTML that one of the attributes of the BASEFONT tag is SIZE. You can set the size of the font by specifying a number such as 5 (the default is 3), or you can specify the size *relative* to 3. In our example, we have set the size as +5, which means we are using size 8 (the default size, 3, plus 5).

NOTE It is usually better to use relative font sizes because your readers have the option of setting their fonts to the default size they prefer. So, for example, if someone with poor eyesight sets their default font size to 18 point, and then you come along and specify a smaller size, it could be a problem. If, however, you use a size that is *relatively larger* to the default size, the reader at least is shown fonts that are larger than the defaults instead of smaller.

Our sample HTML uses another attribute of the BASEFONT tag: the COLOR attribute. You can use it by specifying <BASEFONT COLOR="#hexvalue">, where hexvalue is the hexadecimal value of the color you want to use. If you're not familiar with hex values, you can read more about them in Skills 3 and 16.

Although the BASEFONT tag lets you specify the size and color of text for an entire document in one place, there are definite disadvantages to using this tag. For example, it doesn't allow you to specify a typeface. A larger disadvantage is that the BASEFONT tag is being officially deprecated by W3C in HTML 4.0 in favor of stylesheets. All the major browsers will probably continue to support it, but it won't be official as it was in HTML 3.2. The FONT tag, covered in the next section, is also being deprecated in favor of stylesheets; but, as you'll see, it has at least two advantages over BASEFONT. If you are not going to use stylesheets and you want to specify typefaces, use the FONT tag and its attributes.

Using the *FONT* Tag

The FONT tag is different from the BASEFONT tag in two main ways:

- It allows you to specify not only the font size and color, but also the typeface.

- It can be used anywhere in the document. That is, unlike the BASEFONT tag which applies to an entire document, <FONT> surrounds the words it is modifying and therefore can be used to change the font of selected words, rather than the entire page.

The FONT container surrounds the text that you want to assign a font to. This tag has three attributes: SIZE, COLOR, and FACE. These attributes can be used in any combination or by themselves.

Table 15.1 explains how each of the attributes should be used.

TABLE 15.1: Attributes for the FONT tag

Attribute	How It's Used	Sample Syntax
SIZE	This attribute is used in the same way as the SIZE attribute is used for <BASEFONT>. You can specify absolute sizes from 1 to 7, or relative sizes such as +3. Relative sizes which are larger than the defaults are recommended. That is, use sizes which begin with a + (plus) sign.	`<FONT SIZE="+2">Web design is fun!</FONT>`
COLOR	This attribute is used in the same way as the COLOR attribute for <BASEFONT>. You can specify the color by name (such as "red"), or by hexadecimal value (which gives you much more control over the color).	`<FONT COLOR="#000099"> Web design is fun!</FONT>`
FACE	This attribute defines the typeface. You can specify more than one typeface and the browser looks for the first one you specify. If it can't find that one, it will look for the next, and so on. If the user's computer has none of the typefaces you have specified, the page will be dislayed in the default face. Commas separate the names of the fonts.	`<FONT FACE="Arial,Helvetica"> Web design is fun!</FONT>`

As always, examples are the most instructive way to learn. For reference, here's our sample HTML without the FONT tag:

```
<HTML>
<HEAD>
<TITLE>Web design is fun!</TITLE>
</HEAD>
<BODY BGCOLOR="#FFFFFF">
Web design is fun!
</BODY>
</HTML>
```

Figure 15.5 shows what this HTML looks like in Navigator 3.01.

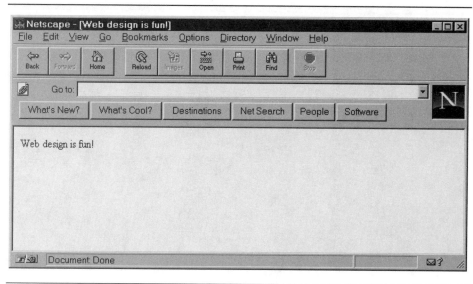

FIGURE 15.5:   The Web page without the FONT tag

To change the size of our text, proceed as follows:

```
<HTML>
<HEAD>
<TITLE>Web design is fun!</TITLE>
</HEAD>
<BODY BGCOLOR="#FFFFFF">

<FONT SIZE="+2" FACE="Arial,Helvetica">
Web design is fun!
</FONT>

<P>

Web design is cool!

</BODY>
</HTML>
```

This latest addition is shown in Figure 15.6.

FIGURE 15.6: The Web page with the SIZE attribute for the FONT tag

Just to give you one more example that uses different values for the attributes, here's another HTML sample:

```
<HTML>
<HEAD>
<TITLE>Web design is fun!/TITLE>
</HEAD>
<BODY BGCOLOR="#FFFFFF">

<FONT COLOR="#5F005F" FACE="Courier">
Web design is fun!
</FONT>

<P>

Web design is cool!

</BODY>
</HTML>
```

To find out what this HTML looks like in a browser, see Figure 15.7.

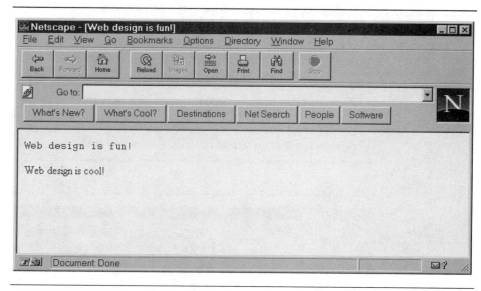

FIGURE 15.7: Another Web page that uses the FONT tag

Fonts and Browser Support

When choosing fonts for your Web pages, there are two main issues you should be considering. One is the technical issue of browser and computer support for what you want to do, and the other is the aesthetic idea of font design.

In this section, we'll look at browser and computer support for fonts and how it affects what you might want to do with them. In the next section, we're going to look at the process of selecting and mixing fonts. Once you are more aware of the possibilities and limitations of fonts on the Web, we'll discuss workarounds for times when your plan won't work on certain browsers and computers.

 NOTE If you want to specify fonts using stylesheets, please see Skill 7, which shows you how to use stylesheets and discusses browser support for them.

There are two things that need to work in order for your audience to see the font you want them to (whether you use the FONT tag or stylesheets). First, they have to have a browser that supports font changes in HTML. Second, they need to have the font installed on their computer.

The browsers that support the FONT tag are Netscape 1.1 and higher, IE 2.0 and higher, and WebTV 0.9 and 1.2. Remember, <BASEFONT> is supported by all versions of Navigator, IE 2.0 and later, and WebTV 0.9 and 1.2, while stylesheets are supported by Navigator 4.0b2 and IE 3.01b and higher.

 **WARNING** Depending on the browser, the user may have the option of overriding the attributes you have set. For example, in Navigator, the panel for Options ➢ General Preferences ➢ Colors (shown in Figure 15.8) contains a checkbox that says, "Always Use My Colors, Overriding Document."

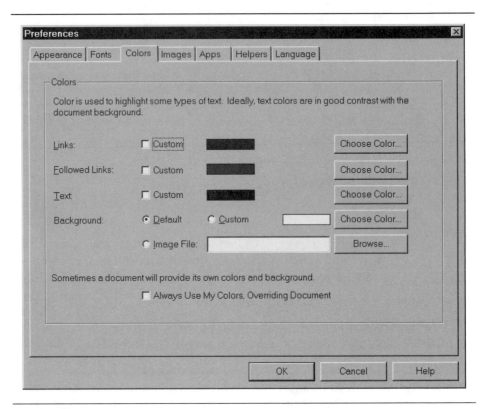

FIGURE 15.8: The colors preference screen in Navigator 3.01

Font Support

The browser needs to have the font you specify installed on the computer. If the browser does not have the correct font, it will use the default font as set in its preferences. It's a good idea to stick to the fonts that normally come installed with operating systems.Another thing you can do is to specify more than one font, as discussed earlier in the skill.

As we mentioned before, this means that the browser will look for the first font you list and, if it doesn't find it, will move on to the next one. You can specify up to six fonts if you like, although most designers specify no more than three.

TIP This is a good way of specifying fonts for different platforms. Arial is an automatic system font for Windows, and Helvetica is automatically included with the Macintosh operating system. By including a font that works for each of these two operating systems, we have included more of our audience in our font selection process.

Sometimes the same font has more than one name on different computer platforms. Table 14.2 shows some of the most common fonts for the Web and their equivalents on Windows and Macintosh platforms.

TABLE 14.2:   Font equivalents

Windows Font	Macintosh Font
Arial	Helvetica
Times	Times New Roman
Courier	Courier New
Century Schoolbook	New Century Schoolbook

TIP We've already covered one of the basic things to think about when choosing typefaces for the Web—it's best to choose faces that are probably already installed on the computers of your target audience. If you design the pages with these faces in mind, you'll have a much higher chance that your audience will see your pages as you intended. If you use a face that looks good, but few people have it, then what's the use? Better to use the obscure face but also specify more common ones and make sure that the page still looks good when you use those instead.

Knowing When to Use Which Font

Choosing the right font and the right *combinations* of fonts can make your pages more useful and attractive. If you include many different fonts and font sizes simply because you *can*, your Web pages will be cluttered and difficult to read.

This following overview is not intended to make you an expert in font design, but it will give you a start. Design principles that don't apply directly to fonts are covered in Skill 13.

Choosing a Typeface

You also want to make sure that you choose typefaces that show up well on a screen. Some faces, such as Geneva and New York, were designed for the computer screen. Experiment with the faces and look at the page. How do they look? With computer screen resolutions, they just won't look as good as they do in print. Make sure you keep that in mind when deciding.

Because people's eyes become strained when they read on the computer for a long time, there are also a couple of other things to keep in mind when choosing a typeface. One is that it is difficult to read when words use all capital letters. Another is that it is often easier to read typefaces that have serifs.

Serif versus Sans Serif Typefaces

Serif typefaces are those which have those small extra strokes on the ends of the lines which make up the letters. One example of a serif typeface is `Courier`. Another example is Times Roman. Do you see the extra strokes? If not, look at the bottom of the letter "r". It could have just ended with the vertical line, which makes up the stem of the r, but there's a small horizontal line at the bottom. That's the serif.

An example of a sans serif typeface (a typeface with no serifs) is Avante Garde. Note that there are no little lines at the ends of the main lines, which make up the letters. Another example is **Franklin Gothic Book No. 2**.

Serif fonts tend to be easier to read than sans serif fonts because the serifs lead the reader's eyes to the next letterform. That is, there is a smoother transition from one letter to the next one. That's not to say that

continued on next page ▶

sans serif fonts should not be used—they can be quite useful, especially to provide contrast to serif fonts, which are more common in text. You just might not want to use them for pages and pages of dense reading. You can see this principle in action if you look at any book that contains a lot of text.

Choosing Colors for Your Text

Colors for the Web are covered in much more depth in Skill 16. But there is one thing about color that is font-specific. There are some colors in a browser-safe palette that look good in images but do not read well as type, depending on the background color. On a white background, for example, any yellow, tan, or pastel will not be easy to read as text, although it may be okay for an image. You might want to have a tan stripe on across the top of a white page, but you would not want to make all of the text tan. The best thing to do is to look at the pages when you are done. If they are difficult to read because of the font color, it's time to pick a different color.

You should also avoid choosing colors that are close to the default colors for hyperlinks in browsers. Some browsers give users the option of not underlining the hyperlinks. Instead, users rely on the hyperlink colors to know whether a particular word is a hyperlink. They will become irritated if some colored words are not links.

In deference to people without color monitors, you should probably avoid saying things like, "The main headings are indicated in red."

 **WARNING**   Don't underline words on the Web unless they are hyperlinks. People with black and white computer screens often rely on the underlining to tell them whether a word is a hyperlink.

Choosing Size

As far as choosing the size of fonts, just be sure to pick something large enough to be legible. With their low resolutions (relative to print), screens can make it impossible to read small fonts which would have been perfectly fine on paper.

Sometimes people set their font sizes fairly large because they have difficulty reading smaller type. If you set a font to an absolute size, it can be very unhelpful. It is best to use relative font size (like +2) and to avoid making fonts smaller than the default font the user has set.

Mixing Fonts

There are some general principles you can follow which will help you get started with putting fonts together.

One of the most important principles of mixing fonts is to make sure that the fonts you use contrast with each other. To achieve good contrast, you should choose fonts that differ in more than one way. For example, you could select fonts that are not only different typefaces but also different sizes. An easy rule of thumb is to combine a serif and a sans serif font. Two serif fonts or two sans serif fonts are often too similar, and the small differences can look like mistakes or can simply be displeasing to the eye.

Let's take a look at a couple of examples. In the first example, two fonts that are very similar to each other are used. First take a look at the HTML below and then see how it looks in Navigator 3.01 in Figure 15.9.

```
<HTML>
<HEAD>
<TITLE>Example which uses similar fonts</TITLE>
</HEAD>
<BODY BGCOLOR="#FFFFFF">

<FONT SIZE="+2" FACE="Times New Roman">We like the Web because it's
    ➥ </FONT><FONT SIZE="+2" FACE="Rockwell">COOL.</FONT>
</BODY>
</HTML>
```

There's not much contrast, is there? It looks like there might be a different font for the word "cool", but then again, maybe not. Let's try making the contrast obvious. Here's our new HTML:

```
<HTML>
<HEAD>
<TITLE>Example which uses noticeably different fonts</TITLE>
</HEAD>
<BODY BGCOLOR="#FFFFFF">

<FONT SIZE="+2" FACE="Garamond">We like the Web because it's
    ➥ </FONT><FONT SIZE="+2" FACE="Beesknees ITC">COOL.</FONT>
</BODY>
</HTML>
```

You can see the results in Navigator 3.01 in Figure 15.10.

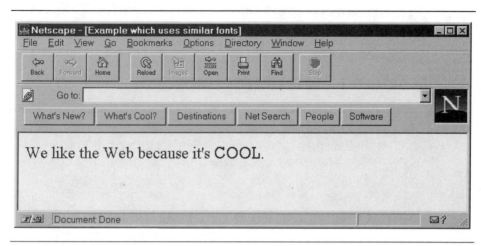

FIGURE 15.9: Two similar serif fonts together

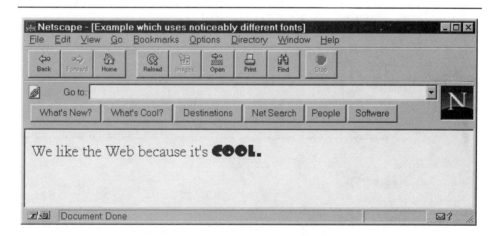

FIGURE 15.10: Two fonts with greater contrast

A deep study into design and typography is beyond the scope of this book. The biggest tip we can give you is to use contrast. The example above contrasted the fonts not only because one was serif and the other sans serif, but also because one was bolder than the other.

When it comes to mixing fonts, just use your best judgement. Do the fonts bring out what you want the reader to see? Is the combination pleasing to the eye? Is it easy to read? If you're not sure, ask. User feedback is great!

Providing Font Alternatives

There will be times when members of your audience won't be able to see the fonts you want them to. They may be using an older browser or a speech-based one. They may have their link colors set to override your specifications, or they may not have the fonts installed on their system. How do you work within these constraints?

Make Your Site Work without the Fonts

You should design your site so that it works without the fonts. That is, it should look well-designed and well-laid out with the default browser settings, on both older and newer browsers.

You should avoid linking typeface to meaning. That is, don't say that all the examples are in blue type, or that a certain typeface represents a vocabulary word. Use the fonts for aesthetics and design, and make sure that the site can be handled gracefully by browsers that do not support your fonts.

 **COMPATIBILITY NOTE**   Don't forget, you can specify more than one font in the FACE attribute. Make sure your site looks good in all the fonts you list, and you'll increase your chances of someone seeing your page the way you intended.

Use PDFs

PDF, or Portable Document Format, is a way of generating files which look the same as the original but can be read across platforms. If you have a document in which fonts or layout are very important, such as a document about typefaces you have designed, you might want to use PDFs.

There are a two ways to make a PDF. The first is to write a PostScript file from an application such as Microsoft Word or Adobe PageMaker. You do this by printing to file instead of printing to a printer. After generating the PostScript file, you use Acrobat Distiller (a commercial product from Adobe Corporation) to make a PDF file. The second way is to have an application write the PDF file directly, which is a new feature on some applications. The PostScript/Acrobat Distiller method produces smaller files, at least so far.

Your readers can look at a PDF file using the Acrobat Reader, which is either a browser plug-in (see Skill 20) or a stand-alone application, depending on what they download. Acrobat Reader is free and comes on many platforms. We've included it on the CD that comes witht this book. Your files will look like the originals, and you can even add some new features not found in the original document, such as hyperlinking. For more information, check out Adobe at `http://www.adobe.com`.

The downside? Your readers have to download the Acrobat Reader. They will need RAM to view your pages, especially if they get the plug-in, which allows them to read the pages in the browser window. If they get the stand-alone reader, they can at least exit the browser before running the reader if they need to.

Use Images (Cautiously)

While this is not a recommended method, people sometimes make images out of the words and fonts they want to use. Often, when you look at a great headline on a Web page, it's not a font specification, it's an image of the headline.

On the positive side, this method can be useful if you really need to use a certain font not commonly installed on machines. If you do use an image, be sure to also use an ALT tag.

What are the drawbacks? Well, if your image is a lot of text (something that couldn't easily be spelled out with an ALT tag) speech-based browsers and browsers that don't show images won't be able to see it.

The other drawback is that images take more bandwidth than text. That means that users may have to wait a lot longer for your image than they would have to wait for text.

Have You Mastered the Essentials?

Now you can. . .

- ☑ Use the *BASEFONT* tag and the *FONT* tag to specify fonts.
- ☑ Understand that your readers will maintain a certain level of control over how they view your content.
- ☑ Select and mix fonts effectively.
- ☑ Add pizzazz to your text by using color.
- ☑ Provide alternatives to specified fonts.

## sixteen

Color on the Web

- ❑ A color primer
- ❑ Using color in your designs
- ❑ Color and your computer

Color is one of the most exciting aspects of designing for the Web. In traditional publishing, color is usually reserved for high-cost publications due to the labor-intensive production methods discussed later in this skill; but on the Web, adding color is relatively easy even for the novice Web designer. By following a few guidelines, you can employ vibrant colorful graphics and photographs to help deliver your message.

Producing effective graphics to enhance the appeal of your Web site design is extremely important. In this skill, you will learn the basics of color and how to work with it; you'll also learn how to choose colors effectively for your designs, and we'll give you some guidelines for producing high-quality color images for the Web.

A Color Primer

We are surrounded by color every day—from the colors we decorate our homes with to the advertising we see on television. In most cases, we don't think much about the colors around us unless we are purchasing a gallon of paint or a new article of clothing. Suddenly, the choice of color becomes an enormously important decision. How do you select colors? What colors go together? Do they match? Does it matter?

Before you can choose effective colors and color combinations, it helps tremendously to have a basic understanding of color theory. Once you have a grasp of how colors relate, the task of choosing colors becomes much easier.

The easiest way to develop familiarity and comfort with color is to spend a bit of time studying the color wheel. The color wheel is the most common tool used for introducing basic color principles because it's fairly intuitive. Colors change incrementally as you go around the wheel.

The wheel, as shown in Figure 16.1, has 12 *hues* (hue is another word to describe color). In particular, this wheel illustrates the three primary hues—red, yellow, and blue. To achieve a new color, you mix various percentages of each primary hue.

 NOTE   To get the most out of this skill, you need to see the figures in color. So take your book to the computer and place the companion CD in your CD drive. You'll find all the figures in the graphics\Skill16 folder. We've included the file names for each figure along with the figure captions. You can open the graphics using a Web browser such as Netscape or Internet Explorer (both are included on this CD)—just enter the file's path name in the place where you usually enter the URL. Trust us—you're in for a treat.

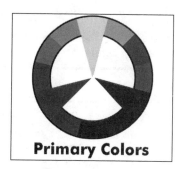

Primary Colors

FIGURE 16.1:   The primary colors of the color wheel (f1601.jpg)

Mixing equal portions of two primary colors produces a secondary color. (Think back to kindergarten and finger painting!) For example, if you mix red and yellow you will get orange. Orange is found on the wheel halfway between yellow and red. The same relationship exists between yellow and blue (green) and between red and blue (violet). We refer to green, orange, and violet as *secondary colors* because they are the result of mixing equal amounts of two primaries.

But, where did that yellow-orange color come from? If you mix the primary yellow with the secondary orange, you get yellow-orange, which we often refer to as a *tertiary color*. You can see this same logic of mixing a primary and a secondary color to achieve a tertiary color all around the wheel.

Color wheels do not always have only 12 hues. Depending on what you are trying to achieve, they can contain as few as 3 colors (the primaries) to as many as 30 colors. The point is that color proceeds in an orderly progression around the wheel and that you create the wheel by mixing the primary hues.

TIP   A color wheel is a terrific tool when you're designing Web sites or any other graphics. You can obtain a cheap color wheel at nearly any art supply store. These little devices, particularly those that show colors in varying tints, are extremely useful time and time again in the design process.

Figure 16.2 shows some adjacent colors (colors next to each other) on the color wheel. Usually, three or four colors are used in adjacent color palettes. Such color schemes are an excellent choice for the novice designer—they are predictable and easy to select.

NOTE   In design terms, a *palette* is a range of colors to be used in a composition. For instance, a decorator's palette for a nursery would likely have pinks, blues, and soft yellows or greens in it, but not purple, chartreuse, or other dark and jarring colors.

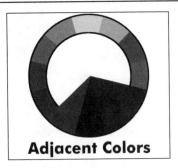

Adjacent Colors

FIGURE 16.2:   Adjacent colors on the color wheel (f1602.jpg)

Complementary colors are colors that are opposite on the color wheel. Figure 16.3 shows blue and orange. These combinations of colors are certainly attention-grabbing; however, as you will see later in this skill, complementary color schemes can also produce undesirable effects when used excessively.

Complementary Colors

FIGURE 16.3:   Complementary colors are very eye-catching when used together. (f1603.jpg)

Figure 16.4 shows an example of *triads*—colors that are equidistant on the color wheel. In this example, you can see orange, green, and violet. The primary colors (red, yellow, and blue) are another example of a triad colors. Palettes based on triads are a popular design choice. Microsoft's home page uses the red/yellow/blue triad (`http://www.microsoft.com`), as does Symantec (`http://www.symantec.com`).

FIGURE 16.4:   Triad colors (f1604.jpg)

In the previous color wheel examples, we were looking at fully *saturated* hues. Saturation refers to the intensity of a particular hue. An intense hue is fairly pure in color—for example, a fully saturated red is bright and intense, not the red of a weathered barn or brick. Fully saturated hues are "simple" colors, much like a child's first set of crayons.

Figure 16.5 shows the color wheel with full saturation on the outer edge, and increasing levels of de-saturation as you look toward the center of the image.

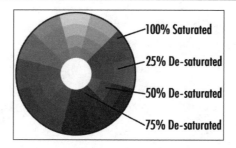

FIGURE 16.5:   Desaturated colors (f1605.jpg)

A fully saturated hue is the most vibrant and intense. As you desaturate the color, it becomes more gray, more dull in tone. The original hue is retained in desaturation; it just becomes less intense.

The last "color basic" to consider is *value* or *brightness*. In Figure 16.6, you can see a stripe of blue that ranges from a high value at the left to a low value on the right. Value is a measure of brightness, or light and dark, in a color;and it determines a hue's placement somewhere between black and white on a scale.

Value

FIGURE 16.6:   Color values (f1606.jpg)

Don't confuse value with saturation; many people do. Value is purely a measure of light and dark, not the amount of gray or dullness within a particular hue. It may be easiest for you to think of value in terms of light and shadow. If an object is brightly lighted on one side and shadowed on the other, the color hasn't changed. The hue's value is different—from a high value on the lighted side to a low value on the shadowed side.

COLOR THEORY: A COMPLEX TOPIC

The color wheel represents only one school of thought on color theory. Although it is the simplest approach to understanding the use of color in design, it isn't ideal for explaining color on computer monitors. The color wheel was actually developed for mixing pigments to paint canvas.

Color theory is a complex topic, and experts from diverse fields have addressed it in great detail—from the physiology of the human eye and perception of color to the mechanics of color monitors.

continued on next page ▶

If you are interested in learning more about color theory, check out the following URLs:

"Basic Color Theory" by Douglas Barkey, is a good page with lots of information. Find it at:

```
http://exchange.coa.edu/HEJourney/polcom/colort.html
```

"Understanding Color" is an excellent tutorial on color, with additional resources. Find it at:

```
http://humboldt1.com/~color/index.html
```

Another excellent tutorial on color with additional resources is Poynton's Color FAQ. This is probably the most comprehensive documentation regarding the creation of computer graphics and digital imaging. Find it at:

```
http://www.inforamp.net/~poynton/notes/colour_and_gamma/
    ColorFAQ.html
```

"Exploring Color" by Bob Hoffman, is a very accessible description. Find this article at:

```
http://edweb.sdsu.edu/edweb_folder/EET/Color/Color.html
```

As we mentioned earlier, a lot has been written about color theory. Here are some titles that we think are particularly helpful:

- *Designer's Guide to Color*, Ikuyoshi Shibukawa and Yumi Takahashi, Chronicle Books,1990
- *The Psychology of Color and Design* (Second Edition), Deborah T. Sharpe, Nelson Hall Inc, 1982
- *The Color of Life*, Arthur G. Abbott, McGraw-Hill, 1947
- *Colour for Professional Communicators*, Andre Jute, Batsford Ltd., 1993

Skill 16

Using Color in Your Designs

Using color effectively depends on understanding and following some simple rules about how our eyes perceive color and how color affects us. Now that we have a common vocabulary, let's dive into some choices that you as a Web designer will have to make. What are your options when choosing colors and combinations of colors to present your message?

Color Relationships

Colors affect the way we see other colors. This phenomenon is used over and over in advertising, design, and decoration. You choose colors to enhance and emphasize other colors much as you would select a mat or a frame for a painting or a print.

Have you ever heard people describe themselves as a "winter" or an "autumn"? They are talking about their personal coloration—their skin tones, hair color, and eye color. When you purchase clothing, you automatically sense this—often unconsciously. Have you ever tried on a sweater that looked great on the shelf but appeared to make you look pale or ill? Do some clothes just make you look good? This is a common example of a color relationship between your personal coloration and the sweater.

Figure 16.7 shows our first example of color illusions. The pink squares in the center of each of the two larger squares are the identical shade of pink; but they sure don't look the same, do they? This is because of the background color on which the pink square rests. The yellow background appears to increase the vibrancy or intensity of the pink; and the gray background seems to cause the pink to appear less intense or less saturated.

FIGURE 16.7: Do both pink squares have the same saturation? (f1607.jpg)

Figure 16.8 illustrates a similar principle; the green in the smallest boxes is identical in both images. However, concentrate on the green on red graphic for a few seconds—does the small box appear to be vibrating? Does it appear to move toward you and then away from you? This is an optical illusion that is common when two complementary colors are next to each other. (Complementary colors are opposite each other on the color wheel, as we described in the previous section.)

FIGURE 16.8: Optical illusions are common with complementary colors. (f1608.jpg)

If the previous image didn't seem to vibrate, the next certainly will! Figure 16.9 illustrates how readability of type can be affected by its presentation against a background color. In this case, the two hues are both high intensity and pure—your eye has a difficult time focusing on the type in this image.

FIGURE 16.9: The background color competes for attention with the text color. (f1609.jpg)

As we mentioned earlier, a complementary color scheme grabs your attention, but it is also hard on your visitor's eyes. If you use a complementary color scheme, do so sparingly in small areas. Overdosing your visitor with vibrating color is likely to be confusing and annoying.

Figure 16.10 illustrates another way background color can affect your viewing of the foreground color. In this example, the red-violet lines and boxes in the graph are on a graduated blue-violet to red background. The red-violet line appears to change color as a result of its relationship with the graduated background; however, the line and the boxes are the identical color.

FIGURE 16.10:   Background color can impact how other objects are seen.
(f1610.jpg)

Using high-contrast hues can improve the readability of type on a color background. Figure 16.11 compares white text against a light green and a dark green background. The only difference in the colors is the value of the green. The type is much easier to read against the darker green because of the high contrast.

> Readability of type
> depends on contrast

FIGURE 16.11:   Choosing high-contrast text and background colors enhances readability. (f1611.jpg)

The Psychological Impact of Color

Color has a strong impact on us emotionally. Consider the following phrases:

- They're seeing red right now.
- I'm having a blue day.
- She has a yellow streak.
- He's still rather green.
- She told him a little white lie.

Each of these statements is immediately understandable without a description of the situation or the emotions involved. Color has the same effect on the viewer—it sets a mood or a feeling.

We commonly refer to colors as "warm" and "cool." Figure 16.12 shows where these "temperatures" of color fall on the color wheel.

Warm Colors

Reds, oranges, and yellows are warm colors, as shown on the color wheel in Figure 16.12. Warm colors appear to move forward in an image, and they convey a sense of energy.

FIGURE 16.12:   Colors arranged by "temperature" (f1612.jpg)

A viewer's response to color depends on the saturation or intensity level of the hue. For example, the photograph in Figure 16.13 (a neon sign at night in Hong Kong) has predominantly high-intensity hues of red and yellow. These colors stimulate the eye, and the viewer can feel the excitement generated by the colors in the image as well as by the subject of the image. This image literally glows with energy — particularly the contrast of the bright hues against the night sky. Do you have an urge to get involved—perhaps go dancing or explore the nightlife of Hong Kong?

Bright red is known to attract attention—often unwelcome attention if you happen to be the driver of a sporty cherry red car. Some studies have shown that red cars tend to be driven faster and are stopped more often by the police for speeding than any other color car. Consider that red is often used for emergency vehicles, for flashing lights on ambulances, and for stop signs—all situations that require prompt attention.

FIGURE 16.13: The bright neon streetscape of Hong Kong (f1613.jpg)

Figure 16.14 illustrates another use of warm color, this time the hues are much less intense and have less energy overall. The sunset colors of yellow, pinks, and oranges still have the ability to evoke energetic emotions in the viewer. Does it feel romantic to you? Do you have a strong urge to watch and see the sun drop below the horizon? The average viewer finds it hard to withdraw from this image.

Copyright 1997 John Lock

FIGURE 16.14:   Sunsets and their colors inspire romantic thoughts.
(f1614.jpg)

Cool Colors

As you saw in Figure 16.12 earlier in this skill, the cool colors are purples, blues, and greens. Cool colors appear to recede into the background and evoke a feeling of released tension.

Figure 16.15 shows a scene at Yosemite National Park. The blues of the skies and water and the greens of the landscape are low-intensity, cool colors. Your eye finds these images soothing. Do you feel a sigh of relaxation as you look at this image? An urge to kick off your shoes, pull up a hammock, and relax in the peace of this landscape?

Copyright 1997 John Lock

FIGURE 16.15: Do you find the cool colors of this scenic spot relaxing? (f1615.jpg)

In Figure 16.16, another example of cool colors, the greens are higher intensity than the hues in the previous photo, but they still evoke a feeling of restfulness. While your eye travels around the image to take in the various details, you can feel the relaxation. Can you hear the dripping of water and the soft sounds of wind in the trees?

Choosing Colors

So, now that you've read all this stuff about color and the emotional aspects of color, what good is it? How does this apply to Web page design?

The impact of color in graphic design is easy to see with a little bit of study. Designers use color to draw your attention to specific elements of a, in the same way that they use the basic art principles outlined in Skill 14. By combining those principles and the tips for using color in this Skill, you can create attention-grabbing pages that will keep your visitors at your Web site, hungry for more!

Copyright 1997 John Lock

FIGURE 16.16:   A lush green forest scene (f1616.jpg)

TIP   Once you've read through this skill, take some time to look at information and advertising sources both in print and on the Web to see if you can understand how color is being used. By looking at other designs with an analytical eye, you will begin to see patterns in the use of color that you can utilize for your own designs.

For the beginning designer, choosing colors feels like an overwhelming task. There seem to be so many choices! Keep your color schemes simple in the beginning. Experiment with the color wheel, apply the color basics we have provided here, and study the color schemes used by other designers. As you experiment, you will begin to get a feel for working with color.

Color is a subjective for most people. Although the rules may tell you that yellow is a happy color, all the rules in the world aren't going to make yellow feel happy for you if you personally don't like yellow. Start with colors that you like and feel good about; trust your gut reactions. After all, when you design your first Web site, you are likely looking to please yourself—not a rule book!

Figure 16.17 shows a fictitious company's Web site done in a one-color scheme with varying tints of violet and black for the text. This is a simple color scheme that can be surprisingly versatile and easy for the novice designer to work with. Graphical text is always white, and buttons are one of two tints of violet. The background is a very light violet. You can easily make color decisions as you add features to the site.

FIGURE 16.17:   A simple single-color design scheme (f1617.jpg)

Figure 16.18 shows the look you get when you add violet's complementary color—orange. The graphical text really jumps out at you now, doesn't it? Again, this is a relatively simple color scheme to work with. The complementary color is used for text, and a very light tint is used for the background. For zing, you could also add orange bullets to this page.

FIGURE 16.18:   The addition of orange really jumps off the screen.
(f1618.jpg)

TIP

Earlier, we warned against using complementary colors inappropriately. The example in Figure 16.18 illustrates the use of complementary colors; however, the violet is not a fully saturated hue. The toned-down violet tint reduces the potential for a "vibrating" image, which is hard to look at, particularly on a computer monitor. The vibration effect is most often seen with two very pure hues of complementary colors. Let your eye be the judge if you are considering this type of color scheme.

In Figure 16.19, we've used a color triad made up of tints of the primary colors (red, yellow, and blue) and white as a background. This color scheme is still relatively easy to work with. The stripe on the left side of the page is a desaturated tint of the blue.

As a designer, you will need to choose which tints of the hues to use primarily based on what feels good to you. You may notice that the blue chosen for the banner and buttons is not a pure hue. Pure hues are intense and are hard on the eyes. Experiment with hue intensity levels until you find a combination that has sufficient contrast to be readable, but isn't difficult to look at on your computer monitor.

FIGURE 16.19:   Incorporating a color-triad into the design (f1619.jpg)

Figure 16.20 shows an adjacent hues color scheme—red-orange through yellow. Again, the designer has used varying tints and saturation levels to achieve a pleasing combination of colors and sufficient contrast for legibility of graphical text. When you use this color scheme, you'll need to experiment to find the right colors—a fun and educational process.

FIGURE 16.20:   The same design using an adjacent palette (f1620.jpg)

And now for a rather intense and dramatic experience, take a look at Figure 16.21. It uses nearly all of the colors on the wheel at full intensity, plus black and white. This color scheme can work; however, the process for deciding which color to use for each element takes careful consideration and a great deal of experimenting. The site is bright and has a great deal of energy. Subsequent pages will be a serious challenge. Which color should dominate throughout the site? Should secondary pages be as dramatic or perhaps toned down a bit?

FIGURE 16.21: Bright colors are eye-catching, though care must be taken not to overwhelm. (f1621.jpg)

Color and Your Computer

So, now you are ready to get busy and create, right? Well, not just yet. You also need some details on just which colors you can use on the Web. But first, we need to look at how your computer handles color.

The RGB Color Model

Artists think in terms of the color wheel. It's the easiest model to understand color because usually artists work in pigments—paint, crayons, pastels, or markers. Artists apply color to (usually) white paper or canvas and build colors by mixing pure hues to form other colors.

Your computer, however, thinks about colors of light, specifically red, green, and blue light—and it handles color with the RGB (Red, Green, Blue) color model. So, for now, put away your color wheel.

The Basics

Your computer, whatever flavor—PC, Mac, Unix, or what-have-you—uses beams of colored light cast onto the black screen of your monitor to make colors. These colored lights "mix," or combine, to create all the colors you use in making computer graphics. Figure 16.22 shows the RGB color model with all lights shining at full intensity. Red, green, and blue are the primary colors that your computer uses.

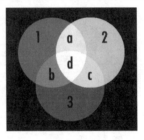

FIGURE 16.22: The RGB colors are blended to produce colors on your computer screen. (f1622.jpg)

The circles show Red (1), Green (2), and Blue (3) overlaid to form other colors. As you can see, Red and Green combine to form Yellow (a), Red and Blue overlay to form Magenta (b), and Blue and Green overlay to form Cyan [c]. At the conjunction of all three circles, you can see White (d)—the resultant color of all three colors of light shining at full intensity.

The next figure illustrates how specific colors are formed with the RGB model. Most colors are combinations of each of the constituent lights of Red, Green, and Blue. The white square in Figure 16.23 illustrates how the RGB model forms a sort of lavender shade as a result of Red and Blue at 100% and Green at 60% intensity. All colors are created by this process in the RGB model.

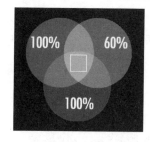

FIGURE 16.23:   By varying the intensity of one component, new colors are achieved. (f1623.jpg)

THE CMYK COLOR MODEL

You've probably heard of CMYK (*C*yan, *M*agenta, *Y*ellow, blac*K*) color—perhaps when reading ink jet printer reviews or when perusing the help files in your favorite graphics software. What's CMYK all about? Why yet another color model?

As you saw in Figure 16.22, Cyan, Magenta, and Yellow are the secondary colors of light. (Remember, secondary colors are formed by mixing equal portions of primary colors.) However, Cyan, Magenta, and Yellow are also the primary colors of printing inks. As in the RGB color model or on the color wheel, mixing various percentages of Cyan, Magenta, and Yellow will yield all other colors. Combined with Black, these are the colors use in four-color printing.

Color printing requires a separate printing plate for each of the four ink colors. The individual plates are made by using "separations"—the separated colors of your image. Separations used to be generated by using different colored filters to photograph the full-color image and capture it onto film. Now, we use sophisticated software to separate the full-color image into its constituent percentages of CMYK and generate a printing plate for each ink.

continued on next page ▶

To create a four-color image, the paper must pass through the press four times—once for each printing plate. Each successive pass applies another ink, starting with the lightest ink through to black. The individual plates must be carefully registered to assure that the elements in the image are aligned properly.

Sound complicated? You betcha! And it's expensive to produce a four-color print job. Web publishing never looked so good!

The Numbers of RGB

So, now that you understand how light is used to create colors in RGB, how do you name or specify these colors? That depends on the software you use. Typically, graphics software uses one of three scales to describe colors: 100%, 256, or hexadecimal.

The 100% Scale   Although not all software supports it, the easiest way to understand color specification is in terms of percentages of intensity of light. Figure 16.24 shows a swatch of blue starting at 100% intensity and declining in 20% increments to 0% intensity.

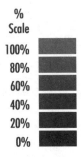

%
Scale
100%
80%
60%
40%
20%
0%

FIGURE 16.24:   Colors brighten with an increase of intensity. (f1624.jpg)

As you can see, 0% intensity is black, and 100% intensity is a fully saturated, very intense blue.

The 256 Scale   Most graphic design software, such as Photoshop, CorelDraw, and FreeHand, describe RBG colors in the 256 scale. This is because computers actually think in a scale of 256. In other words, your computer recognizes 255 levels of light intensity for each of the three colors of light—from 0 (off) as the lowest, to 255 (full light or 100% light) as the highest.

In Figure 16.25, you can see that the computer assigns the number 51 to 20% light intensity, 102 to 40%, and so on. It doesn't matter which color of light you are using; the scale is consistent for all colors.

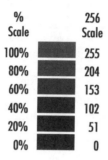

% Scale		256 Scale
100%		255
80%		204
60%		153
40%		102
20%		51
0%		0

FIGURE 16.25:   Intensity values measured in both percentages and the 256 scale (f1625.jpg)

> **TIP**
>
> How many colors are possible in the RGB color model? Would you believe 16,777,216? Why such an odd number? Each beam of light can provide 256 levels of intensity for three colors of light. If you multiply 256 levels of red by 256 levels of green by 256 levels of blue, you get 16.7 million possible colors. RGB color is also referred to as "true color" or 24-bit color.

The Hex Scale   Hex is the geek version of color scales—honest. Hex is short for hexadecimal, the numeric language of computers. As you learned in Skill 4, computers do everything in terms of bits, whether it is measuring file size or specifying colors. In Skill 4, you also learned about using colored backgrounds for your Web pages with a background color tag that includes the hex description of the color you want. Here is an example of how color works in hex. Figure 16.26 shows a modified chart with the colors of blue now described in the 100% scale, the 256 scale, and the hex scale.

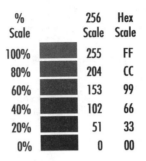

% Scale		256 Scale	Hex Scale
100%		255	FF
80%		204	CC
60%		153	99
40%		102	66
20%		51	33
0%		0	00

FIGURE 16.26: All three scales measuring intensity (f1626.jpg)

Each of the previous figures showed a simple hue, using only different intensities of blue light to illustrate the naming conventions for RGB color. In reality, you will most likely be creating graphics that use combinations of all three colors of light.

Figure 16.27 illustrates a color that is typical for use in a Web design and the three naming conventions that describe that color.

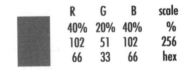

	R	G	B	scale
	40%	20%	40%	%
	102	51	102	256
	66	33	66	hex

FIGURE 16.27: The value dusky violet in each color scale (f1627.jpg)

Web Colors: The Netscape Palette

Now that you understand how your computer creates colors, it's time to start thinking about which colors you will use in your Web designs. At this point, you're either feeling overwhelmed at the idea of choosing just a few colors from a potential of 16.7 million or thinking that it will be a snap to choose with so many different options.

Well, depending on your point of view, it's good news or bad news. Your choice of colors is actually limited to a much smaller palette than the full 16.7 million. In fact, in most cases, you can only choose from a palette of 216 colors or possibly 256. Why? Read on…

Hardware Issues

Why are we talking about hardware? Well, the images you can see on your computer monitor—or perhaps more important, the images that your Web site visitors can see—are only going to look as good as their hardware will allow.

Computer monitors and video cards (video adapters) come in a variety of prices and quality. Many Web designers have relatively high-end equipment, meaning that they can view 24-bit color images in all their colorful glory, and they tend to assume that the rest of the world sees the Web as they do.

However, most people surfing the Web are actually using equipment that can only display images at 8 bits, meaning a maximum of 256 colors in the computer system's color palette. This means that your Web site visitor may not be seeing your images as you intended. In fact, your images may look downright ugly on a 256-color monitor.

COMPATIBILITY NOTE   When developing graphics for the Web, it is important to determine who your audience is and what type of equipment they are likely using. Although it is becoming rare, some systems can display only 16 colors. If your Web site will be primarily viewed by people who are working on older computer systems with low color capability, you need to consider your Web site design carefully.

Side-Effects of a 256-Color Monitor

When a graphic is drawn in a Web browser, the browser uses its own palette to display the image. Depending on the capabilities of the computer, the Web browser's palette, and the actual palette used in the graphic, your images may not appear as you intended. Quite often, the effect is unsettling for the visitor.

Palette Shift   A particularly ugly problem is what is known as *palette shift*. When the visitor loads an image onto a computer that supports 256 colors or fewer, things look fine. The problem arises when a second image or a second window is activated on the screen. In an effort to accommodate the differences in the palette of the new image or window, the computer system "shifts" the palette, causing all colors to change.

The visitor sees a flashing effect on the screen, and many colors appear "off" or "strange." All in all, it's an unsettling experience for visitors, particularly when you are hoping to draw their attention to your Web site's message! Instead, you manage to annoy or bewilder your visitors.

TIP   You will only see the palette shift effect if you are using a computer system that has a 256 or fewer color palette. You might want to check this out by changing your system settings to a 256-color palette. It's good to have some idea of what your Web site visitors experience when palettes are inconsistent.

Dithering   Another problem with 256-color systems is image *dithering*, which is also known as "those strange speckles and dots in my logo." Because your Web browser uses a particular internal color palette, the browser attempts to render the image by "dithering," or faking the colors if an image contains colors not within that palette. This is done via a mathematical formula that colors individual pixels of the image to fool your eye into seeing a simulation of the color not contained in the browser's palette. Dithering gives the appearance of speckles and dots—a sort of pointillistic look. Dithering is most obvious in areas of solid and ungraduated color such as logos and background colors.

The Solution: Browser Palettes

Because of the differences in computers and the undesirable effects on images that these differences produce, something had to be done to create a level playing field for Web images. After all, who wants to create amazing graphics in which the skin tones sometimes appear green because of computer system palette differences? Or your lovely shade of blue in your corporate logo turns a sort of speckled brownish blue?

The companies that develop Web browser software have come up with some solutions that may make it possible for your graphic masterpiece to reach most of the surfing public. Most of the common Web browsers such as Netscape Navigator and Internet Explorer have adopted a common palette called the *Netscape palette*, or the 6 × 6 × 6 palette, to reduce palette problems.

This palette, as shown in Figure 16.28, contains 216 colors that are common to all computer platforms. "But, wait a minute, you said that the palette would contain 256 colors, the number of colors that the monitor could actually display! What happened to the other 40 colors?" They are reserved for the computer's operating system's needs. (Your operating system requires some colors to display window frames, button bars, icons, and other graphic interfaces.)

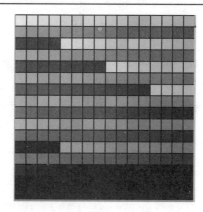

FIGURE 16.28: The "browser safe" 216 color palette (f1628.jpg)

 NOTE   It is possible to use some of those "reserved colors" in your designs. For example, the 6 × 6 × 6 palette does not include white or black. However, most computer systems do include black and white in their system palette, so it is likely a safe bet to add these without any detrimental effects. We will talk about these options in Skill 17.

When the Netscape palette is used to display images that were not created using this palette, the results are often less than desirable. In other words, as a Web designer, using the Netscape palette to create your images is your best insurance that your images will look consistent across platforms.

Using the Netscape Palette

The best rule when creating brand-new images for the Web is to use the Netscape palette whenever possible. This is actually easier than it sounds; the Netscape palette is available from many sources on the Web:

- As a GIF image that you can use with the eyedropper tool in graphics software

- As a color swatch file for Photoshop

- As a text-file with the actual RGB values and the hex values to be entered into the color picker tool in your graphics software

THE NETSCAPE PALETTE ONLINE

The Netscape palette is available in a number of formats that can be downloaded off the Web.

You'll find Photoshop color swatches for Windows at:

```
http://www.adobe.com/newsfeatures/palette/LIBRARY/WEB216.ZIP
```

Photoshop color swatches for Macintosh are available at:

```
http://www.adobe.com/newsfeatures/palette/LIBRARY/WEB216_CLUT.hqx
```

You'll find a GIF file for all platforms at:

```
http://the-light.com/netcol2.gif
```

And you'll find an HTML page with hex values at:

```
http://www.netscapeworld.com/netscapeworld/nw-11-1996/
    216_hexcodes.html
```

So does using the Netscape palette solve all your image problems? Most of the time. In some situations, however, the Netscape palette isn't ideal. In Skill 17, we will provide you with more information on how to optimize your image productions for size and colors and how to choose the file type. You must make a number of choices when prepating images for the Web, including file size, formats, and palettes.

More on Browsers and Palettes

It's impossible in this book to cover every nuance of Web color issues, but here are some online resources that will help:

"Consistent Color on ALL Browsers—10 Easy Steps," by Geoff Baysinger, is an excellent discussion about the issues involved in browser palettes. Find it at:

```
http://www.netscapeworld.com/common/nw.color.html
```

"The Discriminating Color Palette," by Lisa Lopuck, is useful for the Adobe Photoshop user. It contains tips for creating GIFs and copies of the Adobe version of the Netscape palette to download. Find all this at:

`http://www.adobe.com/newsfeatures/palette/main.html`

"The Web Publishing Resource Guide" is an excellent HTML-based Web color chart with the 256 scale and hex scale numbering of colors. Find it at:

`http://members.aol.com/thewprg/htm/wprg_frm.htm`

Have You Mastered the Essentials?

Now you can. . .

- ☑ **Apply color theory to develop a color scheme.**
- ☑ **Utilize color relationships to enhance your Web page designs.**
- ☑ **Work with the RGB color model.**
- ☑ **Develop Web graphics that will display consistently across platforms.**

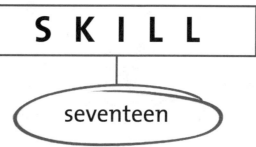

Creating Professional Graphics

- ❑ Digital image basics

- ❑ Creating professional gifs and jpegs

- ❑ Tools of the trade

- ❑ How those who can't draw survive

Digital images, whether graphics or photographs, provide much of the appeal for the Web. They add color, excitement, information, illustration, and fun to Web pages when they are "done well." However it's not enough to design attractive images; you also need to produce technically good images that will load quickly and be consistent across computer platforms.

Have you seen graphics that just don't work for one reason or another? Huge images as the first element on a page, photos with "off" colors, strangely dithered or spotted graphics, or palette shifting? There are a number of common problems that can occur with Web images.

In this skill, we will provide you with the information that you need to create professional graphics for your Web site: graphics that will load quickly, look good consistently across platforms, and enhance your site's image.

NOTE   To help you to get the most out of this skill, we've provided some of the graphics in color on the CD that comes with this book. You'll know which ones they are because we've included their file names along with the figure captions. You can open the graphics using a Web browser such as Netscape or Internet Explorer (both are included on this CD)—just enter the file's path name in the place where you usually enter the URL. The figures for this skill are located in the graphics\Skill17 folder.

Digital Image Basics

Before diving into the details of producing Web images, let's take some time to understand some basics about digital images. Digital graphics come in two primary types: vector and raster.

Raster Images

Raster images are the type of images that Web designers are most familiar with. They include gifs, jpgs, and tif files. Raster formats are always used for photographic or "continuous tone" images. By looking at a magnified raster image such as the one we have in Figure 17.1, you can see that a raster image is made up of individual colored pixels. Each of the individual little rectangles you can see in this image is a "pixel."

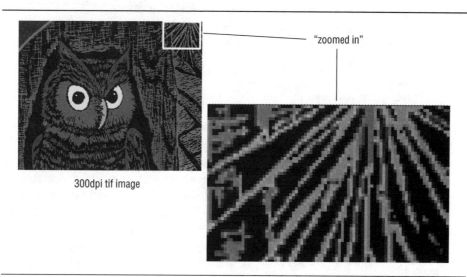

"zoomed in"

300dpi tif image

FIGURE 17.1: A raster image (f1701.jpg)

Raster images are "resolution dependent" meaning that they are not easily stretched or scaled to a larger size without losing image quality. As you can see in Figure 17.2, the rocket on the left is sharp and clean. This image was created for the Web as a "top of page" button. It was saved at 72 ppi (pixels per inch). The image on the right is a scaled up version of the original; it was resized by 200% in an image editing program. The larger version is fuzzy and blurry looking, with some jaggy edges on the diagonal lines forming the top of the rocket. This is what happens when you attempt to scale or enlarge raster images. The image is dependent on the resolution at which it was created.

Original image

Scaled up 200%

FIGURE 17.2: A raster image scaled up 200% (f1702.jpg)

Raster images are often referred to as "bitmap" images, which isn't always completely accurate. In technical-speak, the term bitmap actually describes a black-and-white raster graphic. Technically, "bitmaps" do not contain any color data.

Vector Images

Vector graphics files contain a series of mathematical instructions for drawing a picture in a particular language. Postscript is the most commonly used language for generating vector graphics. The most common vector graphics file formats are eps, ai, and cdr. Vector graphics are most commonly used for print media images.

Vector graphics are easily scaleable or stretchable and as a result are "resolution-independent". This provides the designer with plenty of advantages—you can easily resize the image whether you want to fit it on a business card or on a bill-board without loss of image quality. As you can see in Figure 17.3, the images on the left and the right are the same image. The only difference between the images is that the righthand image is 200% larger than the left image.

FIGURE 17.3: A vector image scaled up 200% (f1703.jpg)

Resizing vector images does not produce the same problem as resizing raster images: a resized vector image does not have jaggy edges Vector images work especially well for logos, branding graphics, symbols, and other images that you may need to re-size for various uses.

Vector graphics sound like the ideal type of image to use, but you cannot directly use a vector image on a Web page. However, vector graphics can be converted to raster images using graphics conversion software.

Graphic File Formats

While there are two primary "types" of digital images, there are seemingly endless flavors of digital images. These flavors are technically known as "file formats". The *format* of a graphic file refers to the specific method of storing the image data within the file on your disk. The format of the file tells your software how to open the image and display it on your monitor.

Web File Formats

There are two primary file formats that are commonly in use for Web graphics: gif (Graphical Interchange Format) and jpeg (Joint Picture Experts Group). These two formats are supported by most graphical Web browsers and as a result, are the file format of choice for most Web development. A recent introduction, png (Portable Network Graphic), may eventually replace gif; however it is not currently supported by most Web browsers.

Gif

Gif files are the most common graphic file format used on the Web. They are usually small in file size and are therefore quick to download and display in a Web browser. Gif files may contain a maximum of 256 colors or 8-bit color.

In most cases, a gif image is created from another raster file format such as tiff. The artist begins with an image created in a raster image editing program such as Photoshop and uses tools within Photoshop to convert the original image to a gif file. When a file is converted to gif, the resulting image is much smaller than the original and the file is now able to be displayed by Web browsers. (Later in this skill, we will look at how to create quality gif images using the Netscape palette.)

Gif is the file format of choice for Web graphics containing line art, large areas of flat color such as logos or banners, small icons, and other graphics that are non-photographic in nature.

COMPATIBILITY NOTE   If you expect that your audience will be primarily using computer equipment that can only display 256 colors, you may want to experiment with converting your continuous tone images to gif format using an adaptive palette as described later in this skill.

Jpeg

Jpeg is the file format of choice for displaying photographs or continuous tone images on the Web. Jpeg files use a *lossy* method of compression for full color RGB files, 24 bit or 16.7 million colors. If the viewer has a monitor capable of displaying 24 bit color, jpeg images can capture the full color range of a continuous tone image and display it in a graphical Web browser.

Lossy compression means that in reducing file size, some image data is removed from the original file. The impact of this removal of data is governed by the choices made by the user of the graphic conversion software. Most raster image editing programs can convert an image to a jpeg file format. The artist begins with a 24 bit image and saves it to jpeg format after choosing image quality levels. (Later in this skill, we will address choosing image quality levels appropriate to your image.) Once the file is converted to a jpeg, the file size will be much smaller than the original image.

Jpeg is the file format best suited for continuous tone images on the Web. While jpeg files are usually smaller than gif files, jpeg does not work very well for line-art, logos, or other images that contain large areas of flat color. One of the side effects of the lossy compression algorithm used in jpeg produces some speckles or other "artifacts" in the final image. These artifacts are usually not noticeable in continuous tone images; however, speckles in your logo typically do not improve its appearance!

Png

The World Wide Web Consortium (W3C), the Internet specification organization, has endorsed png as the newest of graphic file formats for the Web. While png is likely to be the best way to produce consistent Web graphics, not all Web browsers can display png files. The most recent releases (Versions 4.0) of Netscape Navigator and Microsoft Internet Explorer are the only Web browsers currently supporting this file format.

Png offers the file size reduction of gif and jpeg files; yet it also works well across computer platforms as it allows the graphic creator to include image information such as the palette used within the file itself, thus insuring consistent appearance on all systems. Png files are expected to be about 30% smaller in size than most gifs, which provides another advantage in the Web graphics creation process. Once the format is supported by most Web browsers, it will likely become the file format of choice for the Web.

Non-Web File Formats

As you develop images for your Web site, you will create some yourself, you will obtain some by scanning photographs or other printed materials, and you will already have some in digital form. The graphics that are already in digital form may not be "Web ready," in other words, they may be in a file format other than gif or jpg.

When you have a digital image in an unfamiliar file format, you need to know how to open the image and convert it to a file format that can be used on the Web. The following table shows some of the most common file formats whether those formats are vector or raster, and what software products are used to create the formats. Armed with this information and the appropriate software, you can tackle the task of getting your image converted and ready for the Web.

TABLE 17.1: Common file formats

File Format	File Type	Notes
gif	Raster	A common Web format. Many software programs can read it.
jpeg	Raster	A common Web format. Many software programs can read it.
tiff	Raster	A common format. Many software programs can read it.
psd	Raster	A file type created in Adobe Photoshop.
pcd	Raster	A file type created in Kodak PhotoCD, supported by many software programs.
cpt	Raster	A file type created in Corel Photo-Paint. This file type is not widely supported.
bmp	Raster	A file type created in Microsoft Paintbrush. Many software programs can read this format.
pcx	Raster	A file type created in Microsoft Paintbrush. Many software programs can read this format.
targa	Raster	A file type usually created by video industry software. Many software programs can read this format.
pict	Vector	A file type created in MacPaint. This file type is platform dependent.
wmf	Vector	A file type created in Microsoft Draw. Other software programs can read this format.
cgm	Vector	A file type created in various software programs. Other software programs can read this format.

TABLE 17.1 CONTINUED: Common file formats

File Format	File Type	Notes
dxf	Vector	A file type created in AutoCad. This file type has some compatibilty with other software.
ai, eps	Vector	A file type created in Adobe Illustrator, CorelDRAW, and others. Many software programs can read this format.
cdr	Vector	CorelDRAW creates this file type. Some software programs can read it.

Once you have identified the file format of your image, you will need to either use the software it was created in to open it or work with a graphics conversion program such as CorelDRAW, Hijaak, or Lview Pro. We have provided additional information about conversion software later in this skill.

Creating Professional Images

Now that you have a good basic understanding of Web image file formats and when to use which one, it's time to work on developing your Web image production skills. We will take a look at the different ways to prepare images and some of the choices that you will need to make depending on your own Web site and your goals.

Gifs

In Skill 16, you learned about the problems of 256 color monitors and cross platform inconsistency in displaying images. The Web browser companies, namely Netscape, came to the rescue of surfers everywhere with the Netscape palette. This palette, containing 216 "browser safe" colors, is the solution for Web designers around the world. By using the palette, you can provide cross-platform consistency for displaying Web images.

Of course, by now, you have a copy of this palette downloaded and ready to go with your paint program, right? If not, get yourself a copy (Victor Engel has provided a very nice one at http://www.onr.com/user/lights/netcol.html) and then dive into learning when to use the Netscape palette and when not to use it.

Flat Color Images

You almost always want to use the Netscape palette with line art or flat color images like logos. The ideal situation is to have created the image originally using the Netscape palette colors in your paint program. If the image was not created using the Netscape palette, the next best thing is to load the image into your paint program such as Photoshop and save the image as a gif file using the Netscape palette.

Figure 17.4 illustrates the fictitious Tropical Escapes logo in its original RGB file. As you can see there are several areas of flat color in the palm tree and in the squiggly blue line. The rest of the name is a smooth gradient that ranges from a hot red to a bright yellow. The color change in the text is gradual and shows no *banding* or stripes of color. The original file size for this image in tiff format is 46,900 bytes. (On the CD we've provided the image in jpeg format, so you will be able to view it using IE or Navigator.)

FIGURE 17.4:   The original version of the Tropical logo (f1704.jpg)

Figure 17.5 shows the same logo after it has been converted in Photoshop to a gif file using the Netscape palette. The file was saved using the No diffusion option. If you look at the image carefully, you can see that in the flat areas, there isn't a great deal of change, just that the original colors have been converted to Netscape palette colors. The area that shows the most difference is in the gradient in the text, which shows some sharp changes or "banding." While this image doesn't demonstrate extreme banding, the bands are noticeable. The gif file saved with no diffusion is 7,880 bytes.

FIGURE 17.5: The Tropical Escapes logo using the Netscape palette with no diffusion (f1705.jpg)

Figure 17.6 illustrates the logo once again, but this time the original logo was converted to the Netscape palette with diffusion turned on. Careful examination of the image shows that it doesn't have a great deal of change overall and that the "banding" problem seen in the previous version is gone. Instead, under careful examination, you can see that in the areas of color change in the text, there is some diffusion of the colors—a few pixels of each color mixed together to make the change in color less obvious. Of the two gif images, this one is the better looking image. The gif file saved with diffusion turned on is 6,974 bytes.

FIGURE 17.6: The Tropical Escapes logo using the Netscape palette with diffusion (f1706.jpg)

TIP

If you have an image that contains a few solid areas of areas of color, it's worth experimenting with converting those colors to the Netscape palette by hand. This process allows you to choose the color combinations that look best instead of relying on your paint program's conversion algorithm. Just use the eyedropper tool to select the Netscape colors from your swatch palette or your Netscape color file and "pour" those colors into the solid areas of your image. You may discover that you can make a more pleasing image than expected!

Photographic-Type Images

We've said that for continuous tone and photographs that jpeg is the file format of choice. However, if you are a control freak (and most Web designers are) and you expect that most of your audience will be viewing your Web images on a 256 color monitor, you may choose to present your photos as gifs. By doing this, you will insure that your audience will see the image just as you intended, rather than as the Web browser chooses to render the image.

This is where it gets a bit trickier to decide whether to use the Netscape palette in your file conversion to gif. In some cases, the choice will be very obvious: the image degradation that can occur by gifing a photograph containing a wide variety of colors can be truly appalling. (Try gifing a photograph of an image with many levels of light and shadow with lots of different colors. Ick!) There isn't any hard and fast rule on whether to use the palette; what will count is your personal preference in the images that result from experimenting.

Figure 17.7 shows the original RGB photograph of a happy soccer player and her father (Linda and Dave Navarro). As you can see, this image doesn't contain a really wide spectrum of color; however but does have many changes in value and intensity of color in the light and shadows of the image. Particularly notice the changes in tone of the clothing and skin tones. The file size of the original tiff file is 325,062 bytes. (On the CD we've provided the image in jpeg format, so you will be able to view it using IE or Navigator.)

FIGURE 17.7: The original version of the soccer photo (f1707.jpg)

Figure 17.8 is a prime example of what happens when diffusion is turned off when converting a photographic image to gif using the 216 color Netscape palette. Well, this is alarming! You can see the loss of detail in the image. It has been "posterized" very badly, meaning that the color conversion has flattened out all of the colors, making them appear like a flat poster treatment. The photo has lost all depth, the colors of skin were converted especially poorly. Skin tones have turned green, red, or gray in the highlights and shadows. The file size of the gif image is 35,872 bytes.

FIGURE 17.8: The soccer photo using the Netscape palette with no diffusion (`f1708.gif`)

Again, Figure 17.9 shows the same photo with the 216 color Netscape palette and diffusion turned on. Although it is quite an improvement over the previous version, the image still isn't very good. The colors are still not right and the diffusion causes a great deal of speckling in the image that is distracting to look at. Do you find yourself staring at the spots in Linda's soccer shorts or perhaps at the way Dave's leg blends into the green of the grass behind him? The file size of the gif image is 65,721 bytes.

FIGURE 17.9:   The soccer photo using the Netscape palette with diffusion (`f1709.gif`)

In Figure 17.10 you can see the effect of using an adaptive palette with diffusion. The "adaptive palette" refers to the paint software's algorithm for selecting the most common colors in the original image to create a 256 color palette for the gif conversion. Depending on your software program, the adaptive algorithm is different and more or less effective. This image was converted in Adobe Photoshop.

The image in Figure 17.10 shows less degradation than the previous examples. The skin tones aren't ideal, but they are closer to real skin colors. The image suffers from some posterizing, but not so much as in the previous examples. There are also fewer speckles. While this image is acceptable for Web publishing, it *will* dither on a 256 color monitor as it does not use the Netscape palette. The file size of the gif image is 85,511 bytes.

FIGURE 17.10: The soccer photo using a 256 adaptive palette with diffusion (`f1710.gif`)

Figure 17.11 shows the last of our gif examples of photographs. In this image, the adaptive palette was once again used; however this time with a limited palette of 64 colors. Again, there is a significant loss of detail in the image; but the colors are better than in the Netscape palette examples. This image is marginally acceptable, but it has the same problems as the previous adaptive palette image: it will dither in Web browsers if the user is viewing it on a 256 color monitor. The file size of the gif image is 60,022 bytes.

FIGURE 17.11: The soccer photo using a 64 Adaptive palette with diffusion (f1711.gif)

Sizing Files

Did you note the file size information for each of the previous images? In the case of the Tropical Escapes logo, the best looking gif image actually turned out to be the smallest image: 6,974 bytes.

Original tiff image	46,900 bytes
Gif Netscape palette without diffusion	7,880 bytes
Gif Netscape palette with diffusion	6,974 bytes

The Soccer photograph worked somewhat differently. The smallest image (35,872 bytes) was the worst looking image: the Netscape palette without diffusion that gave people purple legs. The second smallest image (60,022 bytes) was the 64 color adaptive palette. This image was acceptable for publishing; however, it is not ideal.

Original tiff image	325,062 bytes
Gif Netscape palette without diffusion	35,872 bytes
Gif Netscape palette with diffusion	65,721 bytes
Gif 256 Adaptive palette with diffusion	85,511 bytes
Gif 64 Adaptive palette with diffusion	60,022 bytes

Let's take a look at jpeg versions of the same soccer photograph for comparison of file sizes and image quality.

Jpegs

Jpeg is the file format of choice for continuous tone images on the Web. It allows you to provide a file with full 24 bit (RGB) color at greatly reduced file size. However, 24 bit images will only display as 8 bit images on a 256 color monitor. This means that your jpeg image will be force-dithered into the computer's operating system palette if displayed on a low color monitor.

That said, let's look at the choices that you will need to make for creating professional jpeg images. Jpeg conversion is much less complicated than gif conversion; there are no palette issues to consider. The only decision that needs to be made is one of image quality versus the final size of the file.

Most paint programs offer three or four levels of compression for jpeg images. They range from maximum quality image (lowest amount of file compression) to low quality image (highest amount of compression). Again, the choice is a personal one: how much image quality are you willing to trade for file size? Most of this is dependent on the specific image, so the only real way to decide this question is to once again experiment with the images.

Figure 17.12 shows a maximum quality jpeg version of the familiar soccer photo. (You can compare the image to the original shown in Figure 17.7.) In this instance, there is very little difference in the overall image's appearance. The place to look for image degradation (posterizing) is in the shadows. In this image, the shadow cast by the man's arm hanging at his side is a good place to look for changes in the levels of shadow colors. There is very little difference between this image and the original. This jpeg image is 163,859 bytes.

FIGURE 17.12: The soccer photo saved as a maximum quality jpeg (`f1712.jpg`)

In Figure 17.13, you can see the medium quality jpeg image. This image is beginning to show the effects of compression: there is a bit of deterioration in the shadows and there are a few "artifacts" or speckles that have been introduced by the jpeg compression process. If you look carefully at Linda's forehead, you can see some areas of light speckles that don't appear in the original image. This jpeg image is 28,210 bytes.

Figure 17.14 shows the lowest quality of jpeg. This image shows more posterization in the shadows than either of the previous images. And there are some additional jpeg-induced artifacts. However, the overall image quality is fine for Web publishing. This jpeg image is 21,265 bytes.

FIGURE 17.13:   The soccer photo saved as a medium quality jpeg (f1713.jpg)

Jpeg file sizes are almost always much smaller than comparable gif file sizes. Based upon looking at the images themselves and the file sizes, the low quality jpeg would be the best bang for the buck on the Web. The Maximum quality image is a beautiful photo and about half of the original image; however, few visitors will wait for a 163K photo to download. While a 21K image requires some download time, the quality of the image is worth the wait.

Original tiff image	325,062 bytes
Jpeg Maximum quality	163,859 bytes
Jpeg Medium quality	28,210 bytes
Jpeg Low quality	21,265 bytes

FIGURE 17.14:   The soccer photo saved as a low quality jpeg (`f1714.jpg`)

TIP

Providing small "thumbnail images" that are linked to larger photographs is an excellent way to provide your visitor with the ability to preview an image without forcing them to download the entire image. This technique works especially well when your Web site has a large number of images, such as a travel site or photographer's portfolio page. Consider using this presentation, especially if your audience is primarily connected to the Net via modems rather than T1 lines. Your visitors will thank you for it!

Resources

We've covered some important issues of working with the various types and formats of digital images, but we've really only scratched the surface. For more information about digital file formats and Web imaging, check out the URLs listed in Table 17.2.

TABLE 17.2:   Web resources for information about digital file formats and Web imaging

Web Page	Description
Understanding image file formats `http://www.cobb.com/tma/9508/tma89501.htm`	This article provides a fairly comprehensive and easy to understand description of file formats, bit depth, raster and vector images, and some good tips for working with images from a Mac perspective.
Graphics File Formats FAQ Home Page `http://www.ora.com/centers/gff/gff-faq/index.htm`	This is about the best resource on the techie (and not so techie) details of file formats.

Usenet's version of Fileformats FAQ
`http://www.cis.ohio-state.edu/hypertext/faq/`
`usenet/graphics/fileformats-faq/top.html`
	Another good collection of information.

Consistent Color on ALL browsers - 10 easy steps `http://www.netscapeworld.com/common/nw.color.html`	Good description of the Netscape palette and discussion of tradeoffs.
WC3's png (Portable Network Graphics) `http://www.w3.org/Graphics/PNG/`	A good description of png and information about the future.
The Discriminating Color Palette `http://www.adobe.com/newsfeatures/palette/main.html`	An excellent Photoshop-centric discussion of working with both gif and jpeg files and the choices you need to make.

Tools of the Trade

So, now that you have a basic understanding of digital image types and formats, you're probably wondering how to dive into actually working with those images.

What software do you need? What imaging program will dependably produce professional graphics for your Web site?

There are a wide variety of tools available for image creation and manipulation. Which you choose to use will depend on several factors:

- Your graphic design needs

- Your software budget

- Your patience for and commitment to learning to use graphics softaware

We've provided a brief overview of the most popular graphic design software products below.

Adobe Photoshop

Adobe Photoshop is indisputably the product of choice for most professional graphic designers working with Web images. Photoshop has a breadth of tools and image manipulation facilities that other software manufacturers try to emulate. Photoshop is also one of the most expensive imaging software products and has one of the steepest learning curves for the graphic design novice.

Whether you want to scan a photo and retouch it, create an image of a "painting," or create the standard buttons, bars, and backgrounds, Photoshop can do it. Photoshop's interface is fairly intuitive once you become familiar with where the various tools are located. Figure 17.15 shows Photoshop's standard palettes.

The term *palette* refers to the individual tool windows offered by Photoshop. The palette system is user-configurable and very convenient to use. The Help menus and tutorials are well-designed and fairly comprehensive technically; however, for most Photoshop novices, it is a good idea to purchase one of the third party reference books, such as *Mastering Photoshop for the Web* by Matt Straznitzkas, as neither the tutorial or documentation is geared toward the non-graphic designer. In other words, if you think a "screen" is what keeps out the flies in summer then make a visit to your bookstore.

Photoshop creates raster image files but is quite capable of working with a number of vector file formats, particularly AI (Adobe Illustrator) and EPS (Encapsulated Postscript). It also is capable of working with and converting most raster image file formats to gif and jpg files. Photoshop will allow you to work with almost all of the images that you may come across.

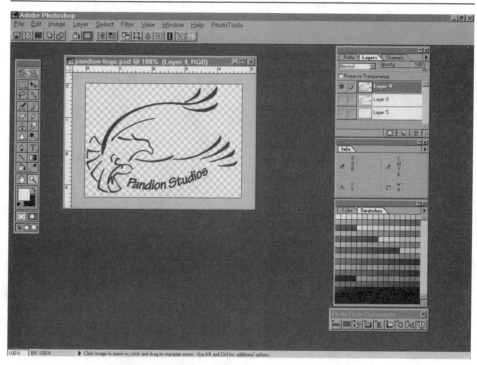

FIGURE 17.15: Adobe Photoshop

Photoshop will also allow you to manipulate palettes for gifs, including palettes for animation files. It will not create animations directly; however, it will create the individual animation frames that you may then assemble in an animation tool.

For more information about Photoshop, check out the Photoshop demo on this book's CD or visit Adobe's Web site at: http://www.adobe.com/prodindex/photoshop/main.html.

CorelDRAW

Remember the discussion of vector images and various vector file formats? Corel-DRAW is one of the best tools available for working with vector images. CorelDRAW can handle almost any vector image that you can find and most importantly, it will allow you to edit the image and convert it to a Web image. CorelDRAW isn't cheap, but it includes raster image handling software, a 3D image creation package, and a variety of other graphics tools in the suite. If you are working with a variety of file formats, CorelDRAW is some of the best software you can buy.

Figure 17.16 shows CorelDRAW's main window and "rolldowns," Corel's version of Adobe's palettes discussed above.

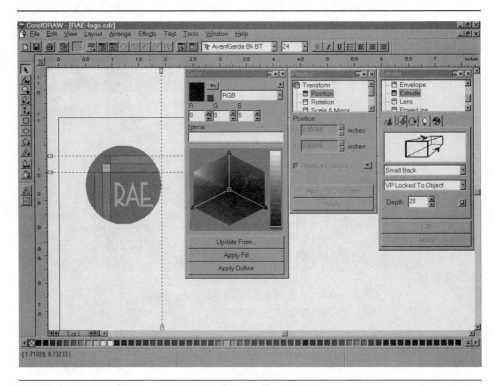

FIGURE 17.16:   CorelDRAW's main window

CorelDRAW is configurable and offers an excellent help menu and tutorials. The documentation is written for the novice user and the novice can actually use the manuals to learn how to use the software effectively. The user interface is easy to understand and the Help menus are also good for the novice user.

Perhaps the best feature of CorelDRAW is the clipart and photo-CD collection that is included in the package. The clipart and symbols include well over 30,000 graphics, and the photos exceed 1,000 images. This library is an excellent way to get started providing your own graphics.

Included in the CorelDRAW package is PhotoPaint, Corel's raster image manipulation software. PhotoPaint performs many of the same functions as Adobe Photoshop but is not nearly as robust.

For more information about Corel Corp. products, visit their Web site at
http://www.corel.com/.

Microsoft Image Composer

Image Composer offers raster image processing without the technical details
to worry about. As an add-on to Microsoft's Web authoring tool, FrontPage,
Image Composer works with raster files, including gif and jpg. Best of all, Image
Composer is free. Image Composer is easy to learn, and you can be creating
images in just a couple of hours.

Figure 17.17 shows Image Composer's main window displaying one of the test
images provided by Microsoft.

Image editing is made easy by replacing the technical details with new terms
coined by Microsoft. "Sprites" are actually raster images that are used to "compose" an overall image. You can use the provided filters and tools to edit photographs and create your own images.

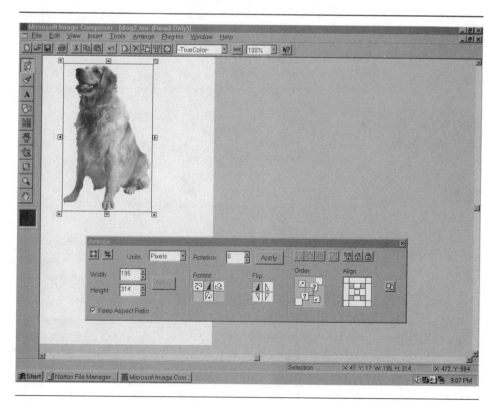

FIGURE 17.17:   Microsoft Image Composer's main window

Microsoft Image Composer is available on the Microsoft Front Page CD-ROM or for free download in beta version at Microsoft's Web site: `http://www.microsoft.com/imagecomposer/aboutic/icinfo.htm`.

How Those Who Can't Draw Survive

Want to know a closely-kept secret? Not every Web designer is an artist. Not everyone can draw; in fact, many Web site designers can't draw a straight *or* curved line. So, what do they do? How can you produce a professional Web site without being an artist? Read on, several solutions are easily available for the non-artist Web designer.

Stock Photos

If you're not a whiz at photography, don't worry. There are many photographic resources just waiting for you to come to them! Using stock photos is an excellent way to provide images for your Web site, whether you need illustration of particular topics or just some decoration, stock photography can provide color and look at a reasonable price.

Stock photographs are available on nearly any subject, in a wide variety of media. You can purchase stock photos in a number of ways and on various media, such as:

- CD-ROM image collections

- Individual images downloaded from the Web

- Slides

- Individual high resolution scans on digital media of your choice

For Web use, you typically won't need high resolution images as your Web output is likely to be at 72 ppi. Getting individual stock photos off of the Web or as a part of a topical collection CD is likely to be the Web designer's most cost-effective way to purchase images.

 **WARNING**   Be sure to check what rights you are purchasing when you buy stock photos. Stock photos are sold with varying usage rights; sometimes they havre only "one-time-use rights" which is inappropriate for the Web. Also be sure to find out whether you must use the image "as is" or if you may edit the image and add an altered image to your Web site.

The following will give you a start in your search for stock photography:

PhotoDisc (`http://www.photodisc.com/`)   PhotoDisc offers a wide variety of images via CD-ROM and on the Web. Some images include clipping paths.

Comstock Stock Photography (`http://www.comstock.com/`)   Comstock offers both one-time use photos and a royalty free collection through their "Comstock Klips" collections.

Digital Vision (`http://www.imageclub.com/digitalvision/`)   Digital Vision sells CD-ROM collections of photographs by topic. These images include clipping paths.

Artville (`http://www.artville.com/`)   Artville offers a collection of royalty-free photographs on CD-ROM.

Clipart

Clipart is another "must-have" resource for Web designers, artists, and non-artists alike. While they won't always confess to it, most graphic designers keep a collection of clipart catalogs and often CD-ROMs around for use in their own designs or as "idea files." While clipart can have a "same old, same old" sort of look to it, there are plenty of creative ways to utilize clipart in your designs that will still look fresh.

Clipart usually comes on CD-ROM in either raster or vector format (vector format is the most common). Vector clipart lends itself to being "customized" by the user. This clipart can be modified by changing its color, removing elements from the image, adding other clipart elements, or by processing the image (in a raster image editor such as Photoshop) with various filters.

As you can see in Figure 17.18, a little creativity and some image editing goes a long way toward customizing clipart. The original vector images, the safari hat and the construction guy, were combined in a drawing program to create the "safari guy". His original hardhat was removed and replaced with a safari hat. The shirt was re-colored in shades of green to give him a "jungley" feel. Of course, he's really not quite ready for a safari Web page yet—it would be a good idea to replace his sledgehammer with a camera or other suitable tool.

Once the changes to the original vector art had been made, the image was exported to a tiff file and opened in Adobe Photoshop for some more image editing and eventual conversion to a gif image.

Skill 17

FIGURE 17.18:   From construction guy to safari guy (`f1718.jpg`)

Figure 17.19 shows our safari guy changed to a more textured image that will display nicely on the Web. After we use some filters in Adobe Photoshop to add noise and alter his colors a bit, safari guy doesn't look much like a standard piece of clipart. Once you have experimented with clipart and done some customization, you'll never see clipart in quite the same way.

FIGURE 17.19:   From smooth vector image to textured Web image (`f1719.jpg`)

As with stock photos, clipart comes with differing usage rights. Always be sure to verify that you can edit and use the art on a Web site before you add it to your Web page.

The following list will give you a start in your search for clipart:

Artville (`http://www.artville.com/`)   Artville offers a excellent collection of unusal clipart on CD-ROM.

Artworks (http://www.dgusa.com/)   Artworks has a wide variety of clipart images in varying styles on CD-ROM.

Corel clipart (http://www.corel.com/products/clipartandphotos/ gallerymagic65/main.htm)   Corel Corp offers a huge collection of vector clipart, photos, and other graphics.

Image Club (http://www.imageclub.com/)   Image Club, a division of Adobe, has one of the more comprehensive collections of clipart, photos, tools, and a terrific monthly catalog.

Subcontracting

Many Web designers subcontract their graphics work to an outside graphic designer. Whether you need assistance with the creation of a couple of images or the overall look and feel of your Web site, an outside designer will be willing to provide their expertise.

Finding a good match with a graphic designer is critical to the success of your Web site project. Forget all the stories you've heard about temperamental artists: they aren't that difficult to get along with. Finding the right designer is quite possible with a bit of research and some planning time on your part. Roll up your sleeves and get out that notepad again. It's time for some analysis of the task.

Define the Task

Perhaps the most important part of working with a graphic designer is being able to clearly articulate what you want them to do. You will need to assess your Web site plan and determine just which pieces of the visual presentation you need help with and then develop a list of the discrete tasks for your graphic designer to accomplish.

As you look through your Web site plan, do an honest assessment of which pieces you can personally accomplish and which pieces would be best done by a professional artist or designer. Once you have identified which pieces will belong to you and which would be good candidates for subcontracting, you can begin thinking about what sort of budget you have for hiring an artist.

 TIP   Depending on your personal inclination and the complexity of your needs, you may wish to develop a formal RFP (Request for Proposal). An RFP is used to solicit a proposal or estimate from individuals or design firms that you will consider hiring as a subcontractor.

CONTRACT INFORMATION

When you do work for a company or you subcontract work to another individual or firm, the best advice is to always have a contract. There are many obvious reasons for having a formal written contract that outlines exactly who will do what for what price and when it will be accomplished. And having an attorney look over any contract that you personally write or are considering is extremely important.

If you are looking for more information about contracting, running a Web site design business, and other business issues, the following URLs may be of some help:

- http://www.business.gov/ A comprehensive resource provided by U.S. Business Advisor.

- http://www.creativebusiness.com/ Business resource company and newsletter for people in creative fields.

- http://www.irs.ustreas.gov/ Business resources are never complete without visiting the IRS.

- http://www.excite.com/business_and_investing/other_business_topics/small_business/ An excellent list of small business resources.

- http://provider.com/contracts.htm This site is a gem with lots of resources for those in need of Web contract-writing help.

- http://www.hwg.org/ The HTML Writers Guild provides excellent resources for Web design.

Choosing a Graphic Designer

Choosing a graphic designer isn't that complicated, but some important issues need to be addressed. Finding a compatible style and developing a good working relationship is crucial to the success of subcontracting whether it is with a designer or a programmer.

You can start your search on the Web. In your travels, you've seen graphics at Web sites that impressed you; it's time to go back to those sites and find out who created the images. Another good source for finding graphic designers is to talk to your online friends. Ask people whom they would recommend for graphic design.

> **TIP** If the artist isn't listed directly on the Web page, try sending e-mail to the site's Webmaster. Most people are delighted to receive a compliment. Tell them you like the site, and they will happily tell you who designed their images.

Once you have compiled a list of designers, contact them and ask if you can view their portfolio. Most designers who do Web graphics will have an online portfolio for you to view or will be happy to send you a list of URLs that contain their work. As you review portfolios, be sure to take notes on what images you liked, what you didn't like, and whether the images are technically well-done.

> **TIP** When looking at Web images on a portfolio page, check and see if the images are created with technical know-how. Do they load quickly? Present well at 256 colors? Succeed at accomplishing their purpose on the Web site?

Once you have narrowed your list of designers, spend some time talking with them via e-mail or telephone. You will need to get a sense of working with the person: Do you have compatible styles and can you communicate? Do your budget expectations match? Be sure to be upfront about any issues that you anticipate will be a problem. And always include a copy of your task list or RFP so you're talking about the same issues!

Have You Mastered the Essentials?

Now you can. . .

- ☑ Work with the many varieties of graphic file formats.
- ☑ Evaluate when to use gif or jpeg images.
- ☑ Produce a quality image for the Web.
- ☑ Produce quality images even if you can't draw.

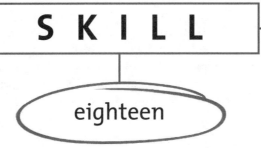

Movement and Animation

- ❑ What is GIF animation?

- ❑ Creating animation from a single image

- ❑ Blending two images with transition effects

- ❑ Providing animation in response to mouse movements

The Web is evolving constantly into a sophisticated multimedia experience. One of the simplest ways to incorporate that feeling into your Web site is through the use of animation. In this Skill, you'll learn how to create animated GIF images and use JavaScript to provide other interactive changes based on your visitor's movement around the screen.

Animated GIFs

In Skill 17, you learned about the GIF graphics file format, an 8-bit or 256-color image file. One of the features of the latest GIF format, GIF89a, is the ability to create a single file that contains multiple images, or *frames*. When the file is viewed, the frames display one after the other, becoming a short animation. The GIF89a specification also allows for data that determines the time lapse between the display of each frame and embedded comments, and the selection of a transparent color is encoded into the file.

These files, which we'll call animated GIFs from here on, have become popular on the Web for several reasons:

They're easy to create. You need to create only a few individual images, which are then combined by special software tools into a single animation file.

They don't require programming knowledge. To create other animation effects, you must often rely on knowledge of Java, JavaScript, or other programming languages. If you can create a simple image file, you can create animated GIFs.

Most Web browsers can display them. Netscape Navigator and Internet Explorer version 2 and newer generally support animated GIFs as you intend, without plug-ins or any other special accommodations.

In this section, you'll learn how to create animated GIFs from as little as a single image file, as well as how to combine a series of image frames into one.

Special Effects with a Single Image File

In this section, we'll create several GIFs using the GIF Construction Set from Alchemy Mindworks, Inc. This program is available for Windows 3.1 or Windows 95/NT platforms. You can download a shareware version from Alchemy's Web site at `http://www.mindworkshop.com/`.

THE SHAREWARE CONCEPT

Shareware is the ultimate "try before you buy" experience. For the end-user, it can be difficult to know whether a new software program will be useful without experiencing its functionality. For the programmer, finding distribution channels for new releases or for low-cost applications can be an exercise in frustration if you are unknown.

Enter shareware. The programmer uploads a new title to a Web site, BBS, or online service for the public to download and try. If they like the program, they mail the programmer a *registration fee*—the price of the software. If it doesn't meet their needs, the user is supposed to delete it from their system. No harm, no foul, and nobody is out any money.

Since not everyone out there performs well under the honor system, many shareware authors have taken to incorporating "features" in the unregistered versions of their programs that will motivate most honest folks to register them. Motivators often include the disabling of key program functions, preventing the user from saving files, or repeated "nag screens" that pop up periodically, asking the user to please send in their payment. When the user does, they are sent a *registration key*—either a password or a small update file—that will tell the program that it's been registered, enabling the functions that were disabled previously and putting a halt to any nag effects.

Quality in shareware, like quality in retail software, varies greatly. Some true gems, including the GIF Construction Set featured in this skill, have come through this channel. If you like the work, support the author—register your shareware today!

Choosing Transitions

We'll start with the file hand.gif, seen here.

TIP

Someone with little artistic talent created this graphic. It's simply the asterisk (*) character in the font type Zapf Ding Bats, with a small drop-shadow added to it. Proof you don't need to be able to draw to create original images!

Launch the GIF Construction Set program, either by clicking its Program Manager icon in Windows 3.x or by selecting it from the Windows 95/NT start menu. The program will open with the directory tree visible in the main window, as shown in Figure 18.1. (In this skill, we are using Windows 95/NT for all screen samples.)

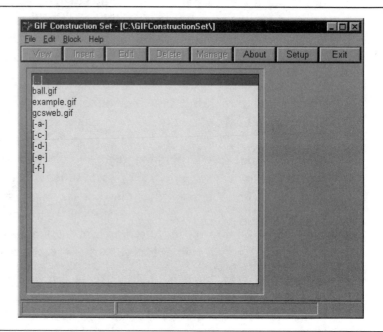

FIGURE 18.1: The opening GIF Construction Set screen

To create the animation, follow these steps:

1. Choose File ➢ New to open a new file. A gray bar with the text "HEADER GIF89a Screen (640 × 480)" will appear at the top of the main window.

2. Click the Insert button to display the Insert Object toolbar shown here.

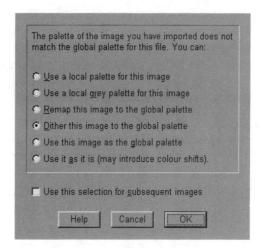

3. We want to insert the hand.gif image file, so click the Image button to open a traditional Windows Open File dialog box.

4. Locate your file on your hard drive, highlight it, and click the Open button. Alternatively, type the file name and path in the File Name box, and click the Open button to open the Palette dialog box shown here.

The palette of the image you have imported does not match the global palette for this file. You can:

- ○ Use a local palette for this image
- ○ Use a local grey palette for this image
- ○ Remap this image to the global palette
- ⦿ Dither this image to the global palette
- ○ Use this image as the global palette
- ○ Use it as it is (may introduce colour shifts).

☐ Use this selection for subsequent images

| Help | Cancel | OK |

5. Because this is the only image that we will use in this animation, choose the *Use this image as the global palette* option. Click OK to return to the main program window. The image file will now be visible in a small pane on the right side of the program screen (see Figure 18.2).

6. To set the transition effect, choose the Edit ➢ Transition. (Use the menu; don't click the Edit button.)

At this point, you're finished creating the animated GIF. A pop-up dialog box will tell you that the image has been changed and prompt you to save it. (It's probably the least intuitive message the GIF Construction Set will present to you. Just remember that at this point, you're done creating the image, and the next part is editing it.)

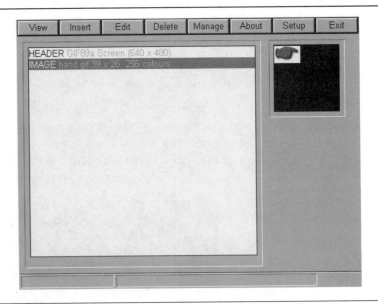

FIGURE 18.2: The image you inserted will appear in the small pane to the right of the main window.

7. Click Yes to save the image and open the Edit Transition dialog box.

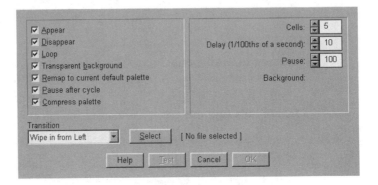

The Edit Transition dialog box has a number of options, almost all of which are selected by default. In the left pane, you'll find the following:

Appear, Disappear These two checkboxes control how the animation moves into view. Should it come out and move back in again? If so, leave both options selected. If you want the animation to only slide into place, unmark Disappear.

Loop   Do you want the animation to repeat? Leave this box selected to activate this option.

Transparent background   If your animation needs to maintain the transparency of the original file, be sure to check this box (it isn't selected by default).

Remap to current default palette   You shouldn't need to use this option often because you've made your palette selection previously.

Pause after cycle   Should there be a break between loops of the animation? If so, leave this option selected to create the pause.

Compress palette   This function removes duplicate colors from the image's palette, resulting in a smaller file size if fewer than the allowable 256 colors have been utilized.

The right-hand pane holds the controls for the number of *cells* (Alchemy's term for frames) and the animation timing:

Cells   The higher the number, the more frames that will be created. Creating more frames results in smoother action. It also increases the file size. You might need to experiment to find a good balance. We chose 8, enough to provide a smooth motion.

Delay   The delay value, measured in 1/100ths of a second, measures the amount of time between each frame. A value of 1 is only 1/100th of a second between frames and is the smallest unit of time. We chose 5/100ths.

Pause   This value determines how long the animation pauses before repeating itself when looping has been selected. We chose 200—a 2-second pause between cycles.

The bottom pane contains a select-list with the available transition types. To begin editing, follow these steps:

1. In the Transition drop-down list, click the down arrow and choose Wipe in From Left, which will begin the animation from "off camera" to the left and bring it into full view "on screen."

2. Click the Select button to open the Open File dialog box, select the file name for the image you just created, and then click Open.

The program will now compile your animation. When it's finished, all four buttons at the bottom of the Edit Transition dialog box will become active (Help, Test, Cancel, and OK), and your file name and path will be shown to the right of the Select button.

3. Click Test to preview your animation. It will appear full screen on your monitor. Right-click your mouse to return to the Edit Transition dialog box.

4. When you're satisfied with the results, click OK to finish compiling the GIF file. You'll be returned to the main program, which will show a list of all the image frames and *control blocks* (the animation instructions) in the main window.

5. To save the file a final time, choose File ➢ Save As.

When you're done, click the Exit button to close the program. Easy, wasn't it?

Developing Banners

This transition takes positively zero artistic ability. If you can type, you can create a scrolling banner! Follow these steps:

1. Choose File ➢ New to create a new file.

2. Next, choose Edit ➢ Banner to open the Edit Banner dialog box.

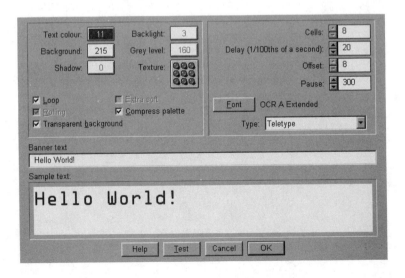

3. Choose a text and background color by clicking the colored buttons. The number in the middle of each button represents the color's palette position. (Aside from helping you perhaps to remember which shade of blue you'd chosen previously, this number isn't critically important.)

4. Click the Font button to open the Font dialog box.

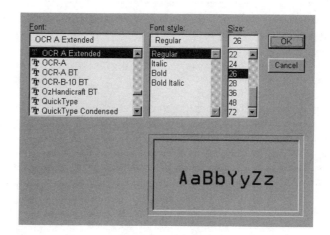

5. Choose the Font face, Font style, and Font size, and then click OK.

6. Click the down-arrow in the Type select-list to identify the type of scrolling that will occur in your banner. We've chosen Teletype, which mimics the one-character-at-a-time appearance of old-fashioned teletype machines.

7. Check the Loop, Transparent Background, and Compress Palette checkboxes to select looping behavior, to use a transparent background, and to compress the GIF palette.

8. In the Cells drop-down list, set the delay between cells, measured in 100ths of a second.

9. In the Pause drop-down list, set the pause between loops if you selected that option.

10. In the Banner Text input box, type your message.

11. Click the Test button to preview your animation. It will play at full screen. Right-click to return to the GIF Construction Set program.

12. When you're satisfied with the results, click OK. You'll be returned to the main program screen.

13. Choose File ➤ Save As to save your GIF and name it.

That's all there is to it!

SPIN, BOUNCE, BLINK, BONK, HELP!

Have you ever been to a Web site that has so many animations going that it seems as if a few of them are about ready to leap right off the screen and bonk you in the nose?

Animations can be both fun and effective, but they can also be overwhelming and distracting. The key is to decide when an animation *enhances* your message. If you create a site about yo-yo tricks, an animation that shows how to perform a trick is a great enhancement. Even a spinning yo-yo as a small bullet or button could be a fun addition, though not as practical as the demo. Here are some tips that can help you find the right balance:

- Resist the temptation to add animation for the sake of having animation.

- Every image that moves or blinks draws your visitors' attention to itself. Be sure that it doesn't distract them from your message.

- In general, limit yourself to one or two animations on a page.

- Consider setting a finite number of loops within each animation file. What's cute the first time can become grating by the thirtieth time.

Easy Animations with Multiple Images

Even more variety in your animations becomes possible when you begin to blend more than one base image. Ulead Systems' GIF Animator (the trial version is available for download at http://www.ulead.com/) makes quick work of the task.

The program opens with the Startup Wizard screen, as seen in Figure 18.3. (Here we're using the Windows 95 version of this product.)

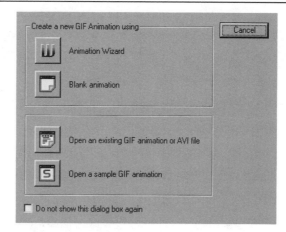

FIGURE 18.3: GIF Animator's handy Startup Wizard

To begin creating your animation, follow these steps:

1. Click the Animation Wizard icon to open the Select Files dialog box.

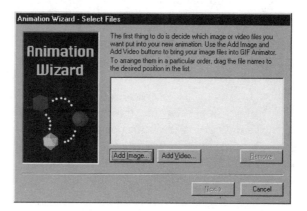

2. To add your images, click the Add Image button to open the File Open dialog box. Locate and highlight the file you want to add, and then click Open to return to the Select Files dialog box.

3. Continue adding files until you've added each of them. For this example, we'll be using the two images shown here:

4. Click the Next button to open the Source Type dialog box. Here you're asked if your source files are primarily text oriented or primarily photo oriented. The program makes decisions on *dithering* (the reduction and combining of palettes to maintain the required 256 maximum colors for a single GIF image) based on your answer. We'll select text oriented. Click Next to continue.

5. In the next dialog box, you set the frame *duration*, that is, the amount of time the frame remains visible (similar to the pause value in the previous examples using GIF Construction Set). We'll be editing this information later, so we'll accept the default. Click Next to move on.

6. GIF Animator now announces that you're done and gives a few tips on optimizing your images. Click Finish to return to main program screen, as shown in Figure 18.4.

Now that we've built the basic GIF file, we'll add the special effects. GIF Animator offers a variety of effects, including transitions similar to those in GIF Construction Set and a cube effect, which gives the appearance of your images being on the sides of a cube and rotating. Explore the options in the Layer menu, shown to the right.

Add Images...	Ins
Add Video...	
Add Comments	
Add Banner Text...	Ctrl+B
Add Transition Effect...	Ctrl+T
Add Color Animation...	Ctrl+L
Add Cube Effect...	Ctrl+K
Export Images...	Ctrl+E
Merge Images...	Ctrl+M
Move Layer Up	Shift+Up
Move Layer Down	Shift+Down

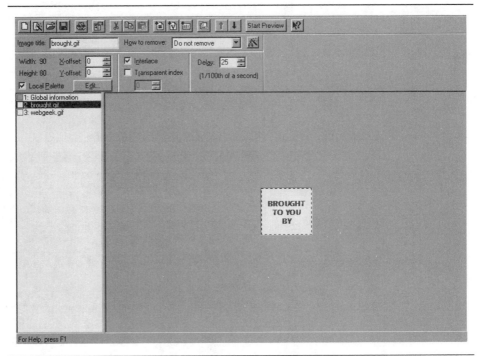

FIGURE 18.4: The main GIF Animator screen, showing our work in progress

We'll use one of the transition effects for this animation. To begin, follow these steps:

1. Choose Layer ➢ Add Transition Effect to open the Add Transition Effect dialog box.

2. Choose the desired transition from the top select-list. The effects are demonstrated in the thumbnail image window immediately to the left. For this animation, choose Wipe(Downwards).

3. The Transition Length is the time it takes for one image to completely wipe down over the other. It is set in seconds. We'll set it to 2.

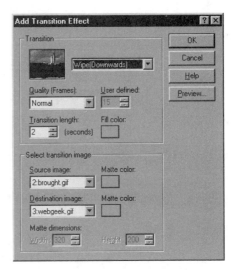

4. The Select Transition Image section is already filled out for us. The program inserted the two images in the order in which we added them to the animation file. Click OK to accept these settings and go back to the main program screen.

You'll notice in Figure 18.5 that the program has created 15 new files and placed them in the left pane between our two original files. These are the interim steps of the wipe effect, moving between the two images.

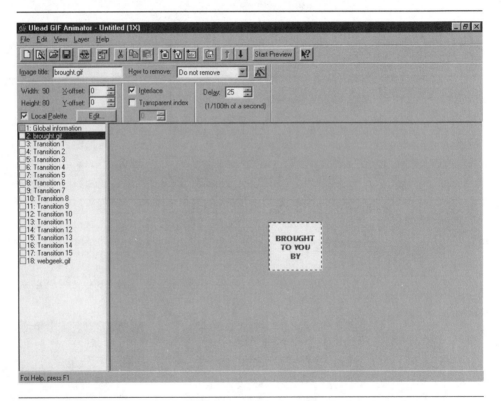

FIGURE 18.5: The new files interpolated by the program

We said earlier that we were going to edit the frame delays on the original images. The effect we'll be trying to achieve is a one-second display of the first image, followed by the wipe-down into the second image (which lasts two seconds), and then the second image remains in place for three seconds before the animation loops and starts back at the first image again. To achieve this, follow these steps:

1. Highlight the first image in the list (actually item number 2, just below the Global Information item).

2. Increase the value in the Delay box to 100 (a full second, since the values are measured in 1/100ths of a second).

3. Highlight the last image on the list. Increase the value in the Delay box to 300.

4. To test the animation before completion, click the Start Preview button.

5. When you're satisfied with the results, choose File ➤ Save As to save your work.

You can see the finished product in the middle of its transition in Figure 18.6.

FIGURE 18.6:   The final image, in transition

Each animation we created in this section has taken advantage of the power of software to interpolate images from one or two source files. You aren't, however, limited to creating animations in this fashion. You can create many highly creative scenes by hand, making small changes in an original graphic a bit at a time and saving them into the individual frame images. To put them all together, simply use the add images process in any GIF animation program. Use your imagination!

Animation through JavaScript

JavaScript is a computer programming language that has been included in the Netscape Navigator (and several other) browser executable program. It's an *interpreted* language, which means that the program instructions, or *scripts*, are processed by the browser at the moment they are run—an event known as *run-time*. JavaScript is also a basic *object-oriented* programming language. This system of programming development views each portion of the Web page and browser as an object—the browser window itself is an object, as is an image within the HTML file being displayed. Object-oriented simply means that the programming instructions identify individual objects and then direct instructions to them specifically.

NOTE   Despite its name, JavaScript is a wholly different language from *Java*, the programming language developed by Sun Microsystems. Unfortunately, the similarity in names has lead to some confusion within the Web community. At this point, you only need to be aware that they are two different languages that serve different functions for Web designers.

Mastering the JavaScript language is a topic worthy of a book all its own. However, in this section you'll learn the basics necessary to include simple animations based on responses to *events*—actions that are perceived by the browser, such as placing your mouse pointer over a hyperlink. The browser recognizes that event and changes your pointer into a hand. You'll learn to handle these *mouseovers* yourself.

Adding JavaScript to Your HTML File

To introduce JavaScript in your pages, you first need to let the browser know you're about to do so, using the SCRIPT tag. SCRIPT is a container tag (it contains the JavaScript itself); therefore, it has a closing /SCRIPT tag as well. The tag uses the LANGUAGE attribute to define which scripting language you'll be using (there are scripting languages other than JavaScript). You can place this container anywhere within the BODY container of your Web page.

To get started, let's create a short script that mimics the traditional first program completed by those learning almost any programming language—the Hello World! program. Figure 18.7 shows the display of this file in Navigator 4.03.

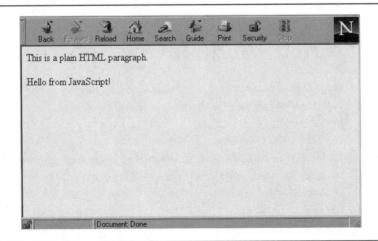

FIGURE 18.7: Hello from JavaScript!

HelloJavaScript.html

```
<HTML>
<HEAD>
<TITLE>Hello from JavaScript!</TITLE>
</HEAD>
<BODY>
<P>This is a plain HTML paragraph.
<SCRIPT LANGUAGE="JavaScript">
document.write ("<P>Hello from JavaScript!")
</SCRIPT>
<BODY>
</HTML>
```

Hiding JavaScript from Noncompliant Browsers

According to the HTML specifications, a browser that doesn't understand a tag is supposed to ignore it. Unfortunately, that depends greatly on the programming processes used to create the browser. Not all of them behave properly when encountering the SCRIPT tag and may display the contents of that container in the page as plain text. To prevent this, you can use an HTML *comment* to hide the script from these browsers.

A comment is a unique tag. It opens with the traditional < symbol, but things change right after that. To differentiate comments from regular HTML tags, you begin them with an exclamation point (known as a *bang* in some programming contexts), which is followed immediately by two dashes. A comment ends with two dashes, followed immediately by the closing >. Anything in between is then hidden from view by the browser. A comment looks like this:

```
<!- this is an HTML comment ->
```

In order not to confuse browsers that *do* understand JavaScript, you use the JavaScript comment notation of a double slash (//) before the end of the HTML comment. So our comment now looks like this:

```
<!- this is an HTML comment with JavaScript notation added //->
```

TIP   Although the browser won't display the comments when the page is viewed normally, they are visible if someone chooses to view the source file. Never place sensitive information in comments.

When the comment is incorporated into the original file, it ends up looking like this:

HelloJavaScript2.html

```
<HTML>
<HEAD>
<TITLE>Hello from JavaScript!</TITLE>
</HEAD>
<BODY>
<P>This is a plain HTML paragraph.
<SCRIPT LANGUAGE="JavaScript">
<!-
document.write ("<P>Hello from JavaScript!")
//->
</SCRIPT>
<BODY>
</HTML>
```

TIP   You can spread comments over more than one line, as seen in HelloJavaScript2.html. This allows for improved readability and lets you immediately locate the beginning and end of each comment.

Ready to get into the animation? Keep reading!

Animation through the Mouseover Event

The first thing your script needs to do is to determine whether the visitor's browser not only supports JavaScript, but also supports the image object within JavaScript. Currently, the major browsers that do support this object include Netscape Navigator 3 or higher and Internet Explorer 4.

COMPATIBILITY NOTE   One of the frustrations of Web development is the slightly different implementations of browser features. JavaScript encounters this on several fronts: First, there are two versions of Netscape's JavaScript, 1.0 and 1.1. Second, Microsoft's implementation—known as JScript—is more a dialect than a true implementation. It's similar, but different enough to make it a distinct language (rather like U.S. English versus British English). Most of the time, the "reader" (the browser) understands what you mean, but occasionally it scratches its electronic head!

To test whether a browser supports the javaScript image object, the first portion of our script includes the *conditional statement* if. A conditional statement operates like it sounds here: *if* this condition is met, proceed with these directions. In JavaScript, it appears as:

```
if (document.images) { … }
```

This statement says that *if* the browser understands the statement document.images—which defines a single object that consists of all the images in the document the script resides in—continue with the actions enclosed in the curly braces (which is represented by the ellipse for example purposes only).

Defining Variables

Next, we need to define several *variables*. A variable is a word or *string*—a set of alphanumeric characters undivided by spaces—that is assigned a value. This concept is probably familiar to you from basic algebra class. For example, in the following equation:

$$x + 3 = 10$$

x is a variable. The letter *x* holds the value of 7 ($x + 3 = 10$ is the same as $x = 10 - 3$, which is the same as saying $x = 7$).

In JavaScript, a variable can hold a numeric value as in this example, or it can hold words, phrases, file names, complex mathematic operations, or HTML markup.

Our variables will hold file names—the names of the image files to be used in the animation. We'll be animating three images, so we'll create six variables—one for both the on and off state. These are for three images that serve as links to the services, portfolio, and "about us" section of Ann Navarro's WebGeek Communications Web site, at http://www.webgeek.com/.

Variables are named with the following syntax:

```
var ServicesOn = new Image()
        ServicesOn.src = "serviceson.gif"
```

This code says: I've created a *variable* named *ServicesOn*, which is being assigned the value of a new image. The second line defines the source (.src) of the image that's now referenced by the variable *ServicesOn* as the file serviceson.gif.

TIP   Wondering about the variable name chosen here? Programmers have long found that by naming variables with words or phrases that have real meaning, rather than nonsense words or simple alphabet letters, it's easier to read through the code and know what the program is doing. In this case, ServicesOn refers to an image and link combination for "services," with "on" indicating the "on" state of the animation versus the off state.

WARNING

In JavaScript, variable names are case-sensitive. That is, *ServicesOn* in the previous example is distinct from *serviceson*. You must maintain the same case throughout when referencing variables.

Here is the entire list of variable definitions:

```
if (document.images) {
    var ServicesOn = new Image()
    ServicesOn.src = "serviceson.gif"
    var ServicesOff = new Image()
    ServicesOff.src = "servicesoff.gif"
    var PortfolioOn = new Image()
    PortfolioOn.src = "portfolioon.gif"
    var PortfolioOff = new Image()
    PortfolioOff.src = "portfoliooff.gif"
    var AboutOn = new Image()
    AboutOn.src = "abouton.gif"
    var AboutOff = new Image()
    AboutOff.src = "aboutoff.gif"
}
```

Defining Functions

Next, we need to define two functions. A *function* is a piece of JavaScript code that actually gives an action instruction; that is, it says "Do this!" to the browser.

The first function tells the browser to pull the "on" image file into the image source. Line by line, this says: We're creating a function named *on* that will operate on the object *imgName* (we'll talk about this in a moment). If you're a browser that understands the document image object, concatenate (add together) the image name and the string On.src, and equate it to document[imgName].src.

If that still sounds confusing, stay with us for another minute here, and it should become clearer.

```
function on (imgName) {
        if (document.images)
            document[imgName].src = eval(imgName + 'On.src')
        }
```

This second function does exactly the same thing, except that it deals with the Off state images:

```
function off (imgName) {
        if (document.images)
            document[imgName].src = eval(imgName + 'Off.src')
        }
```

Now all that's left is closing out the SCRIPT container. Here is the entire container:

```
<SCRIPT LANGUAGE="JavaScript">
<!-
  if (document.images) {
     var ServicesOn = new Image()
     ServicesOn.src = "serviceson.gif"
     var ServicesOff = new Image()
     ServicesOff.src = "servicesoff.gif"
     var PortfolioOn = new Image()
     PortfolioOn.src = "portfolioon.gif"
     var PortfolioOff = new Image()
     PortfolioOff.src = "portfoliooff.gif"
     var AboutOn = new Image()
     AboutOn.src = "abouton.gif"
     var AboutOff = new Image()
     AboutOff.src = "aboutoff.gif"
  }
  function on (imgName) {
     if (document.images)
          document[imgName].src = eval(imgName + 'On.src')
  }
  function off (imgName) {
     if (document.images)
          document[imgName].src = eval(imgName + 'Off.src')
  }
// ->
  </SCRIPT>
```

Now all we need to do is add a few new attributes to HTML tags that you're already familiar with—anchors and image tags.

Adding Event Handlers to Your HTML

An *event handler* is a function that you've defined in your JavaScript that is assigned to a particular event. We'll be dealing with the onMouseOver and onMouseOut events.

 NOTE   JavaScript event names all begin with *on*, indicating that they are activated when the event occurs.

The following HTML snippet includes the anchor and image tags for the first animation:

```
<A HREF="services.html"><IMG SRC="serv.gif" WIDTH="129" HEIGHT="59"
   ALT="services" BORDER="0" ALIGN="left">
```

When you add the information necessary to trigger the JavaScript event, the tags look like this:

```
<A HREF="services.html"
onMouseOver="on('Services')"
onMouseOut="off('Services')">
<IMG SRC="servicesoff.gif"
WIDTH="129"
HEIGHT="59"
NAME="Services"
ALT="services"
BORDER="0"
ALIGN="LEFT">
```

 NOTE　We've shown these new examples with each attribute on a new line, in order to allow you to read and digest them more easily. Once you're comfortable working with them, you can compose them on single lines if you want.

These two newest attributes are these event handlers:

```
onMouseOver="on('services')"
onMouseOut="off('services')"
```

These say: When the mouse is over this linked area (defined as the space occupied by the image), perform the function on, operating on the image named services. When the mouse moves out of the linked area, perform the function off on the image named services.

Look back at the function on:

```
function on (imgName) {
     if (document.images)
          document[imgName].src = eval(imgName + 'On.src')
     }
```

We can now insert the pieces that were missing earlier. This function, when called from this anchor and image tag set, now says: If you're a browser that understands the document.images object, the source file for document.services.src should be

ServicesOn.src (the combination of the imgName (Services) and the string On.src), which was previously defined in the variables section of this script (serviceson.gif).

The entire set of anchor and image tags now looks like:

```
<A HREF="services.html"
onMouseOver="on('Services')"
onMouseOut="off('Services')">
<IMG SRC="servicesoff.gif"
WIDTH="129"
HEIGHT="59"
NAME="Services"
ALT="services"
BORDER="0"
ALIGN="LEFT"></A>

<A HREF="portfolio.html"
onMouseOver="on('Portfolio')"
onMouseOut="off('Portfolio')">
<IMG SRC="portfoliooff.gif"
WIDTH="129"
HEIGHT="59"
NAME="Portfolio"
ALT="portfolio"
BORDER="0"
ALIGN="LEFT"></A>

<A HREF="about.html"
onMouseOver="on('About')"
onMouseOut="off('About')">
<IMG SRC="aboutoff.gif"
WIDTH="129"
HEIGHT="59"
NAME="About"
ALT="about"
BORDER="0"
ALIGN="LEFT"></A>
```

Figure 18.8 shows the Portfolio image in the on state, mimicking the main WebGeek logo when the mouse is placed over the image.

To see it all put together for live use on the Web, view the source of this page at http://www.webgeek.com/.

Skill 18

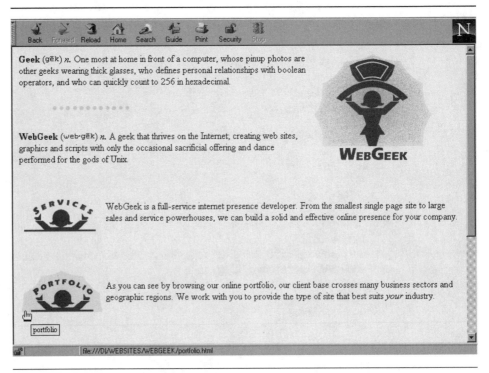

FIGURE 18.8: The onMouseOver event in action

ONLINE RESOURCES FOR JAVASCRIPT

A wealth of JavaScript information and tutorials is available on the Web. Here are some of the better site to check:

- JavaScript Tip of the Week is an archive of 30 JavaScript coding tips, complete with source code. Find it at `http://webreference.com/javascript/`.

- Doc JavaScript is a biweekly column. Find it at `http://webreference.com/js/`.

continued on next page ▶

- WebCoder.com is a brand-new reference on JavaScript and Dynamic HTML. It contains a useful JavaScript support chart. Find it at `http://www.webcoder.com/`.

- Netscape's JavaScript Authoring Guide is available straight from the source at `http://home.netscape.com/eng/mozilla/Gold/handbook/javascript/index.html`.

Have You Mastered the Essentials?

Now you can...

- ☑ Create animation effects from a single GIF image.

- ☑ Develop smooth transitions between images using animated transition effects.

- ☑ Judge when and how to use animation on your Web site.

- ☑ Incorporate mouseover events into your Web pages using JavaScript.

Audio and Video

- ❑ Downloading versus streaming

- ❑ External applications versus plug-ins

- ❑ Producing audio

- ❑ Adding audio to HTML pages

- ❑ Producing video

- ❑ Adding video to HTML pages

- ❑ Providing alternatives to audio and video

Used effectively, audio and video—multimedia—can bring your Web site to life. A few simple mistakes in judgment, on the other hand, can seriously detract from a visitor's experience at your site. For example, suppose a wildlife hospital and education center wanted to let people know about its newest patient, a rescued mountain lion. A link on the center's home page could show a video clip of a staff veterinarian working with the big cat, explaining in a voice-over what she's doing. Or maybe someone had a DAT recorder running when the lion roared for its supper—imagine a sound like that coming out of your computer speakers! But now consider how this would look and sound to visitors with a slow dial-up link or with an older browser. They might have to wait quite a while for the audio or video, and they might prefer a description of the movie or the sound. The sight and hearing impaired there might not have a choice about whether they want to experience your multimedia. The key to accessible multimedia on the Web is to use it effectively to enhance the visitor's experience, while ensuring that visitors who don't experience it feel included.

In this skill, we'll look at the ways you can implement audio and video on your Web site. We'll go over the two methods for transferring this information to browsers—streaming and downloading—and we'll discuss the advantages and disadvantages of both. We'll also consider how your audience is going to listen to or view audio and video, and we'll examine the hardware and software you need to produce them. Last, we'll go over accessibility issues and workarounds for visitors who can't or won't be accessing your multimedia.

When to Use Audio and Video

Not long ago, Web sites could offer only HTML pages and forms. Then inline images came along, bringing new possibilities and new challenges. Among those challenges were making sites work for visitors who didn't see graphics for whatever reason and producing those images so that they worked best for the Web. (For more information on producing graphics for the Web, see Skill 17.) Perhaps the biggest challenge has been to use graphics that are not gratuitous—to actually have a reason for every image.

Although the technology for presenting sound and video on the Web has been around for awhile, most Web sites do not take advantage of this capability, and for similar reasons. Making the site work gracefully for those who cannot hear your audio or see your video is a challenge, and producing the content involves a steep learning curve. Most of all, and probably even more so than with images, it's important to choose audio and video content that has a *reason* for being on the site and is not simply gratuitous. As you might expect, sound and video take up even more digital data than static images, and so bandwidth issues are even more important.

TIP   Certain types of sites almost beg for video and audio clips: sites covering musical events, breaking news, or any other industry that's dependent on sight and sound for content.

On the other hand, truly useful sound and video are great! To be able to show how something actually works or what it sounds like is a capability you should take advantage of if it's appropriate. Just be aware of who can and cannot access your multimedia and how to accommodate those who can't. This skill will help you do that.

Some Web sites make great use of audio and video. For example, National Public Radio (NPR) at http://www.npr.org/ lends itself well to multimedia content—visitors can listen to shows they may have missed or perhaps download an interview. The MTV site at http://www.mtv.com/ features live reports from the music industry.

The Alternative Entertainment Network at http://www.aentv.com/ produces the World Business Review, a technology series for executives. Currently, most Web sites that use audio and video are media sites such as news stations and record companies.

Multimedia Web sites from non–media industries include the CargoLifter site at http://www.cargolifter.com/ which uses video to explain how the company's products work. The Global Cogenics site (http://www.cogenix.com/) includes an interview with its CEO.

Downloading versus Streaming

Once visitors decide to watch your mountain lion video or hear the lion roar, how will you transfer that content to their browsers? For both audio and video files, you have two choices:

- Streaming files
- Downloadable files

Streaming audio or video begins playing before the entire file arrives at the client computer; downloadable audio and video files must be received in their entirety before they can be seen or heard. If you can use streaming files, why would you ever make your visitors wait for downloadable files? Although streaming lets you see or hear the file quickly, the quality usually suffers. On the other hand, downloading complete audio and video files can take a long time. In addition, your visitors will use different software mechanisms to hear or view your content, and you essentially make that decision for them when you decide what to use. With these factors in mind, let's take a look at the advantages and disadvantages of downloadable versus streaming files for your mountain lion video and the audio roar.

 NOTE   As you'll see shortly, all audio and video are not the same. Several (incompatible) formats are in common use. In order to offer multimedia on your site, you need to encode the files before putting them on your Web server (mainly to compress them properly). How you encode the files will determine what your visitors use to listen to them or to view them. We'll go over this in more detail in a later section, *Plug-ins versus External Applications,* but this is an important point to keep in mind as you read through this skill. Sometimes encoding simply involves saving a file as a certain type of format. Other times, you have to purchase the encoder (a piece of software) and use it to convert your files into a proprietary format.

Downloadable Files

Downloadable multimedia files work like any other file on the Web—they are stored on the server, and you link to them using a standard HREF tag:

```
<A HREF="filename">Hyperlink text here</A>
```

For example, the following HTML code produces the results (in Navigator 3.01) shown in Figure 19.1.

```
<HTML>
<HEAD>
<TITLE>The mountain lion roars!</TITLE>
</HEAD>
<BODY>
Are you ready for a <A HREF="roar.au">sound bite?</A>
</BODY>
</HTML>
```

The suffix of the file name depends on the file format—we'll talk about that later. But in every other respect, the file is treated like any other file.

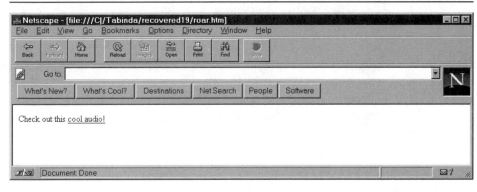

FIGURE 19.1:   The mountain lion soundbite

The Advantages of Downloadable Files

You can usually get much higher sound and video quality from downloadable files. Audio in a downloadable file can be as good as CD quality, but the video will not be as good as VHS. Because the entire file is downloaded, all the data are already on the visitor's machine before the file starts to play.

Downloadable files also provide more flexibility, in several ways. For example, a visitor browsing your site from behind a firewall may not be able to get streaming audio or video (as we'll discuss shortly.) However, he or she will probably be able to get a downloadable file. So if you anticipate that many of the visitors to your wildlife hospital Web site may be coming from behind a firewall, you probably want to offer downloadable files.

And because multimedia files are treated like any other downloadable files, your visitors can select external applications to hear or see the content. For example, visitors who don't run the plug-ins required for streaming files can use the browser to download all the files, quit the browser, and then use another application without the browser running at the same time.

Another advantage (or disadvantage, depending on how you look at it) is that the visitor gets to keep the file after downloading it. This can be an advantage if you want visitors to be able to easily experience the files repeatedly. For example, suppose you are using video to teach your visitors how to safely escape from an encounter with a mountain lion. People may want to see it over and over again. And, remember, the high quality of downloadable files—a bonus for teaching purposes.

On the other hand, if you make a file easy to download, there is always a chance that someone will steal and reuse the content. Whether you own it or whether someone else owns it and you've been licensed to use it, this can be a problem. Although you might not feel it is worth pursuing if it is your own content, you will have to be involved if someone steals content that you have been licensed to distribute. An advantage of streaming media is that a copy does not remain on the visitor's computer.

Because multimedia files are treated like regular files on a server, the server doesn't need to do anything special to serve them. The server simply sends the file when a request comes in, the same way as, say, it sends a GIF image.

Disadvantages of Downloadable Files

Two disadvantages are associated with downloadable files. The first is obvious— it's simply not as "slick" as streaming. Visitors like the idea that they click something and it starts playing right away. The mountain lion roar is probably much more effective if visitors hear it right away, rather than waiting for the roar to download!

The other disadvantage, and the main one, is the wait. A typical file size for a one-minute compressed video file, for example, is 5MB. Over a slow 28.8 connection, downloading might take 20 minutes. In the meantime, the visitor just waits instead of being entertained.

File Types

Like other computer files, audio and video file formats are traditionally associated with computer platforms, or operating systems. That is, at a time when the platforms were even more independent than they are today, you needed a particular type of computer to use a file format. Slowly, people wrote programs that allowed users of a particular computer platform to read files traditionally belonging to another platform. In that regard, the file formats are no longer platform-specific, although they remain so in many people's minds. Table 19.1 lists the different types of downloadable files and the platforms with which they are traditionally associated.

TABLE 19.1:   Common file formats for downloadable files

File Format	Platform
WAV	PC audio
SND	Macintosh audio
AIFF	Macintosh audio
AU	Unix audio
MID, MIDI	All platform audio
AVI	PC video
QT	Macintosh video
MOV	Macintosh video

Although you can find a wealth of technical information about these file types on the Internet and in print, you can use multimedia effectively without worrying much about the internal details behind the different types. Whatever hardware and software you use to create your audio and video files will save them as files of a specific type, probably one of those listed here. Many computers can play files of more than one type, and almost any computer can play any of these types of files as long as it is running the correct client software. (We'll discuss the main categories of multimedia clients—plug-ins and external viewers—later in this skill.)

If you decide to offer your mountain lion video and audio as downloadable files, here's what you do. First, you create and produce the audio and video. That means that you actually record it, listen to it, edit it, and clean it up. You usually use software on your personal computer, unless you have a lot of money and access to a more professional recording system such as an Avid system. For more tips on creating and producing audio and video, see the sections *Producing Audio* and *Producing Video* later in this skill.

When the file is the way you want it, use the editing software to save the file in the format you want. Different types of software let you save in different formats, but any commercial product should provide you with the most popular options such as WAV. Check your saving options before you begin, though, to make sure the software saves files in the format you want. As we mentioned, any format should be okay, but if you anticipate a lot of visitors on a particular platform, choose a format that is traditionally associated with that platform. Once the file is saved in the preferred format, you can put it on the server and link to it like as you would link to any other file, using HTML code that is similar the code we showed you earlier in this section.

There's one last step. Be sure to provide a link to a helper application or a plug-in that can play your format. You'll find more information about helper applications and plug-ins later in this skill. See Tables 19.2 and 19.3 for some helper applications that can play different formats. To find a list of plug-ins that you can link to, try `http.//home.netscape.com/comprod/products/navigator/version-2.0/plugins.index.html` (which works for later versions of Navigator and for IE, despite what the URL implies). The Netscape site is the best place to get plug-ins, even though they are supported by IE, probably because Netscape first produced the architecture and has a vested interest in promoting it. Once you have linked to helper applications and/or plug-ins that your visitors can use, you're all set to provide downloadable files!

Streaming Files

Now that we've taken a look at downloadable options for your mountain lion content, here's some information about streaming files. Streaming files are different from other files from the server's point of view. To send a stream, servers usually need additional software, both to send the stream and to take advantage of the bandwidth in a connection. It's also important that everything in the file arrives in the order that the visitor needs it, with little "dropping out." As with downloadable files, the file type depends on the software you use to encode the files.

Advantages of Streaming Files

The playback of streaming files begins almost immediately and, provided the connection continues uninterrupted until completion (regardless of speed), continues smoothly. This applies if the connection is at least 28.8. Slower modems may have a problem with streaming. If you want visitors with a slower modem to experience your mountain lion audio or video, you will want to provide downloadable files and let them know the file sizes before they begin downloading.

Another advantage of streaming files is that they are used for live broadcasts, which is not possible with downloadable files. You'll often find live broadcasts at radio and television sites and at conference sites (perhaps broadcasting a keynote address. One of the best things about live Web broadcasts is being able to see or hear content that you couldn't hear easily if you weren't using the Web! It's great to hear radio shows in other parts of the world or listen to bands that don't get a lot of air time on regular radio.

For your wildlife shelter, you might want to broadcast live the birth of lion cubs or a healed animal being released into the wild. A live broadcast can involve a lot of setup between the servers and audio or video input (what you need to do depends a great deal on your software), so be sure that you are investing your time in a worthwhile broadcast.

TIP   We'll discuss RealPlayer later in this Skill, but a great place to find out about live broadcasts that use RealPlayer is http://www.timecast.com/.

As of this writing, it appears that visitors have more options for viewing or hearing your content if it is streaming rather than downloadable.

Disadvantages of Streaming Files

Generally speaking, the quality of streamed content is not as good as that of downloaded content. Over a slow connection, streaming audio or video can come across as choppy because frames are sometimes dropped. Like all things on the Internet, quality improves as the connection gets faster.

As mentioned earlier, visitors can save downloadable files on their hard disk; they cannot save streaming files. On the one hand, your visitors may be annoyed at having to watch or hear the stream repeatedly over a Web connection if they need to see it more than once. On the other hand, not leaving a file on your visitor's hard disk does protect you from having your content "borrowed."

To view streamed content, visitors need a browser that supports it or, more likely, a plug-in that can read the type of file format that you've used to encode the audio or video.

Visitors behind a firewall may or may not be able to see or hear your streaming multimedia content, depending on how the local administrator has configured the firewall. (Many companies don't want employees browsing the Web during working hours and don't want them visiting "inappropriate" sites from work at all.) Firewalls are much more common in mid-size to large companies and are hardly ever used on home sites, so this may not be an issue with, for example, a family or recreational Web site. On the other hand, if your site is business-oriented, streamed content might be more of a problem. Our mountain lion example would probably be perceived as a more family-oriented site.

File Types

Once you decide to offer the audio and video as streaming files, you need to choose a file format. File types for streaming media can be a bit trickier than those for downloadable files. Basically, any scheme that involves streaming files needs three kinds of software:

- An editor
- An encoder
- A plug-in or an external application

You use audio or video editing software to edit and clean up the files. You use an encoder to convert the files to streaming files, and in the process, you usually convert the files to a proprietary format. You use a plug-in or an external application later to view or listen to the files.

 NOTE If you are not familiar with these terms, see the sidebar *What Are Plug-ins and External Applications?* later in this skill.

For example, let's say that you decide to offer your mountain lion video and audio in RealAudio and RealVideo formats because they are the most popular streaming formats on the Web. First, you record, edit, and produce the files until they are satisfactory. (For more help in these realms, see the sections "Producing Audio" and "Producing Video" later in this skill.)

The first difference between generating a downloadable and a streaming file is in the way you save the file. As we mentioned earlier in this Skill, you save a downloadable format in the format you want to offer. Saving streaming formats is a two-step process. After saving the audio or video in your editing program, you use the saved file as input into the RealEncoder, which you can get from RealNetworks at http.//www.realnetworks.com. (You can download the smaller and simpler RealAudio encoder rather than the RealEncoder if you want to offer only audio.) Because of this second step, it's important to save the file in a format that the encoder can use as input.

The second difference between generating downloadable and streaming formats is in the encoding process. Generally speaking, the encoder is software that changes the format of your files into a streaming format. So, in our example, the encoder converts your mountain lion audio and video into RealAudio and RealVideo. In doing this, the files not only become streaming files, they also are converted to a format that requires your visitors to have RealPlayer in order to hear or see them. For this reason, you should also provide a link to http://www.realnetworks.com/products/player/index.html so that visitors can get the player.

Although we are emphasizing RealAudio and RealVideo in our example, the same is basically true of whichever streaming format you decide to use. In general, the file type for a streaming file depends on what you use to encode it. There is no standard format for each platform.

Making the Choice: Downloading or Streaming?

As you can see, you have many factors to consider when deciding whether to offer your mountain lion content as downloadable or streaming audio and video. As with any content on the Web that is not a basic HTML file, it's best to consider your visitors.

Leaning toward Downloadable

You probably want to offer downloadable files if you expect your visitors (or a significant portion of them) to be working with:

- Older browsers (earlier than version 3) or browsers such as Lynx
- Dial-up connections running at 28.8 KBPS or slower

Downloadable files are also preferable if any of the following apply:

- You think your visitors will want to experience your multimedia several times or to save it.
- Your visitors might be behind firewalls.
- The quality of the audio or video is important.
- You don't operate your own server, and your ISP doesn't offer support for serving your streaming files.

Leaning toward Streaming

You probably want to offer streaming files if:

- Your visitors have newer browsers (version 3 of Navigator or IE or higher).

Skill 19

- Your users are using speedy connections (28.8 or faster).

- You want to discourage the saving of audio and video files on hard disks.

- You think a lot of your visitors are not behind firewalls (that is, individual users and small businesses, although this is no guarantee).

- The quality of the audio and video is less important than the timeliness of the content.

- You operate your own servers and can install software that optimizes streaming to clients, or your ISP lets you use theirs.

Offering Both

One of the best things you can do for your visitors is to offer both streaming and downloadable multimedia. The only disadvantages are the time to produce both types of formats and the additional space on the server to store both types.

 TIP Audio files and especially video files can take up a lot of room on your server. Be sure to remove them and store them elsewhere when you are not offering them to your visitors.

If you offer both formats, visitors equipped for streaming audio or video receive it as the data comes across from your server to their computer. You could then provide a link for visitors who were not getting the data. Because these files can be so large and can take a long time to download, provide a good description of the file and its size. This prevents visitors from downloading a huge file only to find it's not what they thought it was at all, or worse, just to find out what it is in the first place.

External Applications versus Plug-Ins

Another issue to consider is whether you want your visitors to use a plug-in or an external application for playing back your mountain lion audio and video. Remember, there are lots of file types on the Web, and browsers typically support only a few. The rest have to be handled by other software—external applications or plug-ins. Audio and video files often fall into this category. As we mentioned at the beginning of this skill, your choice of format determines what your visitors will need to access your files.

WHAT ARE PLUG-INS AND EXTERNAL APPLICATIONS?

We'll discuss plug-ins and how they work a lot more in Skill 19, but for purposes of this discussion, here's a summary of the similarities and the differences between plug-ins and external applications.

In the early days of the Web, there was only one way to utilize files that were not directly supported by a browser: external applications (also known as "helpers"). A helper application is described as "external" because it opens its own window to display or run the file and because it is typically stored in a separate directory on the hard disk. In order to get the external application to open the file, you had two options:

- Save the file to disk and then open it separately using the external application. Although reliable and an option that worked for everybody, this was a bit cumbersome.
- With Navigator and later with other browsers such as IE, you could tell your browser to open the external application automatically when it came across a file of a certain type. You mapped the file type to the application in the browser's user preferences dialog box.

This second method is still used frequently. To see your own mappings in Navigator, choose Options ➤ General Preferences ➤ Helpers; in IE, choose View ➤ Options ➤ Programs.

Beginning with Navigator 2, Netscape introduced the plug-in architecture. With this architecture, users can extend the capabilities of their browsers by adding small pieces of software, called plug-ins, to the browser's own directory on their computer. When the browser comes across a file of the appropriate type, it uses the plug-in to open it directly within the browser window. To the user, there appears to be a more

continued on next page ▸

seamless integration with the browser. The file type and the plug-in still have to be mapped, but most plug-ins do this automatically when you install them. The plug-in architecture was also adopted by Microsoft for IE, beginning with version 3.

Streaming files require a plug-in and usually a separate application. For example, when you download RealPlayer and install it, you get a plug-in and a separate application. The separate application is not really a helper application, in that it uses the plug-in to stream files over the Web. You can use it locally, though, to view files that are not streaming in.

As we've mentioned, when you save your files in the recording software—whether audio, video, streaming, or downloadable—you encode them in a particular format, and this determines the software your visitors need to take advantage of the files. That said, let's look at each option.

External Applications

There are many types of external applications for taking advantage of sound and video, both downloadable and streaming. You can think of an external application as a standalone application. That is, you can use it to listen to audio or look at video even without a Web browser on your machine. It's a regular application that is mapped to be launched automatically by the browser to help with unsupported file formats. External applications are almost always used for downloadable files; streaming requires a plug-in. When an external application opens a file, the data—for example, a movie—appears in a window belonging to that application, not in the browser window.

External Applications for Audio

All the applications listed in Table 19.2 play audio of various file formats. Once you select a format in which to deliver your audio, find a player that supports it and provide visitors a link so that they can download it if they need it.

TABLE 19.2:   External applications for audio by platform

Platform	Audio Applications	URL
Windows	Awave	http://hem.passagen.se/fmj/fmjsoft.html
	MidiPlus	http://www.hivolos.com.cy/midiplus/
	WinAmp	http://winamp.lh.net/
Macintosh	SoundApp	http://www-cs-students.stanford.edu/ ~franke/SoundApp/
	SoundMachine	http://www.anutech.com.au/tprogman/ SoundMachine_WWW/welcome.html

External Applications for Video

There are also external applications for viewing video. Table 19.3 includes the information you need to link your audience to the applications they need.

TABLE 19.3:   External applications for video by platform

Platform	Video Applications	URL
Windows	NET TOOB	http://www.duplexx.com/
	QuickTime Player	http://quicktime.apple.com/
	Video Launch Pad	http://www.galttech.com/
Macintosh	Sparkle	http://www.shareware.com/
	MoviePlayer	http://www.shareware.com/
	QuickTime Player	http://quicktime.apple.com/

Some programs have elements of both external applications and plug-ins. QuickTime, for example, comes as a plug-in or as a system extension. It's not really a standalone application, so it doesn't fit neatly into the external application category. The Apple technology is closely integrated with the operating system, and people used the system extension for a long time before plug-ins were around. When the Web arrived, people made a plug-in so that all the QuickTime content could be used over the Web. Today, QuickTime sometimes means the plug-in, and it sometimes means the original system extension/application used on Macintoshes before the Web. The plug-in is now available for PCs.

Plug-Ins

Once the plug-in architecture caught on, there seemed to be plug-ins for everything. A characteristic that distinguishes plug-ins from external applications is that plug-ins are integrated with the browser—they cannot work without one. Again, they also need to be mapped in the browser preferences, but since they are designed to work with the browser, the installation program usually handles this.

Although external applications almost always handle downloadable media, plug-ins are always used with streaming files, although some plug-ins can work with both types (see the "RealPlayer" later in this chapter). Plug-ins almost always display data *inline*, meaning in the browser window itself. This is also true of ActiveX controls.

 **COMPATIBILITY NOTE** Browsers other than Navigator and IE cannot support plug-ins. Even these two browsers could not work with plug-ins until Navigator 2 and IE 3.

Many helper applications were not originally developed for the Web—they already existed, and browser programmers devised ways of mapping to them. Plug-ins, on the other hand, were designed for presenting multimedia (and other files) on the Web. As a result, these technologies typically play both audio and video. For that reason, it does not make sense to list sound and video clients separately. Instead, we'll look at some relevant plug-ins. We'll discuss them in more detail in the next skill, which also covers plug-ins used for media other than audio and video.

QuickTime

QuickTime is an Apple technology that is also available on Windows platforms. It allows for the playback of synchronized content. Like many of the other technologies, it is proprietary, and users needs the plug-in before they can access the file. QuickTime is included with Navigator, and it has a component called QuickTimeVR that allows the user to navigate through virtual reality 3-D models. The plug-in supports the viewing of QuickTime VR, and in addition it supports AU, MPEG, and WAV files. You can find more information about QuickTime at `http://quicktime.apple.com/`.

CineWeb

The CineWeb plug-in from Digigami supports streaming, but of commonly accepted file formats, not proprietary ones. For audio, it supports WAV, MID, and MP2 files. For video, it supports AVI, MOV, and MPG. NET TOOB by Duplexx works the same way, in that it also plays commonly accepted formats. You can get more information about CineWeb at `http://www.digigami.com/`.

RealPlayer

RealPlayer, from Progressive Networks, is probably the most common streaming audio and video format plug-in on the Web today. It is also a bit different from a lot of plug-ins, in that it displays an application window you can use to control playback with buttons such as pause and stop. However, it can't do the streaming without the plug-in, so you need both parts.

RealPlayer is available for many platforms: Macintosh 68K, Macintosh Power Mac, Windows 3.*x*, Windows 95, Windows NT, OS/2, Irix, Sun OS, and Linux. This is a huge advantage—if you encode your audio and video using the Real-Encoder, a lot more people will be able to use it. Still, it is a proprietary format (users need RealPlayer to take advantage of your media), and you need to purchase the server in order to distribute it. You'll find more information about RealPlayer at `http://www.real.com/products/playerplus/index.html`.

VivoActive Player

The VivoActive Player, made by Vivo Software, is another streaming video player. As with RealPlayer, users need the VivoActive Player to view the files. This option is good for those who want high-quality video on a budget. To make files for VivoActive Player, you can use the ViviActive Producer. This technology does not use a proprietary server; the files can be served from other streaming servers like RealServer. For additional information, go to `http://www.vivo.com/`.

Producing Audio

Once you've decided which type(s) of client software you want to allow for, you are ready to begin producing the mountain lion audio and video content. First we'll look at producing the audio of the mountain lion roar. Although a detailed description of audio production is beyond the scope of this book, here are some basics.

To be distributed on the Web (or on computers at all), your audio must be in digital format. It may already be digital (if the sound was made directly on your computer), or you may need to digitize it. In our mountain lion example, the sound is obviously not made by the computer, so you'll have to record the sound digitally.

MAKING DIGITAL SOUNDS

You may be wondering what type of software is used to make sounds digitally. There is a lot of MIDI (musical instrument digital interface) and other synthesizer software available for computers. They are often used to make electronic music, but they can also imitate human voices and other nonmusical sounds. If you've ever had the experience of a computer talking to you, you are familiar with computer-generated voices.

MIDI is a standard that is used to allow software that is MIDI-compliant to play MIDI music. The input can be a microphone or other device but is usually a keyboard. MIDI software often comes bundled with sound cards.

Technical Equipment

You can record digitally in a couple of ways. You can record on Digital Audio Tape (DAT) and then use an audio sound board and sound editing software to move it from the tape to your computer, where you can manipulate it using audio production software. How you get the audio onto your computer for manipulation depends on the type of DAT deck. Many decks have an output that plugs directly into your computer audio input (microphone) jack so that the audio can be copied over. Software that comes with the deck (or with audio editing software, covered later in this section) can then use the files as input. Refer to the manual that comes with the DAT deck for specific instructions. A second way is to record using a microphone directly plugged into the computer and save the file, using a sound recording and editing program.

The first method usually results in better quality but is more complicated. It also works well if you need a way to easily send a method of digital recording to a remote location. If you want to record on DAT, you should do some research into the best techniques for recording and moving the data onto a computer.

More easily, just research the best techniques for recording and then hand the files over to an audio production house. A good audio place can transfer, edit, and produce the audio in whichever format you prefer. Depending on how much you want done, fees can range from $50 to $150 an hour. The low end of the price range is for simple digitizing and encoding, and the high end is usually for sending an audio expert to a location for recording. This can be a real timesaver because sometimes the compression can tie up your computer for a long time. The compression process can be speeded up by using hardware instead of software-only methods, but the hardware is expensive. Again, examine your options.

 TIP

It is useful to have high-capacity and fast hard disks for good performance with sound editing. Disk drive manufacturers sometimes offer an AV type of hard disk that is optimized for the real-time nature of digital media. This is a good way to go if you need to do a lot of digital audio because over time, disks will suffer from data fragmentation, which causes track seek times to vary.

Taping

If you decide not to record professionally, here are some tips:

- Write out what you are going to say and rehearse it.

- Get a good microphone. The ones supplied with most computers are not very high quality and make the *S* and the *P* sound fuzzy.

- To reduce echo, record in a well-padded room, with carpeting, curtains, and as much furniture as possible.

- Place the recorder on a folded towel to muffle vibration.

- Test the microphone at different distances from the source of the sound. After running a few samples, select the best distance and stick with it.

- If your recording method is digital, record at 44.1 kHz sample rate, 16-bit (sample resolution) settings if you have space on your hard disk. If you have these options, they will be set on the DAT recorder or will be part of the software you are using to record directly onto your computer. An analog recorder or less sophisticated software won't let you set these.

Sampling Rates and Resolution

The process of recording sound into digital information is known as *sampling*. A *sample* is essentially a snapshot of the sound at a given instant in time. (The term is also sometimes used more broadly to mean any piece of digital sound.) The *sampling rate* and *resolution* determine both the quality of the sound and the size of the resulting file or stream. As you might expect, more lifelike sound requires more bytes of data; so on the Web you need to strike an optimal balance between quality and file size.

The sampling rate is the number of samples recorded per second. The optimal sampling rate of 44.1 kHz means that your sound will be sampled 44,100 times per second. Although this results in huge files that you will later have to make much smaller, it gives you more data from the original recording to work with. That is, when you *sample down* (reduce the sample size to get a smaller file) and you lose data, you'll still get a better recording because the original sample size was high. Consult your audio production software documentation for more information on sampling down files. It's the same concept as taking a high resolution, full-color graphic image and sampling it down to a more portable file size.

The sample *resolution* is the number of bits used to store each sample. Again, a bigger chunk of digital data stores a more detailed snapshot of the sound. As a default for recording, go with 16 bits—you can always sample down later.

In all cases, the idea is the same: start with a very high quality original recording, and then sample it down to find a balance between file size and audio quality. You'll probably downsample to 22 kHz and 8-bit, but it will vary.

Editing the Audio

Any good audio production application will allow you to save your files in the commonly accepted formats. As we mentioned earlier, if you want to save your file in a proprietary format, such as RealAudio, you need the encoder for that format. Encoders are usually free or relatively inexpensive, as are players. Manufacturers typically make their money from the servers. You need to go to the company's Web site and find out how to get the encoder. Encoders usually need your files in a particular format, so find out before you save all your files. The typical process for our mountain lion example looks like this:

1. Make the audio digital (however you choose to do it). For good quality, you can do this by recording the roar with a DAT deck or by getting the lion to roar into a microphone attached to a computer. The first option seems safer!

2. Edit the file—you can use the audio production software to edit out pauses and other mistakes. (This is easier than getting the lion to roar correctly.)

3. Once the file sounds the way you want, save it—either directly in the format you want to use on the Web (if you plan to serve it exactly as it is) or in whatever format the encoder uses as input (if you plan to encode it into a proprietary format). The RealEncoder supports AIF, WAV, MOV, AU, and SND.

Figure 19.2 shows the interface for RealEncoder for Windows 95. Many audio-editing software programs are on the market. A popular one for the Windows platform is SmartSound (`http://www.sonicdesktop.com/`). Probably the most popular programs for Web audio development on the Macintosh are SoundEdit and Deck II, which come together from Macromedia (`http://www.macromedia.com/`).

TIP   If you plan to purchase video-editing software (see the section *Video Editing Software* later in this Skill), check its audio-editing capabilities. Sophisticated video software packages will usually do everything mid-range audio packages will do, so you'll only need to purchase one piece of software.

Figure 19.3 shows the Macromedia SoundEdit interface on the Macintosh. It's a typical application for affordable audio production. The separate floating controls act like tape recorder controls, and segments of voice can be cut, pasted, and added like any other application. In the bottom-left corner of the application window, you can see that the audio was recorded at 16 bits and 44.1 kHz.

Skill 19

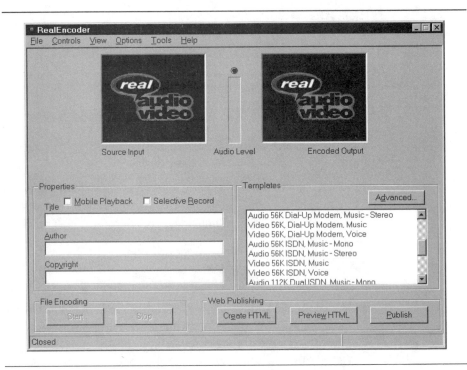

FIGURE 19.2:   The RealEncoder interface for Windows 95

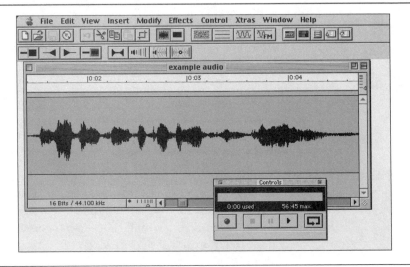

FIGURE 19.3:   The SoundEdit interface. Copyright Macromedia, Inc. 1995.
All Rights Reserved. Used with Permission.

Adding the Audio to Your HTML Pages

How the audio of the mountain lion roar goes out to your visitors depends on the file format, and you should consult the documentation of your product if encoding or setting up a server is involved.

You may also just put a link to the audio in your HTML page and choose a format supported by the browser. For example, the more recent releases of Navigator support AIFF files so that when the link is followed, the sound begins playing. You can add the sound contained in an AIFF file named example.aiff (or whatever name you used for the sound file) by using the following HTML:

```
<html>
<head>
<title></title>
<body bgcolor="#ffffff">

Check out this <a href="example.aiff">cool audio!</a>

</body>
</html>
```

Again, this works like any other HTML link, and it causes the file to begin playing when the link is followed. This works because the file format is supported by the browser itself—there is no external application or plug-in to make it play.

Figure 19.4 shows the page in Navigator 3.01 on the Macintosh. The floating window pops up automatically when a visitor clicks the Cool Audio link This small window belongs to the browser, which opens it when the link is followed. The browser itself plays the audio.

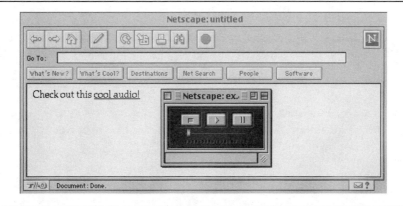

FIGURE 19.4:   An AIFF audio file, which is supported by Navigator 3.01

Embedded background audio starts playing when the page is downloaded; the user doesn't need to select it. You add background audio to a Web page with either the EMBED tag or the BGSOUND tag. The differences between them are in browser support and attributes. The EMBED tag, introduced by Netscape, is supported by Navigator 2 and later versions, by IE 3 and later, and by WebTV 1.2. The BGSOUND tag, which was later introduced by Microsoft, is supported only by Navigator 3 (but not by 4), by IE 2 and later versions, and by WebTV.

Using the *EMBED* Tag

You'll find a particularly nice example of the use of embedded audio at:

```
http://www.best.com/~jylian/journal.html
```

This page can take a while to load, but the music is really fitting. As you look at the pages from an art journal, you hear haunting yet relaxing music. If you view the source code of a Web page with embedded audio, you'll see that the HTML for embedding audio in QuickTime looks something like this:

```
<EMBED SRC= "audio/sample.mov" CONTROLLER=FALSE LOOP=TRUE
    AUTOPLAY=TRUE>
```

The audio is embedded in the page with the EMBED tag, which uses SRC as an attribute in the same way that the IMG tag uses SRC—it points to the location of the file. In this case, the audio file is *sample.mov*, located in the audio directory (replace *sample.mov* with the name of your file). You can hide the controls for the sound by using the attribute CONTROLLER=FALSE. The default value for CONTROLLER's default value is TRUE. The LOOP=TRUE attribute causes the sounds to loop back to the start when it reaches the end so that the sound is continuous. The AUTOPLAY=TRUE attribute causes the sound to play automatically when the page loads. The default value for AUTOPLAY is FALSE.

 **WARNING**   Use care when looping or autoplaying media. Many times, visitors become annoyed when the music or movie keeps repeating.

You can also set the height and width of a movie using the HEIGHT and WIDTH attributes as in HEIGHT="100". The numbers represent pixels.

Using the *BGSOUND* Tag

The BGSOUND tag works in the same way as the EMBED tag, but it is not completely supported by Navigator. The two attributes for BGSOUND are SRC and LOOP, which have the same meanings as they do for the EMBED tag, although the LOOP attribute can have a different value. If you want the audio to loop indefinitely, set the LOOP attribute equal to INFINITE (LOOP="INFINITE").

Producing Video

Although a complete description of the mountain lion video production process is beyond the scope of this book, we can give you some idea of the basic processes.

Online Resources

If you need more information about video production, check out the following:

- The Digital Video Information Server at
  http://www.radius.com/Support/DV/mainDV.html.
  (Scroll down to get to the good stuff.)

- Terran Interactive's Codec Central at
  http://www.terran=int.com.CodecCentral/.

- The Complete Guide to Non-Linear Editing on Your PC at
  http://members.aol.com/simmike/beguide.htm.

- Digital Movie News, which is Macintosh-specific, at
  http://www.el-dorado.ca.us/~dmnews/.

Technical Equipment

To create video for the Web, you need two basic pieces of equipment:

- Something to capture the video, such as a camcorder

- A video capture card that goes in your computer

Not to be confused with the standard video adapter that every computer uses to drive a monitor, the capture card converts the analog video into a digital format that computers can store and use. (Digital camcorders are also available and do not require this conversion.) Some high-end computers already have these cards, but you'll need to install one on most (including most "home multimedia" systems). Check the documentation that came with your computer to find out if you need to purchase and install a card. A typical video capture card runs between $1,000 and $2,000. The price difference mainly reflects the speed of the conversion. Video conversion can take a long time, so purchase the fastest card you can afford.

To move the analog video from the camcorder to the computer, you need video-editing software. The video capture card, which comes with a driver, sometimes also comes bundled with video-editing software such as Adobe Premiere. Using the video-editing software, you can move the video over a cable such as an S-cable. The type of cable required depends on the camcorder and the video capture card. The video card takes the analog video, converts it to digital information, and stores it on the disk.

If you need to purchase a camcorder for this purpose, be sure it has two features:

- The ability to capture high-quality video (such as Hi-8)

- An output jack that can work with a cable connected to the video capture card in the computer

Image stabilization is not required, but is a good idea if you are not going to use a tripod.

Planning Your Video

Be sure to take the time to plan your video. Plan each scene—determine who is going to be in it, where you will film it, and what props you need. Use this information to make master lists of people, locations, and props.

 TIP Preplanning for video really pays off. If you are renting equipment, the more prepared you are before you begin, the more money you can save. Do as much planning as you can before renting equipment or taking up people's time.

Filming

Finally, film the video. If necessary, you can rent the equipment, and you can hire someone to shoot the film if you don't feel comfortable. Rates vary, but if you provide the props and other non-video equipment, you can probably hire a camera person for about $150 an hour. You can see why preplanning is so important.

 TIP   Taping sound for video is more challenging than taping audio alone, especially if people or animals are involved and they are moving around. But the same basic principles apply: buy a good microphone, test the best distance for the microphone, and occasionally listen to the sound as you proceed.

Digitizing and Editing the Video

After the filming of the mountain lion is complete, you need to digitize the video so that it can be stored, edited, compressed, and delivered from a computer. As you edit the files on your computer, you'll want to save them. As with audio, if you plan to compress them later using an encoder, check the encoder to find out what file format it accepts for input, and then use the editing program to save the files in that format. If you want to serve the files to your visitors in a more commonly accepted format such as MPEG, save the files in whichever format you eventually want to use.

Popular video-editing software includes Macromedia Director (for both Windows and Macintosh) and the Adobe ® Premiere ® product. Figure 19.5 shows the interface for the Adobe Premiere product, which is available for Macintosh, Windows, and the SGI platform. For more information, try `http://www.adobe.com/`.

You can use the Adobe After Effects product (for both Macintosh and Windows) to add even more slick transitions and put together images with different resolutions. Effectively used, it can make your video content into a more professional-looking production.

 TIP   Video editing software for personal computers can be expensive, easily on the order of $500 to $1000. Be sure that you are comfortable with the software you purchase and that it does what you need it to do. Also check out the plug-ins for each piece of software, because plug-ins can add a lot of functionality not included in the original product.

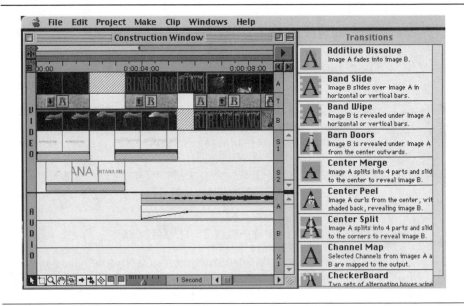

FIGURE 19.5: The Adobe Premiere interface. Adobe and Premiere are trademarks of Adobe Systems Incorporated.

Adding Video to Your HTML Pages

Adding your movie of the mountain lion is just like adding the audio. You provide a link to the file, and if the video is downloadable, visitors can download it as they would from any other link. If it's streaming video, it will begin playing when visitors decide to look at it, provided they have the appropriate plug-in. Remember to add a link to whatever software is needed to view your video files so that visitors can download it if necessary.

You embed video with the EMBED tag, just as you embed audio. For video, you'll definitely want to use the HEIGHT and WIDTH attributes so that the browser can set aside space for the movie as it loads the page. This makes everything load faster.

 TIP

You may have to add pixels to the actual height of the movie if you want to display the controller. For example, for QuickTime, add 24 pixels to the height of the movie to accommodate the controller if you are not hiding it. It's usually best to display the controller for movies, as movies rarely make good background media.

Providing Alternatives

If you are going to offer audio or video, provide alternatives for visitors who cannot use your content. Throughout this skill, we've mentioned some reasons that visitors might not be able to see or hear your content. Here's a brief summary:

- Firewalls may not allow the data through.
- Older browsers may not support audio and video.
- Some visitors are hearing-impaired or visually impaired.
- Slow connections may make audio or video prohibitive.
- Visitors simply choose not to hear or view your content.

Workarounds

You can use any of several workarounds to allow visitors to get a feel for the content they are missing. Although these substitutes are not perfect, it's much better to give your visitors options rather than leaving them in the dark, wondering what they are missing.

First, you can provide a narrative explanation of the content. Be descriptive, and replicate the tone of the audio or video in your explanation. If you are using the audio as background music for the page, you can simply describe its mood as, for example, "cheerful" or "dramatic." In our example, you might want to describe the audio as "a ferocious roar."

For spoken audio (and possibly for song lyrics), you can provide transcripts. You can include a link to another page, along with some text that directs the visitor there. Because a transcript doesn't always convey the tone of the information, you might want to also include your own narrative explanation before the transcript. A couple of brief sentences should do it.

You can provide a video transcript of sorts by combining text with images from the video. Your video-editing program should allow you to make individual video frames into images. Be sure to save them as GIF or JPEG. For more information about optimizing photo images, see Skill 17. Be sure to use the ALT tag for those visitors who are not viewing your images.

An Example of a Web Site with Transcripts

The WBGH radio Web site is a good example of accommodating visitors who don't want to or cannot use multimedia. Find it at `http://www.boston.com/wgbh/`. We looked at this site in Figure 19.4, earlier in this chapter, as an example of a site that offers both downloadable and streaming audio. Figure 19.6 shows the front door to this Web site.

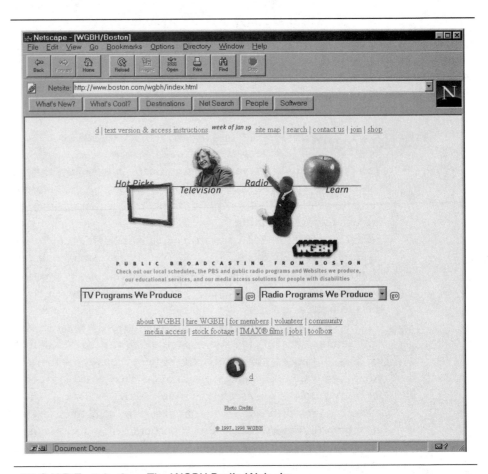

FIGURE 19.6: The WGBH Radio Web site

Notice the *d* in the upper left corner of this page. Clicking here takes you to the page shown in Figure 19.7. This page describes the images to readers who cannot see them. It also provides text links to the same places as the images.

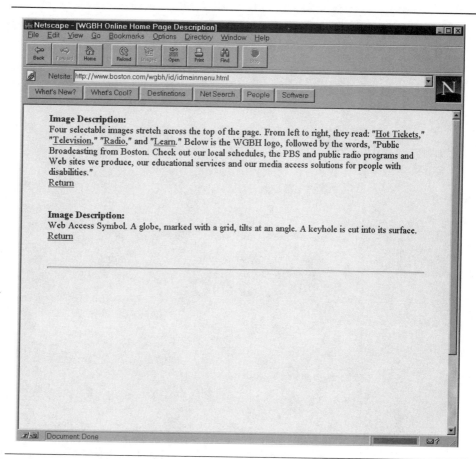

FIGURE 19.7: The image descriptions for the main WGBH Radio Web site

---

TIP

Most eyes go first to the upper left corner of a page. That's also the location at which a speech-based browser begins reading the page.

Next to the *d* on the main page is a link that says "text version & access instructions." Clicking here takes you to a text version of the site and to an area for people with disabilities (see Figure 19.8). If you follow the links, you learn that all the information can be found in text-only pages, that all pages with images have the *d* for image descriptions, and that all audio and video pieces have transcripts.

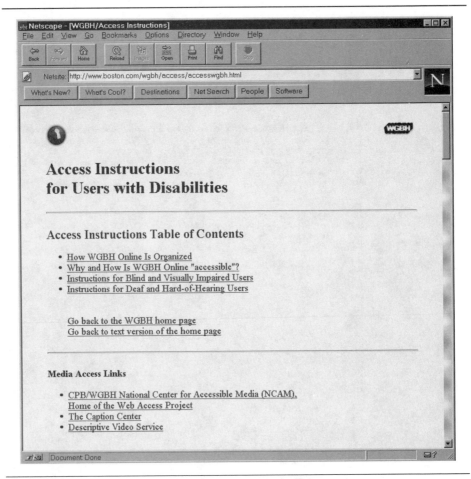

FIGURE 19.8: The WGBH accessibility page

One of the links on the WGBH accessibility page shown in Figure 19.8 is for Descriptive Video Service. There you can see an example of the video transcript, as shown in Figure 19.9.

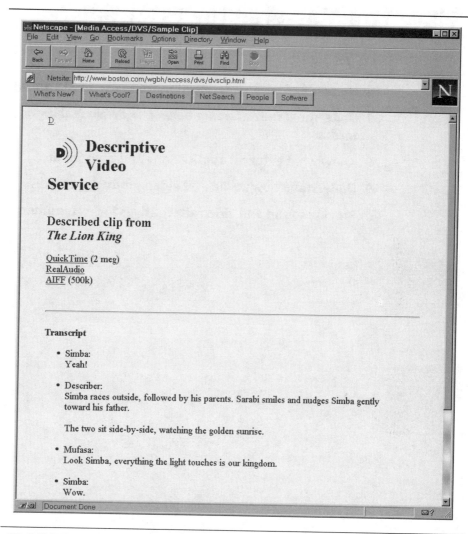

FIGURE 19.9: An example of a video transcript

Although the adaptations at this site are designed for those with disabilities, they also benefit visitors with older browsers, slower connections, and so on. Easy, cross-platform access to information was the driving force behind the invention of the World Wide Web, and sites designed with options such as these clearly keep this philosophy in mind.

Have You Mastered the Essentials?

Now you can...

- ☑ Understand when it is appropriate to use sound and video.
- ☑ Understand the difference between downloadable and streaming media.
- ☑ Know what external applications and plug-ins are.
- ☑ Understand how audio and video production works.
- ☑ Provide sound and video alternatives for your audience.

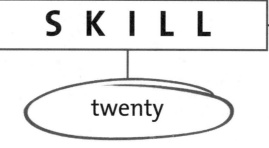

Evaluating Plug-Ins

❑ What are plug-ins?

❑ How plug-ins work

❑ Popular plug-in interfaces

Welcome to the world of plug-ins. Using plug-ins can be an easy way to make your Web site more dynamic and useful. In this skill, we are going to look at the concept of plug-ins, how they work, and which browsers support them. After this background information, we'll look at several popular plug-ins, what you need to make them work, example sites, and alternatives for those who can't or don't use them.

The Plug-In Concept

Plug-ins are not a new concept. The idea originated with hardware; vacuum tubes were referred to as plug-ins, and later, plug-in components were used to add functionality to oscilloscopes. Later, the term was applied to software. An early example was software that you could add to Adobe PhotoShop to enable it to perform tasks that it couldn't do off the shelf.

Plug-ins for browsers add functionality that the browser can't perform by itself. They are similar to helper applications, but plug-ins are much more entwined with the browser. Plug-ins are not standalone applications; they need the browser to work. But remember that not all browsers support plug-ins.

More importantly, when dealing with plug-ins, keep in mind that visitors to your Web site will have to download and install a plug-in to get all the features you added. (They only have to do this once per plug-in. That is, once the plug-in is installed, it works for all sites that need it.)

The History of Plug-Ins

Plug-ins for Web browsers were first introduced by Netscape. In January 1996, Netscape made available to the public the first 15 plug-ins based on its plug-in architecture. In the months that followed, many developers hopped on the band-wagon and developed plug-ins that did everything from allowing users to open spreadsheets in browsers to browsing 3-D VRML Web sites. By June 1996, more than 100 developers were making plug-ins.

Plug-ins were a big advantage for Netscape. Because they added functionality that did not have to be included in the browser itself, Netscape could get new versions of the browser out the door faster. From the user's point of view, plug-ins were both a liability and an asset. Although they had to be acquired and installed, once installed, plug-ins behaved as part of the browser and provided a "customized" approach.

Microsoft began supporting plug-ins with Internet Explorer 3, but also introduced ActiveX controls, which compete on some fronts with plug-ins, although they are not as popular since they are limited to the Windows platform. Today, plug-ins continue to grow in popularity, and the browser companies depend on them for added features.

Occasionally, new releases of a browser incorporate technologies that were previously supported by plug-ins, and then the plug-in is no longer necessary for that version of the browser.

WHAT IS ACTIVEX?

ActiveX controls are based on the OLE technology often found in non-Internet applications, called OCXs. ActiveX allows Web designers to create controls that add functionality to Web sites. Generally speaking, ActiveX controls are used for site-specific functionality, whereas plug-ins are more a means to an end, delivering content that needs special handling. Navigator users can use a plug-in to view certain ActiveX-enabled sites if they prefer, but to take full advantage of ActiveX, it's better to use IE.

In this skill, we are going to focus on plug-ins rather than ActiveX, since plug-ins fit the cross-compatibility model of Web design and ActiveX does not.

Skill 20

The Architecture of Plug-Ins

Without getting into too much technical detail, let's take a look at how plug-ins work. Basically, browsers support different Multimedia Internet Message Extensions (MIME) types. MIME is a file format that each browser handles in its own way. Web browsers inherently support certain MIME types, such as text/html. Support for other MIME types depends on the browser. For example, most browsers support the image/gif MIME type for images, but some don't. The MIME type of each file is provided by the Web server for each document when it is sent to the browser.

Plug-ins support MIME types that the browser can't handle. When you install a plug-in, you sometimes have to update the browser preferences in order to map the MIME type to the plug-in. That is, you need to tell browser to use the plug-in when it encounters a file of a particular MIME type.

 TIP   To install a plug-in, you usually download it, place it in the appropriate directory, and then launch your browser. To install most of the newer plug-ins, however, you use an installer. The MIME types update themselves.

Figure 20.1 shows the interface for selecting helper applications for MIME types in Netscape Navigator. (Choose Options ➢ General Preferences and then select the Helpers tab). Although the tab is called Helpers by tradition, it also includes plug-ins. (Note the LiveAudio and QuickTime plug-ins.)

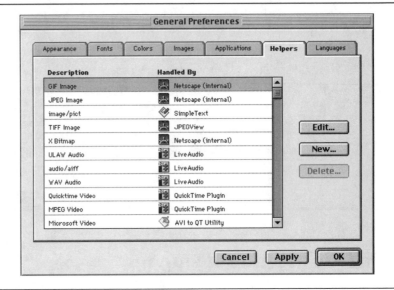

FIGURE 20.1:   The Navigator helper application interface

To map a MIME type, click the New or the Edit button, depending on whether your MIME type already exists in the left column. Figure 20.2 shows the dialog box that Navigator displays if you click Edit for the QuickTime MIME type.

In the Description box, you enter the name of the plug-in, and in the MIME Type box, you enter its MIME type. In the Suffixes box, enter the file name suffix associated with the MIME type. Now you can choose how Navigator is to handle the file. You have the following options:

- Specify a plug-in

- Choose an application

- Save the file to your hard drive

- Have Navigator ask you what you want to do with the file

Figure 20.2 shows the mapping for the QuickTime plug-in.

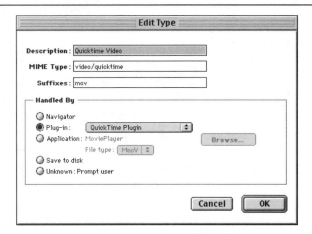

FIGURE 20.2:   The interface for mapping the QuickTime MIME type

Support for Plug-Ins

As of this writing, plug-ins are supported by Navigator 2 and higher and by IE 3 and higher. The latest version of both browsers supports ActiveX: IE inherently, and Navigator via a plug-in. Another browser that supports plug-ins is Opera, which is becoming increasingly popular.

Navigator 4 automatically downloads the required plug-in when you try to load a page that needs it. Depending on how you feel about files being downloaded automatically to your computer, this may be good news or bad news. On the one hand, it's convenient. On the other, if you don't like adding mystery files to your computer and/or have limited disk space, it might not be as helpful as it sounds.

Keep in mind that plug-ins are available for many platforms, although not all plug-ins are available for all platforms. Like all software, it depends on what the developer supports. For example, RealPlayer (discussed below in the section *Popular Plug-Ins*) is available for Macintosh, Windows 3.*x*, Windows 95, Windows NT, OS/2, IRIX, Sun OS, and Linux.

Why Plug-Ins?

These days you can make Web pages more dynamic in several ways. You can use Java, JavaScript, and ActiveX, to name a few. So why do developers make plug-ins? Most make their money not via the plug-in, but from the people who want to create Web sites that use the plug-in. This is a rather typical Internet philosophy of giving software away because market share is more valuable than anything else and then making money elsewhere based on the recognition and popularity.

If you want include material on your Web site that requires a plug-in, chances are that you'll have to buy software to do it. What you'll have to purchase depends on the plug-in. For example, you might have to purchase a server that can send the files over the Web for you, or you might need an encoder that converts files into the format needed for the plug-in.

Using plug-ins is usually an easy way for a developer to add bells and whistles to a Web site. Java and ActiveX require programming knowledge, as does JavaScript. Adding material via a plug-in usually involves converting files to the correct format and then putting them up on the Web. Some server configuration may be involved, but this is commercial software with documentation. It's still much easier than learning a programming language.

Using plug-ins also sometimes allows a Web developer to reuse existing material. For example, if you have a lot of material created with Macromedia's Director software, it's a fairly easy to convert it to Shockwave (discussed below). Or, if you have a lot of documents in a word-processor format, it's a rote job to convert them into Acrobat files for viewing.

Plug-ins lend themselves better to some applications than to others. They are great for audio, video, and interfaces where the user clicks on objects to perform actions (see the Shockwave example Web site later in this chapter). On the other hand, if you wanted to add a loan calculator or a stock ticker to your site, you'll want to develop it with Java or JavaScript. As you gain experience working on the Web, and as you spend more time surfing, you'll come to know which methods of adding bells and whistles works best for what you'd like to do. There is simply no substitute for spending time on the Web and studying how sites have implemented features you like. Take the time to note which plug-ins are required in order to use the site, if you need a Java-enabled browser to view the site, or if the site simply states what technology they are using.

Popular Plug-Ins

With all the plug-ins available, it can be difficult to decide which ones to use for your site. This section showcases a few of the most popular plug-ins on the Web. It's a good idea to use the most popular plug-ins whenever possible, because often people will already have them, or if they have to download them, it's more like they'll be able to use them at other sites. Some of the more obscure plug-ins perform specialized functions. If you need visitors to download a plug-in they probably won't be using anywhere else, be sure your content justifies it.

Shockwave and Shockwave Flash are plug-ins from Macromedia, Inc., located at `http://www.macromedia.com/shockwave/`. These versatile plug-ins are used for animation, movies, and sounds on the Web. More recently, Macromedia announced a Flash player that takes advantage of Java. Using this player obviates the need for a plug-in; Flash content works in any browser that supports Java. Because this product is new and because most Web surfers who want to see and hear Shockwave have the original Shockwave and Shockwave Flash plug-ins, you should support them also.

Shockwave is a proprietary format, and you can use many Macromedia products to make Shockwave files. Macromedia makes many multimedia authoring tools, including software for audio and video production. Most of these applications give you the option of exporting content as Shockwave or Shockwave Flash. There is no way to make Shockwave files free of charge, unless you download the unsupported trial versions. As is the case with many other plug-ins, the Web site developer purchases the software to make the materials, and the plug-in is free to visitors. Macromedia is currently pushing Flash as the standard, not plain Shockwave, but Shockwave has a large installed user base.

Skill 20

You can use Flash to create streaming animation, graphics, banners, and maps. Content is played back to the viewer in the Flash player. Plain Shockwave is played back in the page in which it is embedded.

The Shockwave plug-in is available for Windows 3.1, Windows 95, Windows NT, Macintosh 68K, and Macintosh PowerPC.

An Example Web Site

The Bullseye site, located at `http://www.thing.net/~bullseye/`, is a really good example of what you can do with Shockwave. Before you go there, be sure to get the plug-in from `http://www.macromedia.com/shockwave/`. A series of Shockwave movies and sounds, combined with linked images that appear as you proceed, lead you through an art exhibit.

When you first arrive, you see the page in Figure 20.3. Rolling your mouse over any of the gray ellipses plays a sound and displays the name of an art

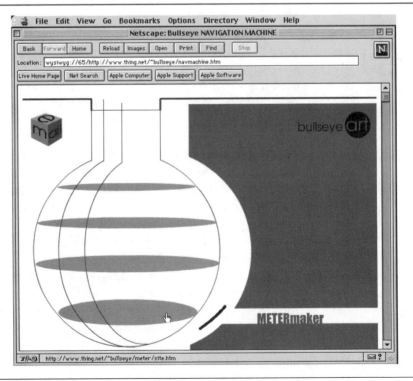

FIGURE 20.3: The opening page of Bullseye

exhibit, METERmaker in this case. Clicking METERmaker displays an animation of blooming flowers, and then that page refreshes to automatically take you to the screen shown in Figure 20.4. Clicking a shape plays music and displays another shape, until the page is filled with shapes, as shown in Figure 20.5.

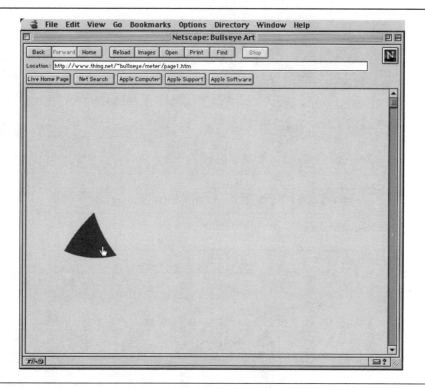

FIGURE 20.4:   The first of the musical shapes

After the page is full, clicking random shapes and playing music eventually leads to a page full of words that change when you roll a mouse over them. Clicking the words causes them to change, until they say the same thing over and over, as shown in Figure 20.6.

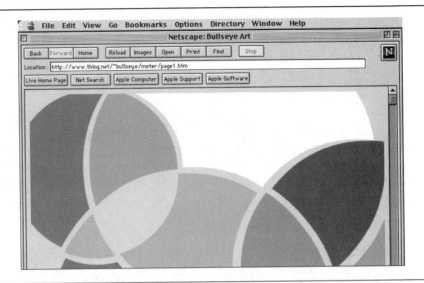

FIGURE 20.5: All the musical shapes

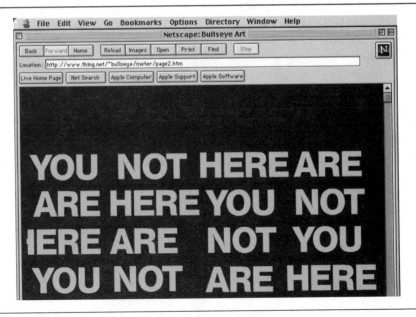

FIGURE 20.6: You are not here (but you are).

Finally, the page refreshes and goes automatically to the screen shown in Figure 20.7. When you roll the cursor over the cubes on the right, they animate to form a curved surface. This is another example of what Shockwave can do. Clicking the arrow in the bottom right corner leads to the page shown in Figure 20.3, earlier in this chapter, where you can select a different art exhibit.

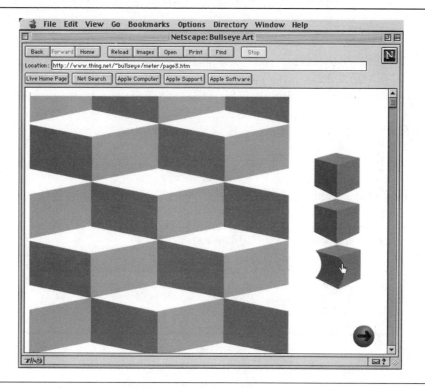

FIGURE 20.7:   The final page of the exhibit

What You Need

This section contains information about what you need to provide Shockwave content—the content itself, what you need to convert it to Shockwave, and how to configure the server.

The Content   To generate Shockwave files, you first need the actual content. As we mentioned at the beginning of this section, you can use many Macromedia products—such as Director, Freehand, and SoundEdit—to generate movies, animations, and sound. These applications provide high-level options that you can use to develop professional-looking content. You can then export your masterpieces as Shockwave files.

In other cases, there might be a plug-in for the application itself. For example, if you already own SoundEdit, you can get the Shockwave plug-in for the SoundEdit application. SoundEdit can export AIFF (a Macintosh audio file format) files as Shockwave audio (SWA) files.

The HTML   To embed Shockwave media into Web pages, you use either the OBJECT or the EMBED tags. Using both makes the media run well in both Navigator and IE. Here is the HTML recommended by Macromedia for embedding Shockwave media:

```
<OBJECT classid="clsid:D27CDB6E-AE6D-11cf-96B8-444553540000"

  codebase="http://active.macromedia.com/flash2/cabs/swflash.cab#version=2,1,0,7"

  width=100 height=80>
  <PARAM name="Movie" value="moviename.swf">

  <EMBED src="moviename.swf" width=100 height=80

  pluginspage="http://www.macromedia.com/shockwave/download/index.cgi?P1_Prod_Version=
➥ ShockwaveFlash">
  </EMBED>
```

 TIP   Substitute your own movie name, height, and width in this example.

In addition to supporting IE, the OBJECT tag works for any browser that supports the Shockwave Flash ActiveX control. The EMBED tag supports the browsers that support the plug-in, which includes Navigator 2 and higher. By using both, you can cover most of your bases.

 WARNING   Be sure to put the OBJECT tag first, followed by the EMBED tag, as shown. The other way around will not work as well!

If you use this code, be sure to leave classid and codebase and their values alone—they are set to work with Shockwave and to tell the browser where to find the player. It's also a good idea to leave `pluginspage` alone—it tells the browser where to get the plug-in if the visitor wants it. If you are going to offer the plug-in from another location, say from your own site, change this HTML code to reflect the correct URL to your alternate plug-ins page.

The NOEMBED tag is used for browsers that don't support plug-ins or ActiveX. (We'll look at this is in more detail later in this chapter.)

The Server   Be sure that your Web server is set up to serve these files according to their MIME type. The MIME type for Shockwave Flash is application/ x-shockwave-flash, and the file suffix is .swf. The Macromedia Web site contains information about additional MIME types for all the different media.

Alternatives to Plug-Ins

One way to accommodate browsers that do not support plug-ins is to use the NOEMBED tag. Macromedia suggests that you use the following HTML to substitute a GIF image in place of the Shockwave file. Of course, you can substitute whatever you like by using the appropriate file name.

```
<NOEMBED>
<IMG src="moviename.gif" width=100 height=80>
</NOEMBED>
</OBJECT>
```

This GIF file could be an animated GIF, which might add more excitement or might even replicate what Shockwave does. You can also use imagemap buttons to lead visitors to new content or to refresh the pages. To replicate the effects you can achieve with Shockwave, you would need to use JavaScript, and browsers that support JavaScript usually support plug-ins or ActiveX.

COMPATIBILITY NOTE   Try to make your Web site work for visitors who do not have Shockwave. In general, it's a bad idea to require a plug-in for your front page. Allow your visitors to see what you're about. They can then decide if getting to the rest of your content is worth getting or running the plug-in.

It's a good idea to provide a text description of the animation, sound, or movie for visitors who cannot access multimedia. We'll discuss accessibility issues such as this in more detail in Skill 23.

Acrobat Reader

Acrobat Reader, available from Adobe Systems at http://www.adobe.com/, is a free utility that you can use to view Acrobat files. We've included the Acrobat Reader on the CD that comes with this book. Acrobat files are in PDF (Portable Document Format) and are generated in various ways (we discuss this later in the section "What You Need"). PDF files are completely cross-platform. As long as you view them with the Acrobat Reader, what you see is exactly what you'd see viewing them in the application in which they were created. You cannot, however, edit PDF files.

To edit the file, you need the original file from which the PDF document was made. The closest a user can get to altering a PDF file is to interact with it as a form. When you convert a file into a PDF file, you can add forms that contain objects such as radio buttons and drop-down menus, and you can add audio and video controls. The visitor can then interact with the file using these methods. Visitors can also add comments to the file that sit on top of the original file like electronic Post-Its, but they cannot change the actual file. People often use PDF so that they can offer files that retain their original formatting. This can be useful if the formatting is really important, and it can save time if you already have the files and don't want to convert them to HTML.

The Acrobat Reader is available for many platforms as a standalone application (for those who don't have access to the Web) or as a browser plug-in. In this section, we'll be looking at how to use Acrobat Reader as a plug-in.

A PDF document can contain hyperlinks, both to links within the document and to other Web sites, and you can embed movies in a PDF document. It is fully searchable and indexable. A PDF document tends to be large, much larger than a comparable HTML file. For example, the Mars example PDF in Figure 20.8 was about 250 pages and was about 10.5 MB, including images Depending on the size of the images, a comparable HTML page with the same information might be 2–4 MB in size.

To view the PDF files at your Web site, your visitors must have the reader or the plug-in; both are available at http://www.adobe.com/prodindex/acrobat/. Like all other plug-ins or helper applications, the browser MIME type must map the Acrobat plug-in.

TIP In graphical Web browsers, the user usually has an option to decide if the graphics and text should be rendered together or if graphics should load after the text. The latter is usually better, because the visitor can read the text while the images load. Acrobat Reader works the same way—it loads the text first and then the images, so that your visitors can begin reading as soon as possible.

Adobe makes many software products, including PhotoShop, PageMaker, and Illustrator, and they invented PostScript and many electronic fonts. The Acrobat Reader is available for Windows 95, Windows NT, Windows 3.1, Macintosh, Linux, IBM AIX, Sun SPARC SunOS, Sun SPARC Solaris, SGI IRIX, HP-UX, Digital Unix, and OS/2 Warp.

Two PDF Examples

Now, let's look at two examples of PDF documents at the Adobe Web site. Each illustrates different features.

Figure 20.8 shows a PDF document from the Mars Pathfinder mission to Mars. Opening this document with the plug-in displays a PDF-specific toolbar at the top of the browser window. You can use these tools to navigate, change the magnification, print, and view the document in outline format. It also offers an option to view the PDF in outline mode, with links on the left side. This outline option is not used in Figure 20.8, but it is in Figure 20.9.

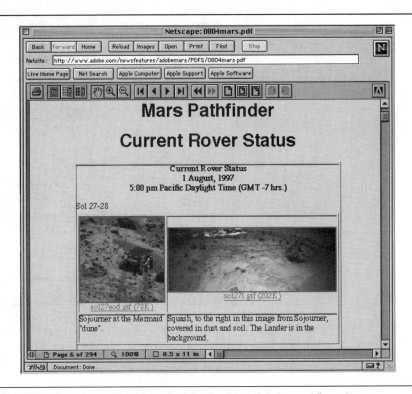

FIGURE 20.8: The Mars Pathfinder PDF. Adobe and Premiere are trademarks of Adobe Systems Incorporated.

Although the PDF is displayed in a Web browser, it is not HTML. The plug-in is programmed to display the PDF in the browser window. It has text, layout, and images—all of which were in the original document that was converted to PDF.

Figure 20.9 shows two other features of the Acrobat format—navigation elements and thumbnails. The navigation elements, also known as bookmarks, are in the column on the left. Bookmarks can be textual or graphical, as those shown here. Each image (thumbnail) represents a page of the PDF document. Obviously, this work best when pages contain images. Distinguishing one page from another in a heavily textual document would be almost impossible.

The icons in the bottom right corner are hyperlinks to Help, Contact Information, and the next page. Any image within a PDF file can be hyperlinked.

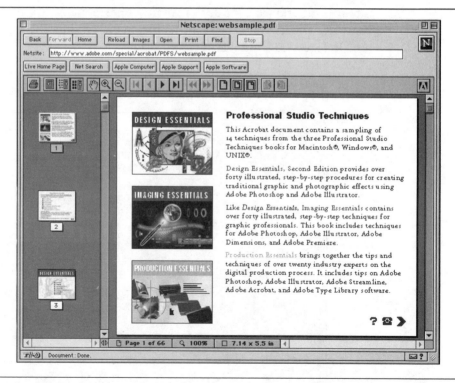

FIGURE 20.9: Professional Studio Techniques PDF. Adobe and Premiere are trademarks of Adobe Systems Incorporated.

What You Need

In order to provide PDF files for your visitors, you'll need to convert the original files to PDF format. You can then add features such as hyperlinking and bookmarks. Finally, you put the files on the server and make sure it understands what these files are.

The Content   You can create the content for a PDF file in any application and then convert the file to PostScript. In most applications, you do so by printing to a file. You then convert this PostScript file to a PDF file, using Acrobat Distiller, another Adobe product. Distiller accesses only PostScript files, and its only job is to make PDFs.

TIP   If you need help creating PostScript files, see the documentation that comes with your application.

You can also convert files to PDF using two other Adobe products:

- PDF Writer allows you to print an application directly to PDF format

- Acrobat Capture allows you to do batch conversions for large numbers of documents

PDF macros are available for both Microsoft Word and Microsoft Excel on the Windows platform. If the macro is installed, you can directly write PDF files from within Word or Excel by choosing File ➢ Create Adobe PDF.

TIP   Although you can create PDFs in several ways, using PostScript/Distiller route usually results in the smallest file sizes.

To add bookmarks, hyperlinks, and other features you use Acrobat Exchange. Although each document can be searched, true indexing and searching of multiple files over a network is not possible without Acrobat Catalog and Acrobat Search. You can purchase these all in one package.

The HTML   Linking to a PDF file is like linking to any other document. The .pdf suffix is added automatically when you convert the document. A typical link to a PDF file that is in the same directory as the HTML file might look like this:

```
We've put our cheese catalog in the form of a <A HREF="cheese.pdf">PDF
    file.</A>
```

Clicking the words *PDF file* sends the user to the document, which opens using the plug-in so that it looks like the examples in Figures 20.8 and 20.9. It's that simple. This will only work, of course, if the browser is mapped so that the PDF MIME type opens the file using the plug-in.

The Server   The server needs to know that files with the suffix `.pdf` need to be sent with the MIME type application/pdf and that they are binary. Update your server if you run it yourself, or be sure that your ISP's server is configured to handle this. Because PDF is a common format, your ISP probably already has the server configured appropriately.

Alternatives to PDF

PDFs are convenient because all your visitor needs to view them is a free reader. However, there's nothing in a PDF file that can't be duplicated in HTML, including links, indexes, images, sounds, and movies. To keep it simple, provide your content as straight HTML as well as PDF.

You might even want to provide a link so that visitors can download the original file from which you created the PDF. It probably won't have the nice features such as hyperlinks, and your visitor will need the application in which it was created to view it, but this might work for some people. Keep in mind, though, that if you provide the original file, people will be able to modify it easily.

QuickTime

QuickTime is an Apple technology that was in use on media such as CD-ROMs long before the Web became popular. Apple describes it as a synchronizing mechanism, which, simply put, means that you can coordinate video and audio. You can also use QuickTime for audio or video alone. A related technology, QuickTime VR, allows the user to move the view 360 degrees. QuickTime movies can be streaming and can begin playback before the browser receives the entire file. Apple refers to this as "Fast-Start."

The QuickTime plug-in ships with Navigator, and that is one reason that QuickTime content is common on the Web. According to Apple, currently more than 20,000 Web sites use QuickTime. Recently, Apple released QuickTime for Windows.

If your user has the plug-in, the QuickTime media that you embed in your HTML will display the same as any other embedded object. (For more information about producing video on the Web, see Skill 18.) The QuickTime plug-in, in addition to supporting QuickTime video, also plays MPEG video.

> **TIP**   To download QuickTime, go to http://quicktime.apple.com/.

Two QuickTime Examples

Figure 20.10 shows what a QuickTime movie looks like while it is loading. The image near the middle of the screen is the QuickTime logo. Figure 20.11 shows what the movie looks like once it is loaded.

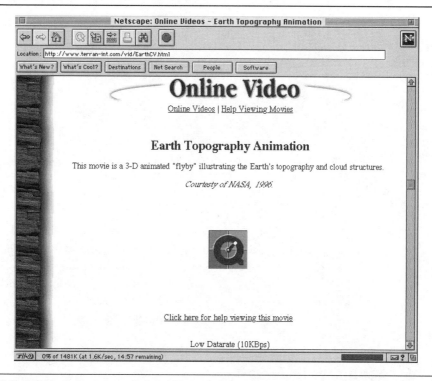

FIGURE 20.10:   A QuickTime video loading. Web page courtesy of Terran Interactive, Inc. Copyright 1997, all rights reserved, www.terran-int.com. Video courtesy of NASA, 1996.

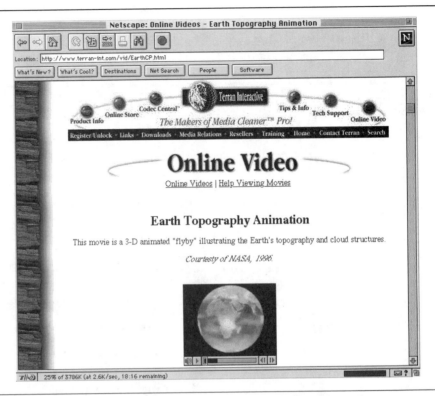

FIGURE 20.11: The loaded QuickTime video. Web page courtesy of Terran Interactive, Inc. Copyright 1997, all rights reserved, www.terran-int.com. Video courtesy of NASA, 1996.

Figure 20.12 is a scene from a QuickTime VR (Virtual Reality) movie. QTVR movies are not really movies with movement and sound. Rather, they are scenes in which users can look around 360 degrees by moving the pointer. Depending on filming techniques, the user may also be able to look up or down. Figure 20.13 shows the view in the movie if the user scrolls about 30 degrees to the right. The trees shown on the right side in Figure 20.12 are in the middle of the image shown in Figure 20.13.

What You Need

Making QuickTime movies is a fairly simple process, similar to other methods of converting content for plug-ins. Making QTVR content can be a lot trickier, because you need to use additional software to piece together your images. Let's take a look at what you need to make each type of content.

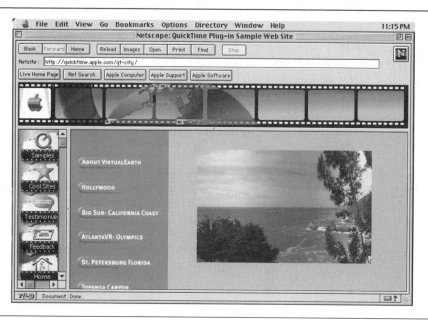

FIGURE 20.12: A QuickTime VR scene

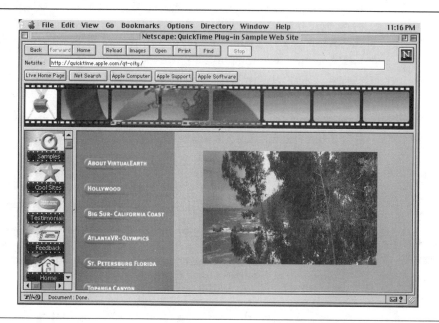

FIGURE 20.13: Another scene from the same QuickTime VR movie

The Content   The content for QuickTime is digital audio and video. (You'll find more information about these types of media in Skill 19.) The current version of QuickTime is 2.5, and it comes with MoviePlayer.

Typically, you use the MoviePlayer utility to convert video to QuickTime. You can also use Internet Movie Tool to batch process entire directories simultaneously and to convert files to the Fast-Start format. The Fast-Start format is one of the few streaming technologies that does not require special server software. QuickTime Fast-Start moves information that is necessary for playback to the beginning of the file so that playback begins right away.

 TIP   When converting video using the Internet Movie Tool, it's possible to display the first frame of a movie while the rest of the movie is downloading. Choose File ➢ Save As, and then click the Make Movie Self-Contained and Make Movie Playable on Other Computers boxes.

Making QTVR content can take more effort and additional software. To provide the special effect of rotating in a 3-D space, you have to obtain multiple images of the space you are going to show, and they need to overlap. For example, if you want to show a QTVR movie of a living room, you need images of the entire living room, and they have to overlap a bit. So if you stand in one place and slowly turn 360 degrees with your camera to take photos, be sure that the right edge of one photo overlaps with the left edge of the next one. It doesn't matter if you take the images with a digital or a regular film camera, but if you use the film camera, you'll need to scan the photos. Once the images are on the computer, you'll need special "photo stitching" software, such as PhotoVista, that blends all your images seamlessly into one panorama. You can then convert this to QTVR.

The HTML   Here is Apple's sample HTML for embedding a QuickTime movie that is in the same directory as the HTML file that references it:

```
<EMBED SRC="SampleQT.mov" HEIGHT=176 WIDTH=136>
```

Replace the name of the movie with the name of your own movie and its height and width. The file name suffix of a QuickTime movie is traditionally `.mov`.

 TIP   To find out the size of your movie, choose Movie ➢ Get Info ➢ Size. If you want the controller to appear as it does in Figures 20.10 and 20.11, add 24 to whatever number you have for the height.

Table 19.1 shows the attributes for the EMBED tag that can be used to add functionality to the QuickTime movie and its display.

TABLE 19.1: QuickTime Attributes for the EMBED Tag

Attribute	What It Does	Required or Optional	QT, QTVR, or Both?
HOTSPOT	QuickTime VR tools give the author an opportunity to specify a hotspot, n. If you set n = "url", the browser goes to the specified URL when the user clicks the hotspot.	Optional	QTVR only
CACHE	If you set this parameter to TRUE, Netscape 3 and higher caches the movie on the hard disk.	Optional, default is TRUE	Both
VOLUME	Setting VOLUME= "value" specifies the volume of the movie. Values are from 0 (mute) to 256 (loudest).	Optional, default is 256R	QT only
SCALE	Setting SCALE=value determines the size of the movie. If value is TOFIT, the movie will be the value of the HEIGHT and WIDTH. APSECT is the same as TOFIT, but it maintains the aspect ratio. Setting SCALE equal to a number multiplies the size of the movie by that number.	QT, not recommended for QTVR	
PLUGINSPAGE	Set PLUGINSPAGE equal to a URL where the user can download the plug-in. Apple recommends: http://quicktime.apple.com/.	Optional	Both
WIDTH	This is the width of the image in pixels, with a minimum value of 2.	Required	Both
HEIGHT	This is the value of the width in pixels, with a minimum value of 2.	Required, unless you use HIDDEN	Both
HIDDEN	Using HIDDEN will hide the file.	Optional, and should only be used for sound-only files	QT

Skill 20

TABLE 19.1 CONTINUED: QuickTime Attributes for the EMBED Tag

Attribute	What It Does	Required or Optional	QT, QTVR, or Both?
AUTOPLAY	Setting AUTOPLAY to TRUE causes the movie to automatically begin playing, rather than waiting for the user to click the Play button.	Optional, the default is FALSE	QT
CONTROLLER	Setting CONTROLLER to TRUE displays the CONTROLLER; FALSE hides it. If you set CONTROLLER to TRUE, you must add 24 pixels to the height of the movie.	Optional, default is TRUE	QT
LOOP	If you set LOOP to TRUE, the movie loops repeatedly. Setting LOOP to PALINDROME plays the movie forward and then backward, alternating endlessly	Optional, the default is FALSE	QT
PLAYEVERYFRAME	Setting PLAYEVERYFRAME to TRUE displays every frame of the playback, no matter how slow the connection, and turns off audio.	Optional, the default is FALSE	QT
HREF	If you set HREF equal to a URL, clicking the movie takes the user to another page.	Optional	QT
TARGET	If the page contains frames, TARGET can be used to specify which frame the movie will be in.	Optional	QT
PAN	This value, which is in the range 0 and 360, specifies the initial pan angle for the camera.	Optional, default is 0	QTVR
TILT	This value, which is in the range −42.5 to 425, specifies the initial tilt angle for the camera.	Optional, default is 0	QTVR
FOV	This value, which is typically in the range 5 to 85, specifies the initial field of view angle.	Optional, default is 0	QTVR

The Server   You don't have to do anything special to the server to serve QuickTime media. The MIME type for QuickTime is video/quicktime, and the typical file extensions are `.mov`, `.moov`, and `.qt`. As long as the server recognizes these types, there should be no problem.

TIP   Video files can consume a large amount of disk space. For this reason, it's usually best to store those that are not available to the public on a separate disk or on some other medium rather than on the server.

Alternatives to QuickTime

QuickTime is a good alternative if you want to support only Macintosh and Windows users. Creating the media is straightforward, you have lots of display parameters, and you can have streaming without setting up a server.

On the other hand, if you want to support all users who can see video, you might want to go with MPEG. There are many more players for the MPEG format, and as we mentioned, the QuickTime plug-in supports MPEG.

There is no really good substitute for QuickTime VR, but if you want to show a 360-degree view of an image, you can substitute a series of images, made while rotating in a circle.

For accessibility reasons, it's always a good idea to include plain HTML transcripts and descriptions of multimedia.

RealPlayer

RealPlayer, from Progressive Networks, is an application that lets users listen to streaming audio and video, both live and previously recorded. Although RealPlayer is also a standalone application for local use, it works via a free plug-in for Web content. You can find it at `http://www.realplayer.com/`.

RealPlayer media is a popular form of streaming content over the Web. Not only did RealPlayer arrive early in the streaming media game, it is available for many platforms, including Macintosh 68K, Macintosh PowerPC, Windows 3.*x*, Windows 95, Windows NT, OS/2, Irix, Sun OS, and Linux.

The RealSystem package from Progressive Networks contains the following:

- RealPlayer, which is used to view or listen to RealAudio and RealVideo

- RealServer, which serves the content

- RealEncoder, which converts content

Skill 20

Brand-New: RealFlash

To make things more complicated, as this book was being written, Progressive Networks combined forces with Macromedia to introduce RealFlash. RealFlash is a new technology that combines the animation of Flash with the streaming of RealPlayer. One player plays everything.

The RealFlash Content Creation Kit is available from Progressive Networks, and Flash is available from Macromedia.

What You Need

Converting content to RealAudio or RealVideo streaming format is easy with the RealEncoder. The most complicated part usually involves setting up the server. Let's take a look at what you need to provide RealAudio and RealVideo content on your Web site.

The Content   To create RealAudio and RealVideo, you use the Progressive Networks RealEncoder. RealEncoder 5 is a free encoder that converts files for RealPlayer playback. For input, the encoder accepts WAV, AU, AVI, QuickTime, and AIFF files. At the time of encoding, you can add additional information such as the author, the event, and the copyright.

TIP   RealAudio and RealVideo conversion can take some time. If you plan to do more than a few files, be sure to set aside several hours.

TIP   When a file is encoded into RealAudio or RealVideo format, it is optimized for a certain modem speed. The minimum is 28.8, but helpful sites will often offer more than one speed so that people with fast modems can experience a higher-quality version of the content.

The HTML   In terms of HTML, adding RealAudio and RealVideo to Web pages is just like linking to any other file. The traditional suffix for these files is .ram.

Here is a sample link to a video file named sample.ram, which is located in the same directory as the HTML file:

```
<A HREF="sample.ram">Here is a sample movie in RealVideo format.</A>
It is optimized for 28.8. If you need the RealPlayer, you can get it
from <A HREF="http://www.realplayer.com">here</A>.
```

The Server   Progressive Networks offers several ways to serve streaming content. Basic Server is free, and it can serve RealAudio and RealVideo, but that's about it. It cannot handle a lot of traffic and is therefore more suitable for personal Web sites. Basic Server Plus is a commercial product that includes technical support, the option to make RealFlash content, and upgrades—all features that Basic Server lacks. You can purchase RealFlash for an additional fee.

RealPublisher is an all-in-one product with which you can both create and publish RealAudio and RealVideo. Content created with RealPublisher does not need to be served with any extra server software, but the files are still in a streaming format. Like the Basic Server, this is not intended for sites with high traffic—those sites should have server software dedicated to serving streaming media. The highest level of server is the Real Server, which is designed for higher traffic sites and supports RealFlash content.

If you do not manage your own server but use an ISP, check with the ISP or system administrator about installing these servers.

Alternatives to RealAudio and RealVideo

Many of the alternatives to RealAudio and RealVideo are covered in Skill 19. It is always a good idea to offer streaming files as downloadable files also. In addition, plain HTML transcripts of audio and video provide accessibility to users who cannot see or hear the content.

Have You Mastered the Essentials?

Now you can. . .

- ☑ **Understand what plug-ins are and how they work.**
- ☑ **Know which browsers support the plug-in architecture and which don't.**
- ☑ **Get the software you need to prepare materials for Shockwave, Acrobat, QuickTime, and RealPlayer and understand the factors to consider when creating content.**
- ☑ **Provide alternatives for visitors who do not have a plug-in.**

Attracting and Retaining Visitors

- ❏ Offering valuable content

- ❏ Keeping your site up-to-date

- ❏ Avoiding visitor turn-offs

- ❏ Advertising on your site

It doesn't matter how good the content of a Web site is if it isn't visited. Now that you've spent so much time and effort making it work well, look good, and be accessible, be sure that people know about it! There are a lot of Web sites, and visitors are only one step away from easily going on to another one. You can do a lot to attract visitors to your site, to keep them there once they've arrived, and to make them want to return.

Offering Valuable Content

The most important thing that any Web site can do is offer valuable content. It's often said of the Web that "content is king" and that all that matters is "content, content, content." Many of the busiest sites on the Web are not the best designed with the most sizzle, but droves of visitors return to them regularly because they have the information that people want.

A common misconception is that because much Web content is free (except for the connection), people should somehow be satisfied with whatever they can get. But in the competition to get the visitor's attention, people are often surprised at how much truly valuable content is given away. The Web as it stands today was built on the concept of the free exchange of resources, from information to software. This is especially true for commercial sites. Unless a site is selling a unique item or service that cannot be purchased elsewhere on the Web, one of the biggest mistakes is to offer only the product or service, with no extra information. For one thing, other sites will offer additional content. For another, offering additional support and information is a way to get people to return time and again.

For example, Figure 21.1 shows the Flifo site, which is at `http://www.flifo.com/`. Here, you can book air travel and purchase tickets. In addition, you can link to a page and check flight times. This service is handy and is always accurate. You can find out when a flight took off, if it landed, and when it's expected to arrive. You can even find out the flight number if you know the airline.

Although this service is free, it pays for itself because a lot of people come to check flight times but eventually think of Flifo when it is time to purchase tickets. To purchase tickets, you must become a Flifo member, which involves giving them information such as an address for mailing tickets, a credit card number for charging the payment, and customized items such as meal and seating preferences. Flifo even tracks frequent flyer plans and has a Fare Beater feature that checks for a money-saving similar flight, maybe an hour or so later or perhaps on a different airline. Flifo is a good example of how free service and additional content can attract visitors.

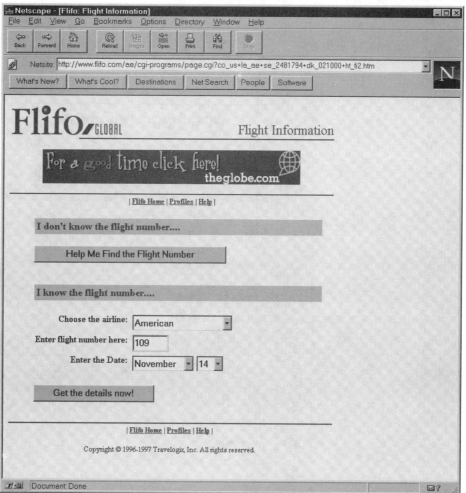

FIGURE 21.1:   Checking flight times on Flifo

Figure 21.2 shows a page from the Web site of Garden Escape, located at http://www.garden.com/. This site, which resells plant seeds from growers, claims to have the largest horticulture database on the Web. Visitors can access this database to find plants that match their specifications in a virtual garden planner. Among the factors the visitor can enter are soil composition, sun exposure, soil pH, soil moisture, flower and foliage color, and season of blooming.

FIGURE 21.2:   Choosing plants at Garden Escape

The horticulture database then returns a page which looks like that shown in Figure 21.3. It includes the price of the plants that match the criteria, photos, and links to additional information. By providing this extremely valuable information in addition to an online seed catalog, Garden Escape makes it more likely that a customer will eventually make a purchase. The information not only helps the customer, but also achieves the company's objective of showing potential customers how products work for them.

FIGURE 21.3: Plants that match the visitor's criteria

Even if your site is not commercial, it's important to offer good solid content. Quality information and a fulfilling browsing experience encourage visitors to send the URL to their friends, to bookmark the site, and to return.

Update, Update, Update!

The slang term for a Web site that never changes is a *cobweb*. Take great pain to ensure that your site does not earn this reputation. When content is printed on paper, readers understand that the information is only as current as its print date. Web visitors, however, expect content to be absolutely current. They need return only once to a site that hasn't changed since their last visit to assume that it never changes. Let's take a look at some ways to keep content fresh.

Good Old-Fashioned Updating

There is no substitute for really updating the content. Maybe the company has a new product, you just had a baby, or a noteworthy advance has been made in the topic your Web site covers. Add these items as they happen. No matter what a Web site is about, there is probably something new, even a link, that you can add every day. In addition to updating major content, you can do some simple things to keep a Web site fresh.

Simple Daily Updates

One way to keep new content coming is to design a site so that you can update content easily, every day, without touching the rest of the site. An example of this is the Dilbert cartoon Web site, located at `http://www.unitedmedia.com/comics/dilbert/`.

This high-traffic site is updated daily with a new comic strip, but the rest of the site does not have to change. The designers made it easy on themselves by simply substituting a new comic every day in the same place. They also update the archive, though you don't necessarily have to store all your old content.

Updating content is easy if you do it in the same place. If you update an image or a table with one of the same size, it's even easier. Design a site with these easily swappable components in mind because nobody wants to go back and fix lots of links every time a minor change comes along.

Contests and Polls

Another way to update content regularly and to encourage visitors to return is to use interactive polls and contests. Polls allow your visitors to submit an opinion about a topic and then return later (the sooner the better) to see the results. Once the system is in place for tracking responses and calculating results, updating content daily or weekly is a simple matter of changing the question and posting the results of the latest poll.

In addition to updating daily content, the ZDNet site (located at `http://www.zdnet.com/`) posts a new poll every day. Once visitors submit their opinions on a topic, they can see the current overall results. Each day you can see the results of the current and the previous day.

Web sites also often have contests. To enter the contest, a visitor usually fills out a form that collects data that can later be used for marketing purposes. A recent contest on ZDNet involved surfing to different areas of the ZDNet Web site and clicking a contest logo. Each additional click-through increased a visitor's chances of winning, so there was incentive to surf as much of the site as possible. Announcing the results of a contest only on the Web site entices visitors to come back and check often.

Message Posting and Chat

Another way to easily and regularly update content is to let visitors do it in chats and on bulletin boards. Once you set up such a system, these areas involve minimal maintenance for the site owner if you are willing to put up with the occasional spam or inappropriate comment. If you are not willing, you can spend a bit more time and monitor the messages, even checking them before they are posted. Several commercial software packages, for example, WebCrossing, are designed for developing and maintaining Web-based chat and discussion.

Although there is certainly more to creating an online community than simply adding a discussion area to a Web site, it's a great way to update the content of your site without actually doing all of it yourself.

Again, there is no real substitute for making solid and regular content updates to your site about whatever is new. However, fostering a true feeling of community by encouraging visitors to share or even asking a few to participate as "invited experts" can help keep the site's content fresh during slow news times or when you're otherwise occupied.

Skill 21

The Top Seven Visitor Turn-Offs

In general, whatever turns you off when you're surfing the Web also turns off other visitors. We've identified seven pitfalls that really send visitors packing at a Web site, never to return. With a little time and effort, you can avoid making these mistakes and retain the visitors you've worked so hard to attract.

Slow Servers

Probably the biggest turn-off for visitors is a Web site that is slow to load. Although you can make graphics smaller, limit the number of images on a page, and make tables simple, your most important asset is a server that is as fast as you can afford.

If you are purchasing your own machine, get as much RAM as you can afford, be sure to hire a good contractor to code any CGI scripts so that they are as efficient as possible, and purchase the fastest Internet connection you can afford. A common setup is to place your machine (the server) at an ISP's location—this is referred to as co-locating or co-hosting. Typically, connecting your machine to an ISP's T1 runs about $500 a month. You usually get a card key so that you always have access to your machine.

If your site is being hosted by an ISP, ask about the company's available bandwidth. If its servers are connected only by a single T1 line, it won't be able to handle as many clients as an ISP that has redundant T3s. In addition:

- Go to the ISP's home page and see how quickly it loads.

- If an ISP hosts several popular sites, it might be better to find one whose machines do not get quite so many hits.

- If at any time it appears that the ISP cannot handle the traffic, start looking for another one. Many a good site is left unexplored by visitors who become impatient and leave.

 WARNING   Remember, another site is always just a click away.

Sounds That Play Automatically

If you've visited a site that plays sounds automatically as it loads and if you've searched in vain for a way to turn off this sound, you know how annoying such a "feature" can be. When designing your Web site, include audio that is quiet and soothing and that the visitor can turn off easily. Keep in mind that visitors not only surf from home, but also surf from work and libraries.

If you feel that audio is integral to your site, keep the clips short, and be sure that they do not loop endlessly. For an example, go to `http://www.warnerbros.com/`, the Warner Bros. site.

Huge Graphics

Waiting for a huge graphic to load is a huge turn-off. If a graphic takes more than 20 seconds to load over a 28.8 modem, you can rest assured that most visitors will become impatient. In certain cases, you may feel that larger, more sophisticated graphics are justified, but always provide a text version of the page. And put the link to the text version near the top of the page, where those who are already tapping their fingers can find it easily.

 **WARNING**   If your server is slow and you also employ huge graphics, you're virtually assuring a mass exodus from your site.

Figure 21.4 shows the home page of the corporate Web site for Silicon Graphics (`http://www.sgi.com/`), a company known for its high-end graphics workstations. Because of SGI's reputation and its target market, the designer no doubt felt justified in using large graphics, but they also included a text-only alternative. Visitors get to the text-only version by clicking the Text Only link at the top of the page. Figure 21.5 in the next section shows the text version of the SGI site.

No Text Alternative

Designers are often surprised by the number of people who prefer to get information quickly rather than be dazzled by a collage of sizzling graphics. The truth is that one of the best ways to retain visitors is to provide a text-only alternative. When you do so, you accommodate those using older browsers, those who have slower machines or a slow connection, those using speech-reading browsers, and anyone who wants to get to the meat of the site quickly and easily.

As we've said before in this book, the easy sharing of information is central to Web philosophy. The lack of a text-only version of a largely graphical site presents a barrier to visitors rather than an enticement. By providing both alternatives, you satisfy the needs of more visitors. We'll talk more about accessibility issues in Skill 23.

Skill 21

FIGURE 21.4:   The Silicon Graphics Web site

Figure 21.5 shows the text version of the Silicon Graphics site. This site works for people who don't want graphics. It's also an excellent example of applying good design principles in the absence of graphics. Text-only pages don't necessarily have to be ugly.

Notice that the text version includes links back to the graphics version and to the Java-enabled version. Many people browse the Web with graphics turned off, turning them on when they decide that something sounds interesting enough to load. For that reason, it's a good idea to include an easy way to head over to the graphics area. At the Silicon Graphics site, visitors can go to the graphics and Java areas easily, even if they are several layers into the text site.

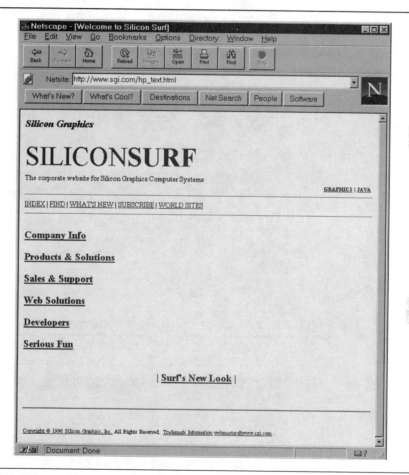

FIGURE 21.5: The text version of the Silicon Graphics site

Broken Links

If you've browsed the Web at all, you've clicked links that took you nowhere or to those cryptic "File Not Found" messages. If you're like most of us, you deal with this annoyance by retracing your steps or going to a site that you know is up and running. You don't usually attempt to find the new location of the site.

There is no reason to have broken links on a Web site, yet you encounter a lot of them on the Web. Figures 21.6 and 21.7 show two typical broken links. More helpful sites provide a cross-reference to the new URL, and some send visitors to a search page so they can attempt to locate the information, but neither solution is as good as simply not having broken links.

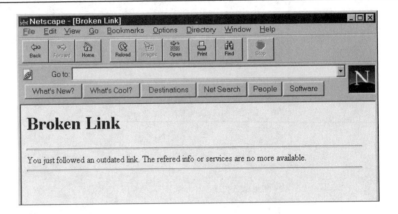

FIGURE 21.6:   An example of a broken link

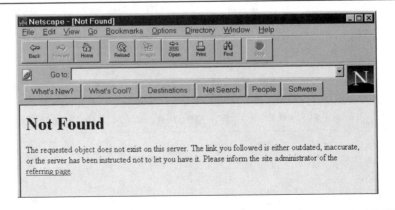

FIGURE 21.7:   A second example of a broken link

LINK-CHECKING SOFTWARE AND WEB SITES

You can automatically check the links on your Web site in two ways. First, you can purchase software that you install locally that goes through a site and checks all the links. One such program is InfoLink Link Checker from BiggByte Software (`http://www.biggbyte.com`).

The other option is to go to a Web site that will check the links at the URL you specify and give you a report. An example of a free service is Dr. Watson, located at `http://www.addy.com/watson`.

A good option for beginners is to go to the Weblint site (`http://www.unipress.com/cgi-bin/WWWeblint`) and pay a subscription fee of $9.95 for six months of link checking. Weblint also checks HTML, not just links. (An HTML checker is usually referred to as an HTML validator.)

One popular link-checking utility and HTML validator is Dr. HTML (`http://www2.imagiware.com/RxHTML/`). It's a hybrid service. You can go to the Web site and enter a URL for limited checking, or you can purchase the software and set it up on your local site for more robust validation.

Skill 21

Here are some steps you can take to avoid broken links:

- Regularly go through your site and check all links to other sites. (You can do this manually, or you can use link-checking software.) This is the area over which you have the least control, so be prepared to remove outdated links.

 NOTE   An outdated link leads to a nonexisting URL or to a site that no longer contains the content you wanted to reference.

- Keep a map of your Web site handy. This tree structure shows how documents are related within the site, and you can use it to determine which links need to be updated if a page moves or is renamed. If your site is small, maybe fewer than 20 pages, you can create a site map by hand. If it's large or if mapping seems tedious, you can use site-mapping software.

- If you move your Web site, either to another server or to a different domain, place a link at the old site to send visitors to the new one. Also, register the new address with search engines and directories as soon as possible.

SITE-MAPPING SOFTWARE

We don't recommend the WYSIWYG HTML editors that are currently on the market because they usually write improper or inefficient HTML code. However, they often include useful site-mapping features. A good example is Claris Home Page (http://www.claris.com).

One site management tool that does mapping is Abobe SiteMill (http://www.adobe.com). It works in conjunction with Adobe PageMill, a WYSIWYG editor, but it can also be used alone. Both Home Page and SiteMill are available for Macintosh and for Windows 95 and NT.

Some utilities allow users to map remote sites and download the content for reading offline. There's nothing to keep you from running the utility on your own site, though. One example is WebSnake, from Anawave (http://www.anawave.com/websnake/), which is only available for Windows 95 and NT. A similar product is FlashSite (http://www .incontext.com/products/flashsite/index.html), also available for Windows 95 and higher. For Macintosh, try Big Brother, which needs System 7.5 or higher. It's available from http://pauillac.inria.fr/ ~fpottier/brother.html.en.

Requiring Plug-Ins

As we discussed in Skill 20, a plug-in is additional software that the browser needs to access a site or part of a site. Many visitors will not stay on a site that requires a plug-in, period. And almost all visitors balk at needing a plug-in to view the home page of a site.

Before you include a plug-in for your site, be sure that the value it offers is worth the risk of alienating visitors. And, if you do require a plug-in, give your visitors an alternative to it.

The AppleTree Multimedia site, located at `http://www.appletree.com/`, is a good example of a home page that offers alternatives (see Figure 21.8). Visitors can go to the low-bandwidth version, and if the site seems interesting enough, they can then get the plug-in and move to the area where the plug-in is needed.

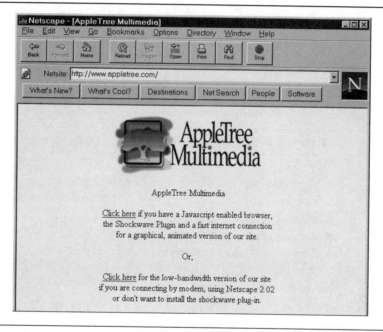

FIGURE 21.8: A Web site that offers options. Notice the easy-to-follow Shockwave link. ©1997, 1998 AppleTree Multimedia, a division of AppleTree Technologies Inc. Web Site Design and Production by AppleTree Multimedia, a full service multimedia development company.

Sites Under Construction

Although every Web site that is updated regularly as it should be is always "under construction," we're referring here to sites or portions of sites that are not ready for public consumption. You've no doubt encountered sites that consist wholly of an "under construction" message. Figure 21.9 shows one such site. Don't you wonder why its developers even bothered? If a site or a certain area is not fully ready for public consumption, don't link to it.

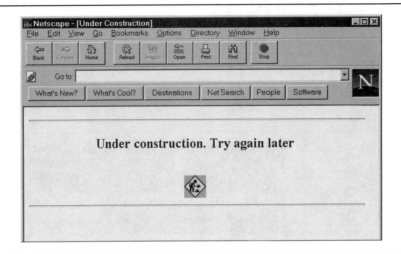

FIGURE 21.9: A Web site that is under construction

More common is finding areas of a site under construction. Naturally, as a Web site evolves and grows, areas will be added to it. However, you can develop a new area and not link to it until it's ready. Your best bet is to develop on a server that is not connected to your Web, just to make sure that the area is not found accidentally. If you must develop on your Web server, don't link to the new area and, in general, don't advertise it. If you must publicize it, mention that it's coming soon or on a certain date—and then be sure that it appears on time.

Onsite Advertising

In addition to publicizing your site via flyers, billboards, or even commercials and placing your URL on marketing collateral, products, and business cards, you'll want to take advantage of onsite advertising. Like the radio, television, and the daily newspaper, one of the primary ways to finance a Web site is through advertising, and it's also an important avenue for attracting visitors and customers.

Onsite advertising involves advertising on your Web site itself or on other, related Web sites. Keep in mind, though, that once people come to your site, the content is what entices them to explore it and to return to it for future reference.

Using Banners

On the Web, banners are images that announce a Web site. Banners are usually found at the top of a Web page, although they can be found anywhere. You can use banners to announce the current site, another part of the site, or a different site altogether. In this section, we are most interested in the last option, because you can often advertise your Web site by putting banners on another Web site. The sites where you put your banners may or may not be related to yours in subject matter. Figure 21.10 shows an IBM advertising banner for a site for Webgrrls, located at `http://www.webgrrls.com`. The Webgrrls group is devoted to women in new media, and the ad banner is about computers—a logical tie-in.

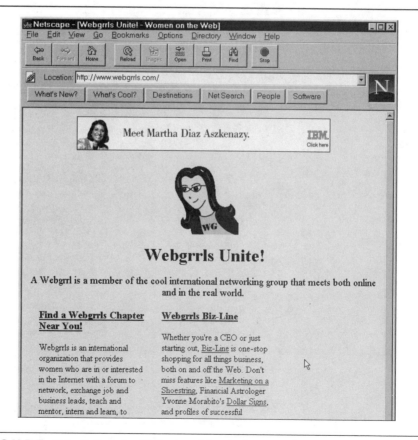

FIGURE 21.10:   An IBM advertising banner on the Webgrrls site

How Much Does Displaying a Banner Cost?

In the early days of the Web, banner charges were based on the number of page views, or on how often people would see a banner based on site traffic. Because site developers soon realized that they were not always getting the response they wanted, a system of paying only for click-throughs emerged. A click-through occurs when a visitor actually clicks the banner and links to the Web site.

These days, prices for banners vary. For example, displaying your banner on the Netscape site is much more expensive than displaying it on the site of a smaller, lesser-known company. You, of course, must determine whether the greater exposure is worth the money.

Prices are often negotiable and depend on the size of the banner, how long it will remain up there, and how often it will be shown. Prices are generally quoted in CPM, or cost per thousand impressions. (M is the roman numeral for 1000 and is used in financial circles to represent that number. An impression is a single display instance of the banner.)

Many Web sites use CGI scripts to rotate a series of banners so that a new one comes up every time the page is served. If you are paying for an ad banner to appear on a site, be sure to find out how many banners are rotating.

CGI scripts are usually written so that banners can be weighted. That is, just because your banner is one of ten, it doesn't necessarily come up only 10% of the time. You can usually pay more and have it come up a larger percentage of the time.

Do Banners Work?

The average click-through rate, according to *Advertising Age* (`http://www.adage .com`), is about 3.6%. Clever, enticing banners and those offering bargains or announcing contests might get rates as high as 6%. Although these numbers may not sound high, they can add up if the site that carries the banner receives a lot of traffic.

Because banners are relatively new to the realm of advertising, it is difficult to get good statistics and accurate information about effectiveness. Naturally, sites that sell advertising space want to emphasize how many visitors will see your banner, but that doesn't necessarily translate to click-thoughs or purchases on your Web site. The best way to determine if a banner is working for your Web site is to do a controlled study. First, put your banner on only one site and see if the traffic to your site increases. Then add your banner to another site. Keep doing this incrementally to get an idea of whether banners work for you. Also, trying different styles of banners on the same site will give you an idea of which designs are most effective.

Banners can be useful advertising vehicles, but be sure to judge their effectiveness compared with the price you pay for them. And if you are going to pay for them, be sure they are enticing and well-designed. A poorly designed banner costs just as much to post as a well-designed one!

Designing Banners

The first issue to consider when designing an ad banner is the requirements of the site that is going to post it. Sites often limit size (in terms of both pixels and bytes). You'll also want to find out if there are any other rules, such as a ban on animations.

Once you determine the requirements, start thinking about design. This realm is a lot more like traditional advertising; try to think of catchy phrases, and use bright colors that display well. If you are running a contest, announce the prize on the banner. The most successful banners are simple and contain a small amount of intriguing information that makes the visitor want to know more.

Like all design, banner design is trendy. One current trend is to make banners that appear to rotate, but that are actually animated GIFs, so all the banners lead to the same place. Another trend is to make the banner look like part of the Web page it is on, sometimes with buttons or fake drop-down menus. Although both techniques are effective in getting visitors to follow the link, some people feel tricked and are not happy when they end up at your site.

Skill 21

SHOULD YOU OFFER BANNERS?

You may be wondering if you ought to offer banner space for sale on your Web site. Here are some things to consider.

First, your site should receive enough traffic to warrant offering advertising space to other sites. A good way to tell if a site generates enough interest is to wait until someone asks what needs to be done to advertise on your site. Whether it should be done is a separate question.

If a Web site is not used to sell goods or services online, advertising is often the only way it can generate the revenues that justify it. On the other hand, it's often not a good strategy to send visitors elsewhere as soon as they arrive. The general rule is to not accept banners if the money is not needed to support the site, but to try to put banners on other sites.

Using Link Exchanges

Generally speaking, link exchanges are agreements between Web sites to link to each other's site for a certain amount of time. This type of reciprocity is representative of the nature of the Web. It not only occurs in the spirit of community, but also takes advantage of the ability to hyperlink documents.

Of course, when you engage in this sort of linking agreement, you risk sending visitors to a site other than your own. On the other hand, they may never see your site if not for a link exchange. In addition, these types of exchanges can be a good way to experiment with banners and such without spending too much money.

You can participate in a more formal arrangement by joining the Link Exchange (http://www.linkexchange.com/). Figure 21.11 shows the home page. Basic membership is free and includes a listing in the member's directory and the use of the Link Exchange logo in your banners.

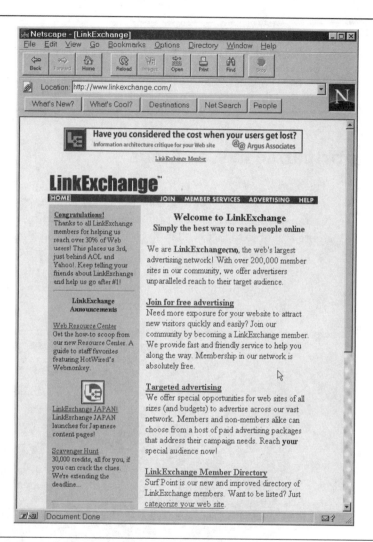

FIGURE 21.11: The main LinkExchange page

Many link exchange programs don't limit the types of sites that can participate in the exchange. Consider that by participating, your site selling gourmet salsa may wind up with a banner ad for a competing food emporium!

NOTE Create a small logo for your Web site and ask people to copy and use it to hyperlink back to your site. This makes it easy for people linking to your site to maintain your brand and identity, without feeling they have to duplicate your logo or get permission. Be sure to say that the logo is for linking back to your site and not for other uses. It should be fairly small.

Participating in Web Rings

The term *Web ring* refers both to the "official" Web ring site, at `http://www.webring.com` and shown in Figure 21.12, and to informal agreements among site owners to link their sites into a sort of virtual tour. According to the official Web ring site, there are more than 15,000 Web rings covering just about as many topics, and the services are generally free.

When you visit a site that is part of a Web ring, you will find a link to the next site in the ring. In this manner, viewers are lead from one site to the next in the ring, rather than traversing a list of links.

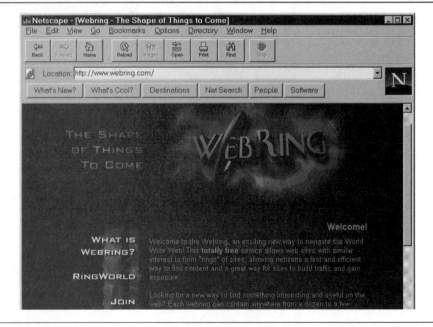

FIGURE 21.12: The official Webring site

Figure 21.13 shows the Modern Pet Web site that is part of the Dog Ring. The home page contains a logo signifying that the site is part of the Dog Ring, and it contains an icon linking this site to the next site in the ring. As you can see, the Modern Pet site is also a member of Link Exchange. Many site owners participate in both rings and link exchanges.

TIP

Be sure not to clutter your site with too many banners and logos—you want your message to come through loud and clear.

FIGURE 21.13: The Modern Pet Web site, billed as "the place where cats and dogs use their master's credit cards"

Announcement Lists

Another way to keep visitors returning to a Web site, especially to a commercial one, is to maintain an announcement list. An announcement list consists of the e-mail addresses of people who want to be notified of updates. These updates might relate to the Web site or to the product or industry specific to the Web site. A personal Web site might even maintain an announcement list for sending news about family events.

 **WARNING** Be sure that your list contains only the names of those who asked to be added to it. It is considered a major breach of Internet etiquette (a.k.a. Netiquette) to add someone to a list without their permission. Also, don't sell or give out your announcement list to others. People who receive unsolicited e-mail from your Web site are not likely to become loyal fans.

The trick is to establish a quick-and-easy way for visitors to add their names to your announcement list. The RealNetwork's area for downloading RealPlayer at http://www.realplayer.com, is a good example. To join this list, you simply check a *Please notify me of RealAudio and RealVideo events and new software* box. The placement of this box is effective. It follows the description of the product that the visitor is choosing to download. Also, visitors can choose whether to join the list. Simply downloading the product does not signal assent. In addition, the default is that the box is checked.

Once you set up an announcement list, it becomes an effective tool for attracting visitors. They'll return to read new material, get product updates, and download software. And they can easily forward your announcements to other interested parties.

Have You Mastered the Essentials?

Now you can. . .

- ☑ Understand the need for free, yet valuable content.
- ☑ Generate ideas for ways to easily update a Web site.
- ☑ Avoid the pitfalls that make people quickly leave Web sites.
- ☑ Find ways to advertise your site.

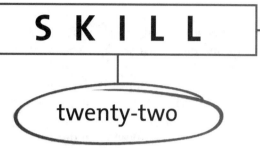

Doing Business on Your Site

- ❑ Understanding Web server security issues

- ❑ Introducing firewalls

- ❑ Protecting your private data

- ❑ Dealing with commerce and Internet security

- ❑ Looking at how secure servers work

- ❑ Exploring payment alternatives

- ❑ Using virtual shopping carts

- ❑ Getting a handle on tax matters

Congratulations! Your sales pitch was a smashing success. Your site is informative, useful, and pleasing to the eye. Your visitors can't wait to buy your products! Now what?

The key to a successful volume of sales online rests in *customer convenience*. If visitors can't easily order or obtain your goods, they aren't likely to purchase them, especially if the same items are commonly available elsewhere. The forces at work are similar to those involved in the popularity of mail-order catalog sales. Customers can browse a catalog at their leisure, taking time to review their choices before purchasing, and ordering at any time via a handy 24-hour toll-free telephone line or by mailing or faxing a printed order form—all without ever leaving home.

Online, however, the average consumer expects faster results, since the Internet gives every appearance of being "instantaneous." At the same time, consumers are concerned about security on the Internet and want assurance that their identity and purchasing methods during the transaction are protected.

Web Server Security Primer

If you plan to do business on the Net, you must address two major security concerns in order to have a safe and secure Web presence:

- The server itself
- The data

When considering the security of your server, you need to ask the following questions:

- Is your server connected to your company's LAN?
- Does it store sensitive documents, even though they aren't linked to the Web site?
- Can an unknown individual execute commands on the host machine that could change, damage, steal, or destroy data?
- Does your server have adequate protection against misuse by others, including denial of service attacks and the routing of unsolicited e-mail through your gateways?

When considering the security of the data that are passed back and forth between you as the vendor and your customers, you need to ask the following questions:

- Can someone eavesdrop on a network connection point? Such activities can occur anywhere between the customer's browser and your server, including:

    - At your customer's ISP

    - At your ISP

    - At an ISP's regional or "backbone" provider

    - Even on your own servers, if you have a full-time connection

- Have you protected against such eavesdropping on commerce transactions by providing a secure server for consumer use?

Firewalls: (Carefully) Bringing the Outside In

The whole process sounds simple enough: All you need is the phone company to install a new line (often called a "pipe"), connect the pipe to a router, connect the router to the Web server, and then connect the Web server to your LAN. Ta-da! Your company is on the Net!

But just as you wouldn't show off your brand-new office building with its gleaming new furniture and computer systems with a swank soiree and then leave the doors open and unlocked when you go home, you shouldn't wire up your company and then not take measures to keep the curious and the bad guys out.

A *firewall* is a hardware and software system for your servers that allows approved traffic both in and out according to the constraints you impose when setting it up. It consists of two primary pieces:

The Screening Router   This device provides the primary connection between the "trusted" network (your LAN) and the "untrusted" network (the Internet at large). It sends the data packets to the appropriate servers or blocks packets based on their machine names, IP addresses, or protocol types.

 NOTE   An IP address is a numerical identifier for a specific machine or device connected to the Internet or an internal network.

The Application Gateway   The screening router performs what are known as the *low-level functions*—the basic tasks that don't require much decision making beyond an approval or a denial of a request. The application gateway handles more complex tasks, such as the routing of incoming FTP or Telnet requests and determining where password authentication takes place before access is granted.

Because a firewall protects expensive equipment and confidential data, it should be installed and configured by experts. A poorly designed system is like a cheap dead-bolt lock: It gives you a false sense of security, while making it easy for even the most casual snooper to break in. Contact your system administrator for assistance in locating a qualified individual to assist you.

Keeping the Private Stuff Private

Some of the ways that you provide security can be quite technical; others, however, are just plain common sense. While ensuring that you've taken all the appropriate technical steps, don't overlook the practical aspects, such as the following:

Store only public documents on a public Web server. Keep items such as the following on a server that does not directly connect with the outside world:

- A map of your company network
- A list of hardware and software configuration
- The company address and telephone directory
- Internal letters and memoranda

Although a good firewall may prevent someone from rooting around where they shouldn't, don't tempt fate by storing these documents where they'd be immediately available after a security failure.

Keep centralized records of all access accounts. Designate one person on your staff to approve and distribute all log-in accounts for your Web server. Typically, this is someone in your Information Systems division or whoever is responsible for your current LAN access.

Change passwords frequently. Require users to change passwords frequently (at least every two months). A good password is a combination of at least six letters and characters. Never allow users to use their birthday, a family member's name, or any other readily "guessable" word or phrase.

Audit all access logs periodically. Your Web server's access logs provide detailed information on what type of requests were made when and by whom (identification may be only by an IP address or a machine name, rather than by user ID). Reviewing this data can alert you to potential trouble spots or allow you to identify malicious individuals by their attempted usage patterns.

Security on a Virtual Server

Not every company has the resources to maintain a full-time connection to the Internet. In those cases, most companies contract with an ISP to set up what's known as a *virtual server*—space on an ISP's Web server. Through software configuration, the outside world sees your site as its own machine; hence, the *virtual* in virtual server.

The security of your data on a virtual server is only as good as the security the ISP has in place for the entire system. Here are some questions to ask an ISP system administrator in this regard:

- What security measures have you taken against unauthorized access to Web documents?

- Do you allow users to run command-line tasks from CGI scripts or Server Side Includes? (This opens a potential security hole, though it isn't always indicative of immediate danger.)

 NOTE   Server Side Includes (SSI) are processes that run on the server. Using SSIs, a Web designer can instruct the server to *include* material from another source in the document currently being processed. SSI is often used to insert the current date and time or to incorporate repetitive blocks of HTML markup, such as navigation bars or address and copyright notices.

- Who in your organization has access to your data? Only the Webmaster and system administrator, or can anyone in the company get into the server?

- Will access logs be available to me?

- Will you assist you in dealing with any attempted breaches to the system?

- Do you subscribe to the CIAC-Bulletin, distributed by the U.S. Department of Energy's Computer Incident Advisory Capability group? If not, how do you keep abreast of new developments in Internet security?

On your end, you can take several steps to protect your virtual Web server:

- Don't share your account with anyone: neither the dial-up access nor your Web server space. Internet access accounts are available for as little as $5.00 a month, not to mention that most ISP contracts prohibit sharing an account.

- Don't use the same password for multiple access accounts or services, such as your dial-up password and your FTP access password. If one is compromised, all others will be.

- Test all CGI scripts for security before uploading them to your live site. If you aren't comfortable judging this, consider hiring a professional programmer to review them.

Commerce and Internet Security

Now that you know how to protect your servers and the data residing on them, the next step is to protect your customer's data while it's in transit to you.

Recent waves of public concern over the security of Internet transactions have ranged from the conservative to the paranoid. Unfortunately, a lot of misinformation is floating around out there. In order to wade through it all, let's take another look at a short form that might be used on a commercial Web site (for brevity's sake, we've removed many fields).

 NOTE   For a quick review of forms and processing, see Skill 8.

Below is the HTML that produced the form shown in Figure 22.1.

```
<FORM>
<P>Yes! Please rush me a case of widgets immediately!
<P>Please enter your name: <INPUT TYPE="text" NAME="name" WIDTH=20>
<P>What kind of credit card would you like to use?
<P><INPUT TYPE="radio" NAME="card" VALUE="Visa"> Visa
<INPUT TYPE="radio" NAME="hardware" VALUE="MC"> MasterCard
<INPUT TYPE="radio" NAME="hardware" VALUE="AmEx"> American Express
<P>Card number: <INPUT TYPE="text" NAME="number" WIDTH=20>
<P>Expiration: <INPUT TYPE="text" NAME="exp" WIDTH=6>
<P><INPUT TYPE="submit" VALUE="Submit!">
</FORM>
```

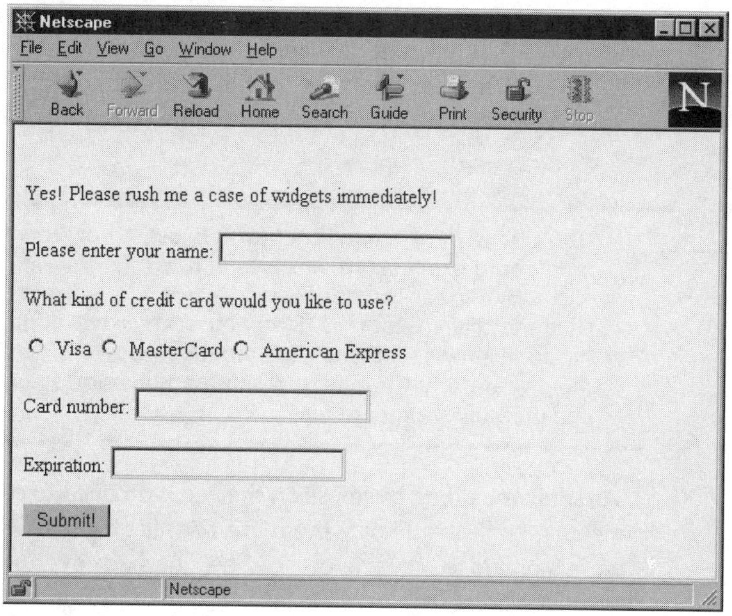

FIGURE 22.1: A simple form for ordering on the Web

Clicking the Submit button on this form sends the data to the CGI script for processing in URL encoded format. Here's how this really looks:

```
name=Jane+Smith&card=Visa&number=4444-4444-4444-4444&exp=02%2F98
```

Pretty obvious what this data is, isn't it? For the most part, no one (or nothing) but your CGI script sees the data. Although it is sent "in the open", or unencoded, it's not quite as bad as wearing a name tag.

To obtain this data, someone must purposefully go out and hunt for it, a process that's usually done with packet sniffers. A *packet sniffer* is a program designed to capture and read each packet of data that is sent to or through a specific Internet hub or subnet (a *subnet* is loosely defined as a network of computers such as the LAN in your office). Such programs have legitimate uses—they can help network administrators locate system problems or aid in security checks. Unfortunately, they can just as easily be used to snoop for account names and passwords or unencrypted credit card data.

Some Internet users feel that the risks associated with sending personal data through e-mail or as a form transaction are minimal. In concept, we agree. You're

Skill 22

probably far more at risk every time you hand your credit card to a waiter at a restaurant or give credit card information to a telephone catalog sales person. (We realize that most waiters and sales reps are honest individuals. We certainly don't mean to imply otherwise, but theft does happen.) In reality, however, the common perception is that you should avoid sending such data unencrypted at all costs.

TIP   Don't have a merchant account? Browse dozens of companies offering credit card processing services at http://www.yahoo.com/Business_and _Economy/Companies/Financial_Services/Transaction_Clearing/Credit_ Card_Merchant_Services. Many companies will contract with new, Internet based business whereas traditional banks won't. Be sure to read all agree- ments carefully for fees, including application fees, cost per transaction, and monthly statement fees.

As someone doing business on the Net, you need to consider these legitimate concerns. You can alleviate them in a couple of ways. One way is to allow first- time customers to contact you "offline," perhaps over the phone. You can obtain the relevant data—name, address, shipping information, and payment method— and then issue an account number. When customers are ready to make an online purchase, they need only enter this account number. You look up the customer's data in your database that's not connected to the Web and then process it as you would any online sale.

The most popular way to deal with security issues is to use what's known as a secure server. A *secure server* is an extra layer of software that encrypts specified transactions, such as sending URL-encoded data from a form to the CGI script for processing.

Transaction Security through the Secure Sockets Layer

The Secure Sockets Layer (SSL) was developed and proposed to the W3C by Netscape Communications Corporation. It's an encryption scheme that protects *transactions* (the exchange of data between computers, regardless of content) for HTTP requests (Web site transactions). It allows for the browser and the server to verify each other's identity, and it encrypts all data in transit between the two. Netscape Navigator and Internet Explorer, as well as a handful of other browsers, support the use of SSL.

The identity verifying portion of the process involves a *server certificate* that is granted by a certifying authority. There are several authorities with varying application processes and fees, including:

- Verisign (http://www.verisign.com/), which was the first and continues to be the most widely used

- GTE CyberTrust (http://www.cybertrust.gte.com/)

- Thawte Consulting (http://www.thawte.com/)

NOTE   Before choosing a certifying authority, be sure to investigate which browsers recognize its certificates. Navigator and Internet Explorer, as well as many other browsers that support SSL, recognize Verisign and Thawte certifications, but support for others isn't universal.

TIP   If you'll be hosting your site at an ISP, rather than running your own Web server over a full-time Internet connection, consult with them before purchasing a certificate of your own. Many ISPs allow clients to use their general site certificate, saving you considerable cost and effort.

Applying for a Certificate

Once you've decided on a certifying authority, it's time to complete the online application process. The steps that follow are for Verisign but will be similar for other certifying authorities. Before you begin, you need to generate a key pair—basically, a digital password—and a certificate signing request (CSR). You'll find instructions for doing so in your server software documentation, and you can also find details for several popular secure servers at this Verisign site:

https://digitalid.verisign.com/ss_help.html#keygen

In the process of filling out the form, you'll also be asked to supply a Dun & Bradstreet number (DUNS number). Verisign must verify your company's identity, and the quickest way to do so is through your DUNS number. If you don't have one, you can make application by using a form at the Verisign site, https://digitalid.verisign.com/dnb_query.htm.

NOTE   Dun & Bradstreet is a respected business resource that compiles background information on companies and their executives.

Skill 22

If you don't have a DUNS number or would rather not use your DUNS number, you can verify your company's identity by providing, via postal mail, a copy of one of the following:

- Articles of incorporation

- Partnership papers

- Business license

- Fictitious business license

- Federal Tax ID confirmation

Once you've generated your key pair and CSR, it's time to fill out the enrollment form, at `https://digitalid.verisign.com/ss_getCSR.html`. Follow these steps:

1. Copy and paste the CSR into the online enrollment form.

2. If you received a special promotional offer from one of Verisign's business partners, choose the appropriate code from the Select box; otherwise, choose None. Continue to the next page.

You'll now be asked for the following information:

- Your secure server software vendor.

- A challenge phrase. This phrase will be used as a password of sorts between you and Verisign, to authenticate requests to revoke a certificate.

- Name and contact information for the following:

    Technical contact   This person must be employed by your organization and be authorized to run and maintain the Web server. (If you are purchasing a certificate to be used on an ISP, your ISP will need to complete the ISP online enrollment form for you.)

    Organizational contact   This person must also be employed by your organization and must be someone other than the technical contact. He or she must have the authority to enter into a binding agreement with Verisign (generally a corporate officer, business owner, or other individual that enters into contracts for your company).

    Billing contact   This person will receive all invoices from Verisign and can be the technical or organizational contact as well.

- The type of service you need. Are you applying for a new digital ID? An additional ID or a renewal?

- Payment method. Verisign accepts credit cards, purchase orders, and checks (POs and checks must be received before your application is processed). For fastest service, use a credit card.

Once you've submitted the application, the technical and organizational contacts will get e-mail confirming enrollment. Once approved, the certificate will also be forwarded via e-mail. Instructions for installing it are provided with your secure server software documentation.

Collecting the Data

To secure your customer's data once the CGI script has finished processing it on the secure server, the data needs to remain on the secure server. If you're running your own Web server, that's not a problem: You can collect the data from inside your firewall and distribute it appropriately. But what if you're using a virtual server?

Downloading the data via e-mail, Telnet, or FTP subjects it to a trip across the Net in an unsecured environment—something that undoes all your earlier precautions and may well land you in trouble with the server certificate authorities or the credit card companies if the data is compromised along the way. To maintain the required confidentiality, you'll need to access your orders on the secure server itself. You can do so by programming your CGI scripts to alert you via e-mail each time an order comes in, or you can make it a part of your routine to check the system periodically.

Alternatives to Secure Servers

At times, you may find that using a secure server is impractical or not an available option. You can still provide your customers with an immediate online ordering experience by doing a little custom programming or by using one of several third-party solutions.

CyberCash

Rather than a new form of money, CyberCash (http://www.cybercash.com) is a secure transaction system that endeavors to create a seamless experience for both the consumer and the vendor using three distinct products.

Credit card payments   CyberCash links your virtual store directly to your credit card processor for real-time authorizations and transaction processing. A secure interface is provided for the merchant to capture and close out transactions.

CyberCoin™ Service   Designed for purchases with values ranging from 25 cents to $10.00, this product is ideal for fee-for-information sites or subscription-based Web sites.

PayNow™ Service   This product allows for payments directly debited from checking accounts, both for product purchases and bill payments.

The software that drives the system is known as the CashRegister. If an ISP hosts your site, the ISP must install and execute the software license for this application.

 **WARNING**   Before proceeding too far with plans for CyberCash support, check with your ISP for availability of the software and/or its willingness to install the software for you.

Here's how the payment process works:

1. Installing CashRegister on your Web site incorporates a Pay by CyberCash logo that is a link.

2. When the customer clicks this link, the browser sends a CyberCash payment request message to the CyberCash client software installed on the customer's computer.

3. The client software launches itself automatically and asks the customer to choose a credit card to use for the purchase and to accept the transaction.

4. The client software then sends a message to the CyberCash Merchant Payment software (a part of the CashRegister product) running on your server.

5. The Merchant Payment software validates the request and then passes it and the entire digital "document" on to CyberCash in encrypted form for processing.

6. When CyberCash receives the document, it verifies the document's authenticity, decrypts it, and forwards it to the appropriate merchant bank for authorization against the customer's credit card.

7. Receipts come back through the process in reverse.

8. Depending on which type of transaction-capturing your merchant agreement requires, you then close each transaction or batch automatically or manually (albeit online) to tell the bank that the transaction is complete.

First Virtual

The First Virtual concept works similarly to CyberCash: The customer has a VirtualPIN (a personal identification number) that represents the credit card data on file at First Virtual (`http://www.firstvirtual.com/services/`). The primary difference is that First Virtual Holdings becomes your merchant processor (actually handles the charging and payout of credit card receipts). If you are an established merchant who already offers credit card purchases, you have no significant incentive to use the First Virtual system. First Virtual requires additional credit qualification for the seller and high application and annual renewal fees, and the minimum settlement period (the time from the date of the charge against the customer's credit card for the merchant processor to deposit the funds into the vendor's checking account) is at least four business days. (The industry average is one to two days.)

If you are an individual or a small business just starting out or if you have less than stellar personal credit, you might want to investigate using First Virtual's Pioneer Seller account. No credit qualification is required for the seller, and the application and renewal fees are minimal. There is, however, one significant drawback to this arrangement: The minimum settlement period is *ninety-one* calendar days—a full three months. The *discount rate*—the percentage of the sales price that is kept as the merchant processor's fee—isn't bad though. Currently it's 2% plus 29 cents a transaction.

Skill 22

The Virtual Shopping Cart

One of the more challenging design issues on a commerce site is how to lay out your virtual store. You want your visitors to be able to locate products quickly, and you want to provide an easy-to-use interface for finalizing the order.

A popular visual metaphor for handling multiple product selections is the virtual shopping cart. Consumers are familiar with selecting products individually and placing them in a cart while they continue to shop. Once they're done, they head to the checkout line to have their purchases rung up and to conclude the transaction with a payment for the entire order.

Figure 22.2 shows a fairly typical shopping cart interface for the Kropps & Bobbers WebStore. (You'll find this store at `http://www.kropps.com`). Shoppers can click the hyperlinks to see details about each product or simply enter the amount of their purchase directly into the form. A convenient calculator will tally up the total price of your selections at any time—helpful if you want to make sure you're not splurging *too* much before adding these luxurious soaps to your cart!

Tracking Items in the Virtual Cart

The process looks easy—a form and a little JavaScript script to do the calculating. All things considered, not really complex, right? Not quite so fast. Complicating things is the inherent *statelessness* of the Web. *State* is the concept of a computer "remembering" which events occurred recently. For instance, the word-processing program we used to compose this text remembered what we typed between save requests. On the Web, once the server sends back the page that the browser requested the server completely "forgets" ever having had any contact with the page.

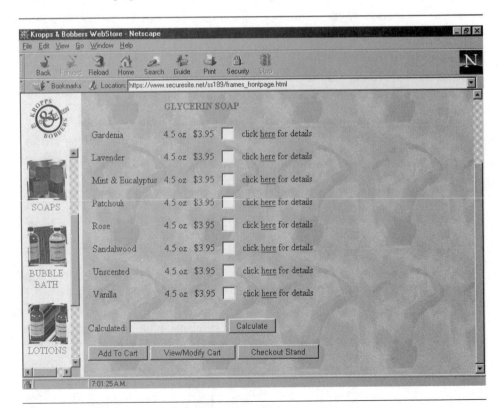

FIGURE 22.2: A virtual shopping cart

Keeping track of which items the shopper has placed in a virtual cart is made possible by a state-tracking technique known as cookies. A *cookie* is a small bit of data that the Web server sends to the browser, which then either keeps this data in memory during your browsing session or stores it in a text file (known as the cookies.txt file) on your hard drive. At a later date, that *same* server can retrieve the information it stored there by sending the proper request to the browser. Only the server that *set* the cookie can retrieve it—rather like a safe-deposit box that can only be opened by the person who has the key.

This data is simply plain text. The cookie file on Ann's computer looks like this:

```
# Netscape HTTP Cookie File#
http://www.netscape.com/newsref/std/cookie_spec.html# This is a
generated file!  Do not edit.
www.download.com  FALSE   /       FALSE   946598442      csr
    /=/PC/FrontDoor/0^1^0-0^01.html.netscape.com      TRUE   /      FALSE
    946684799    NETSCAPE_ID    10010408,110a4d5a.microsoft.com      TRUE
    /    FALSE   937422000      MC1
    GUID=21de1634224511d18b1d08002bb74f3f.sfnb.com     TRUE   /      FALSE
    946684813    INTERSE pm4-168496873575945.yahoo.com TRUE   /
FALSE      915145264      T      z=3436ff9dsupport.microsoft.com      FALSE
    /    FALSE   903769234      ANSWERWIZ
    COUNT=1&1=cd+changer.amazon.com     TRUE   /      FALSE   880790440
    session-id-time      880790400.amazon.com   TRUE   /      FALSE
    880790440    session-id     7814-9198713-551054.amazon.com      TRUE
    /    FALSE   2082787235     ubid-main      7814-0090564-
584339www.eudora.com      FALSE   /      FALSE   978307881      Am_UserId
    cdb3ff3053252638www.surplusdirect.com      FALSE   /      FALSE
    946602061    SOURCESITE     default11|0.00|0www.pcuniverse.com   FALSE   /
    FALSE        946684868      EW3_ID
    205.179.255.75.4144.878771698www.laptopsuperstore.com     FALSE   /
    FALSE        946684870      EW3_ID
    205.179.255.75.11667.878782895ads.softbank.net   TRUE   /      FALSE
    1893456321   uid    0x0.0xcdb3ff8ewww.ual.com      FALSE   /      FALSE
    937396826    MC1    ID=aa429a7c56ff11d1817400805ffe4cdb
```

Most of this data wouldn't mean much to the casual observer, and it shouldn't. You can discern only a few things other than the domain that set the cookie (the first column of data). Line 6, beginning with support.microsoft.com, shows a cookie that was set when Ann searched Microsoft's Knowledge Base for information relating to drivers for a CD-ROM changer (notice the last entry on that line).

The remaining data may track where Ann came to this site from or, in the case of the download.com entry, that she selected the PC-specific version of a site. Sensitive information, such as the credit card information used to purchase a book from Amazon.com, should never be stored in the cookie itself. Rather, the cookie stores a unique identifier, such as the session-id number listed in the amazon.com entry, which allows the server to look up that data in the *server's* files. Think of it as the electronic version of being asked for the last four digits of your telephone number by the sales clerks at Radio Shack.

Skill 22

NOTE   For those of you not familiar with the practice, Radio Shack has a chainwide policy of tracking the name, address, and telephone number of all customers. This data is sorted by the last four digits of your telephone number. When you provide that information on repeat visits, the clerk can immediately pull up the rest of your information. The jury of public opinion has found this practice to be unpopular, especially with those customers making purchases with cash, but we digress.

Cookies and Privacy

As often occurs with anything that seems a little mysterious or that we don't quite understand, rumors and urban legends begin to spread until reality and "what's out there" are no longer recognizable as being related. This has happened with cookies. Let's try to debunk a few myths.

A cookie file is a plain text file.   Just like any other plain text file on your system, it cannot of its own accord record, send, read, or do anything. Your browser, acting on a request by the server, reads or write to the `cookies.txt` file.

NOTE   A cookie file is similar to an ATM. You can put your card in and ask, How much money is in my account? and the machine will tell you. You cannot put your card in the machine and ask, How much money does the guy that was in line ahead of me have in his account? You can only access your data. Same with the `cookies.txt` file—a site can access only the data it previously "banked" there.

The *cookies.txt* file does not indiscriminately give out your name and e-mail address.   If you submit such data to a site that uses cookies, it may store that information in your `cookies.txt` file (or in a server-side database referenced by an ID set in the cookie) for its own use later, but only because you gave this information (typed it in) to the site. The server cannot look for your e-mail address elsewhere, not even in the browser configuration files.

The *cookies.txt* file does not give out your IP address or tell other sites where you've just been.   However, sites can glean this information in a variety of ways. Each time a you load a Web page, your browser and the site's server have exchanged information. Your browser says, "Hi, I'm Navigator 4 from IP address 165.227.94.172, and I want the file `foo.html`, please". The server needs that information (at least the IP address and the file name) to send the requested information back to your browser for display. This data is contained in what's called the *environment variables* that get passed between the browser and server with each request.

ENVIRONMENT VARIABLES: *CALLER ID* OF THE INTERNET

Have you ever visited a site that says something like, "Welcome to our site. We show that you're associated with Nitelog, Inc., and are connected in or near Monterey, CA"? The site got this information from the environment variables. When Ann got this message, she was "near" Monterey, CA, and was only remotely associated with Nitelog, Inc. Nitelog owned Ann's dial-up ISP, Redshift Internet Services. And that's all the information about most users that any site can get from the environment variables.

The IP address that most SLIP/PPP systems use comes from a "pool" available to your ISP. A local ISP might have 500 IP addresses to hand out "dynamically" as each user logs in and out. You're never guaranteed to have the same IP address twice—or even twice in a row. Your e-mail address cannot be gleaned from the environment variables unless the domain sent back within those variables is a specific machine name or "static" IP address assigned only to you. Even then, your e-mail address can only be "guessed at."

For example, Ann used to connect through a company that assigned specific machine names to their customers. They assigned her a machine name of navarro.mry.someisp.com. That's the data that was passed back in the environment variables. This machine name breaks down like this:

> navarro (Ann's account name there)
>
> mry (the Monterey node where she logged it)
>
> someisp.com (the domain)

Logic says that navarro@someisp.com could have been Ann's e-mail address, and in fact it was. Did she have Spam overfilling her mail box because of it? Nope. As a matter of fact, she had only one e-mail message during that six-month period that was directly traceable to someone following this path of reasoning to resolve her e-mail address.

You cannot get a virus from a cookie exchange.   As we've mentioned, data written to your `cookies.txt` file is plain ASCII text. Viruses (even Word macro viruses) are *binary* data. Viruses (binary data) must be executed to create any harm. Binary data cannot be written to a plain text file. Plain text does not execute; it's simply read (interpreted or translated, for a more literal image). Therefore, a virus cannot reside in or be written to your `cookies.txt` file.

If you'd like to learn more about cookies, you might want to start by checking out these Web resources:

- The Unofficial Netscape Cookie FAQ by David Whalen at `http://www .cookiecentral.com/unofficial_cookie_faq.htm`

- Persistent Client State HTTP Cookies (the real scoop from Netscape) at `http://home.netscape.com/newsref/std/cookie_spec.html`

Additionally, the State Management subworking group of the Internet Engineering Task Force's HTTP Working Group has been working on a proposed specification for the handling of cookies. It's available online at `http://www.internic.net/ rfc/rfc2109.txt`.

With the addition of the cookie exchange between the browser and the server, the virtual shopping cart system now works smoothly. A cookie can be set at the beginning of the session, identifying the user to the server. Each time items are added to the cart, the server notes the shopper's unique id number and associates each selection with it in a database on the server. At checkout time, the browser passes the shopper's id number back to the server, which then retrieves all the selections.

Tax Issues

Setting up a virtual store-front immediately presents the new or small business owner with a unique set of commerce issues. With traditional retail stores, shop owners only need to learn about and comply with local sales or use tax laws since their customer base is primarily residents and businesses from the local area. Move that store to the Internet, and your customer base instantly becomes the global "wired" population. Does that really have any consequences beyond figuring out how to ship something to Sri Lanka? Unfortunately, the answer is, it all depends.

New legislation pending before both the U.S. Senate and the House of Representatives is known as the Internet Tax Freedom Act. It intends to institute a moratorium on new taxes on electronic commerce and will prevent new sales and use taxes on Internet access. Smoothing out conflicting local regulations is a key goal. Situations cited by sponsoring Senator Ron Wyden's (D-OR) office include:

- New York levies taxes on gross receipts on the "furnishing of information" but not on personal or individual information.

- Ohio taxes electronic transmissions and real estate databases as providing objective data but exempts news services as providing analysis.

- Texas taxes the transmission of electronic information and software in whatever form but does not tax software sent out of state on a disk.

In California, our home state, whether sales tax must be collected depends on whether the seller has a *nexus* within the state. The definition of a nexus is rather vague—it's a determination of whether the seller has a "significant connection" with the state, which would result in the seller being subject to a requirement to collect sales tax. Not very helpful, is it?

California has determined that the physical location of a Web server in that state does *not* constitute a nexus if that is the only "presence" the seller has in the state. Further, the U.S. Supreme Court has ruled that a seller is not obligated to collect sales tax if it does business in a state only by mail order.

CALIFORNIA'S LONG ARM ACROSS THE NET

While making the collection of sales tax a fairly simplistic issue, California has muddied the waters on another front. In addressing a growing fear of online fraud, a statute enacted in early 1997 applies consumer-protection provisions previously enacted for telephone and mail order sales outlets to online sales. Specifically, California requires that *any* seller that makes a sale to a California resident or business, regardless of nexus within the state, is required to provide on a Web site or via e-mail information regarding refund policies, a physical address for the business, and contact telephone numbers for complaint and dispute resolution. Additionally, vendors who don't perform within the bounds of those policies—perhaps not shipping products or not providing refunds within the prescribed time frames—are subject to prosecution.

continued on next page ▶

Skill 22

> This new law is relatively untested, as it takes a "long-arm" stance toward out-of-state vendors. California has taken the position that anyone making sales to its citizens must follow its rules—above and beyond the rules of the vendor's home state or country. Since the information the law requires is consumer-friendly, providing these details is a good idea, regardless of any statute that attempts to regulate it.

Collecting Sales Tax

An old cliché says there are only two sure things in life: death and taxes. Even then, taxes often seem as if they'll be the death of business owners! To help you wade through the widely varying regulations on the collection of sales taxes from state to state, Table 22.1 provides information "straight from the source" at each state's Web site (with notations for states that don't have sales tax).

TABLE 22.1: Sites for state sales tax information

State	Web Site
Alaska	No state sales tax. Contact local authorities.
Alabama	http://www.ador.state.al.us/salestax/Rules/index.html
Arizona	http://www.revenue.state.az.us/tpt/specevent/specevnt.htm
Arkansas	http://www.state.ar.us/revenue/eta/sales/salesusetax.html
California	http://www.boe.ca.gov/
Colorado	http://www.state.co.us/gov_dir/revenue_dir/TPS_dir/drp1002.html
Connecticut	http://www.state.ct.us/drs/
Delaware	No state sales tax.
Florida	http://fcn.state.fl.us/dor/html/taxguide.html
Georgia	http://www.state.ga.us/Departments/DOR/taxinfo/surates.htm
Hawaii	http://www.state.hi.us/tax/tax.html
Idaho	http://www.idwr.state.id.us/apa/idapa35/0102.htm
Illinois	http://www.revenue.state.il.us/statinfo/st25.pdf (Adobe Acrobat format)

TABLE 22.1 CONTINUED: Sites for state sales tax information

State	Web Site
Indiana	http://www.ai.org/dor/pubs/bullets/salesib.html
Iowa	http://www.state.ia.us/government/drf/taxtypes.html#sale
Kansas	http://www.ink.org/public/kdor/96forms.html#11
Kentucky	http://www.state.ky.us/agencies/revenue/pdf/salestax.pdf (Adobe Acrobat format)
Louisiana	http://www.rev.state.la.us/dirserv.htm
Maine	http://www.state.me.us/revenue/bulletin/bulletin.htm
Massachusetts	http://www.state.ma.us/dor/publ/sls_use.pdf (Adobe Acrobat format)
Michigan	http://www.cis.state.mi.us/tax/
Minnesota	http://www.taxes.state.mn.us/factshts/salestax.html
Mississippi	http://www.mstc.state.ms.us/taxareas/sales/main.htm
Missouri	http://services.state.mo.us/dor/
Montana	No general sales or use tax.
Nebraska	http://www.nol.org/home/NDR/info/352.pdf (Adobe Acrobat format)
Nevada	Not available online.
New Hampshire	No state sales tax.
New Jersey	http://www.state.nj.us/treasury/taxation/publsut.htm
New Mexico	http://www.state.nm.us/tax/
New York	http://www.tax.state.ny.us/Forms/239e.htm
North Carolina	http://www.dor.state.nc.us/DOR/
North Dakota	http://www.state.nd.us/taxdpt/resource.htm
Ohio	http://www.state.oh.us/tax/SALES/SALESTAX.HTML
Oklahoma	http://www.oktax.state.ok.us/oktax/publicat/copo397.pdf (Adobe Acrobat format)
Oregon	No state sales tax.
Pennsylvania	http://www.revenue.state.pa.us/
Rhode Island	http://www.tax.state.ri.us/info/faqs/faqs&u.htm
South Carolina	http://www.dor.state.sc.us/su.html
South Dakota	http://www.state.sd.us/state/executive/revenue/revenue.html

Skill 22

TABLE 22.1 CONTINUED: Sites for state sales tax information

State	Web Site
Tennessee	http://www.state.tn.us/revenue/faq.htm#SALES
Texas	http://www.cpa.state.tx.us/taxinfo/taxforms/01-forms.html
Utah	http://txdtm01.tax.ex.state.ut.us:80/sales/salestax.htm
Vermont	http://www.state.vt.us/tax/
Virginia	http://www.state.va.us/tax/sales.htm
Washington	http://www.wa.gov/dor/pub/struc/fsmajtx.htm
West Virginia	http://wvweb.net/taxrev/taxdoc/WV-TAA/INDEX.HTM
Wisconsin	http://badger.state.wi.us/agencies/dor/faqs/sales.html
Wyoming	http://revenue.state.wy.us/excise/taxguide.htm

Have You Mastered the Essentials?

Now you can. . .

- ☑ Discuss security issues with your Information Systems personnel or your ISP with confidence.
- ☑ Understand how state is maintained using cookies and virtual shopping carts.
- ☑ Apply for a server ID certificate from a certifying authority.
- ☑ Implement alternative payment processes for your customers.
- ☑ Research sales tax and other consumer issues on the Web.

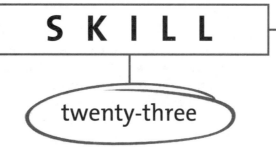

Accessibility Issues

❑ Understanding the Web Accessibility Initiative

❑ Looking at how the Americans with Disabilities Act
impacts the Web

❑ Evaluating your site's accessibility

❑ Exploring the Web Access Project

❑ Employing accessible design methods

It has been estimated that at least 45 million Americans have some form of impairment when it comes to processing visual or auditory information. When you add to that number the figures for those with mobility or cognitive disabilities, the total represents a significant percentage of the U.S. population. With more and more Americans (and persons of other nationalities) accessing the Internet every day, the potential impact of barriers to access becomes an important issue.

The Web Accessibility Initiative

In April 1997, the W3C announced the commencement of the Web Accessibility Initiative (WAI—pronounced *way*), which belongs to its Technology and Society domain of programs. The project is designed to promote and provide increased functionality on the Web for individuals with disabilities—from those with visual or auditory impairments to the physically handicapped.

The program will move forward with the opening of an International Program Office, a body that will coordinate the traditional W3C Project work along with the efforts of organizations for the disabled, governmental entities, and individual companies. The targeted objectives include work in the following areas:

Technology   Work will continue on HTML markup that is complementary to the existing ICADD (International Committee for Accessible Document Design) structures. Current projects include converting HTML documents to a DTD that supports Braille, large print, and voice synthesis and enhancements to forms and tables. This group will also work on enhancing Cascading Style Sheets to include support for speech output.

New tools   A style guide for tool developers will include suggestions for the creators of HTML-authoring programs and other Web-related software. This project will give advice on how to incorporate accessibility features into programs that will prompt authors using those tools to generate accessible Web sites.

Guidelines for use of new technologies   Although the W3C doesn't intend to suggest policy, it is dedicated to providing the necessary mechanisms for authors to produce accessible documents. Existing mechanisms include ALT tags for images that allow the visually impaired to receive information in place of the designated image.

Education of Web developers   Many developers and designers may not be aware of how their design choices affect those with disabilities.

Research and development This group will continue to work with the W3C host institutes—INRIA, Keio University, and MIT—on automatic certification tools for Web content and accessibility in scripting interfaces and HTML display tools.

The WAI's author guidelines were released just as this book went to print. For more information, check out `http://www.webgeek.com/ewd/`.

The Americans with Disabilities Act

The equal dissemination of information to all citizens is one of the goals of the Americans with Disabilities Act, commonly known as the ADA. In general lay terms, this law asserts the rights of the disabled to gain equal access to public services. This includes familiar accommodations such as wheelchair ramps at public buildings, sign-language interpreters in courtrooms, and official documents converted to Braille for the blind.

Cities, states, and other public entities are required to provide reasonable alternatives if information or services are normally delivered by means that aren't accessible to an individual with a qualifying disability. As more public entities develop a Web presence, these concerns apply to the online world.

Here are some excerpts from this act. You can find the entire text in Section IV at `http://www.usdoj.gov/crt/ada/t2hlt95.htm`.

> *State and local governments must ensure effective communication with individuals with disabilities.*
>
> *...Where necessary to ensure that communications with individuals with hearing, vision, or speech impairments are as effective as communications with others, the public entity must provide appropriate auxiliary aids. "Auxiliary aids" include such services or devices as qualified interpreters, assistive listening headsets, television captioning and decoders, telecommunications devices for deaf persons (TDD's), videotext displays, readers, taped texts, Brailled materials, and large print materials.*
>
> *... Public entities are not required to provide auxiliary aids that would result in a fundamental alteration in the nature of a service, program, or activity or in undue financial and administrative burdens. However, public entities must still furnish another auxiliary aid, if available, that does not result in a fundamental alteration or undue burdens.*

Most current legal interpretations also apply these requirements to online presentations, and many local governments are working hard to make their Web sites as accessible as possible.

ADDITIONAL ONLINE READING

The regulations that safeguard accessibility for disabled individuals can be complex. If you're designing sites for a public agency of any kind—from a city's informational Web site, to a publicly funded university site—you may be required to provide certain kinds of access that a private enterprise would not. Your organization probably already has an ADA compliance officer or has assigned those tasks to someone as part of a broader job title. Be sure to consult with that person early in the design phase of your Web projects.

You'll find additional information at the following Web sites. Remember, interpreting these statutes and requirements is a task for specialists.

- Technology-Related Assistance for Individuals with Disabilities Act of 1988 as Amended in 1994: `http://www.itpolicy.gsa.gov/coca/tech_act.htm`

- The Rehabilitation Act Amendments of 1992: `http://www.itpolicy.gsa.gov/coca/sect508.htm`

- The U.S. Dept. of Education's Requirements for Accessible Software Design: `http://gcs.ed.gov/coninfo/clibrary/software.htm`

The Web Page Accessibility Self-Evaluation Test

This test is a means for Web designers to evaluate their own efforts by answering questions about layout, markup, and presentation habits. It looks at issues that could impact accessibility for individuals with one of several hurdles to overcome, including:

Coordination or mobility impairment   These users may find fine control over a mouse or pointing device positioning difficult or impossible.

Deaf or hard of hearing   Sound clips or video that depends on the sound component to deliver the message may create a barrier to information for these users.

Cognitive, learning, or developmental disabilities   Heavy reliance on metaphorical graphics and icons can impede understanding.

The test questions are crafted in a manner that will suggest methods that will be helpful not only for the groups mentioned above, but for all users. Accessibility points are awarded based on this critical question: How much information is lost to challenged users due to specific design choices? Scoring does consider whether a design feature presents a "dead-end" for users. In other words, does it leave them unable to access critical information, or is the feature primarily an embellishment?

A few questions are outdated—referring to HTML 2 rather than the current HTML 4 proposal or even the previous HTML 3.2 recommendation. If you answer these questions in terms of current specifications, you can still obtain a useful score.

 NOTE   Two versions of this test are available online. The first, at *http://www.psc-cfp.gc.ca/dmd/access/testver1.htm*, is in HTML 2 compliant markup. The second, at *http://www.psc-cfp.gc.ca/dmd/access/javascri/jan97tst.htm*, uses JavaScript to track your score if you're using a JavaScript enabled browser.

The Web Access Project

CPB/WGBH National Center for Accessible Media (NCAM) is an organization committed to making media accessible to what they call "underserved populations such as disabled persons, minority-language users, and people with low literacy skills." Public broadcasting groups were instrumental in creating the closed-captioning systems used on television that first became available 25 years ago. The NCAM group is an extension of those efforts, broadening their work into exciting new electronic media formats.

Skill 23

NCAM announced the Web Access project in 1996. It has been researching and testing methods for integrating access technologies, such as captioning and audio descriptions, into Web site design. The public access TV channel WGBH's Web site, WGBH Online (`http://www.wgbh.org/`), serves as the test-bed for the group's project. In 1997, it began to focus on assisting other public television stations in making their individual Web sites accessible to those with visual or hearing impairments by creating a set of accessibility guidelines.

The project has developed and donated to the public domain a Web Access Symbol that is intended to identify sites that have made efforts to accommodate the needs of the Internet community with disabilities.

One of this group's more interesting experiments is the process of providing captioning and audio descriptions on Web sites by using QuickTime multimedia movies. Figure 23.1 shows a sample in action. The traditional movie clip is playing at the top, while a text window has been added at the bottom, providing an interface that closely mimics the familiar closed-captioning system available on television. You can view the original online at `http://www.boston.com/wgbh/pages/ncam/ currentprojects/captionedmovies.html`; it's the ManHole Covers selection.

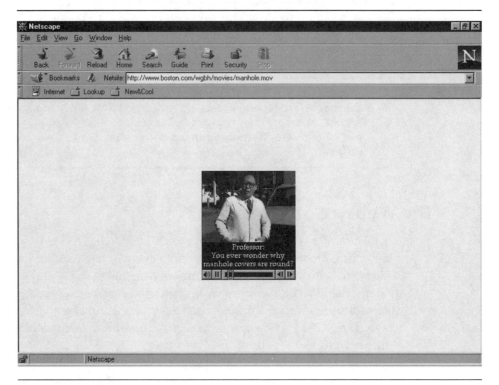

FIGURE 23.1:   A QuickTime movie with a text caption component

A link to a text transcript of the movie is provided at the same location as the QuickTime and AVI versions of the clips. Figure 23.2 shows the transcript. A set of >> symbols denotes a new speaker. The transcript is clear, even when it switches "voices," and provides an exact copy of the information relayed on the audio track of the movie.

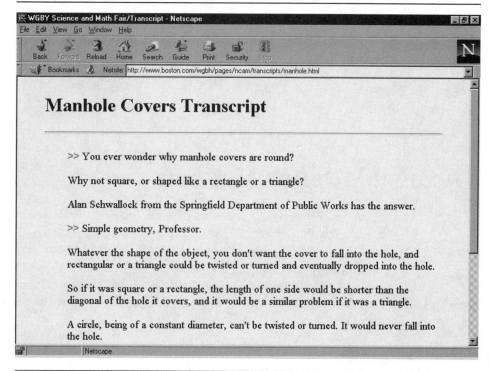

Manhole Covers Transcript

>> You ever wonder why manhole covers are round?

Why not square, or shaped like a rectangle or a triangle?

Alan Schwallock from the Springfield Department of Public Works has the answer.

>> Simple geometry, Professor.

Whatever the shape of the object, you don't want the cover to fall into the hole, and rectangular or a triangle could be twisted or turned and eventually dropped into the hole.

So if it was square or a rectangle, the length of one side would be shorter than the diagonal of the hole it covers, and it would be a similar problem if it was a triangle.

A circle, being of a constant diameter, can't be twisted or turned. It would never fall into the hole.

FIGURE 23.2:   A transcript of the QuickTime movie shown in Figure 23.1

TIP

When creating transcripts of audio events, don't give in to the temptation to edit out such "extras" as sound effects or "off-camera" responses. In order for readers to experience the event as everyone else did, they need to be presented with the same information. If, for instance, a speaker's comments are received with a chuckle from the audience, a notation in the transcript such as <audience laughs> can reinforce the effect and tone of the content with little effort on your part.

NCAM has provided details on its captioning process that you can follow to create your own files at `http://www.boston.com/wgbh/pages/ncam/qtcaptionhowto.html`. The instructions provided are for Macintosh systems, though the steps are similar for Windows users.

The center has also developed an icon that's freely available to Web designers who are developing accessible sites. Here are two of the available images:

Accessible Design Methods

If you've been working your way through this book, you have probably already incorporated many accessibility features in your design. It's no accident that *effective* Web design is frequently *accessible* Web design. Although we've briefly mentioned features that improve accessibility in previous skills, we're restating them here to reinforce the need to incorporate these techniques in your HTML repertoire and to provide a concise and consolidated reference that you can use as a checklist when evaluating existing designs.

Be Descriptive

Sounds simple—and it is! In every aspect of your design, from the naming of HTML and graphics files to captioning and even creating hyperlinks, using descriptive terminology can greatly increase the ease with which all users experience your site.

Use Meaningful File Names

Whether it's an image or an HTML document, a file's name should reflect its contents. For example, a restaurant site might include a page that re-creates the restaurant's menu. Naming that file `menu.html` is both meaningful and descriptive. Naming that file `page2.html` is not.

File names are just as important for images. A search on AltaVista for the file name `logo.gif` produced 1,310,003 returns. Enough said.

TIP

An added benefit of using meaningful file names is that you will also be able to more readily identify a file's contents without opening it. With cryptic file names, the chances of remembering just which image is the picture of the widgets out of 50 that are on a site you created 6 months ago are slim. If that file was named `widgets.jpg`, you'd find it in a snap.

Provide ALT Text for All Images

Every image, no matter how small or seemingly inconsequential, needs a descriptive ALT attribute. Building on our logo-based theme, an ALT value of "Company Logo" doesn't tell a speech-reader program or someone with a nongraphical browser anything about the content of that image besides the fact that it's a logo. Whose logo is it? What does it say or look like?

For example, PowerBASIC, Inc., is a software publishing company in Carmel, California. Its Web site uses an ALT value of "PowerBASIC on the Net: We put the power in basic!" This line identifies the company and further identifies it as the Web presence logo ("on the Net") and incorporates a text version of the company's slogan. Much more informative than "Company Logo," isn't it?

Where Is Here?

Have you ever stopped to consider how dependent on visual cues the hackneyed "Click here" is? How is a speech-reader supposed to interpret "here"? Rather than using the tired:

```
Click <A HREF="order.html">here</A> to view our online order form.
```

Use:

```
Use our online <A HREF="order.html">order form</A> to purchase your
    very own widget now!
```

TIP

When creating links, keep a balance between making them meaningful and making them verbose. In the example here, we could have hyperlinked "online order form" instead of just "order form." However, the meaning attached to the linked text is just as understandable with "order form" alone. Any extra information is unnecessary, and can produce needlessly long link displays.

Titles Speak Volumes

Every page on your site needs a TITLE tag. Not only is that a requirement of a properly formatted HTML document, but it's also a place where you can provide valuable descriptive information about the page contents. You'll remember from Skill 10 that many search engines and directories award higher rankings to sites that contain a keyword used in a visitor's search than those that don't. Now, this doesn't mean we're recommending that you load your title with keywords. However, the title should consist of a brief—at most one sentence —description of the page's contents. If the page describes your gadget line rather than your widget line, reflect that in the title.

 TIP   Remember that the Web isn't linear. That is, you never know which page of your site will be the first page that a visitor views. One way to diffuse any disorientation that may result from a visitor jumping in on a link or from a search engine is to incorporate your site's overall title in each page's TITLE tag. That is, Gadget Central would begin each title tag with Gadget Central: so that its tags could then be Gadget Central: Kitchen Gadgets, Gadget Central: Garden Gadgets, and Gadget Central: All About Us!

META Matters

In Skill 3, we introduced you to META tags. Two of the most useful define a document's keywords and description. Make good use of this opportunity; you won't find a better way to get your point across!

Here are a couple of ways to use META tags effectively:

Prioritize your keywords. Each search engine processes META information—or doesn't process it—differently. To maximize the effectiveness of your keyword list, place the most important words and phrases at the beginning. That way, if a search engine weights them in the order they are listed or limits the number of keywords it will process, your most important ones won't be left out.

Use listed keywords in your description. Additional "relevance points" may be awarded to your site if a keyword is found in both the keywords META tag and the description META tag (and even further in your TITLE tag).

TIP   Don't overlook placing your own company name in both the description and the keyword lists. You want to increase the chances of your company home page coming up in a search before the page of a reseller that carries your product line.

Provide Text Alternatives

It's never safe to assume that your visitors will all see your images—even those visitors without any vision impairment! They may be using a text-based browser such as Lynx, or they may have the auto-loading of images turned off because they are using a low-speed Net connection or simply because they're searching for hard information and don't want to be slowed down by the large image files that are common on many sites.

Add a Text Navigation Bar

Most sites on the Web today rely at least in part on graphical navigation icons. Although visitors who can't process images can use the ALT attributes you're providing with each image in order to navigate with those links, providing a secondary text-based navigation bar greatly eases the burden placed on those visitors.

In Figure 23.3, the text navigation bar is at the bottom of the page on the Holiday Homes Unlimited Web site (`http://www.dedot.com/holiday`).

When creating a navigation bar, here are some guidelines to keep in mind:

- At a minimum, provide a link back to your main page and to any "critical" subsections on your site.

- Separate each link with easily distinguishable characters. The site in Figure 23.3 uses square brackets to enclose each link. Other sites use the pipe character | to separate them.

- If you use the same navigation bar across your site, provide a cue as to which link is the current page by removing the anchor around it—display it simply in plain text.

Skill 23

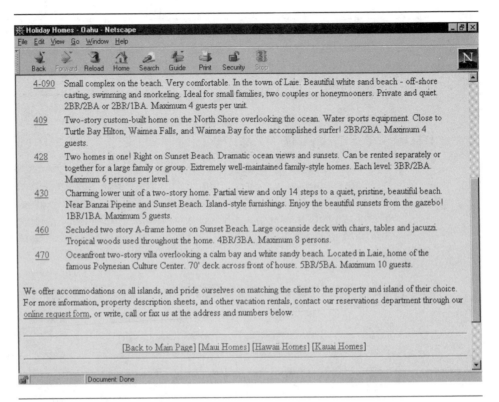

FIGURE 23.3:   Text navigation is simple, yet effective.

Providing alternative text-based navigation is especially important if your primary navigation tool is an image map. Figure 23.4 shows what a Web page looks like in Lynx, when it only has an image map on the front page—no ALT text and no alternative navigation tools. What's a visitor supposed to do with *that*?

Provide the *NOFRAMES* Container

In Skill 2 and again in Skill 5, you learned that not all Web browsers support the use of frames. To accommodate these users, you'll need to provide the framed content and a means for navigation within the NOFRAMES container. This can become a considerable project if one of the motivating factors for using frames is to stabilize a navigation tool.

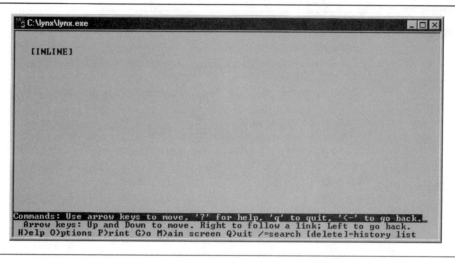

FIGURE 23.4:   The hazards of no alternative navigation

Give Some Assistance for Tables

Tabular formatting can really confuse speech-readers and non-tables compliant browsers. Although overcoming this affliction is difficult without providing a non–tables-based alternative page, you can provide some assistance by always inserting a line break tag at the end of each table cell, such as:

```
<TD>Cell Contents<BR></TD>
```

For browser clients that don't fully render tables but do display the contents of the cells, this will result at least in a line break between each cell's contents, which can bring some clarity.

HTML 4 includes some valuable tools to assist speech-readers that are compliant with the new HTML 4 standard. Several new attributes for table elements were defined, as outlined in Table 23.1, and put into action in headers.html.

TABLE 23.1:   New Attributes for Table Elements

Attribute	Tag	Usage
summary	<TABLE>	A descriptive summary of the table contents.
id	<TH>	Sets an identifier for each table heading. Similar to the NAME attribute in forms.
headers	<TD>	Identifies with which heading the cell should be logically aligned.

headers.html

```
<TABLE border="border" summary="This table charts what kind of sand-
    wiches the Navarro family prefers, including bread, meat and spread
    choices.">
<CAPTION>The Navarro family sandwich preferences</CAPTION>
<TR>
<TH id="t1">Name</TH>
<TH id="t2">Bread</TH>
<TH id="t3" abbr="Type">Meat</TH>
<TH id="t4">Spread</TH>
</TR>
<TR>
<TD headers="t1">Dave</TD>
<TD headers="t2">wheat</TD>
<TD headers="t3">ham</TD>
<TD headers="t4">mayonaisse</TD>
</TR>
<TR>
<TD headers="t1">Ann</TD>
<TD headers="t2">sourdough</TD>
<TD headers="t3">roast beef</TD>
<TD headers="t4">mayonaisse</TD>
<TR>
</TR>
<TD headers="t1">Linda</TD>
<TD headers="t2">white</TD>
<TD headers="t3">pastrami</TD>
<TD headers="t4">mustard</TD>
</TR>
</TABLE>
```

The SUMMARY attribute serves as a description for the contents of the entire table. Consequently, it's used within the TABLE tag itself. You can think of the summary as an ALT attribute for a table.

The ID attribute functions much like the NAME attribute in forms (see Skill 8 to refresh your memory). When each heading is defined in the first table row, it's assigned a unique identifier—for our purposes, t1 through t4.

When filling the main table data cells, each one is assigned to a heading with the HEADERS attribute. For instance, the cell that contains the name "Dave" is assigned to the heading "Name," which was given the ID of "t1." Therefore, the value of the HEADERS attribute for that cell becomes "t1." Figure 23.5 shows our file displayed in Navigator 4.04 on Windows NT.

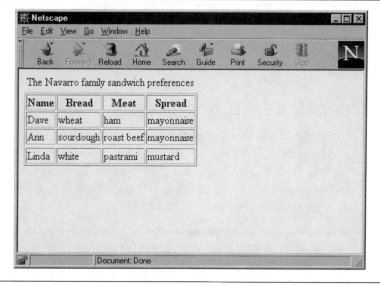

FIGURE 23.5: Tables with accessibility features appear normal in visual browsers.

   Doesn't look much different from the other examples, does it? The key here is what a speech reader can do with the additional attributes. Like graphical browsers, speech-readers aren't required to read (display) these features in one strict manner: the programmers who write them do have some leeway. However, the intended presentation would be similar to the following:

   Caption: The Navarro family sandwich preferences

   Summary: This table charts what kind of sandwiches the Navarro family prefers, including bread, meat, and spread choices.

Name: Dave	Bread: wheat	Meat: ham	Spread: mayonnaise
Name: Ann	Bread: sourdough	Meat: roast beef	Spread: mayonnaise
Name: Linda	Bread: white	Meat: pastrami	Spread: mustard

   This presentation lessens the chance of confusion, by allowing the listener to immediately associate each cell's contents with the proper category.

Skill 23

NOTE   Additional attributes for more complex situations, along with sample tables, can be found on the W3C Web site, at http://www.w3.org/TR/PR-html140/struct/tables.html#h-11.4.

Provide a Substitute for Online Forms

Provide a link to a text-based form—one that can be printed and filled out by hand and mailed to you, rather than submitted online. If this isn't practical, perhaps for forms that don't support ordering or important consumer feedback issues, at least provide a telephone number for voice contact and an e-mail link for additional online communication.

TIP   Don't rely on your HTML forms for printing visitor responses. In most cases, browsers don't pass along the contents of the input fields when sending the data to the printer. Your visitors will wind up with blank spaces where their responses were. A better solution is to provide a form with lines where you want the user to make an entry, just like traditional printed forms.

Transcribe All Audio Content

Always accompany audio files with a text transcript of all content. As we discussed earlier in this skill, you can do so by adding text to video files or by linking to a traditional transcript file.

Document Formats Other Than HTML

Providing important content in formats other than HTML presents challenges to the general Web population, not just to those with disabilities. For example, if you provide a link for visitors to download a white paper on your latest product, but you upload the file in Microsoft Word 97 format, only a limited number of people will be able to open and read that file. By providing an ASCII-text alternative copy, users who don't have the required program can nevertheless open the file. Though formatting and other special details may be lost, critical information will still be delivered.

Consider this approach for documents formatted in word-processor formats, spreadsheets, Adobe PDF files, Quark or Publisher files, and any other format that can't be displayed directly in a Web browser without a special plug-in.

Enhancing Readability

Several design choices can decrease the readability of your site for visitors that aren't generally classified as disabled. Many adults over the age of 40 experience some difficulty in reading small text or text that's set against a background that has little contrast compared with the text color.

Choose High-Contrast Background and Text Colors

In Skill 16, you learned about color theory: how to choose complimentary colors and contrasting colors and how to match hues and densities. You can enhance readability by choosing high-contrast colors for your background and text. Not only does this serve visitors with poor but not completely failed vision, but it also helps those who suffer from color-blindness (it's estimated that about one-third of the male population is color-blind).

TIP Did you know that light text against a dark background may render your pages unprintable? Many browser/printer combinations will result in the background color being "removed" from the print data, yet the text color is interpreted in its appropriate gray-scale classification. The end result is white or nearly white text printed on white paper—in other words, a blank page!

Use Relative Font Sizing

Web designers have more font manipulation options available than ever before, with the features in Cascading Style Sheets and the FONT tag in HTML. When taking advantage of these styles, choose relative font sizing over absolute font sizing. We addressed this concept in both Skills 7 and 15; it's an important issue above and beyond accessibility for the disabled. Predicting what font sizes will be functional for your visitors is next to impossible with the variety of monitors and supported screen resolutions available to today's computing enthusiasts.

Stylesheets

Rather than being viewed as an impediment to accessibility, stylesheets can actually help improve the odds that all your audience will be able to view your site as you intended. In Skill 7, we discussed how to provide links to alternative stylesheets. By supplying sheets that do away with elements that can complicate the experience, visitors with CSS-compliant browsers can choose the display that will serve them best.

A significant advance in stylesheets was announced in June 1997. The W3C made public a working draft of a proposal for Aural Cascading Style Sheets—ACSS. These stylesheets are designed with optimization in mind for audio-based client technologies. The draft is available online at http://www.w3.org/TR/WD-acss.

Have You Mastered the Essentials?

Now you can...

- ☑ Follow development efforts of the W3C and other organizations involved in the Web Accessibility Initiative.
- ☑ Evaluate your own sites for accessibility using the self-test.
- ☑ Incorporate a logo endorsing accessible design methods.
- ☑ Improve the handling of a variety of elements in your HTML markup.

APPENDIX

A

Tag Support across HTML Versions and Browsers

Some of the most common questions that we hear deal with which features of HTML are supported in what manner and by which browser. This list is not meant to be an exhaustive reference of all possible combinations, but instead a guide for the most commonly encountered situations.

TABLE A.1: HTML tags and their support by HTML version and browser type

Tag	HTML 2	HTML 3	HTML 3.2	HTML 4	Navigator 1.x	Navigator 2.x	Navigator 3.x
APPLET			X	X		X	X
BASEFONT			X		X	X	X
BGSOUND							X
BLOCKQUOTE	X	X	X	X	X	X	X
BODY	X	X	X	X	X	X	X
sBOLD	X	X	X	X	X	X	X
CENTER			X		X	X	X
CITE	X		X	X	X	X	X
COLGROUP		X	X	X			
DL	X	X	X	X	X	X	X
DT	X	X	X	X	X	X	X
EM	X	X	X	X	X	X	X
EMBED					X	X	X
FONT		X	X		X	X	X
FORM	X	X	X	X	X	X	X
FRAME				X	X	X	X
FRAMESET				X	X	X	X
H1,H2...H7	X	X	X	X	X	X	X
HEAD	X	X	X	X	X	X	X
HR	X	X	X	X	X	X	X
HTML	X	X	X	X	X	X	X
IMG	X	X	X	X	X	X	X
I	X	X	X	X	X	X	X
LI	X	X	X	X	X	X	X
MAP			X		X	X	X
OBJECT	X	X	X	X	X	X	X

Tag	Navigator 4.x	IE 2.x	IE 3.x	IE 4.x	AOL 3.x	Lynx	WebTV 0.x	WebTV 1.x
APPLET	X		X	X				X
BASEFONT	X	X	X	X	X		X	X
BGSOUND		X	X	X	X		X	X
BLOCKQUOTE	X	X	X		X	X	X	X
BODY	X	X	X	X	X	X	X	X
BOLD	X	X	X	X	X	X	X	X
CENTER	X	X	X	X	X		X	X
CITE	X	X	X	X			X	X
COLGROUP								X
DL	X	X	X	X	X	X	X	X
DT	X	X	X	X	X	X	X	X
EM	X	X	X	X	X	X	X	X
EMBED	X		X					X
FONT	X	X	X	X	X		X	X
FORM	X	X	X	X	X	X	X	X
FRAME	X		X	X	X	X		X
FRAMESET	X		X	X	X	X		X
H1,H2...H7	X	X	X	X	X		X	X
HEAD	X	X	X	X	X	X	X	X
HR	X	X	X	X	X	X	X	X
HTML	X	X	X	X	X	X	X	X
IMG	X	X	X	X	X		X	X
I	X	X	X	X	X	X	X	X
LI	X	X	X	X	X	X	X	X
MAP	X	X	X		X		X	X
OBJECT	X	X	X	X				

TABLE A.1 CONTINUED: HTML tags and their support by HTML version and browser type

Tag	HTML 2	HTML 3	HTML 3.2	HTML 4	Navigator 1.x	Navigator 2.x	Navigator 3.x
OL	X	X	X	X	X	X	X
PRE	X	X	X		X	X	X
SCRIPT			X	X			X
STRONG	X	X	X	X	X	X	X
SUB		X	X	X		X	X
SUP		X	X	X		X	X
TABLE	X	X	X	X	X	X	X
TD		X	X	X	X	X	X
TEXTAREA	X	X	X	X	X	X	X
TFOOT		X		X			
TH		X	X	X	X	X	X
THEAD		X		X			
TITLE	X	X	X	X	X	X	X
TR		X	X	X	X	X	X
TT	X	X	X	X	X	X	X
U	X		X				X
UL	X	X	X	X	X	X	X

Tag	Navigator 4.x	IE 2.x	IE 3.x	IE 4.x	AOL 3.x	Lynx	WebTV 0.x	WebTV 1.x
OL	X	X	X	X	X	X	X	X
PRE	X	X	X	X	X	X	X	X
SCRIPT	X		X	X				
STRONG	X	X	X	X		X	X	X
SUB	X		X	X		X	X	X
SUP	X		X	X		X	X	X
TABLE	X	X	X	X	X		X	X
TD	X	X	X	X	X			X
TEXTAREA	X	X	X	X	X	X	X	X
TFOOT								
TH	X	X	X	X	X		X	X
THEAD								
TITLE	X	X	X	X	X	X	X	X
TR	X	X	X	X	X		X	X
TT	X	X	X	X	X		X	X
U		X	X		X	X		X
UL	X	X	X	X	X	X	X	X

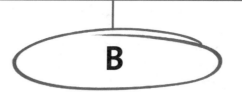

APPENDIX

B

Character Entities

The HTML 4.0 recommendation supports dozens of named character entities, the more common of which are shown in Table B.1. A complete reference of character entities can be found online at `http://www.w3.org/TR/WD-html40/sgml/entities.html`.

Current browsers support these extended character sets with varying success. Always be sure to test-view your HTML files before publishing them, to insure that any codes used here are presented in the manner that you intended.

COMPATIBILITY NOTE More browsers support the numerical usage than support the name usage. In either case, each use must begin with the ampersand (&) character and end with the semi-colon (;). For example, you'd write &*nbsp*; or   for the non-breaking space.

TABLE B.1: Common character entities

Character	Description	Entity Name	Numerical Usage
	non-breaking space	nbsp	
¡	inverted exclamation mark	iexcl	&#161;
¢	cent sign	cent	&#162;
£	pound sterling sign	pound	&#163;
¤	general currency	curren	&#164;
¥	yen sign	yen	&#165;
¦	broken bar	brvbar	&#166;
§	section sign	sect	&#167;
¨	umlaut	uml	&#168;
©	copyright sign	copy	&#169;
®	registered sign	reg	&#174;
™	trademark sign	trade	&#8482;
°	degree sign	deg	&#176;
±	plus or minus sign	plusmn	&#177;
¹	superscript 1	sup1	&#185;
²	superscript 2	sup2	&#178;
³	superscript 3	sup3	&#179;

TABLE B.1 CONTINUED: Common character entities

Character	Description	Entity Name	Numerical Usage
´	acute accent	acute	&#180;
µ	micron sign	micro	&#181;
¶	pilcrow (paragraph)	para	&#182;
¼	one-quarter fraction	frac14	&#188;
½	one-half fraction	frac12	&#189;
¾	three-quarters fraction	frac34	&#190;
¿	inverted question mark	iquest	&#191;
×	multiplication sign	times	&#215;
÷	division sign	divide	&#247;
≠	not equal to	ne	&#8800;
≡	identical to	equiv	&#8801;
≤	less than or equal to	le	&#8804;
≥	greater than or equal to	ge	&#8805;
∞	infinity	infin	&#8734;
<	less than	lt	&#60;
>	greater than	gt	&#62;
–	en dash	ndash	&#8211;
—	em dash	mdash	&#8212;
†	dagger	dagger	&#8224;
‡	double dagger	Dagger	&#8225;

Index

Note to the Reader: Throughout this index **boldface** page numbers indicate primary discussions of a topic. *Italic* page numbers indicate illustrations.

Numbers

Symbols

a

b

e

editing. *See also* changing; text editors
  audio files, 443, *444*
  video files, 449, *450*
EM (emphasis) tags, 68–69, *69*
em spaces, 156
e-mail. *See also* addresses
  e-mail links from surveys, 258
  in Internet Explorer, 24
  in Lynx browsers, 27
  mailto forms for processing responses, 178–179
  mailto links for receiving responses, 258
  in Netscape Navigator, 23
  security of e-mail addresses, 528–529
EMBED tags, 21
embedding
  background sound, 446–447
  QuickTime attributes of EMBED tags, 481–482
  Shockwave files, 470–471
  video files, 450, 480–482
emphasizing text
  with HTML tags, 68–70, *69*
  with stylesheets, 141–144, *143*, 146
empty tags, 82
encoder software, 432–433, 443
encoding multimedia files, 426, 432–433
encryption software for customer transactions, 520–523
Engel, Victor, 372
Enterprise Server software, 243
environment variables, 528–529
E-Quarium Web site, 193–194, *194*
equipment for A/V production, 440–441, 447–448
escaping
  @ signs in Perl scripts, 181
  character entities, 77–79
  characters with entities, 76–78
European Laboratory for Particle Physics. *See* CERN
events, 412. *See also* mouseover events
excluding keywords from searches, 215, 217, 219
"Exploring Color" Web site, 341
Extensible Markup Language (XML), 5
external applications. *See also* multimedia
  for audio, 436–437

  defined, **435**
  overview of, 436
  versus plug-ins, 434–436, 438
  for video, 437
external stylesheets, 145–146, *147*. *See also* stylesheets

f

FACE attribute of fonts, 321–324, *324*, *325*
family font style, 152–153
fantasy font family, 153
Fast-Start format, 480
file extensions
  .css, 145
  .htm or .html, 145
  .mov, .moov, and .qt, 483
  .ram, 484
  .src, 415–416
  .txt, 209–210
file formats
  for downloadable multimedia, 428–430
  for images, **369**, 369–372, 385
  MIME file formats, 461–463, *462*, *463*
  for streaming multimedia, 432–433
file permissions, 182
files
  converting to PDF format, 475
  converting to QuickTime files, 480
  converting to RealAudio and RealVideo files, 484
  converting to Shockwave files, 469–470
  hyperlinks to, 56–57
  hyperlinks to specific places in, 59–62
  naming, 544–545
filming video, 449
finding
  code values for character entities, 74
  movie size, 480
  x, y coordinates for image maps, 193–194, *194*, 196–199, *197*
firewalls for server security, 515–516
First Virtual Web sites, 525
fixed-width fonts, 69, **316**, 317
Flash software, 465–466, 484
FlashSite Web site, 500
flat color GIFs in Netscape palette, 373–374, *373*, *374*, 380

n

t

u

W

X

y

z

EVERYTHING YOU NEED TO KNOW ABOUT
good & bad
WEB DESIGN.

What's on the CD?

The attached CD-ROM contains the code files used in this book, along with useful shareware and freeware. To find out how to access the files on the CD, see the readme file.

Effective Tools

This CD is a collection of some of the most commonly used tools for Web designers including browsers, readers, animators, HTML editors, and more. With this complete set of tools, you'll be ready to start designing for the Web immediately.

For Windows 95/NT Users:

The following shareware is provided for Windows 95/NT users:

- Adobe Acrobat Reader
- Cute FTP
- GIF Movie Gear
- HTML PowerTools Test Drive
- HVS ColorGIF
- Internet Explorer
- Mapedit
- Netscape Navigator
- TextPad
- Ulead GIF Animator
- Web Graphics Optimizer
- WebRazor
- WinZip

For Mac Users:

Mac users will appreciate the following shareware products:

- Acrobat Reader
- Internet Explorer
- HVS ColorGIF
- Mapedit
- Netscape Navigator
- TexEdit